PROTECTIVE PRACTICES

Protective Practices

A History of the London
Rubber Company and the
Condom Business

JESSICA BORGE

Foreword by Lesley A. Hall

McGill-Queen's University Press
Montreal & Kingston | London | Chicago

© McGill-Queen's University Press 2020

ISBN 978-0-2280-0333-5 (cloth)
ISBN 978-0-2280-0426-4 (ePDF)

Legal deposit third quarter 2020
Bibliothèque nationale du Québec

Printed in Canada on acid-free paper that is 100% ancient forest free (100% post-consumer recycled), processed chlorine free

Library and Archives Canada Cataloguing in Publication

Title: Protective practices : a history of the London Rubber Company and the condom business / Jessica Borge.
Names: Borge, Jessica, 1980– author.
Description: Includes bibliographical references and index.
Identifiers: Canadiana (print) 20200250442 | Canadiana (ebook) 20200250604 | ISBN 9780228003335 (cloth) | ISBN 9780228004264 (ePDF)
Subjects: LCSH: London Rubber Company—History—20th century. | LCSH: Condom industry—Great Britain—History—20th century. | LCSH: Condoms—Great Britain—History—20th century. | LCSH: Contraceptives—Great Britain—History—20th century.
Classification: LCC HD9995.C64 L66 2020 | DDC 338.7/681761—dc23

Set in 11.5/14 Filosofia with Trade Gothic Std
Book design & typesetting by Garet Markvoort, zijn digital

For Charley

The traditional story of the male contraceptive is serious drama
played as low comedy.
— *Samuel A. Baker, senior vice president of Julius Schmid*

Contents

Tables

Map

It is very pleasing indeed to see, at last, such a fine study of that very underexplored aspect of contraception, the commercial production and distribution of 'rubber goods', which was a significant factor in providing the material means of birth control to the British population before the advent of the pill in the early 1960s.

This is an area of research that has faced considerable difficulties. During my decades as an archivist at the Wellcome Library many researchers came to me eager to explore this important topic but were thwarted by the discovery that either the records of the businesses in question did not survive (as the businesses were now defunct) or that access was denied (there are passages in this book which may hint at why the London Rubber Company might have been somewhat reluctant to throw open its records ...). This aura of secrecy extended to a case in which a popular history of the condom was, at a very late stage of the production process, refused permission even to use a certain brand name on the grounds that it was a registered trademark, and therefore all occurrences of the word 'Durex' had to be blacked out.[1] Massive kudos, therefore, to Jessica Borge for the way in which she has tackled this challenge and succeeded in locating and analysing sources which illuminate the activities of the London Rubber Company, which played such a major role in British contraception during the twentieth century and whose operations form such a fascinating story.

The trade in the wherewithal by which couples might limit their families dwelt within what Anna Clark has so tellingly characterised as those 'twilight moments' into which so many sexual matters have fallen.[2] It was not, in Britain, actually illegal to purvey birth control devices: however, advertising them too openly and bringing them to the attention of the young and innocent, or those who did not wish to have such matters imposed upon them, was liable to fall foul of laws on obscenity, public nuisance, and what it was permissible to send through the Post Office. What Borge's study reveals is how adeptly the London Rubber Company over the years took advantage of this liminal existence in the 'twilight zone' to the bene-fit of its own profitability.

Historians have, perhaps surprisingly, found it possible to illumin-ate the matter of how couples approached matters of controlling family size, at least by the early twentieth century. A few social surveys in the period after the Second World War addressed the topic.[3] The copious col-lection of letters sent to Marie Stopes by her grateful public from 1918 onwards in response to her popular works has been explored by several scholars,[4] and more recently the possibilities of oral history have been deployed, in particular by Kate Fisher and Simon Szreter.[5] While it now appears, confirming the earlier studies, that until well into the post-war era a majority of couples who limited their families were employing non-appliance methods (withdrawal, abstinence for longer or shorter per-iods, prolonged breast-feeding), nonetheless a significant minority was employing appliances, predominantly condoms.

Claire L. Jones has recently demonstrated that the trade in contracep-tives in Britain, subject to considerable local variations, was not quite so surreptitious and concealed as has been believed, and that although advertisements in the mainstream press might be coded, they were still widespread. Similarly 'hygienic' and 'surgical' stores did not hide their existence even if they were to be found on backstreets rather than main shopping thoroughfares.[6] Clearly the demand for 'rubber goods' and indeed for chemical contraceptives created profitable business oppor-tunities even if these constituted only a small part of the potential market. If it was a niche trade it was a substantial one, and, as Borge proves here, one that was extremely profitable.

There is already a long-standing historiography of the activists who argued the case for birth control and the right of individuals – or rather, for most of the period in question, married couples – to limit the size of their families.[7] This is well documented since by the nature of their endeavour, it was about public debate – even if it was a public debate leading to press attacks and trials for obscenity – conducted in the light of common day, which was where these pioneers thought the question ought to be venti-lated. The consequences of public advocacy – or even suggesting that the topic might legitimately be discussed – suggest one reason why organisa-tions fighting to make birth control a respectable cause might have shied away from any too-close association with commerce, as Borge so tellingly shows was the case with the Family Planning Association (formerly the National Birth Control Association).

In the nineteenth century a few dedicated Malthusians (such as J. Greevz Fisher, J.R. Holmes, and Henry Young) set themselves up in the retail contraceptive trade (but not, as far as one can tell, at the manufacturing end), an enterprise in which falling foul of the law, as Holmes and Young found, was always a risk.[8] There were daunting historical examples of the disinterested desire to promote birth control becoming intertwined in the public mind with an intention to profit from the wish to practice it. In 1866 Lord Amberley (father of Bertrand Russell) chaired a meeting of the London Dialectical Society on the Malthusian question: the knowledge of this being disseminated to a wider public, he subsequently lost a parliamentary election amid scenes of riot and the display of cartoons of him selling abortifacient mixtures.[9] In 1923, the judge sitting on Dr Marie Stopes's libel case against Dr Halliday Sutherland made a calculation, based on a bizarre misunderstanding of the economics of publishing, of the immense profits Stopes must have been making on her admittedly bestselling work on marriage and contraception in order to cast doubt on her idealistic motivation.[10]

It is therefore not surprising that the National Birth Control Association/Family Planning Association, which had a fair amount on their plate already – operating clinics, lobbying for greater acceptance of contraception, and improving standards – preferred to work with existing manufacturers rather than to engage in profit-making activities themselves. It was never really a viable strategy in the British context to emulate the movement in Sweden, which established retail and eventually manufacturing subsidiary organisations to provide contraceptives at low cost but nonetheless at a sufficient profit to subsidise their educational activities on behalf of family limitation and sexual enlightenment.[11] A plan to set up a non-profit-making contraceptive enterprise was mooted in 1928 by a group of several of the contemporary great and good, including H.G. Wells and Julian Huxley, but this does not seem to have come to anything.[12] On the evidence presented by Borge in this book one feels it would have faced considerable opposition, overt and covert, from the London Rubber Company.

While the respectable ladies of the British birth control movement wished to dissociate themselves from the sleazier aspects of the 'rubber goods'/'surgical stores' business, they were in general resistant to restricting access to contraception for those who needed it, but this was a line that required delicate negotiation. Their concern was that the public should have access to reliable safe contraception: the ideal was the cap or the pessary as prescribed in clinics, but that families should be relieved from the burdens of excessive begetting was the desideratum. Thus their pursuit of standards in all forms of contraception – appliance or chemical – currently on the market, was by way of the 'Approved List'. The uneasy symbiosis with the manufacturers into which this led them is very well delineated by Borge: the FPA, in spite of its penuriousness, commanded a good deal of reputational capital and increasingly wide influence, and the advantages of being included on their Approved List led to a string of wrangles with manufacturers claiming this accolade for products which had not, in fact, made the cut (not just the London Rubber Company: there were prolonged tussles with W.R. Rendells over whether the 'Wife's Friend' pessaries could claim to be Approved[13]).

This book is clearly of immense interest and value to the historian of birth control and changing sexual mores, but it also has a great deal to offer to historians in other spheres. It is a fine exemplar of the way in which taking some humble – in this instance, not merely humble but despised – material object can lead one into large and unexpected vistas. So much is there for the business historian – for example why businesses make what appear to be counterintuitive decisions, which we see LRC did on several occasions in order to maintain their monopoly, or in order that their monopoly would not face a challenge further down the line. There is a fascinating contrast between the unscrupulousness of the LRC's business practices and the testimonials from their staff to their benevolence and the perception that they were excellent and humane employers.

They were a paradigm of the 1950s 'second shift' of housewives working in light industry to supplement the family budget. There is perhaps more to be explored around their involvement in questions of packaging and design. They provide a case study of 1950s public relations strategies at a time when this sector was just gearing up in the UK. We are also led to consider the impact of wider international factors, from changes in rubber growing to the effects of two world wars.

This is a work which, while admirably filling in a significant lacuna in the history of birth control in Britain, also opens up a lot of exciting possibilities for further exploration.

LESLEY A. HALL, FRHISTS, PHD, DIPAA
Wellcome Library Research Fellow
Honorary Senior Lecturer, Department of Science and Technology Studies,
University College London

Unpacking the story of the London Rubber Company has been one of the most satisfying projects I have ever undertaken, and the most challenging. Some may say it is a fool's errand to write the institutional history of a company for which there is no corporate archive, but this wasn't the original intention. The idea had been to examine the marketing of the oral contraceptive 'pill' to British women in the 1960s, but the name 'London Rubber' kept popping up and I wondered why. Back in the late 1990s, a friend had cheerily pointed out the old factory during a stroll along the North Circular Road at Chingford, and sniggered. I knew what London Rubber made, all right — Durex condoms. So why were they turning up in my research on oral contraceptives? Needless to say, I 'went off the pill' and tried to unpack the London Rubber story.

During the course of my research, I had the incredible fortune to hold conversations with two former London Rubber employees, Angela Wagstaff and John Harvey. It was in the autumn of 2016 that Angela and I discovered each other, thanks entirely to the kindness of Gary Heales, assistant curator at Vestry House Museum (since retired). Angela generously set up a meeting between John, former London Rubber sales manager, and myself, at her home in Chingford that November, in what was to be the first of several such meetings. To say that John was poorly when we first met is an understatement — he had, at the time, suffered sixteen transient ischemic attacks (or 'mini-strokes'), and yet here he was. Being more of a London Rubber careerist than Angela, and a specialist in marketing (a key area of interest), I focused on John and his experiences, making audio recordings of our sessions on an iPad. Doubtless these chats would have been more one-directional had the meetings occurred at the beginning of my research, when I was less of an expert myself. John was measured and reflective in his answers to my questions, but our chats can't really be called 'interviews' in any traditional sense of the word. John's recollections (and Angela's, to a lesser extent) have been included throughout this book less a basis for discovering London

Rubber's activities, and more as means of adding texture to what is, in the main, revealed or corroborated through original document research. Although I would have liked to trace other ex-staff members, time was against me. I do not make any pretence of having produced an oral history of contraceptive or condom use in Britain, or even to have used an oral history methodology; others have done a much better job of this than I ever could. The Waltham Forest Oral History Workshop, for example, is currently engaged in tracing former staff and interviewing them for the benefit of future researchers. For my part, it was simply not possible to undertake a similar venture for this particular project, and readers should therefore be aware of the circumstances surrounding my chats with Angela and John.

In the case of Lucian Landau (1912–2001), his autobiography is not widely available, and I cite from *Normal, I Suppose: A Rather Strange Story* in chapter 2, in order to bring this account of London Rubber's early years to a wider audience. Landau was the original architect of London Rubber's in-house condom, which facilitated the switch from wholesaling to fabrication. To my mind, this makes Landau the father of the modern condom in Britain, but so far as I can tell, he has been erased from official company lore and is unrepresented in histories of contraception, until now. Some of the claims Landau makes about certain individuals within the company are obviously difficult to corroborate, and readers are invited to weigh his testimony alongside other evidence presented. Nevertheless, it gives me great pleasure to go some way toward restoring Landau to his rightful place as the inventor of the condoms that bore the Durex trademark, back in the beginning.

I have often quipped that the downside of doing an institutional history of Britain's biggest condom maker is that it takes most of the sex out of the subject. This is regrettable, as readers will reasonably expect a fair measure of sex with their condoms. But I have a strong conviction that the less sexy side of the condom business has its own richness and intrigue. It is only fair to let the reader know that this book is categorically *not* the story of sex in modern Britain. I make no claim to be a specialist in the history of sexuality, or of business for that matter. However, I believe the history of the manufacture, promotion, and supply of condoms is at the very bedrock of how many millions of people combined their sex lives with consumer purchasing power. The result is a very descriptive and hopefully interesting book that necessarily blends methods from different schools in order to tell the palimpsest story of a company on the make.

Condom manufacturing left Britain in 1994, after which time the Durex name was passed on. Today, London Rubber exists as a small holding company that does not directly participate in the production of condoms. I would therefore like to stress that the company described in this book bears no resemblance to Reckitt Benckiser, which currently produces condoms under the Durex brand name and which does much for sexual health and education. The history of the London Rubber Company, however, is unique, and its first fifty years was unlike any other time; the particular blend of social, political, and regulatory conditions that allowed it to flourish will never be repeated. With that said, this book also offers a substantial final chapter detailing events affecting London Rubber and the condom between 1965 and 2001. These decades are not the main focus of this study, but any work on London Rubber would be incomplete without dealing with the slippery 1970s, the diverse 1980s, and the difficult 1990s. At the very least, I hope to shed light on the long view, although I recognise that some will still find my choice of subject matter a little *outré*. All I can say to that is: if you had told me twenty years ago that I would be writing a book about the rise and fall of Britain's most successful condom maker, I wouldn't have seen it coming.

JESSICA BORGE
London, 2020

Acknowledgments

Many kind and patient individuals have supported *Protective Practices*. Charley Greenwood gave me the courage to return to higher education and undertake an MA, then a PhD: this book is dedicated to him. Andrea Tanner never turned me away when I needed guidance, and any success I enjoy has a lot to do with her counsel and influence. My doctoral supervisors at Birkbeck, Janet McCabe and Suzannah Biernoff, gave me more liberty than I deserved and I was exceptionally lucky to have them on side. They, along with Adrian Bingham, Jo Cannings, Emma Cole, Alana Harris, Scott Howard, Julia Laite, Joanne Metivier, Claire Nally, Alex Ritchie, Peter Scott, Angela Smith, Michael Temple, and several anonymous reviewers contributed constructive and useful comments to early versions (in part and whole) of this work, as has Lesley A. Hall, who has has kindly written the foreword: she has been unfailingly generous with her time and expertise, for which I offer my warmest thanks. I am grateful to the team at McGill-Queen's University Press who have supported the actualisation of this book, including Lisa Aitken, Victoria Benjamin, Natalie Blachere, Jacqui Davis, Filomena Falocco, Kate Fraser, Kathleen Fraser, Elena Goranescu, Linda Iarrera, Rob Mackie, Andrew Pinchefsky, Jennifer Roberts, Erin Rolfs, and Shannon Wood. My wonderful editor, Richard Baggaley, at MQUP London believed in the project from the moment we met and has been incredibly patient. I thank him unreservedly, and also Mary Clare Martin for introducing us. My thanks to David Drummond for the charming cover design, and Garet Markvoort for the most elegant typesetting and layout.

Many organisations and individuals have supported this research. Financial assistance has come from the Arts and Humanities Research Council, the Dittrick Museum of Medical History (via James Edmonson), the Guinness Partnership, the Wellcome Trust, the Business History Conference, the Business Archives Council, CHARM Association, European Association of the History of Medicine and Health, and Birkbeck College. Percy Skuy supported my attendance at several American conferences in 2015, and gave generously of his time. Warm thanks to him, and to Elsa Skuy. Alison J. Payne, as well as being unwavering in her friendship, has personally sponsored many of the photographs presented in this book, and to her I offer special thanks. Conversations with the following people have greatly helped to solidify my ideas: Greg Anderson, Rowan Aust, Patricia Caillé, Jennifer Cohen, Delia Cortese, Michael Dunn, Richard Evans, Sarah Gibbs, Susan Hawkins, Phil Harvey, Agata Ignaciuk, Claire L. Jones, Cathryn Johnston, Lauren Klaffke, Julia Larden, Ben Mechen, Laura Mayhall, Kate Malleson, Bruce McKay, Michael Mainelli, Lutz Sauerteig, Christabel Scaife, Jonathan Simon, Gordon and Mary Snow, Aisling Shalvey, Leslie Tentler, Lawrence Poos, Caroline Rusterholz, and Sarah Scarsbrook. Special thanks to Christian Bonah, Tricia Close-Koenig, Anja Laukötter, and my colleagues on the ERC-funded 'BodyCapital' project, SAGE UMR7363 Université de Strasbourg, and the Max Planck Institute for Human Development, Berlin. Thanks also to Jane Winters at the School of Advanced Study, University of London.

My gratitude to all of the archival repositories and individuals that have granted me access to their collections, particularly past and present staff at Wellcome Collection, including Amanda Engineer, Phoebe Harkins, Peter Judge, Angela Saward, Ross MacFarlane, and Danny Rees. I thank Alexander Bieri, Bruno Halm, Christian Helm, Lionel Lowe, and Svenja Egli of the Roche Historical Museum and Archive, Basel, and also Regina Pötzsch, for their spirited encouragement. Colleagues from King's College London Archives – including the Liddell Hart Centre for Military Archives, namely Salvatore Bellavia, Katrina DiMuro, Hannah Gibson, Kate O'Brien, Christopher Olver, Frances Pattman, Diana Manipud, Stephen Miller, Lianne Smith, Chloe Jane Thomas, and Catherine Williams – uncovered precious documents and fed me cake. Extra special thanks with bells on to Geoff Browell, Head of Archives and Research Collections at King's, for his continued support and kindness. I thank Gary Heales and Ainsley Vinall at Vestry House Museum/Waltham Forest Local Studies Centre for their thoughtful assistance and enthusiasm, as well as Angela Wagstaff, and John and Pat Harvey ... you have all been smashing. The curators within the Division of Medical Sciences, Smithsonian Institution, and particularly Katherine Ott, accommodated me with care. Katrina M. Brown, Alexia MacClain, Catherine Keen, and Jim Roan at Smithsonian Libraries were unfailingly helpful. Special thanks to Anthony Shepherd of the Birkbeck School of Arts, and Beatriz Ferrer-Quiles at Birkbeck

Library. I am grateful to the British Library, the Science Museum London, the London School of Economics library, the National Archives at Kew, the London Metropolitan Archives, Samantha Blake at the BBC Written Archives Centre, University College London libraries, and the Institute of Education Library – including Beverley Hinton, Bryan Johnson, Christopher Josiffe, Francesca Peruzzo, Freddie Linares, and Daniel O'Connor. Thanks also to Senate House Library, the History of Advertising Trust, the National Institutes of Health in Bethesda, Maryland, Lucas Clawson at the Hagley Museum and Library, Wilmington, Delaware, Jeanie Smith and Jo Wisdom at the City Business Library at Guildhall Library, Mary Rose Barrington and Peter Johnson at the Society for Psychical Research, Iain Logie Baird at the National Science and Media Museum in Bradford, the University of Vienna Library, the Royal College of Surgeons Library, Alice Mackay of the Waltham Forest Oral History Workshop, and Graham Keen of Autonumis.

My personal thanks to Faith Buck, Colin Corbett, Mark Gilfillan, Iain Gray, Robin and Sarah Greenwood, Susan Haines, the gorgeous Susan Jackson, Jeremy Mack, Andrew Malleson, Kate Malleson, Jose Martinez, Scarlett Parker, Oliver Porschmann, Greg "Greggypoos" Rea, Leah Richbell, Jennifer Anne Rowley, Bernard "Scaifey" Scaife, Michael and Fiona Skyers and their beautiful family, Bruce and Pam Tugby, Christin "Super Swede" Vidgren, Simon Willgress, Jeanie Wills, Lynne Williams, and Ness Wood. I know that dear departed friends Peter Cannings and Ronald Falloon have been willing me along. Nigel Fahey started it all when he pointed out the disused LRC factory on the North Circular Road, shortly before it was demolished in the late 1990s. The image stuck. My glamorous assistant, Jemima Jarman, has been there through thick and thin. How lucky am I? Last, but certainly not least, I thank my family for their kindness, understanding, and good humour. I am as surprised as you are!

Condoms – or 'protectives', as London Rubber called them – have always done well as a consumer product in Britain, but the industry has been little understood by outside observers, and historically consumers have not found the subject easy to talk about. This has given the impression that condom makers and users have operated in the shadows, away from public view, ashamed to be seen participating in a trade popularly associated with exploitation and sleaze. Not everybody has felt this way, however, and for a large part of the twentieth century those who dealt in condoms found themselves negotiating the finely drawn line that existed between a product that was 'unmentionable' in the public sphere,[1] but which sold like hotcakes. The London Rubber Company, of Chingford, North London, was by and far the biggest and most successful condom manufactory that ever existed in Britain: it was a 'first mover' in dipped latex condoms, balloons, and gloves, rapidly developing mass production capabilities and squashing competition in the process.[2] This book offers the first major study of the company's rise during its first fifty years, between 1915 and 1965. Using new primary sources, *Protective Practices* delivers a detailed history of London Rubber and Durex condoms, making a critical contribution to our current understanding of the development of mass-produced, consumer-oriented, single-use contraceptives during the early and mid-twentieth century. In combining a general history of the condom with a business history of London Rubber as its dominant supplier, *Protective Practices* argues that the development of the British condom market was substantially influenced by the company's policies and relentless efforts at self-preservation.

As will be shown, London Rubber went to considerable lengths to protect its interests, basing its business strategy around creating, and defending, the monopoly in condom production and supply. It then pursued a high profit, high price strategy based on generous margins for both itself and its retailers. This meant, on the one hand, that marketing and distribution was necessarily focused on a somewhat seedy group of retailers (back street chemists, barbers, surgical appliance shops, etc.), which served to keep the condom outside the mainstream of family planning, closing the industry off to competition. On the other hand, London Rubber tried to widen cultural acceptance (and, therefore, the market) by working with the non-profit Family Planning Association and cashing in on its good reputation. However, London Rubber's tendency towards underhanded dealing and self-interest meant that socially motivated family planners remained wary, and refused to provide an official, public endorsement of the company. The advent of oral contraception as a disruptive innovator threatened London Rubber's monopoly position,[3] triggering a belated drive towards marketing aimed at more mainstream customers, and a 'dirty tricks' PR campaign which largely backfired. Not knowing where the market would go next, London Rubber half-heartedly brought out an own-brand oral contraceptive pill, Feminor, which eventually sank without a trace. But despite these trials and tribulations, London Rubber did not capsize under the combined threats of rival technologies and recalcitrant family planners, and neither did the condom: *Protective Practices* explains why.

Background to This Study

Today, condoms are automatically associated with protection against disease as well as pregnancy, and are widely purchased by men and women for use during sex and sex play. For generations that have come of age since the 1980s HIV and AIDS crisis, it is difficult to imagine a time when the condom was not explicitly marketed for 'safe sex', and yet this was not always the case in Britain.[4] While condoms were undoubtedly bought and sold for self-protection by teenagers at vending machines, men in barbershops, and prostitutes and their clients around Soho and other places, evidence that so-called 'French letters', 'rubber johnnies', or, indeed, 'protectives', provided complete protection against sexually transmitted infections was inconclusive.[5] Gay men, for example, had not yet been targeted by the condom trade's safe sex campaigns,[6] or by public health bodies, or by peers within their own communities. In twentieth-century America, condoms could be legally sold under the label of disease prevention, but not for the purposes of birth control following the 1918 *Crane* ruling.[7] In Britain the opposite was true. The 1917 Venereal Disease Act made it illegal to proffer items for the prevention or cure of VD, and made it an offence to 'advertise in any way any preparation or substance of any kind as a medicine for the prevention, cure or relief of venereal diseases'.[8] The medical status of condoms would be pondered for many decades, but during first half of the twentieth century the majority of makers and advertising vendors erred on the side of caution and did not market condoms for disease protection.

Consequently, condoms were sold as 'contraceptives' rather than 'prophylactics' in Britain, and by the middle years of the twentieth century the prevention of pregnancy within the heterosexual family unit had become the default marketing angle. By this time, quality of life had improved for the average British family, which had become smaller. Aggregate fertility rates had taken a sharp drop in the 1870s, reaching very low levels in the 1930s before climbing again during the Second World War and peaking in the 1960s, but not nearly approaching nineteenth-century levels.[9] Whereas decreased family size contributed to higher living standards and increased leisure time, modern labour-saving innovations and the standardisation of consumer products presented more options for how that time might be spent, even by the working classes (although this group was less likely to use condoms).[10] Condoms fitted well into these new patterns of consumption: they were an incredibly successful product that could be purchased in most towns and cities, or ordered through the post. Unlike in America, where a tradition of female contraception meant that the oral contraceptive pill quickly displaced the condom when it was released in the late 1950s,[11] men took the lead in British birth control practice.[12] Despite the availability of contraception being linked to the fertility decline,[13] condom sales flourished in post-war, post-austerity 'family Britain',[14] following an upward trajectory between 1949 and 1965 that coincided with recovering birth rates and the increased popularity of marriage (appendix 1).[15] A major research study by Rachel Pierce and Griselda Rowntree, which was published in two parts in 1961, showed that condoms were the most commonly used appliance contraceptive, followed by the practice of withdrawal, which was also known as 'pulling out' or *coitus interruptus*.[16] Oral contraceptives broadened the total market for birth control, and condom use only began to be overtaken in the mid-1970s, when the National Health Service made the pill available for free.[17]

Protective Practices presents the first in-depth, historical account of the London Rubber Company. Chapters 1–8 detail its first fifty years of operation between 1915, when the Jackson brothers set up as a contraceptive wholesaler on Aldersgate Street, and 1965, by which time the company dominated the market for condoms, and the steady, cumulative growth in condom sales came to an end. Chapter 9 gives a précised overview of

FIGURE 0.1   Women staff members clocking off, North Circular Road, 1947.

events affecting London Rubber and the condom over the subsequent thirty-five years, including those that led to the closure of the last condom factory in Britain in July 1994. *Protective Practices* tells the story of how London Rubber came to dominate the trade in birth control appliances during five decades of unprecedented social change, encompassing two world wars, and the oral contraceptive pill. For sure, these were extraordinary times. Despite the growth of contraceptive provision for women, the condom remained a lucrative product and London Rubber ruthlessly pursued the monopoly on production and supply, absorbing or otherwise squashing competitors in the process. During its most prosperous years, London Rubber was the key player not only in condoms, but also in the wider contraceptive industry, laying the foundations for the easy-access contraceptive landscape we enjoy today. As will be shown, profits made off the back of condoms bankrolled family planning clinics, subsidising the development and sale of diaphragms, as well as London Rubber's own in-house contraceptive pill. In addition, 'the Rubber' (as the factory complex was known locally) was, for many years, the biggest employer in the Chingford area. Condoms provided regular and reliable employment to thousands of people, including mothers and homemakers, their children, and their friends. By the 1960s, London Rubber was the monopoly

FIGURE 0.2   Small latex tanks leaving North Circular Road factory, 1950.

producer and distributor, and was also the only full-line British contraceptive house.

It was also a secretive organisation that was the subject of no fewer than
three investigations by the Monopolies and Mergers Commission between the 1970s and 1990s. Historians have found the company's early
interests and activities difficult to unpack because of the limited availability of primary sources. Apart from official photograph albums (which
are held at the Vestry House Museum, London Borough of Waltham Forest,
and are published here for the first time), there is no publicly accessible
corporate archive. Prior to this book, short studies about (or otherwise
touching upon) the London Rubber story are all that have been available.
Local historians Leonard Davis and Bill Bayliss have each produced brief
written pieces focused specifically on the company's history in Chingford.[18] Sociologist John Peel's 1963 study on contraceptive manufacturing
and retailing is an excellent starting point for background reading into
how the Victorian birth control boom paved the way for the modern industry, but its account of London Rubber's rise to success is skeletal.[19] As
discovered during the course of this research, Peel was co-opted by the
company at around this time, which calls into question the objectivity of
this account.

More recently, articles by Paul Jobling, Ben Mechen, and Claire L. Jones have revived academic interest in London Rubber.[20] Jobling's article tracks events in venereal disease prevention from 1780, then looks at the promotion of contraception and prophylaxis from 1970 to the 1980s, before examining the paradox between prophylaxis and pleasure. Jobling's corpus is composed of print advertisements for condoms with a focus on London Rubber's Durex brand, which he uses to analyse their iconography and symbolism.[21] Mechen has also produced an engaging case study of the Durex brand using magazine and newspaper advertisements from 1972 to 1979, which explores converging concepts of 'safety' and 'pleasure' as marketing hooks, and advances the concept of 'contraceptive consumerism'.[22] In the absence of a corporate archive, print advertisements offer a useful pathway for beginning to understand the motivations of the company behind the brand, but Jones, a medical historian, proposes a different strategy for finding primary sources in the history of contraception. In her article, 'Under the Covers? Commerce, Contraceptives and Consumers in England and Wales, 1880–1960', which sets London Rubber products in their historical retail context, Jones explains how she looked for information indirectly, exploring underused paper sources such as the archives of social interest groups, parliamentary papers, and trade catalogues.[23] This methodological approach was used to 'trace contraceptive products on their commercial journey to consumers – from production and promotion, to distribution and sales – and [to] identify their relevant significance'.[24] By looking at condoms (and other contraceptives) as material objects that were bought and sold (as well as used), Jones widened her search criteria and found that new information was plentiful.

Responding to what is clearly an interest in London Rubber, and following on from the premise, inspired by Jones, that a company as omnipresent as London Rubber must have left behind more than just adverts, this study brings together a unique and diverse palette of new or otherwise overlooked primary sources (see appendix 5). In doing so, it paints a detailed and highly descriptive picture of the company and its activities that has been lacking in shorter works, drawing from the fields of market research, retail reports, regulation, and autobiography. Many histories of contraception have been written from social science or cultural history perspectives.[25] As such, sources focused on production and supply would normally fall to the side.[26] In *Protective Practices*, however, a source-driven framing pushes beyond the existing social, political, and public health narratives in contraceptive history. The result is a complex, source-led story in that greatly expands upon the current corpus, while filling a gap in our understanding of how the commercial condom trade actually traded. In this sense, *Protective Practices* seeks to tessellate with other, more general studies on the condom by Aine Collier and Jeanette Parisot,[27] as well as with Jones's ongoing work.[28] London Rubber's story is central to this emerging field, and is important for opening up the examination of contraception as a business as well as a social cause because, as the American historian Rosemarie Petra Holz has pointed out, the two are so closely related.[29] While other historians have been interested in the commercial side of contraceptives, the British condom industry — and London Rubber's role in developing and monopolising it — has not yet been explored in depth. Norman Himes offered the first serious historical examination of the contraceptive and condom industries in America and Britain in his influential *Medical History of Contraception* (1936).[30] Andrea Tone devotes a chapter to 'Condom Kings' in her book *Devices and Desires: A History of Contraceptives in America* (2002).[31] However, these accounts do little to illuminate the emergence, development, and significance of the modern *British* condom. Himes's book was published in the 1930s, and Tone's account of commercial contraceptive history from 1873 to the 1970s focuses on America. Tone's discussion of the condom business also drops off abruptly once the contraceptive pill enters the scene, leaving open the question of how traditional contraceptive houses responded to this unknown quantity. Were they worried? Or did they set out to take advantage of the expanding women's market? These questions are relevant to all the contraceptive firms that were around when technological disruptors entered the fray, and are discussed in the closing chapters of this book.

In terms of media attention, condoms never attained the volume or quality of exposure that the pill did in the 1960s. Like the dispersed London Rubber archive drawn together for *Protective Practices*, the condom in British life was both seen and unseen. As late as 1981, marketing experts Aubrey Wilson and Christopher West still considered the condom an 'unmentionable' product in Britain. According to them, condoms shared marketing characteristics with napalm, drugs for terminal illnesses, and funeral arranging.[32] Conceptually, and for the purposes of marketing, the idea of condoms was felt to be akin to 'extreme political ideas', 'emotional preparation for death', 'unconventional sexual activities', 'racial or religious prejudice', and 'terrorism'.[33] In mapping London Rubber's rise to success, this book necessarily takes account of the company's failures, detailing its better-known challenges and some lesser-known embarrassments. For example, it is a testament to the company's early adoption of damage limitation techniques that the original architect of mass-produced latex condoms in Britain, a young Polish chemistry student named Lucian Landau who fell out with the company's founders during the Second World War over alleged black market trading, has long been forgotten. This book dusts off Landau's own story, making it available to a wider audience and restoring his place in contraceptive history. In particular, I ask: what was the business strategy that enabled London Rubber to secure, and retain, its almost monopoly position? In focusing on manufacture, distribution, and market forces, *Protective Practices* explores commercial production and supply as categories for analysing corporate decision-making in the specific case of birth control in Britain. These categories are intrinsically linked to other analytical channels, including innovation, the use of public relations techniques, and the dynamics of corporate protectionism.

Production and supply are presented as conduits to the multifaceted and varied array of actors that participated in contraceptive culture, leading to unexpected discoveries. For example, *Protective Practices* presents clear evidence of London Rubber's systematic intervention into women's contraceptive regimens. As will be shown, the unique profitability of condoms enabled London Rubber to manufacture women's contraceptives at close to a loss throughout the twentieth century. While cervical caps, diaphragms, and spermicidal creams did not contribute very much to profits, the interrelated social, cultural, and business conditions of the time made it strategically useful for London Rubber to continue making them. *Protective Practices* argues that the company's intervention in women's contraception was a significant contributory factor in the survival of cash-starved family planning clinics, even though these weren't especially interested in condom supply. London Rubber enjoyed considerable power in the mid-twentieth century, but as Holz has pointed out, birth control clinics were not without clout.[34] What is apparent here is that, despite the often-made connection of reproductive determination with 'power',[35] control in the contraceptive business was neither one-directional nor linear. As such, this book takes the position that, to use sexuality historian Jeffrey Weeks's words, 'Power does not operate through single mechanisms of control. It operates through complex and overlapping – and often contradictory – mechanisms, which produce domination *and* opposition, subordination *and* resistance, regulation *and* agency'.[36] London Rubber fought tooth and nail to win the custom of the new family planning clinics, and to squeeze this resource both for its customer base and for access to publicity. What *Protective Practices* shows is that, for London Rubber, power to manufacture at scale had to be tempered with being seen to support non-profit contraception as a social cause, as well as upholding popular ideas about the family and marriage.

So far as London Rubber was concerned, expanding the consumer base for condoms was always an aim, but the company nonetheless floated on the periphery of changing norms. As Paul Jobling has suggested, intervention in British sexuality was not the company's goal:[37] on the contrary, the cultural stigma surrounding condoms benefitted business, in that it created a formidable barrier to competition. One need only look to the AIDS crisis, which is covered in detail in chapter 9, to see how the eventual de-stigmatisation of condom use finally made London Rubber vulnerable to competitive forces. In the first fifty years, however, before contraceptives were woven into national health policy for the prevention of pregnancy (in the 1970s), or into public health policy for the protection against disease (in the 1980s), condoms were, by and large, marketed on a normative model,[38] and were sold to straight men, heterosexual couples, and (less obviously) to prostitutes. London Rubber was not the only manufacturer, but it was the biggest and boldest, fabricating condoms under many brand names for itself, for other companies, and for the family planning clinic movement, at home and abroad.

As Lesley A. Hall notes in her foreword, it was not illegal to sell condoms. Compared to America, where their promotion and distribution was initially prohibited under the 1873 Comstock Act,[39] and then loosened under the 1918 *Crane* ruling (see above), government control in Britain was minimal, and advertising in paper media or in shops was theoretically possible. However, restrictions on publicity ebbed and flowed, and came from all directions – from retailers in the pharmacy trade, from advertising vendors (such as newspapers), from regulators, and from the Family Planning Association. These parties and others objected variously to the types of consumers that condoms attracted, and to the quality of the products. Not wanting to rock the boat, London Rubber sat on the fence with these issues, acting most forcibly when the market offered something new. 'We always wanted what we had not got', former London Rubber salesman John Harvey told me in 2016. 'We wanted it both ways … everything was defensive: to protect ourselves'.

Protective Practices is divided into nine chapters, the first eight detailing London Rubber's first fifty years, from 1915 to 1965. The final chapter presents a précis of significant events from 1965 to 2001. Chapter 1, 'Rise of the Condom', gives a brief history of condom retailing in Britain, and outlines the reputational issues the condom faced in the early part of the twentieth century, with particular reference to open retailing, the VD crisis during the Great War, and cultural associations with prostitution. Chapter 2, 'Rise of London Rubber', charts the evolution of the company from its beginnings as a wholesaler to its shift into manufacturing Durex in 1932, encompassing its growth during the Second World War, and the sale of public shares in 1950. This chapter pays close attention to the key personalities responsible for London Rubber's success, including the Jackson family, chemist and inventor Lucian Landau, managing director Angus Reid, and ex-staff members John Harvey and Angela Wagstaff. Chapter 2 also includes a section on company culture, which explains what it was like to work for London Rubber in the 1950s and 1960s.

From this point on, chapters make detailed case studies of specific events and situations that affected the contraceptive trade, and London Rubber in particular, between the 1920s and the 1960s. The business of dealing in contraceptives was never straightforward. By looking at how London Rubber coped with potential crises, we can learn more about the company's motivations, and how these shaped the marketplace for ordinary consumers of condoms. Chapter 3, 'To Be Seen, or Not?', details the methods and problems of retailing condoms from the 1920s to the 1960s. It shows how family planning campaigners attempted to restrict the retail sale of contraceptives and the machine vending of condoms, how retail pharmacy grew as a commercial channel, and how London Rubber responded to challengers. The chapter ends by reflecting upon the 'under the counter' debate, and questioning the idea that condoms have historically been 'invisible' for cultural reasons. Chapter 4, 'London Rubber and the Family Planning Association', is a case study of London Rubber's relationship with the British Family Planning Association from the 1930s to the 1960s. In particular, it unpacks how female methods, namely cervical caps and diaphragms, were used by London Rubber as leverage against the FPA (a woman-centred organisation), and to squash competition from other manufacturers, such as Lamberts of Dalston. This chapter reveals the ways in which the FPA received support from London Rubber, in the form of financial aid and professional guidance on public relations strategy and implementation.

It is at this halfway point that *Protective Practices* turns to events affecting London Rubber between the late 1950s and 1965. Chapter 5, 'All Change: Into the 1960s', describes organisational and motivational shifts that occurred as the company expanded its interests. The condom remained London Rubber's main source of income in this period, during which time it introduced the first lubricated condom under its flagship brand, Durex Gossamer. The 1950s and early 1960s were also characterised by the cultivation of diverse income streams as London Rubber ventured into new areas, and expanded abroad. This was underpinned by changes in consumer relationships in Britain, wherein the company was attacked by the nascent Consumers' Association, and became subject to the new British Standard for condoms. This chapter shows how London Rubber used public relations techniques to turn challenges into opportunities, as a means of attracting publicity that it otherwise could not attract through normal channels.

Chapter 6, 'The Consumer Speaks', explores problems the company faced with consumer advertising at the beginning of the 1960s, considered in the context of London Rubber's response to the nascent oral contraceptive, which was widely publicised. London Rubber went to great lengths to understand the pill and why consumers found the idea of it so attractive as a method of birth control. The chapter is supported by the use of market research reports, which show that consumers also felt that brand advertising for contraceptives was distasteful. Chapter 7, 'The Public Relations Game', explains how London Rubber approached the problem of the pill by both appropriating it and working against it, following market research. The company waged an underground public relations campaign designed to undermine the idea of the pill, which was aimed at both the medical profession and journalists who, it was hoped, would feed doubts back to consumers. Chapter 8, 'Feminor: The London Rubber Pill', details how London Rubber gained insider information on oral contraception by developing, trailing, and marketing its own birth control pill, Feminor, while concurrently running a disinformation campaign designed to undermine oral contraception overall. Finally, chapter 9 gives a detailed précis of the decades following London Rubber's first fifty years, namely the 1970s, 1980s, and 1990s. In particular, this section deals with the AIDS crisis, and London Rubber's disastrous diversification into photographic processing, which contributed to the closure of the Chingford condom factory in 1994. A brief conclusion then offers an overview of the main research findings.

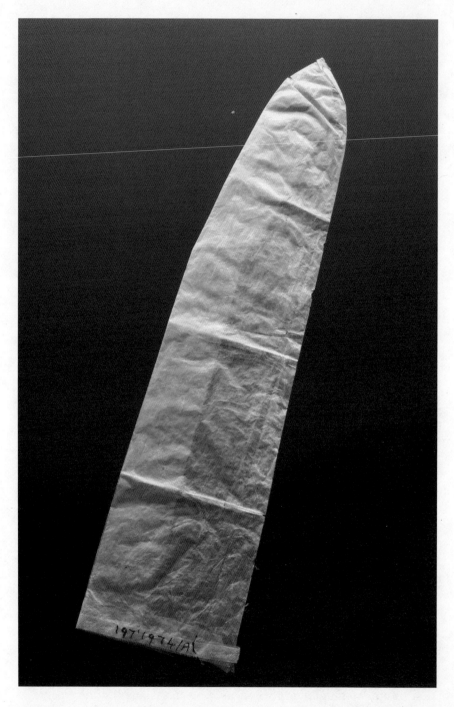

FIGURE 1.1   Condom, London, England, 1901–30. Made from animal skin.

The condom has a long and interesting history, particularly in relation to how it has been made, sold, and discussed. After exploring some of the early history, this opening chapter looks at the manner in which condoms were retailed in the early twentieth century, and how their reputation was affected by debates about venereal disease around the time of the Great War. The social stigmatisation of condoms – particularly the link between condoms, disease, and prostitution – would go on to affect London Rubber once it had become a successful manufacturer, so it is useful for us to understand why pharmacies and chemists' shops would become the preferred retail outlets, and also the way that the condom's history and reputation affected consumers' feelings about using them.

Penis sheaths have existed in one form or another since ancient times.[1] Rather than being employed wholly as a contraceptive, the sheath (or 'condom') in history is widely construed as having had a principally prophylactic function prior to the twentieth century.[2] The Italian anatomist Gabrielle Fallopius (who also gave his name to the fallopian tube) provided the first published account of a linen glans sheath in 1564, in his posthumously published *De Morbo Gallico liber absolutismu*.[3] A syphilis specialist, Fallopius advised the use of 'a small linen cloth made to fit the glans' because of the European syphilis epidemic at the end of the fifteenth century.[4] The origin of the term 'condom' itself is widely contested,[5] but the first published use of the word reportedly comes from a 1706 poem by John Hamilton (Lord Belhaven), entitled 'A Scots Answer to a British Vision'.[6] Later, the physician Daniel Turner referenced a 'condum' in his *Practical Treatise on the Venereal Disease* in 1717, after which time the condom appeared as standard in VD textbooks.[7] Norman Himes traced 'the earliest sheaths of contraceptive form' to the sixteenth century, and Casanova subsequently noted his personal use of them both for prophylaxis and preventing pregnancy in the eighteenth century.[8] It was at this time that London wholesale trade took off, wherein animal skin condoms were manufactured, warehoused, and distributed.[9] These businesses were dominated by women, with prostitutes and madams (among others) acting as distributors. Successful manufacturing warehouses, such as Mrs Phillips's of Half-Moon Street, Strand, London, advertised the sale of 'cundums' through handbills from the 1770s onward. Mrs Phillips also claimed to be a European distributor, with orders from 'France, Spain, Portugal, Italy, and other foreign places'. She supplied 'apothecaries, chymists, druggists, etc.', and 'ambassadors, foreigners, gentlemen, and captains of ships going abroad'.[10]

Skin condoms from this period likely resembled those discovered by the British sex historian Eric Dingwall in a country mansion in the 1950s.[11] These came in three sizes in packets of eight, in blue and white rag wrappings. Seamless skins were secured with a silk ribbon at the base of the penis because they were not elastic, although moistening the skin helped the material to cling. Skin condoms were an expensive luxury item because their manufacture was time consuming and labour intensive. By and large, skins were made from the sheep caecum (the pouch connecting the junction of the small and large intestines). The process consisted of around ten stages, including an alkaline treatment and exposure to brimstone vapour. Some models were polished on oiled moulds, scented, and doubled up for strength.[12] The luxurious status of skins was also due to the fact that there is only one caecum per animal. Nonetheless, their value to butchers was limited compared to other parts of the animal, and most did not take time to separate the caecum after slaughter, making them relatively scarce.[13] The cottage industry around skins depended on the willingness of consumers to pay high prices for an item they felt comfortable using, and proactive marketing to inform users of availability and variety was central to keeping the market competitive.

The rubber condom industry began with the discovery of vulcanisation, or the 'heat curing' of rubber in 1843–44 by Hancock (in Britain) and Goodyear (in America). This made rubber easier to manipulate and handle in the manufacturing process. The first mass production of rubber contraceptives in Britain is attributed to Lamberts of Dalston, an East London firm that began intensive production of vulcanised crepe rubber sheaths in 1877.[14] This is reported as having begun in the 1850s in America.[15] Both accounts coincide with the Brazilian rubber boom, which in the second half of the nineteenth century supplied 'most of the rubber used for gaskets, valves, belts, wire insulation, carriage, bicycle, and automobile tires, boots, shoes, raincoats, condoms, and elastic garters'.[16] Early rubber sheaths were made by manually assembling flat, raw rubber into a tube, and fixing a seam down the length.[17] Sheet crepe was wrapped around a mould, sealed down one side, and then vulcanised.[18] This 'sheet process' method of production was easy and used minimal equipment. Cutting the rubber with dies also meant that a uniform product could be created en masse.[19] Lamberts was producing up to 720,000 units annually from the 1890s, but despite their apparent popularity, sheet process sheaths were thick and crude compared to modern condoms.[20] In any case, available rubber contraceptives were not limited to condoms and included occlusive female diaphragms, caps, and sponges. Variants on the sheath were also made, including glans coverings, as well as a type that could be inverted, making it interchangeable for male (external) or female (internal) use.[21] Though small, the burgeoning rubber contraceptives industry attracted a steady flow of newcomers: eight 'rubber goods' firms, Claire Jones tells us, had clustered in the London India Rubber Works, Dalston, by 1883.[22] Aside from Lamberts, firms operating in the 1890s included A. Dumas Surgical Appliances, the Surgical Rubber Company, and the Hygienic Remedy Company.[23] Further contraceptive producers sprang up in the cosmopolitan hubs of Manchester, Birmingham, and Leeds.[24]

Himes has called vulcanisation the first 'revolution' in condoms.[25] So far as comfort and usability was concerned, the second revolution occurred following the move from sheet process to cement dipping in the late Victorian factory period, allowing for the manufacture of a full-length sheath without a seam.[26] Sources are divided on exactly when this happened. Some say dipping was developed in Germany in the 1880s,[27] while others claim Goodyear carried out the first cement dipping in 1901.[28] Either way, the method was well established by the fin de siècle, allowing for greater economies of scale in production, thereby lowering costs, and facilitating widespread use.[29] In the cement process, natural crepe rubber was masticated and dissolved, then heated with a solvent (such as petrol or benzene), making a liquid solution into which porcelain, wood, or glass formers were dipped. Multiple glass mandrels were arranged on racks for batch dipping. The solvent was then evaporated, leaving the shaped rubber behind, which could be re-dipped until the desired thickness was reached. The cement process was time consuming: drying between coats could take upwards of an hour. 'Finger cots', condom-like forms used for digital medical examinations, typically had six to seven dips with two hours between each, for example.[30] Once fully dipped, mandrels were cold cured using sulphur chloride gas, resulting in a thick, seamless vulcanised rubber sheath.[31] Though comprising many steps, the basic process was simple enough to be adopted by cottage industry producers.[32] In Merthyr Tydfil, for example, Tommy Horton set up a small factory in his garage around 1915, following a consultation with Lamberts, the manufacturer from Dalston. Horton's business would later become known as Bentalls.[33]

According to the London Rubber Company, most cement-dipped sheaths were imported to Britain from Germany.[34] Industrial-scale dipped fabrication appeared with the Berlin-based Fromms Act brand in 1914, whose annual output ran into millions.[35] In America, the cement process was popularised by the New-York based Julius Schmid company, makers of the Ramses and Sheik brands.[36] Schmid, Andrea Tone tells us, was a paralysed Jewish immigrant from Germany who began fabricating skin condoms from sausage casings in 1883.[37] In 1915, he branched out into cement process condoms, and was followed in 1916 by another New York manufacturer, Youngs Rubber, originator of the Trojan brand.[38] The Great War created considerable extra demand and left an opening for exporting condoms to Britain, since they could no longer be drawn from Germany. As condoms were illegal in America until the 1918 *Crane* ruling (after which they could be sold as prophylactics), the supply of American cement condoms to Britain supported these businesses.[39]

Some early sheaths were intended to be reused many times. Durability was partially dependent on the rubber itself (which perished quickly following curing), and partially on the carefulness of the user. Reusable sheaths needed to be rinsed and powdered with French chalk inside and out so that the moist rubber didn't adhere to itself. They also needed to be stored in consistent conditions. Well kept, the reusable sheath might last for three months or longer.[40] Peripherals, such as rolling devices and dusting powder, could also be purchased, making use and care easier and contributing to the ritualization of sheath use. Compared to skins, which were only 0.038 mm thick,[41] cement sheaths were very heavy, weighing around 3–4 grams per unit. Such was the thickness that reusable sheaths were even prescribed for cases of premature ejaculation.[42] Up to this point, then, rubber sheaths had become easier to produce and obtain than skins, but the expensive and difficult-to-produce caecum condom offered a superior user experience – for those who could afford it.

The third revolution in condom manufacture was the introduction of latex rubber.[43] Latex-dipped condoms did not transmit body heat as easily as skin condoms, but they brought rubber closer to the skin experience while keeping costs low and availability high. Latex condoms were also disposable, requiring no aftercare. This had implications for manufacturing and retailing: the condom became a one-off consumable, thus steering consumers toward regular repeat purchasing. Packaging was also tied directly to the intrinsic qualities of the new disposable condom. Unlike reusable sheaths, which were bulky and had to be stored in a long box, disposable latex condoms could be carried inconspicuously about the person in small envelopes just as the historic skin condoms had been, making disposable latex condoms especially suited to casual or spontaneous use.

From a manufacturing perspective, latex made the fabrication process faster, safer, and cheaper. The inflammable solvents used in cement-dipped condoms had meant that factories regularly caught fire.[44] As well as posing a risk to life and limb, fires interrupted production and pushed up insurance premiums.[45] By the end of the 1920s, the American companies Killian, Shunk, and Youngs had all suffered bad fires, and on one occasion the whole of Youngs's cement dipping room was destroyed.[46] On top of being safe to produce, latex condoms could be dipped, dried, vulcanized, and stripped in a fraction of the time it took for cement condoms. This saved on costs in many ways, not least of which was reducing the number of glass mandrels needed, thus reducing capital expenditure on basic equipment.[47] Curing by simple hot water also had the benefit of preserving durability, meaning that latex condoms were thinner, stronger, and more elastic than cement condoms, with a shelf life of five years, as opposed to three months for reusable sheaths.[48] Of course, they still could be used only once.

The European transition from cement process to latex dipping was slow compared to America, where nearly all of the manufacturers (the exception was Julius Schmid) had dumped the old-style condoms by the 1930s.[49] In 1931, the Killian company of Akron, Ohio, patented a highly efficient automated machine system which dipped inverted mandrels on a continuous conveyor or 'chain' at the rate of one per second, dried them with hot air, then dipped and dried again.[50] Once finished, condoms were stripped by rotating brushes that created a beaded edge and then were manually packed. Killian's chain was 500 feet long, contained

4,000 glass mandrels in dual series, and produced close to 173,000 units per day.[51] Fred Killian invented the revolutionary system after a relative died in a factory fire.[52] His technology was protected by a US patent, but also by the prohibitive cost of leasing it, meaning that smaller producers were left behind in the latex condom revolution.[53] Youngs Rubber, however, was big enough to participate in the new style technology and had hitherto been outsourcing production; it leased the technology from Killian in 1933.[54] It was Youngs that exported the first branded latex condom to Britain, the Dreadnought, in 1929.[55] Ostensibly named for a class of British battleship with large-calibre guns that was launched in 1906, 'Dreadnought' had also been the nickname for an early form of VD treatment called Nargol, which was carried around in a tube (below).

As will be discussed in detail in the following chapter, latex dipping in Britain was started in 1932 by British Latex Products Ltd, sister firm of the London Rubber Company, under the direction of Polish rubber technologist Lucian Landau.[56] Initially, this was a semi-mechanised affair: continuous, fully automated latex condom production did not begin in Britain until around 1951. By this time London Rubber was already the leading manufacturer of condoms.[57] It is difficult to overstate the significance of switching to an automated process for the British contraceptives industry, and for the consumer, the leap in quality and yield was correspondingly significant. Non-stop twenty-four-hour fabrication dramatically increased output, affording extraordinary jumps in production volume. Whereas in the mid-1930s London Rubber had been producing around two million condoms per year via semi-mechanised machines, by 1954 the automated lines produced over two million *per week*.[58] Annual yield catapulted to 200 million units by the mid-1960s (see appendix 1).[59] London Rubber relied upon its own technical resources to design everything in-house, meaning that it did not have to purchase technology from America, and was the only fully automated condom manufacturer ever to operate in Britain.[60]

Open Availability

The distribution and sale of contraceptives was not a criminal offence in Britain, and a buoyant retail market existed even before large-scale mass production of disposable latex condoms.[61] Vulcanised rubber sheaths quickly became grouped with other 'rubber goods', as various types of contraceptive were known. In H. Berdot's 1904 catalogue, rubber and skin 'protectors' were offered alongside rubber vaginal pessaries, soluble quinine pessaries, rubber vaginal sponges, and Marvel 'Whirling Spray' syringes (for vaginal douching), all of which were used for preventing pregnancy.[62] Early forms of intrauterine device were also available, but less complicated mass-produced methods such as condoms and pessaries could be purchased off the shelf, and used without a gynaecological examination. These proved very popular.

Having been a long-standing centre for the condom trade, London naturally adapted to the open retailing of mass-produced rubber goods, and contraceptive shops emerged in areas where skin warehouses had previously dominated in the central areas of the city. A 1933 survey of Fleet Street, Chancery Lane and High Holborn, Leicester Square, Charing Cross Road, Camden, Euston, and Victoria found thirty-seven shops 'exposing' contraceptives openly for sale, with twenty-five of them concentrated in the West End (map 3.1).[63] Even a few decades earlier, a doctor visiting from Dublin in 1897 was 'astonished and amazed to see how London chemists display such things in their windows, under the very eyes of the public and the noses of the police, with perfect impunity and probably profit'. The English had become so accustomed to purchasing contraceptives without fuss, Dr McWalter said, 'that here in Dublin, where no respectable house would touch them, visitors look astonished, incredulous, and insulted when they are refused them'.[64] Incredulity and insult were clearly no deterrent to London shopkeepers, who were only too happy to feed the demand for rubber goods.

Dedicated contraceptive retail outlets were known variously as 'hygiene', 'surgical', or 'rubber' shops, which remained popular well into the twentieth century.[65] In addition to stocking contraceptives, rubber shops carried related goods such as abortifacients (substances for terminating pregnancy, such as pennyroyal) and aphrodisiacs.[66] The Stockwell Hygienic Stores, for example, sold impotence capsules and penile 'Sexaids' (the latter presumably serving the same purpose as the former). They also traded quasi-medical rubber items such as lumbago belts, trusses, and elastic hosiery.[67] Both in London and in provincial towns, retailers presented contraceptive supplies blatantly and without embarrassment, so much so that the commercialization of contraceptives was well established by the interwar period.[68] Women and men of any class might purchase them on high streets, especially near manufacturing hubs such as Leeds and York, and in southern areas close to London.[69] The Leeds chief constable, for example, reported a growth in 'Medical Stores' in the 1930s, noting the visibility of 'young women who frequent these shops for the

FIGURE 1.2 Contraceptive sponge, United Kingdom,
1901–30. Made by Elarco ('L.R. Co.').

purchase of contraceptives such as pessaries, sponges etc.', sales of which
were 'on the increase'.[70] Women also continued to act as proprietors of
contraceptive businesses as they had done since the eighteenth century.
Mrs Daisy Stewart-Matthews, for example, operated as a 'Consulting

Gynaecologist' at 369 Edge Lane and 6 Norton Street, Liverpool. From these sites, she gave lectures on birth control and sold appliances at what the chief constable called 'exorbitant prices'.[71] As well as specialist stores, condoms could be purchased through vending machines on the street, in public parks, in garages, and in pubs (more of which is discussed in chapter 3).[72] Dr Alfred Salter, MP for West Bermondsey (in London), noticed that 'contraceptives and appliances and a good many indecent accompaniments' were being openly hawked in a London street market in the 1920s.[73] One chemist even noted their advertisement by means of men carrying sandwich boards.[74]

Rubber and surgical stores notwithstanding, chemists' shops were also central to the general trade in contraceptives. One proprietor of a chemist in Plymouth, while professing not to cater for 'this class of business', admitted that his own contraceptive sales had nonetheless increased 30 per cent by 1932. Men 'inhesitatingly' came in asking both male and female counter staff for 'rubber goods', he reported. Young people, he felt, were increasingly well informed, to the degree that 'even errand boys were asking for them'. On one occasion, a 'widow of three weeks' came in to purchase 'French letters', which this particular shopkeeper found surprising.[75] Contraceptive manufacturers such as London Rubber and W.R. Rendell (who made Rendells soluble vaginal pessaries) saw chemists as the more desirable outlet, and retailers accordingly sought to wear both hats. For example, George's in Green Street, Leicester Square, was ostensibly a dispensing chemist, but also ran a mail order service as a 'Surgical and Drug Store' which offered contraceptive fitting rooms in the back of the shop. George's was also linked to the manufacturer Prentif (also a brand name), which produced branded caps, condoms, and spermicides, demonstrating early vertical integration in the contraceptive business.[76] Herbalists, who operated outside of the chemist trade, were especially free to sell contraceptives, as they were not affected by the gradual restrictions imposed upon chemists' shops by trade bodies. Lloyd's Surgical, a mail order firm from Portsmouth, started out in the herbal trade.[77] According to former London Rubber sales manager John Harvey, who had also been on the road selling condoms to retailers, herbalists were popular in northern cities such as Sheffield and Doncaster, selling condoms alongside natural remedies.[78]

Herbalists, like barbershops, were usually staffed by men.[79] This made them an especially important channel for the condom trade away from metropolitan hubs in the south. Hairdresser-tobacconists' shops were

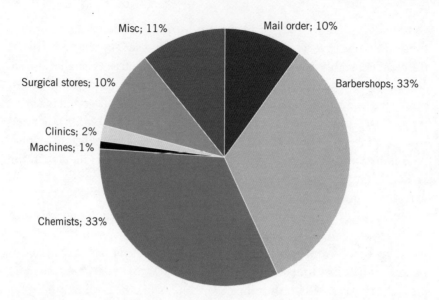

Misc; 11%   Mail order; 10%

Surgical stores; 10%   Barbershops; 33%

Clinics; 2%
Machines; 1%

Chemists; 33%

FIGURE 1.3   Estimated retail distribution of condoms, 1960s. © J. Borge 2019. Misc = pedlars, street markets, herbalists, factory sales, private clinics, etc. Sources: Economist Intelligence Unit, 'Contraceptive Products,' *Retail Business Survey* 92 (1965); John Peel and Malcolm Potts, *Textbook of Contraceptive Practice* (Cambridge: Cambridge University Press 1969); Office of Health Economics, *Family Planning in Britain* (London: Office of Health Economics 1972).

also important. In this type of shop, men could get their hair cut, buy pipe tobacco or cigarettes, and purchase condoms, all at the same time. It was also the type of shop where London Rubber began as a contraceptive wholesaler in 1915 (see chapter 2). By the early 1930s, the number of to-bacconists' shops exceeded 400,000.[80] Barbershops, however, were by far the most enduring of all condom retailers. This exclusively male domin-ion retained a large share of the condom market up to the 1970s (figure 1.3), when hairstyles became longer and demand for men's haircutting reduced.[81] The barbershop had grown out of the tobacconist-hairdresser tradition, which had customarily sold men's services alongside men's products. Unlike surgical or rubber shops, which sold a range of male and female contraceptives, barbershops specialised in condoms.[82] 'The barber', sociologist John Peel says, 'was continuing an activity which arose historically out of the barber-surgeon's concern with venereal disease and for which his shop, with its all-male clientele, provided a singularly convenient agency'.[83] Barbershops were inconspicuous on the high street, and they maintained a bachelor atmosphere where female barbers and clients were uncommon.[84] This allowed men to purchase condoms in relative privacy, but in addition to such cultural reasons, there were economic reasons for selling condoms in barbershops. Compared to female salons (where margins on cutting and styling were customarily higher), profits were relatively low on male haircutting. The sale and display of personal articles and toiletries provided an additional revenue stream, upon which barbershops depended more than women's hairdressers did.[85] Although barbers were prevented from opening on Sundays,[86] they were nonetheless direct competition for surgical stores, which did most of their business after 6 p.m.[87] Indeed, barbershops were so well known for contraceptive sales that F. Gedge, a surgical store proprietor from Stoke-on-Trent who had been trading since 1935, felt justifiably threatened when one opened next door.[88]

In addition to high street retailing, availability was facilitated by mass print culture and mail order.[89] This has a long history. For example, Mrs Mary Perkins and Mrs Phillips, who each ran commercial skin condom warehouses in London, had fought a 'war of the handbills' as early as the 1770s.[90] In the factory era, mail order was as important as shop-based retailing because of cheap postal rates. Manufacturers also printed their own trade catalogues catering to all classes.[91] Printed sales material was highly descriptive, using illustrations as well as text to explain the benefits and methods of various devices as a substitute for personal service in shops. In this sense, mass print culture also served to develop the market for contraceptive users by alerting readers to the latest available techniques, driving the purchasing cycle.

Catalogues were distributed through retailers but were also advertised via small ads in newspapers and magazines, and a common practice was to use mailing lists to send indiscriminate, unsolicited catalogues.[92] As was customary at the time, catalogues were densely packed, making them a form of entertainment as well as information. Hancock & Co., a Fleet Street chemist's shop, sent enquirers a colourful bundle of booklets covering cosmetics, 'glandular rejuvenation' (impotence cures), beauty, and abortion, all topics that were popularly grouped with contraception.[93] The volume of commercial mail order catalogues disseminated far outstripped that of print material spread by social interest groups.[94] Around 15 million pamphlets were in circulation between 1914 and 1938.[95] Far from being 'barely visible', as some historians have stated,[96] the British contraceptive marketplace in the early part of the twentieth century depended on the conspicuous display of products inside stores, in shop windows, and via mass print culture.

Uncertainty and Distrust

Despite their unqualified success as consumer items, condoms have been dogged by a negative reputation. This amounted to a kind of cultural baggage that would continue to impede the public discussion and acceptance of condoms well into the twentieth century. 'Identified as a prophylactic against sexually acquired diseases in a context of illicit sex, its use as a preventive of pregnancy has suffered', public health historian Milton Lewis has said. 'Identified as a contraceptive in a context of pro-natalism, its use as a preventive of infection has suffered'.[97] Condoms have been especially plagued by their historic association with the venereal diseases for which the early skin versions were employed. A culture of resistance emerged as markets developed at the fin de siècle alongside the nascent women's movement. For early feminists, historian Lucy Bland tells us, female VD sufferers were portrayed as victims of male sexual hypocrisy wherein 'trusting, "innocent" wives were the unsuspecting victims of a disease imposed by licentious, lying husbands'.[98] Members of the women's suffrage movement such as Louisa Martindale and Christabel Pankhurst popularised the idea that men, bent on servicing selfish sexual needs (with prostitutes, for example) were responsible for the destruction of women, and, by extension, the nation.[99] Far from being seen as a solution, condoms were regarded as part of the problem. The feminist objection lay in the availability of condoms to men for their own protection. For some social activists, contraceptive use was just as bad because the ability to prevent pregnancy, so it was thought, loosened constraints on sexual behaviour.

So far as VD was concerned, cultural and political struggles came to a head during the Great War because of the evident and devastating effect on manpower. In 1917, for example, nearly 55,000 British soldiers were hospitalised with VD.[100] The venereal diseases are very nasty. Untreated syphilis is a debilitating chronic disease, which can infect almost any tissue. Primary syphilis manifests in genital chancres (ulcers) and lesions, and the secondary stage produces flu-like symptoms. Signs of meningitis occur in around 10 per cent of secondary syphilis, and third-stage infections can kill. Gonorrhoea is an acute genito-urinary tract infection. In men, it results initially in a discharge, an inability to urinate, and the absorption of toxic material into the blood. Untreated, it spreads to other organs. In women, gonorrhoea can lead to infertility.[101] VD was easier to detect in the armed forces than in the civilian community, and servicemen were particularly likely to be infected and to infect others due to their itinerant lifestyle.[102] The practical problem for infected soldiers and sailors was the lengthy post-infection treatment that kept them out of action, especially in wartime. Following the establishment of VD hospitals in 1915, the average soldier-patient's stay was between fifty and sixty days.[103] In total, 400,000 VD cases were treated over the course of the Great War, with gonorrhoea making up 66 per cent of them.[104]

Social interest groups in Britain could not agree on a way to deal with the VD crisis, favouring either abstinence (known as 'moral prophylaxis')[105] or post-infection treatment.[106] Preemptive preventive measures were seen as licensing free sexual behaviour and as an invitation to vice.[107] For example, Mary Scharleib and Dr Edward Turner of the National Council for Combating Venereal Diseases equated prophylaxis against VD with contraception, which was, in turn, felt to promote 'uncontrolled passions'.[108] VD was seen as self-inflicted, with the infected and infecting sufferers respectively divided into the 'innocent' and the 'guilty'.[109]

Finding itself caught between conflicting public debates, the British government delayed action on VD during the Great War.[110] In fact, implementation of a standardised prophylaxis programme for the armed forces was neglected until the conflict's final months, and this did not include condoms.[111] Rather, the eventual preemptive measures consisted of mobile 'prophylactic packs' inspired by American and Dominion forces, although the American packs were withdrawn in 1915 because the secretary of the navy, Josephus Daniels, was morally opposed to them.[112] The term 'prophylactic' has become synonymous with 'condom' in common parlance because of American usage (since American condoms could not be sold as contraceptives for most of the twentieth century), but wartime 'prophylactic packs' did not in fact contain condoms or barrier protection. Rather, they were composed of topical treatments to prevent infection, and the means of applying them to the penis and groin.[113] In the British navy, packs were issued thanks to the wildcat efforts of individuals frustrated by a lack of official guidance. Venereologist Bryan Donkin and civilian medical officer Archdall Reid, for example, designed their own portable packs in 1917. Reid's packs, which were made available to 2,000 men at Portsmouth Barracks, included disinfectant (Condy's Fluid or potassium permanganate/'potash'), cotton wool swabs, and capsules of calomel ointment.[114] Soldiers were instructed to 'carefully and thoroughly swab the penis with the disinfectant before rubbing in the calomel'.[115] Dramatic results were reported: over a period of two years and four months, only seven infections were noted in a cohort of 20,000 men.[116] The British naval officer Commander P.H. Boyden and naval surgeon Halliday Sutherland conducted similar experiments in 1907 and 1914.[117] Boyden's experiments used Nargol Dreadnoughts (tubes of silver nitrate that was squeezed directly into the urethra) but found them to be less effective than potash.[118] These experiments led to the normalisation of preventive measures earlier in the navy than in the army, but it was not until the last months of the war that potash, the most effective of the experimental substances, was distributed across all operational stations.[119]

So far as condoms were concerned, there was no official recognition that they might serve as a stand-alone measure against VD, in America or Britain.[120] In 1916, Frank Kidd, assistant surgeon at London Hospital, told the Royal Commission on Venereal Disease, 'There is a very prevalent idea that the wearing of a condom is sufficient protection against contracting the disease, but I have plenty of evidence that convinces me that it is not so'.[121] The 1923 Trevethin Committee, convened to consider preventive measures against VD, accepted that 'sheaths … afford by mechanical means a measure of protection against venereal disease' but did not offer a 'complete' safeguard.[122] In the case of the Royal Navy, although VD infections reduced after standard issue began in 1933, available statistics did not prove that condom use materially affected infection rates.[123]

Inconsistency in condom quality was also a known barrier to prophylactic effectiveness in condoms. By the 1930s, manufacturing techniques were still in transition, despite technical improvements.[124] End quality was dependent on the purity of latex and the continuity of production conditions. For example, weak tips might result from mandrels being inverted for too long, too soon, or at the wrong angle into liquid latex.[125] Random sampling by biochemist Cecil Voge found structural weaknesses in popular brands, which were caused by holes, dust particles, and other foreign bodies.[126] Storage conditions and shelf life also affected reliability,[127] and uncertainty was not helped by an absence of quantitative data concerning the number of flawed products reaching consumers.[128] Condoms suffered stigmatisation because of a long association with VD and casual sex, but institutional resistance to prescribing them expressly for prophylaxis cannot wholly be attributed to cultural problems when there was a simple lack of evidence of their efficacy.

Condoms were certainly far from perfect and did not offer complete protection. Nonetheless, various alternative quack methods were even worse, and, ironically, it was because of the latter that there was a ban on all medicines for the prevention or cure of VD under the 1917 Venereal Disease Act.[129] This forced constraints on the marketing of condoms for prophylaxis, leading them to become grouped with contraceptives as the standard sales practice, avoiding the subject of disease. For many people, however, condoms remained a symbol of vice, and served as the material means of quantifying it. 'That such articles as sheaths are extensively used can be ascertained by an inspection of the hedgerows and byways near the centres of our large populous areas', Sir John Robertson, the ex-medical officer of Birmingham, reported to the Public Morality Council in 1939. 'Some years ago, complaint was made of the disgraceful conditions in a quiet back road in the north of Birmingham, and I sent an inspector to report. His report confirmed the complaints that had been made, and contained evidence that he had counted no less than twenty three sheaths in the two or three hundred yards of road he had examined'.[130]

The link between condoms, disease, and illicit sex was difficult to shake off, especially when sex was paid for. 'There is no doubt that most prostitutes acquire V.D.', said a 1955 report entitled *Women of the Streets*.[131] According to the same report, most prostitutes also used condoms.[132] Pimps bought them in bulk to sell to their women and girls for extra income.[133] Alternatively, prostitutes might buy condoms from their landladies (or madams) at cost, or could make the saving themselves, purchasing by the gross (i.e., 144 units) at discount rates. Street hawkers targeted prostitutes to sell them condoms on well-known beats.[134] Clients who disliked condoms would offer bonuses to prostitutes who forewent them,[135] and the cycle of infection continued. VD was nonetheless stigmatised among professional prostitutes, who blamed young amateurs and foreign girls for its spread. 'They're the dirty ones, they've got filthy habits; of course you know what the French are like, they are dirty people', said Bessie, an East London prostitute working in Soho in the 1950s. 'They can't even wash their hands, and that's what spreads it to us'.[136] Others claimed that 'most professional girls' went through three bottles of Dettol per week in an effort to stave off infection, presumably using it as a vaginal douche.[137]

Into a Climate of Conflict

Despite the cultural problems and public debates stirred by condom use, campaign groups championed contraception for the purposes of family limitation, working to spread awareness of the benefits and techniques of birth control practice. The Malthusian League was established in Britain in the 1870s, following the exoneration of Charles Bradlaugh and Annie Besant, who had been tried for disseminating a birth control pamphlet, *Fruits of Philosophy*, by the American Charles Knowlton. The Malthusian League was the first organisation to promote the concept of family spacing in the abstract, while the first contraceptive clinic was opened by Dr Aletta Jacobs in Amsterdam in 1882.[138] By 1913, Malthusian campaigner Dr C.V. Drysdale was agitating for clinics to be established in order to practise what had been preached. In Britain, the modern clinic movement officially started when botanist/eugenicist Marie Stopes launched the Mothers' Clinic in Holloway, North London, in 1921. Other non-profit clinics quickly followed, becoming amalgamated as the National Birth Control Association (NBCA) in 1930. This was renamed the Family Planning Association (FPA) in 1939. 'Family planning' was promoted as a practice benefitting matrimonial and familial harmony, for which women would ideally be responsible, under the assertion that men had hitherto been in control of contraceptive practice.[139] Of course, the birth control clinic movement did not automatically make contraceptives acceptable overnight, but this was the long-term goal. At this stage, however, condoms were not especially factored into the plan. Stopes, who broke away from the NBCA/FPA, believed in the "highly stimulating" (by which we can infer sexually arousing) power of semen absorption through vaginal walls, and vetoed the condom on that basis.[140] The FPA was more pragmatic: although they would supply condoms if requested, female contraceptives (such as the cap or diaphragm) were the methods preferred by clinics, this being an overly female organisation formed to serve women.

As this chapter has shown, anyone who wished to set up in the making or selling of condoms in early-twentieth-century Britain would have had significant hurdles to jump, not least of which was that respectable organisations such as the FPA supported female-controlled alternatives. Condoms had long been associated with commercial entrepreneurship, but the business was not for the faint-hearted. The product itself was inseparably bound up with profiteering, disease, illicit and commercial sex, and even anti-social behaviour (e.g., condoms littered in hedgerows): in short, condoms provided the material evidence for the existence of vice. Early feminists and others were concerned with the abuse of contraceptives and/or prophylactic measures against VD. Moral panic was magnified on both sides of the Atlantic during the Great War, but condoms were not officially proven or sanctioned for prophylaxis. War nonetheless shaped patterns of distribution and user demand, in particular establishing a supply relationship between America and Britain, where there was a history of open retailing and mail order. This was greatly aided by print culture. At the turn of the century, condoms were offered as part of a wide range of birth control devices in catalogues, but they also did well in predominantly male retail outlets such as hairdresser-tobacconists and barbershops. Whereas a widow might be frowned upon for purchasing condoms at a chemist's shop, a man might go to any number of retail outlets and purchase with impunity.

Skin condoms were superior alternatives, but the scarcity of the caecum and the laborious means of production meant that they would always be prohibitively expensive for most people. Rubber brought down the cost of protection. Technologically, rubber condoms were subject to three waves of revolution: the sheet process, the cement process, and latex dipping. The emergence of latex as a new material for making condoms pushed manufacturers to find safer and better technology. Patented automatic dipping machinery whittled down competition, and made condoms cheaper and easier to produce in larger numbers. Continuous, automated production led to dramatic improvements in both yield and user experience, although condoms were not yet entirely free from flaws. In any case, demand continued unabated, and there was money to be made. Condoms were purchased for prophylaxis as well as pregnancy prevention (whether approved of or not), and manufacturers such as London Rubber actively responded to opportunities to maximise their consumption. When Lionel Jackson first took over the running of his father's tobacconist's shop and set up as a wholesaler in 1915, his business was moulded around the procurement and distribution of a wide spectrum of contraceptives and peripherals that were commonly sold together. The London Rubber Company, as the Jackson business was called, capitalized upon years of knowledge and networks and carved out a market for itself, developing those products that could be made inexpensively and sold readily. In the event, the disposable Durex condom paved the path by which London Rubber would move from wholesaling in 1915 to manufacturing in 1932, and onto market domination following the Second World War. The story of London Rubber's rise to success, from humble beginnings in Aldersgate Street to a state-of-the-art factory in Chingford, is told in the next chapter.

2 Rise of London Rubber

The previous chapter described a cultural landscape that was, in the early decades of the twentieth century, broadly hostile to the idea of condoms in spite of their obvious popularity. Even so, barriers to entry in the British condom market were relatively few. Fire continued to be a significant risk because of solvents used in the cement rubber production process, but small-scale producers were able to set up manufacturing, for example, in garages. For those willing to navigate the physical and cultural hurdles of condom trading, the business was potentially lucrative. Recognising this, London Rubber set up as a wholesaler of rubber goods in 1915, supplying German and American condoms to the retail trade. In 1932, it funded a venture in which its new sister company, British Latex Products Ltd, began manufacturing the new latex condoms on London Rubber's behalf. This instantly set it apart from other manufacturers, such as Lamberts of Dalston, who were still making condoms using cement. Within seven years, London Rubber claimed a 50 per cent market share for condoms.[1] In 1952, following the installation of automatic dipping lines, London Rubber reported a 95 per cent share for condoms, and 75 per cent for women's diaphragms.[2] By the early 1960s, when the oral contraceptive pill came to market in Britain, London Rubber enjoyed a near monopoly in the condom trade.

This chapter describes how London Rubber grew from a small wholesaler of contraceptives to the biggest condom company in Britain, through accounts of the personalities and events that facilitated this rise to success. In particular, it looks at the internal family dynamic within the company, and how London Rubber's founding father, Lionel Jackson, coloured the company's early good standing with distributors. Lionel's reputation lived on after his premature death, to the extent that he is still seen as Durex's figurehead. This chapter argues that, while Lionel supplied the good business sense to make the early incarnation of the firm fruitful, the forgotten chemist and engineer Lucian Landau should rightfully be seen as the father of the modern latex condom in Britain.

It is further argued that the strong managerial prowess of Angus Reid deserves recognition for expanding the business and keeping it profitable. Like Landau, Reid was brought in from outside of the Jackson family. He served longer than anyone else, and, managing the firm into the early 1970s, Reid negotiated problem after problem to maintain the company's dominance in the market. Whereas subsequent chapters deal with more business-oriented machinations of the firm, this chapter takes the opportunity to present the human face of London Rubber, looking at the internal culture of the company, using testimony from ex-employees like John Harvey and Angela Wagstaff, and drawing on evidence from the internal staff magazine, *London Image*. Despite Landau's ill feeling towards the Jackson family and his eventual erasure from the company's official history, it is argued that London Rubber was generally seen as a good employer to work for, offering opportunity and flexibility to a local labour force of suburban women and men.

London Rubber's Early Days

According to the cultural commentator and management consultant Peter York, 'A backstory is the building blocks of a brand. You can charge more for it, and you can make a higher profit from it. It's a form of modern day magic and it's a sort of substitute religion'.[3] If London Rubber was a religion, then Lionel Alfred Jackson was its god and his brother, Maurice Elkan, was a devoted disciple. Up until the 1994 closure of the main Chingford factory, Lionel's paternal visage gazed down upon the company's upper management and directors from the boardroom walls, where he was painted in oils and held in reverence.[4] The legend of L.A. Jackson unified all who had known him in business, from the factory floor up. 'You're sitting in the chair where Lionel used to sit', sales rep John Harvey was informed, with some gravity, on a visit to an Oxford pharmacist in the 1950s, perching on a tatty old stool.[5] Lionel and Elkan came from a line of Russian-Jewish émigrés – the Jacobys – who arrived in London in the 1860s, lived in St Pancras ward, and worked as hairdresser-tobacconists.[6] The brothers' father, Daniel, was a convicted diamond robber,[7] later a barber with a hairdresser-tobacconists' shop on Aldersgate Street, Clerkenwell. It was this business that inducted Lionel and Elkan into commercial life, the two of them working as travelling salesmen carrying toys and confectionery for the tobacconist part of the trade.[8] Though he died at the age of forty, Lionel laid the foundation of an empire and provided for the lifelong prosperity of condom sellers across the country, as well as the thousands of workers who would pass through the factory gates at Chingford and beyond.

London Rubber strove to be the gatekeeper of its own image. As told to a handful of historians and published internally for *London Image*, the official company history is abbreviated to a few short pages and elides the Jacoby name, beginning instead with the Jacksons (the Anglicised form of Jacoby) at the back of another hairdresser-tobacconists', namely 'A. White's' at 32 Aldersgate Street, in 1915.[9] It was here, London Rubber lore relates, that Lionel set up as a wholesaler of chemists' sundries, including household and 'surgical rubber' products, employing twelve staff.[10] A small room behind the shop was filled with toothbrushes, combs, toiletries, and tea chests of condoms. There were around twenty personnel.[11] At this stage the condom part of the business dealt with imports from Germany and America, and Elkan Jackson was still on the road selling sweets. Angus Roderick Reid was the first hire from outside the family, and would eventually become the managing director and longest serving staff member.[12] It was Angus, legend has it, who devised the concept for Durex condoms – London Rubber's most famous brand – on a commuter journey, which stood for DUrability, REliability, and EXcellence.[13] As it grew, the company moved around the Clerkenwell and City of London borders, taking additional offices in nearby Old Street to house a growing staff and wholesale/mail order stock.[14]

Lucian Landau: Forgotten Founder

In the official record, it was Lionel who founded London Rubber and made it a success.[15] However, while Lionel possessed the business acumen and foresight to facilitate the shift away from wholesaling condoms, manufacturing them was not his idea: in-house production only began after a Polish teenager approached him out of the blue, with a primitive latex condom sample he had made at college.[16] Born in Warsaw in 1912, Lucian Landau was sent to London to study rubber technology by his family, who were small-time industrialists dealing in rubber, perfume, cosmetics, and soap.[17] Lucian was only seventeen; the idea was for him to return home and take over his father's business after completing a course at the North London Polytechnic, which ran rubber programmes targeting middle managers.[18] However, the young Lucian had grown to like North London, and, according to his autobiography, he 'simply could not bear the thought of living in another country'.[19] It was while experimenting with a sample of Pirelli latex and some glass tubing that he hit upon the idea of mass-dipped condoms, saying, 'I knew that these products were all imported from Germany and America and there was no British manufacturer. The plant required would be simple to construct and I could probably make it myself'.[20] It was around this time that Fred Killian, the condom maker from Akron, Ohio, was developing his own machine system for the mass production of latex condoms,[21] but the technology had not yet reached Britain.

Together with fellow rubber students Harry Barron and Jack Skinner, Landau had already set up a rubber toilet sponge business in Shore Road, Hackney, opposite Harry's house. Owning British Rubber Products bought Landau some time to figure out a permanent way to stay in London after completing his studies.[22] Ultimately, though, he felt condoms a more promising venture than toilet sponges.[23] In the event, it was Mr French, a retail pharmacist with a shop at the corner of nearby Mare Street and Well Street, who suggested that Landau might seek out Lionel Jackson.[24] Up until this point, London Rubber had not engaged in producing its own condoms, possibly because cement production was so hazardous. Another likely reason is that, until Landau entered the scene, it would not have been viable to try to produce latex condoms in competition with American firms, and without the technical know-how: while the Jacksons were business people, they were not inventors. The Durex trademark had been registered in 1929,[25] and London Rubber simply brought in American condoms and repackaged them under this name.[26] Landau, however, offered Lionel a chance to branch out, and to use the Durex stamp on a product made in-house. Impressed with Landau's commercial sample, Lionel loaned him £600 for the establishment of a separate firm to produce and supply condoms to the London Rubber Company for sale under the Durex brand. Lionel took a 60 per cent controlling share, retaining Landau at £5 per week, and granting him the freedom to design and organise the plant as he wished.[27] British Latex Products Ltd began small-scale production in 1932, under Landau's direction. The plant was set up at the ground floor of a two-storey factory in the back garden of 20-22 Shore Road, Hackney, underneath the landlord's 'Rock-A-Bye' baby shoe works.[28] Landau was barely twenty years old at the time. Steel fabricators Frederick Braby & Co. Ltd, who operated at the Fitzroy Works (close to Euston Station), produced a manual dipping machine according to Landau's design.[29] The mandrels were made to order by the National Glass Co.,[30] but as the use of this material resulted in regular breakages, the factory employed a resident nurse.[31] Labour came in the shape of young

FIGURE 2.1   Lucian Landau at British Latex Products
Limited, Shore Road, Hackney, 1938.

women and older girls of 'good class' and who enjoyed 'good conditions':
until they left to get married, these production line workers could earn up
to £2 10 (two pounds and ten shillings) weekly in 1933,[32] which was not
insubstantial.

It was the partnership between Lucian and Lionel that created British Latex Products, and, later, the London Rubber Company, as the 'first
mover' in modern, mass-dipped, single-use condoms in Britain. Busi-

FIGURE 2.2   Entrance for workshop of British Latex Products Limited (located to the rear), Shore Road, Hackney, 1938.

ness historian Alfred D. Chandler coined this term to describe enterprises that are not necessarily the first to produce or sell a new product, but are the first to 'develop an integrated set of functional capabilities essential to commercialize the new products in volume for national and usually worldwide markets'.[33] From the early days at Shore Road, British Latex/London Rubber established what Chandler would call 'an integrated learning base in a technologically new industry'.[34] It was an excellent time to establish manufacturing: the purchase price of latex had slumped due to increased competition among rubber plantations in Malaya (now part of Malaysia), which were then under British control.[35] Rubber exports had spiked dramatically, jumping from 1,940 tonnes in 1931 to 14,172 tonnes by 1934.[36] Supply was therefore good, and the price, for the time being, was low. The latex itself was transported in steamer tanks, in iron drums of about 40–7 gallons, and in wooden cases.[37] Initially, British Latex Products bought in pre-vulcanised latex from Pirelli, and all dipping was undertaken manually, wherein the racks of mandrels were submerged into tanks by hand-operated pulleys, then dried on gas burners.[38] Finished condoms were hand-stripped and tested by air inflation,

FIGURE 2.3   Tensile testing of latex condoms at British Latex
Products Limited, Shore Road, Hackney, 1938.

one by one.[39] By the mid-1930s, the plant was gradually improved and expanded to 24 Shore Road.[40] Dipping equipment was electrically assisted
and ovens were installed for drying and vulcanising, meaning that raw
latex could be brought in bulk.[41] As filled drums weighed 450 to 500 lbs
and Landau had a hernia, he designed a frame to make the drums easier to
work with, built by the firm's carpenter, Ernest Ash.[42] Gradually, through
trial and error, these improvements made condoms quicker and cheaper
to produce.

FIGURE 2.4   Maintenance department, British Latex Products Limited, Shore Road, Hackney, 1934.

Landau's original business partners, Harry and Jack, were also part of British Latex Products, although he did not reckon their worth. 'Harry and Jack never made any contribution towards the development process and the equipment', he said. 'They were valuable to me because they could speak and write better English than I could. And, of course, they provided two pairs of willing hands'.[43] Harry, Landau says, left the company after he was caught stealing. Jack, though 'never of great help' to Landau, was at least 'a very nice fellow to have about'.[44] Landau's account is certainly very opinionated, giving the impression that while he found many people disagreeable, he was not always a joy to deal with himself. A good friend from later life, Denise Iredell, used plain words to describe him, saying, 'Modesty about his own capabilities was never evident'. Iredell also felt that Landau 'could be dismissive of others whose views were not in accord with his own, but he never embellished facts, and he had an unusual capacity to assess himself with utter objectivity'.[45] On the whole, Landau's account sounds plausible. By 1933, production at Hackney had already usurped the position of other condom houses, such as the Mitcham Rubber Co., and the Leyland & Birmingham Rubber Co., Lancashire. Between this firm and Landau's operation, four-fifths of home production was covered.[46] While other firms, such as Lamberts, were building up cement process technology, Lionel Jackson had been busy establishing up the company's wholesale connections with tobacconists' and proprietors of chemists' shops, such as Mr French. Unlike Lamberts, a small, private company that had been in operation since the 1880s, London Rubber was not burdened by dated equipment and old brands. Lamberts was weighed down by a coterie of outmoded trademarks such as Lam-Butt and Pro Race (the latter being marketed to eugenicists and promoted by Marie Stopes).[47] Unlike the American companies that had been exporting to Britain, and which leased patented manufacturing processes from Killian (such as Youngs Rubber) or otherwise stuck to old processes (such as Julius Schmid), London Rubber/British Latex Products's self-sufficiency gave it complete freedom to experiment under Landau's guidance.

In 1934, Lionel Jackson died at the Royal Holloway Hospital, North London, from cancer of the spine, which had spread throughout his body and caused him enormous pain. He was only forty years old, and did not leave a will.[48] Consequently, Lionel's brother Elkan Jackson, his sisters Mrs H.M. Collins and Mrs V.M. Power, and the young Angus Reid formed a limited company named Elarco ('L.R. Co.') and sat in directorships on the board, with Elkan taking the chair.[49] Elarco traded as London Rubber Company, and 'Elarco House', previously at 183 Aldersgate Street, moved to new premises at 221 Old Street.[50] So far as Landau was concerned, he had held Lionel in some esteem, but now his business relationship with the company changed forever. In fact, Lionel – who often made visits from the Aldersgate Street office to Shore Road – had been one of the only people at London Rubber that Landau ever actually liked. 'The other three directors never had any business experience', Landau wrote. 'Mr Elkan had a job as a travelling salesman for Mackintosh's toffee. Now he suddenly became the chairman of the company. I regarded all three as of limited intelligence'.[51] Elkan Jackson, in particular, 'proved of no use whatsoever' to Landau.[52] Not everybody shared Landau's assessment, however. Elsewhere in the company, Elkan was appreciated for his amiability and friendliness. 'A very gentle, genial, great big huge man', is how John Harvey describes him.[53] Remembered as a chatty, popular character with a cheerful disposition, Elkan was known for 'his genuine interest in people and his vast, comfortable good nature,' and was especially noted for his generosity with drinks and cakes.[54]

It was Elkan who pushed for expansion during the Elarco period following Lionel's death. By 1936, London Rubber's catalogue carried the full gamut of birth control products, including its own Elarco-branded range of cervical caps, soluble pessaries and condoms, and even pennyroyal for terminating pregnancy.[55] The intention was to make London Rubber the go-to wholesale supplier for any birth control items, with the ultimate goal of pushing contraceptive products of its own manufacture. As German condom imports decreased through the troubled 1930s, forward-thinking London Rubber substituted own-manufactured products to serve the domestic market. Figures on output from batch dipping at Hackney ran at around 72,000 units per weeks, or 2–2.5 million units annually (allowing for variable wastage of up to one-third of production), using high quality latex from the Dunlop plantations in Malaya.[56] This nonetheless accounted for only a fraction of potential condom users, and was known to be insufficient, leaving the market wide open to fulfil aggressive expansionist ambitions.[57] London Rubber thereby extended its expansion programme beyond ordinary retail channels, soliciting the nascent birth control clinic movement, the medical profession, and even the Admiralty, which had begun condom supply to the Royal Navy in 1933.[58] By 1937, London Rubber was the Admiralty's official supplier.[59] It also provided male and female contraceptives to the Family Planning Association, in what would become a difficult but necessary relationship (see chapter 4).

At the end of the 1930s, the Shore Road factory was composed of two small production bays.[60] Increased confidence set London Rubber's sights higher, and manufacturing was transferred to a bigger, purpose-built factory in a wide, green area of farmland on the North Circular Road, Chingford, with Landau in charge of production. The site was perfect for the expanding business, with excellent road and rail transport, ample space to stockpile latex, room to build up mechanical plant, and scope to expand in the future.[61] The Old Street offices, which were by now Angus Reid's territory, were also moved to bigger premises near the new factory, on Hall Lane. By 1939, production at Chingford was fully operational with two semi-automatic, hand-operated batch-dipping bays. Domestic competition paled in comparison because no other producer was so readily equipped to fill the gap as foreign imports dropped off. Lamberts, for example, was still operating modestly out of two Italianate townhouses on Queen's Bridge Road.[62] London Rubber, in the meantime, had half of the market; the remainder divided between Lamberts, Harrison Kent Ltd (Prentif brand), Selka Rubber, and other small condom producers.[63]

Wartime Growth

The war with Germany came just after the move from Shore Road to Chingford. This improved London Rubber's position, as the factory was kept busy with the Admiralty contract and other work brought on by changing market conditions.[64] Although it is impossible to link a rise in production to an increase in sex, there was a surge in sexual activity in London, commercial and otherwise, during the war years.[65] Movement of servicemen within Britain, the arrival of GIs from America, and the mobilisation of women for war work increased sexual opportunities to such a degree that popular historian Joshua Levine has referred to the Blitz (i.e., the 1940–41 German bombing offensive against Britain) as 'The First Sexual Revolution'.[66] According to Levine, illegitimate births jumped from 24,540 in 1939 to 35,164 in 1942, with incidents of VD increasing by 70 per cent over the same period.[67] Watch committees complained of immoral conduct in air-raid shelters, an increase in streetwalkers, and the solicitation of members of the Forces in Shepherd Market and St Johns Wood by aggressive prostitutes.[68] London Rubber reported a considerable demand for its products at this time[69] – so much so that, in Landau's telling, Elkan Jackson and Angus Reid even began selling on the black market. Wartime conditions had brought about many hardships and shortages, and Landau felt that the future of the company depended on his ability to continue production in times of scarcity. He was especially indignant that this apparent black-market trading was going on behind his back, although Elkan did try to slip Landau some pound notes, assuring him it was 'all above board, legitimately made cash'.[70] London Rubber was reported anonymously to the Inland Revenue, and the company's solicitor was instructed to pay the tax on the black-marketed products.[71]

However, these were relatively minor problems compared to the risk of being bombed. Because London Rubber was a large mark on the Chingford landscape, an alternate factory was built nearby inside the Lee Valley Viaduct under the North Circular Road, together with an air raid shelter for the hundreds-strong London Rubber staff.[72] 'Gas gloves' were manufactured for the Admiralty at an extra wartime factory at Park Royal, using another of Landau's ingenious processes.[73] At the same time, production capacity at the Chingford complex necessarily expanded.

FIGURE 2.5   Construction of North Circular Road factory, June 1938.

Naval contract notwithstanding, it was not until 1942 that London Rubber began producing condoms for British soldiers. Despite the crippling effects of uncontrolled VD during the Great War, standard issue of condoms during the Second World War was held back until after the British Army was fully mobilised throughout Europe, the Middle East, and the Mediterranean.[74] London Rubber became the sole domestic manufacturer of condoms under the government's rationalisation of industry scheme in 1942, following the Japanese invasion of Malaya, which threatened rubber supplies.[75] It took a year to bring production up to speed, at which point output tripled.[76] Thereafter, production ran at 36 million condoms per year for the remainder of the war.[77] Labour on the production line was supplied by women and young girls, as it had been since the Shore Road days. As unmarried women between the ages of twenty and thirty had been conscripted into essential war work after the (second) December 1941 National Service Act, London Rubber's female labour was most likely to have fallen outside of this cohort.[78] Watch committees were concerned that many of the girls were simply too young to be involved in

FIGURE 2.6   Latex preparation for (semi-mechanised production), North Circular Road, 1948.

the routine handling of contraceptives. In September 1943, an unnamed vocational guidance officer contacted the Public Morality Council, complaining that girls as young as fourteen were being offered jobs with high wages (which, by now, were up to £2 17 weekly) straight out of school.[79] The council tried to get the matter raised in Parliament, but the minister of labour, Ernest Bevin, could not see his way to issuing an order prohibiting the girls from such employment, and the matter was dropped.[80]

As the company's position strengthened, war conditions further weakened competition, both foreign and domestic. Latex stocks were disrupted following the Japanese occupation of Malaya from 1942–45: exports dropped from half a million tonnes to just 168,000 tonnes for the whole of the occupation.[81] Low supply caused much trouble for Landau. Because of the Admiralty contract, London Rubber did not run short of latex, and condoms for the Forces were accommodated by special

FIGURE 2.7   Dipping and drying line (semi-mechanised production), North Circular Road, 1940.

authority from the Ministry of Supply under the (exceptional) proviso of disease control.[82] However, rubber had to be sourced from countries such as Liberia, and was not up to the quality of the Dunlop latex.[83] So far as female contraceptives were concerned, London Rubber had started to make these in the 1930s and continued during the war with what rubber was available, on one occasion fashioning a batch of cervical caps from a consignment of marbled sheet rubber earmarked for French hotel bathrooms.[84] But the government's Rubber Control only prioritised condoms for prophylactic use, something that would not ordinarily be sanctioned during peacetime. Protection against pregnancy was not considered to fall within the remit of this special medical provision.[85] Whereas the Board of Trade did allocate latex for condoms intended for civilian use, the allocation of sheet rubber allowed for caps or diaphragms was rescinded from 31 March 1944.[86] Liquid latex earmarked for condoms was diverted

FIGURE 2.8　Women traversing dipped condoms into ovens for drying, North Circular Road, 1940s.

to Chingford, making it difficult for smaller manufacturers to survive.[87] One such competitor, Prentif, found their 'small residue of stock of raw rubber' quickly exhausted.[88] Diaphragms, which block the cervix by pressing against the vaginal wall, also required metal springs, but makers were denied steel.[89] Prentif's manufacturer, Harrison Kent, was forced to halt diaphragm production and hand over their remaining stock of steel springs to Lamberts, who produced caps for them from their remaining latex supply, rather than from the usual sheet rubber.[90]

In Germany, rival condom manufacturer Fromms Berlin suffered under the Nazis. Like Lionel Jackson, Julius Fromm came from a Jewish background and had gone into business around the time of the Great War, manufacturing from 1914 and launching the Fromms Act brand in 1916.[91] Unlike the situation in the British Forces, German troops were issued condoms alongside prophylactic salves as part of a systematic VD prevention programme.[92] This meant that Fromm launched his business

FIGURE 2.9   Semi-mechanised condom dipping, North Circular Road, 1940s–50s.

FIGURE 2.10   Durex 'prophylactic' condom from the Second World War, c. 1942–45.

just as state demands enlarged the German prophylaxis market, leading to the company's rapid, early expansion.[93] Thereafter, half of output was exported and Germany's own condom use dramatically increased.[94] In 1926, the sexologist Magnus Hirschfeld attested that Fromms produced no less than 144,000 condoms every day.[95]

As in Britain, German condoms retailed in drug stores, barbershops, and rubber goods stores, as well as through pedlars.[96] Between 1900 and 1927, however, statutory law classed them as 'obscene' objects, and public display or promotion was forbidden.[97] This may go some way to explaining the high levels of exports. In 1937, Fromms tried to break into the British market, offering a range of chemical contraceptives under the Frommag label, but these failed spermicidal tests set by Prentif, the importer. Fromms responded by simply poaching Prentif's head chemist, who then copied his former company's ideas in Fromms' name.[98] By 1938, however, Fromms Berlin stood out as a business run by Jews and was subject to Nazi appropriation. The factory at Köpenick was sold under duress to Hermann Göring's grandmother, Elisabeth Epstein, and Julius Fromm was forced to leave Berlin.[99] Fromm had prepared for this eventuality earlier in the 1930s, having filed for an array of British patents.[100] But his plans for a London Fromms factory were nipped in the bud when war broke out.[101] Fromm made it to England, and died in Hampstead just before the war ended in July 1945, aged 62.[102] His sons Herbert and Edgar, also exiled to London, attempted to realise their father's wishes and set up a small condom plant, but this was squashed by overwhelming competition from London Rubber.[103]

Back on the home front, London Rubber came through the war with its former domestic and international competition no longer existent, although latex supply was still an issue. British plantations in Malaya were reoccupied early in 1946, and, although rubber estates and smallholdings had suffered 'no wanton damage' under the Japanese, transport, the plantation buildings, and local labour forces had been neglected, the plantations having become overgrown by jungle.[104] Bringing rubber tapping back up to pre-war levels took several years, and continued scarcity led to rationalisation at home.[105] Britain faced economic crisis after the war. As historian Dominic Sandbrook sums up, 'hundreds of thousands of British soldiers and citizens had been slaughtered; half a million homes had been destroyed; and the treasury was utterly exhausted'.[106] Britain had borrowed heavily from America during the war and after because almost one-third of the country's wealth had been wiped out: the balance of payments deficit ran at £1 billion and food and raw materials had to be imported from abroad. By 1947, the pound was worth the same as an American dollar and the British economy was in a mess.[107] But so far as condoms were concerned, consumer demand resumed readily once the factory switched back to supplying civilians in peacetime. London Rubber was now bigger and more productive than ever, with no comparable firms on the market. The experience of forcing high production levels under pressure and in difficult wartime conditions ensured that the company grew its technical and operational expertise quickly: it would henceforth focus on expansion, developing its production techniques, and growing the contraceptive market.

Post-War Development

The foundation for London Rubber's post-war success had been laid in the 1930s when Lionel Jackson bet on the future of new latex technologies. Thereafter, the Second World War reduced competition while forcing up production, paving the way for market domination. Although imports of continental condoms resumed in the early 1950s, they did not account for more than a small percentage of British sales.[108] London Rubber's success after the war was also fuelled by incidental factors, which it was uniquely positioned to exploit. Condom provision to the Allied Forces increased familiarity with condom use in both Britain and the United States,[109] and reinforced the presence of Durex in British colonial territories, such as India (where London Rubber had sold condoms since 1932).[110] The supply of Durex condoms to British troops provided unparalleled opportunity for brand marketing to the very demographic – adult British men – who would be purchasing condoms as civilians, meaning future generations were easily indoctrinated to the preeminence of the Durex brand. To quote marketing experts Aubrey Wilson and Christopher West, 'Every schoolboy had a high level of awareness dating from his first dirty joke, and the brand was impossible to forget'.[111] For all intents and purposes, London Rubber was the only significant industrial producer of latex condoms in Britain post-1945.[112] Small manufacturers and start-ups quickly folded in the shadow of London Rubber, as did the London outpost of Fromms. London Rubber was also in a position to deal with competitors by simply buying them out, or, in John Harvey's words, 'to swamp them and get them off the market'.[113] Selka Rubber, for example, restarted condom production after the war but was absorbed by London Rubber in 1954.[114]

Back in the late 1920s, London Rubber had purchased condoms from America and repackaged them under its own brand. After the Second World War, it was offering this service to British manufacturers. Lamberts, for instance, never fully recovered after the war, and did not resume production under the protracted threat of a possession order from the local borough council.[115] London Rubber supplied them with unpacked and unbranded condoms in bulk, which Lamberts made up in their own packets.[116] Other firms sold London Rubber-made condoms under their own brands, such as Phelps (Surgical Appliances), which was run by Annie Phelps in South Tottenham, and the Stockwell Hygienic Co. Ltd in South London, run by Ada Willis.[117] Both operations did a big trade in mail order as well as having retail premises. Although there was hostility between London Rubber and some of the firms they supplied, standing arrangements continued because there was no other source for cheap, unbranded latex condoms, especially for small orders. Some firms, such as Lloyds of Portsmouth, found the arrangement very profitable. 'They had quite a big range, a lovely catalogue, brochure, very pretty', says John Harvey. 'They used to buy everything from us'.[118] Bertie Lloyd, who ran the firm, was well known at London Rubber, and seemed to epitomize the prosperity of the post-war contraceptive business. 'He used to drive a Roller [Rolls Royce]', Harvey says. 'He was a very, very wealthy man. I remember meeting him for lunch once in Knightsbridge … don't forget, the price that we gave him for supplying him with condoms was vastly lower than we were able to charge for Durex. So he made quite a big margin. He knew a bit more about profitability than the ordinary punter, so he had some idea of what the profitability was, so he played on that, but we gave him good prices'. The Lloyds share of the market was virtually invisible from London Rubber's perspective, but the firm focused on mail order and ran with minimal overheads. Clearly, Bertie Lloyd was raking it in, even though he was buying in London Rubber product. Other firms the company supplied included the Midlands mail order house Le Brasseur, which was run by the Desmond family. According to Harvey, this outfit required special treatment because they had another, secret source. Elsewhere, Mrs Hickman of Premier Laboratories, a post-war startup 'packer', also supplied London Rubber products under its own brand.

But whereas London Rubber had always carried a line of contraceptives and would go on to experiment with other dipped latex products, packers were only interested in selling condoms. 'You got to remember these people weren't interested in the finer points', Harvey states with conviction. 'They didn't want to know anything about rubber gloves or anything like that. It was straightforward French letter business'. Barriers to manufacturing in the post-war condom market, which by now included London Rubber's inimitable economies of scale and its vast supply network, only increased as the company expanded its trademark library with new latex products, strengthening its control over stocks of the raw material. In 1947, the company registered trademarks for Pyvex rubber gloves and Ariel balloons, both of which became staples of London Rubber production thanks to Landau's inventiveness.[119] However, the company was aware that these product groups would not yield immediate profit, if at all.[120] Toy balloons, for example, required more manual labour than condoms, as they had to be spread out in packets to display their variety.[121] But controlling British balloon production meant that London Rubber effectively cancelled competition from latex dippers who might, one day, diversify into making condoms with similar technologies. In 1956, for example, the company took over the toy and advertising balloon interests of Lea Bridge Rubber Works Ltd, which had been in operation since 1840.[122]

This strategy of becoming the dominant producer/distributor in all fields peripheral to condoms also saw London Rubber's contraceptive line expand into many variants and sundries. No longer a wholesaler of other people's products, London Rubber produced and distributed for itself. Condoms – the products – were virtually identical, meaning that sales were marketing-led.[123] Accordingly, brands were designed for different types of trade, the idea being to supply all corners of the market but to retain a sense of exclusivity (and the highest margin) for Durex, London Rubber's premium line.[124] For example, Elarco would become the discounted clinic brand.[125] Ona became a barbershop brand, along with Durapac and Nu-Pac.[126] London Rubber also produced diaphragms, foaming vaginal pessaries, lubricants, and spermicides. Duracreme, a spermicidal cream for use with cervical caps and condoms, was sold in chemists' shops and Family Planning Association clinics.[127] In this respect, London Rubber simply continued the practice established in its earliest days as a wholesaler, catering to the contraceptives market at its broadest. However, the company also had one eye on the future.

Secondary Expansion: Going Public and the 1950s
It has been suggested that London Rubber 'rested on its laurels' in the 1950s and 1960s, because its historic market power allowed it to continue

to do well without innovation.[128] It is certainly easy to understand how this might look like the case from the outside. But rather than sitting back, the company was readily inventive in the 1950s, revamping manufacturing processes and expanding yield. This activity was supported by a portfolio of new patents and trademarks. London Rubber delivered, through in-house ingenuity, a better and more uniform product for consumers. This near-monopoly was crystalized by the introduction of sophisticated automated production technology designed by Lucian Landau and his team of engineers. The shift to automatic production was funded by a public flotation in 1950.[129] Automation increased output at Chingford while deepening the technological gulf between London Rubber and its old rivals. Like Killian, London Rubber patented its technology, doing so in piecemeal fashion as different manufacturing stages were designed and implemented. This was especially important because although various contraceptive devices were protected as Class 10 Trademarks (i.e., 'surgical appliances made of India rubber'), the condom itself was not. By safeguarding its technology, London Rubber protected its product. Already outmoded condoms from the Victorian era, such as Lamberts' Lam-Butt, were simply eclipsed.[130]

London Rubber began the move towards these more streamlined operations after the 1948 Companies Act, when British Latex Products was wound down and Lucian Landau was made a director of Elarco Ltd, alongside Elkan Jackson, Angus Reid, V.M. Power, and H.M. Collins.[131] In November 1950, London Rubber converted from a private company to a public one and floated shares in the London Stock Exchange, having first incorporated to acquire the whole of the issued share capital of the remaining, smaller companies that had accumulated over the years (namely Elarco Ltd, London Rubber Company (A.G.), Latex Industries Ltd, and Essex Rubber Industries Ltd).[132] According to Landau, the suggestion to 'go public' was first posited by Charles Sweeny, the American millionaire playboy, stockbroker, financier, golfer, and ex-husband of Margaret Whigham (later the disgraced Duchess of Argyll).[133] But Reid apparently had 'great doubts' and couldn't decide if it was better to have capital or income. 'I had to spend much time trying to explain to him that collecting some cash, and making our shares marketable, did not have to affect our income', Landau says.[134] Indeed, if Landau's account is to be believed, going public landed London Rubber's directors with cash and shares to the tune of £200,000 each, close to £7 million in today's money.[135]

The sale of shares bankrolled modernisation, but the transition to automation was affected by a number of issues, not least of which was the 'Malayan Emergency' (1948–60), in which anti-British insurgents attacked and destroyed rubber plantations, tin mines, and infrastructure in Malaya. At its peak, the Anti-British National Liberation War, which was also viewed as a communist rebellion, saw up to 500 attacks per month by Malayan guerrillas. Having fought the Japanese during the Second World War, these freedom fighters fought a battle of independence against British and commonwealth troops, colonial police, and Ghurkhas, using the jungle as cover.[136] One of the richest territories in the British Empire, Malaya's post-war rubber market struggled to stabilise, causing anxiety for those who depended on latex.[137] Rubber prices, observes historian John Tully, 'have always been mercurial and have always fluctuated wildly', but the Malayan situation was especially difficult for London Rubber to manage after going public, and shareholder confidence was affected.[138] Having stockpiled latex as availability fluctuated, a dramatic rubber slump in 1952 resulted in losses for the company.[139] A bad fire also disrupted production and forced the rebuilding of 'B bay' in 1950.[140]

This run of bad luck melded uneasily with otherwise optimistic activity at Chingford, which included the development of electronic condom testing (introduced in 1953), and the new automated production plant. London Rubber, perhaps in response to instability, worked to build 'London Rubber Co.' as a trustworthy brand in the public imagination, alongside Durex.[141] With future diversification on the agenda, London Rubber's focus in the 1950s remained with dipped latex products for the home and export market, with Landau beginning small-scale production of surgeon's gloves, golf ball centres, finger cots, and pen sacs for Parker pens.[142] Nevertheless, condoms remained the company's core product.[143] It has been suggested that London Rubber may have used creative accounting to disguise the true profitability of condoms, emphasizing rubber glove and balloon production to obfuscate the company's dependence.[144] If this was indeed the case, then balloons and rubber gloves would have helped in smokescreening London Rubber's core business interest to investors, which must have sat uneasily with Landau.[145]

Between 1950 and 1952, the first two automated production lines were installed at Chingford, and the upgrade was paid for without borrowing.[146] Landau had been beta-testing his self-designed automatic machine since the end of the war, but was prevented from developing it earlier because

FIGURE 2.11   Back of automated condom production line, North Circular Road, 1950s.

of Board of Trade restrictions on steel.[147] Once installed, however, the first automated line replaced three preexisting manual lines and was immediately used to capacity.[148] This single line, London Rubber claimed, could produce enough condoms to meet domestic demand.[149] The automated lines were christened 'APs', which stood for 'Automated Protective' plant, 'protective' being the preferred synonym for 'condom' at London Rubber.[150] Production itself took place in several stages. Prior to dipping, the large vats of latex were checked and chemically treated.[151] Latex is an emulsion of tiny, dispersed rubber particles in water. A chemical treatment was used to make these particles receptive to vulcanisation, which is to say, the chemical linking of the particles making the final product strong.[152] Once chemically prepared, latex was decanted into AP tanks, ready for dipping. The APs were each about 100 yards long and had two

FIGURE 2.12   'The first dip' on Lucian Landau's Automated Protective line, North Circular Road, 7 September 1949.

'double decker' production lines wherein hollow glass mandrels passed through two latex baths on a large conveyor. Coated mandrels were heat cured (or 'vulcanised') by passing through a carefully controlled series of gas chambers. The cured latex coating was then washed and rolled up the mandrel by spinning brushes, forming the condom's beaded edge, before being passed through a chalk solution to prevent sticking and into a collecting chute for air testing.[153]

Save for the preparation of latex emulsion and testing, the complete automated sequence took eight minutes. Modifications to the APs were made as London Rubber refined the different stages and improved the end product. In 1953, electronic testing replaced air testing.[154] Four APs were installed between 1951 and 1959, by which time the Chingford complex covered 230,000 square feet over three sites, namely the

FIGURE 2.13 (OPPOSITE)   Beading brushes on Automated Protective line, 1950.

FIGURE 2.14   Engineering department, North Circular Road, 1950.

North Circular Road (original manufacturing division, mainly condoms), Chingford Mount Road (balloons), and Hall Lane (sales division, offices, packaging and distribution and manufacture of gloves).[155] London Rubber reported that production had increased from 2 million units per year in the early 1930s to the same volume per week by the early 1950s. By 1954, weekly production was 2.5 million (appendix 1). It is impossible to use these figures to calculate the total viable output of each AP, because of the many variables involved. For example, information about which of the APs were running at full capacity in 1952 and 1954 is unavailable. In addition, wastage figures were inconstant and could be as much as half of the units produced in the 1950s.[156] Nonetheless, according to a Monopolies and Mergers Commission report, there was a twenty-nine-fold increase in output between 1951 and 1960, due to the automation programme.[157] Angus Reid claimed that no 'official' figures were available, but estimated annual production ran at over 150 million units, with national consumption of British-made condoms at around 93.5 million, the difference being exported. Approximately 3.5 million additional condoms were imported from Germany each year.[158]

Landau's Exit

The completion of the first APs in the early 1950s also marked the end of the line for Lucian Landau, who had been harbouring ill feeling for London Rubber management since the death of Lionel Jackson. Following the black market incident during the war, a man from the Inland Revenue showed up and shadowed Landau for a whole month, while the company was under investigation. Landau was cleared of any wrongdoing, although Elkan Jackson and Angus Reid were fined. 'My relationship with my two colleagues had never been close', Landau says in his autobiography. 'I did not like them and did not trust them'. Landau spent most of his time at the factory and away from Reid and Jackson, which only deepened the gulf between them.[159] The experience of being investigated following the misdemeanours of others left a bad taste, and it was under these circumstances that Landau insisted on being appointed to the board alongside the other four directors. He received one-fifth of the company's shares as recompense, prior to it being floated.[160]

The final straw came in the summer of 1953 when Landau's paramour, a former London Rubber switchboard operator named Alice Maud, committed suicide at the Hotel Russell in Bloomsbury. Landau, who was in the midst of divorcing his second wife, returned to the office after a few days off to find tongues wagging. 'I sensed an air of hostility around me', he said. 'The recent events must have been well known and I had been seen with Alice by various people'. Landau was not worried about being the subject of gossip from people he did not get along with anyway, but September 1953 marked his twenty-one years working with London Rubber and there was some expectation that his work would be recognised, as was the custom after this length of service. Landau began to wonder why he was still toiling at London Rubber, especially when he was overlooked for the usual gift of a gold watch. 'I asked myself why I should continue to work with people whom I did not like, and who did not really appreciate all I was doing', he wrote.[161] On Friday 4 September 1953, Landau announced his departure to the surprise of most people at London Rubber, including his loyal secretary, Florence Knappet, who decided to leave with him, and one unnamed male colleague who, Landau says, 'openly wept'.[162] Jackson and Reid did not stop by the factory to say goodbye.[163]

For Landau, however, the future was positive. In the course of twenty-one years of service, he had not only built up considerable personal wealth, but had also developed a belief in his own spiritual powers as a healer. This latter discovery happened back in the Shore Road days, when a girl from the dipping line had her fingers trapped and crushed by the equipment, only for the injuries to disappear after Lucian clasped her hand, which he would recollect as a some sort of 'miracle'.[164] He went on to lead a happy and fulfilled life investigating the psychic skills of himself and others, lecturing at the College of Psychic Studies, engaging in dowsing, and eventually relocating to the Isle of Man.[165] Landau left London Rubber in good condition for the future, having installed the first of the automated lines and left a team of engineers who would add to and improve them. He was nonetheless erased from the official London Rubber record; Landau's name did not appear on the company's long service plaque, nor in the official company history that was provided in a 1968 press release, nor in the staff magazine, *London Image*, or in John Peel's 1963 account of the company.[166] Peel's account, in particular, claimed that the latex process was begun in 1932 by the London Rubber Company, with no mention of either Landau or British Latex Products.[167] Without further evidence it is difficult to say why this is, exactly, but Landau appears to have left London Rubber abruptly and on bad terms, informing few people about his intentions. He had not seen Elkan Jackson or Angus Reid for over a month at the time of his leaving, and the few people he chose to tell were astonished and upset. We might surmise that Landau's marked dissatisfaction with the work culture at London Rubber was essentially at odds with the vision of senior management, which, as shown below, nurtured a close-knit family atmosphere. Landau – confident in his own abilities but dismissive of others – had eschewed any personal loyalty to senior management following Lionel's death, deliberately locking himself away in his workshop. Is this the sort of person to whom London Rubber wanted to attribute its success? If backstories, as York suggests above, are indeed 'the building blocks of the brand', then perhaps it was simply easier to leave Landau (and his expertise) out of the equation. By crediting the long-dead Lionel Jackson as the unreachable and god-like father of Durex (as many pop histories do), and by magically attributing all ingenuity to 'the company', London Rubber protected its image as it moved forward, maintaining an aura of mystique.

Company Culture

Alhough in later years the company would seek prestige by entering City business circles, from the 1930s to the early 1970s London Rubber was very much a North London operation that valued local labour and was run by senior managers who had worked their way up. This was at a time when British business and industry was increasingly populated by the 'old boy networks' of politicians and ex-public schoolboys, where the institutions of upper-class privilege served as training grounds for business and many industrialist managers were 'elevated to the peerage'.[168] London Rubber was therefore set apart from the better-known British businesses because of its management style, as well its choice of product. With that said, the post-war period was in many respects a boom time for the working classes who secured ready employment in manufacturing,[169] and productive companies unburdened by the obligation to recruit from the City offered solid career opportunities for bright youngsters without university educations. Angus Reid was born in Barnet in 1905 and joined London Rubber in 1924 at age twenty, the first non-Jackson at the company. By the 1950s he was managing director.[170] Upon retirement in 1971, Reid was London Rubber's longest serving member, at forty-seven years.[171] Reid had a quiet home life and a serious workplace demeanour, and is described by John Harvey as a 'solid' and 'reliable' figure.[172] Having been brought in by Lionel as a youth, Reid knew the inner workings of the company, an understanding acquired through hands-on work. 'To the best of my knowledge, although he spoke very well I don't think he was very highly educated', Harvey recalls. 'I never had the impression that he'd been to university or anything like that'.[173] Reid's loyal secretary, Rita 'Steve' Stevenson, left when he did, continuing to manage his affairs in retirement.[174] 'They were both very, very brilliant people', says Harvey.[175] By contrast, Reid's younger brother, Roy, was an extroverted, charismatic and 'good-looking' character, who 'naturally gravitated toward the sales side'.[176] Because of the ten-year age gap, Angus and Roy were thought of more as father and son than as the brothers they were. Roy became sales director, but to many, Angus was very much the 'real' boss. 'I loved him, really', says Harvey. 'A great man, in many ways. Very hard worker. I think his weakness was probably that he couldn't delegate. Everything at Hall Lane at the end of the day revolved around him'.[177]

Like Reid, John Harvey joined London Rubber at age 20. He stayed for almost three decades. Born in 1931 in semi-rural Ongar, Essex, Harvey attended Buckhurst Hill grammar school but forewent university, saying, 'I don't think it would have replaced the other things I got out of life, one of which was an early start at London Rubber'.[178] Following a spate at the London County Council interspersed by two years of national service in Germany, Harvey became a London Rubber sales office clerk in 1951, gradually rising to national sales manager in 1963, and product group marketing manager (gloves and baby pants) in 1966. John was interviewed for his first position by long-serving London Rubber 'legends' Alan Turner, the sales manager who had joined in 1933, and office manager Doris Gunthorpe (née Groom), who joined in 1929.[179] 'She was very confident, very poised, she ran that office', Harvey said. 'She was Angus Reid's right-hand lady, very confident, very assuring'. Harvey accepted the job because he 'liked the look of the people'.[180] However, despite coming into contact with Durex as a sergeant in the Royal Artillery, Harvey was initially unaware that London Rubber made condoms, and nobody told him. The penny dropped a few days into the job, when he was processing invoices and spotted the Durex brand name.[181] Condoms themselves were seldom mentioned in the offices, and the contraceptives division was referred to euphemistically as the 'props department'.[182] 'I don't think I actually discussed it with any of the women on the staff', Harvey says, 'although I could have done because they were very welcoming to me'.[183]

Being on the outskirts of London, Chingford's large, stable, suburban population afforded the company a reliable labour force: local housewives took jobs on the factory floor and ran the offices.[184] The aptly named Mrs L.R. Stevenson is just one such example of a London Rubber local. A supervisor at the Hall Lane site, Mrs Stevenson lived just 200 yards away

FIGURE 2.15   John Harvey, Brentwood, February 2019.

and stayed for twenty-eight years.[185] Latex dipping operated twenty-four hours per day, and the night shift enabled mothers, in particular, to spend their days looking after children and their evenings earning an income. A popular anecdote was that workers from the night shift paid their bus fares with Durex condoms on the way home.[186] In the main, men populated the engineering department, which designed and maintained London Rubber's ever-growing plant, while production lines were staffed by women who worked on dipping, packing, and testing (although

FIGURE 2.16   Offices at Hall Lane, 1950.

there was some overlap in these roles).[187] Many of London Rubber's long-est serving staff members were recruited for this sort of work during the Second World War when production capacity increased, and then were retained into peacetime. Miss A. Want, for example, joined the surgical testing department in 1941 and stayed for thirty-two years.[188] Mrs Minnie Skingley spent twenty-eight years at the Hall Lane stores, having started in 1939. Her daughter later worked at the same site in Data Processing.[189] Mrs Alice Sleap, a charge hand in production tooling at North Circular Road, started in 1941 and stayed for twenty-six years. Her daughter, Joyce Idell, joined later as a secretary, meeting her future husband over con-doms at the AP plant.[190]

According to Harvey, the core demographic in the London Rubber of-fices was middle-aged, 'well-to-do' married women (at least by Ching-ford standards), many of whom had raised families and whose husbands worked in the city.[191] The sales side was populated by male representatives who visited retailers up and down the country, but it was women in the offices who processed orders, dealt with accounts, and generally kept the administrative side running. Harvey has vivid recollections of being a young man among forty or so women office workers: 'It was almost totally female oriented ... there we no more than probably half a dozen men on the office side'. London Rubber did not have a crèche, but women employees with children often stayed on at the company, and, according to Harvey, were well accommodated as working mothers. Evidently, the pre-war practice of women leaving work upon marriage was not universally retained into peacetime. 'Some of them wanted special hours when it came to school holidays and things ... I found they were very generous', Harvey says. 'When the children were sick, say. They wouldn't be hard; they'd be quite generous as to what time they could have off'. Asked why women were so heavily represented, he continues, 'They were cheap, basically. Not that they were ever bad payers, London Rubber. They didn't really do things on the cheap. But women all earned less than men. Crazy now! But it was the case'.[192] Being one of only six or so men in the sales office, Harvey was something of a 'blue-eyed boy' when he started, receiving small gifts of chocolates from his female colleagues and generally receiving plenty of fuss.[193] Harvey was serious about his work, however, and was committed to the company, holding a lifelong belief in the superior quality of London Rubber products.

Spread over three main sites, London Rubber's different departments each had their own personality and calendar of social events. The overall impression of London Rubber's corporate culture during the first fifty years is of a smooth and professional operation that nonetheless took account of family and social life. Lionel and Elkan Jackson, Angus and Roy Reid, and Freddie and Eddie Davis are just three examples of siblings who were recruited early on and achieved high positions in the firm. (Eddie would go on to marry Mrs E. Skinner, who had run the Hall Lane canteen since 1946.)[194] The Sarluis brothers, Michael and Sam, had also been with London Rubber since its earliest days, joining in 1928 and 1933 respectively.[195] Nepotism aside, London Rubber recognized that many employees felt like family even if they were not related. Among the regular soirees was the annual pensioners' seaside coach trip and the Christmas pantomime parties for employees' children.[196] Coachloads of London Rubber children mingled with such stars of stage and screen as Arthur Askey, Tommy Cooper, and Danny La Rue on a special backstage tour at the Golders Green Hippodrome, while workers from the condom lines at North Circular Road enjoyed an annual dance and cabaret at the Walthamstow Assembly Hall.[197]

The staff was also incentivized in other ways. Managers and senior members of the firm were able to buy London Rubber shares at preferential rates. Some of them held onto these as the company expanded and 'made a killing', but Harvey cashed in his shares to buy his family a home.[198] All staff benefitted from a 'prosperity bonus', which was replaced by a profit share scheme in 1959. This gave every employee a direct interest in achieving results, just as London Rubber was taking on new ventures.[199] Employees were also able to buy London Rubber products at discounted rates on regular sale days, and the North Circular Road site had a daily lunchtime shop in its canteen.[200] London Rubber took on many disparate product groups over the years. At one point, this even included wine supermarkets. 'Once we got Wine Ways, a wine dispenser appeared in the manager's dining room', says Harvey. 'It was quite popular, really, no one abused it. I don't remember anyone getting plastered!'[201] Other staff members, such as Angela Wagstaff, never bought Durex in the staff shop, only Tiger Balm for her father, rubber gloves for her mother, and Royal Worcester dinner plates for her sister-in-law.[202]

In terms of understanding London Rubber as a workplace, Angela's testimony is especially interesting because it describes the ordinariness of working for a firm that just happened to make contraceptives. London Rubber would become the biggest employer in Chingford and as such it had an important role for the locale, but aside from the occasional wisecrack, the specific discussion of condoms seemed as uncommon as it was unnecessary. Many thousands of employees passed through the factory doors and for some of them, like Angela, it was just a job. Having been employed in the offices of Westcott's Laundry, it was in 1955 that eighteen-year-old Angela opted for a change and was recruited to the London Rubber wages department. Innocent for her age, Angela lived quietly with her parents, who never had cause to mention contraceptives. 'When I went back to the laundry, into the office where I had been working, and told the girls where I was going to go there was a lot of sniggering, which I didn't fully understand', she says. This was because, like Harvey, Angela was unaware of what the company made when she was first hired. Struck down by tonsillitis after her first day, it wasn't until she properly began her job and had to distribute wage packets that reality dawned. 'Well of course, walking round the factory I saw things I had never seen

FIGURE 2.17   Angela Wagstaff, North Circular Road offices, 1960s.

before, which made me realise what the sniggering was about, though
I still wasn't sure'. Asked what she'd seen, Angela said, 'Protectives. Being
dipped in latex'. Asked how she felt about seeing them, she says,

> I don't think I did know what they were for except that I do remem-
> ber that my mother found one in my brother's pocket. She didn't
> show it to me but she was very upset about it. I can't remember her
> exact words but she said she'd found *something* in his pocket and so I
> probably guessed. I don't know that I thought anything particularly
> about it. It wasn't something I'd come across. I didn't know how you
> bought them, I didn't know how they were used, so it probably went
> over the top of my head and knowledge came gradually I guess.

In 1960, Angela married Harry Wagstaff, a surgical instrument maker
for University College Hospital and a keen sportsman. After a few years,

London Rubber allowed Angela two half-days off per week, wherein she would make bread, wander along Oxford Street, or meet up with Harry. Life was fulfilled outside of work, and although she was friendly, Angela didn't feel the need to join in with London Rubber's social events. In other circles, the fact of her workplace was largely ignored. 'I would say it was more of a joke, really', she recalls. 'Everybody knew what they did at "the Rubber". One way or another they knew ... except me!' Angela moved up through the wages department, becoming data preparation supervisor in the computer department and ending up in financial accounts. London Rubber had a good record of retaining and promoting talented people: it was an ever-expanding, ever-developing firm that readily created opportunities for those who wanted to progress. By the same token, the company gave people like Angela secure and steady employment in order that they might enjoy a decent standard of living outside of work. 'I wouldn't have stayed there for thirty-three years if I'd been unhappy for a lot of the time, I'm quite sure. It was a convenient place to work. I was married and running a home, that probably took up most of my life ... it was a means to an end'.[203]

Onward and Upward?

As this chapter has shown, Lionel Jackson was the face of London Rubber in the early days and was long remembered as a highly respected figure, by both clients and by employees. But while Lionel hand-picked the personnel who ensured the company's prosperity, it was Lucian Landau's technical expertise that took London Rubber into manufacturing via British Latex Products in 1932, and on to greater heights with automatic mass dipping in the 1950s. After Lionel's death, younger family members stepped into the fray and the roles of Angus Reid and Elkan Jackson were greatly expanded, although Landau did not approve of either the new management or their techniques. The company benefitted from war conditions and came through the other side with greatly enhanced production and greatly reduced competition, both at home and in Germany.

In its post-war heyday, London Rubber rewarded loyalty among its staff and gave opportunities to those without formal training, allowing them to rise through the ranks. For others, the three sites at Chingford offered reliable, regular work with good conditions, but even here the condom remained outside the realms of everyday conversation. Although condoms were readily available and had become especially familiar to men during the war, neither Angela Wagstaff nor John Harvey were privy to what London Rubber made when they joined the company. And while many employees met their husbands or wives at 'the Rubber', and sent their own children and relatives to find jobs there, others felt a deep sense of shame. The grandson of one ex-employee, who asked not to be named, told me in hushed tones that his grandmother 'never admitted it to anyone as it was akin to working in a concentration camp'.[204] These accounts remind us of the complex and many-layered status of the condom in the broader culture at the time. Condoms were an undeclared necessity, their production, purchase, and use being a private matter that, for many people, did not warrant extended deconstruction or discussion.

As a rapidly growing company, London Rubber learned how to negotiate the complex attitudes of its market on the fly. If Landau is to be believed, the directors themselves were feeling their way after Lionel's death, defining the market as they went. London Rubber's product was controversial while also being incredibly popular, and there was no model for a manufacturer/supplier such as this in Britain. The company's future strategy would be reactive, responding quickly to cultural and societal change, sniffing out gaps in the market, and fighting to deflect competition when new opportunities occurred. By the 1960s, London Rubber would embrace regulation to make condoms more reliable, and venture into such alien territories as the oral contraceptive pill in order to stay in the game. In terms of publicity, it was important for London Rubber to be perceived as taking these measures, because ongoing barriers to display and advertising otherwise retarded the company's image programme. The next chapter explores the background to these barriers, and especially the issue of retail display.

The previous chapter gave an account of how London Rubber became successful, first as a wholesaler and then as a manufacturer, exploiting the demand for extra product during the Second World War and rapidly becoming the biggest condom manufacturer in Britain. Having provided a broad view of the contraceptive landscape and London Rubber's place in it, the aim of this and subsequent chapters is to present detailed case studies of situations and events affecting the sale and of promotion of condoms, and London Rubber's response to these events. This chapter deals with the public visibility of condoms from the 1930s to the 1960s. Retail display in shops was a necessary reality of the contraceptive business, but it was also problematic because it made some observers uncomfortable. In the interwar period, shop displays of bright, attractive, branded contraceptives drew the attention of campaigners who sought to enact regulation to restrict public display. This Contraceptives (Regulation) Bill was ultimately dropped when the Second World War began, but it resulted, as this chapter argues, in derivative successes elsewhere. Parts of the abandoned bill were incorporated into the regulation of machine vending, and the enforcement of a professional code of conduct among retail pharmacists in the 1940s and 1950s. These developments created a situation wherein the display of saleable birth control products remained legal, but was complicated by the vestiges of a law that was never enacted.

London Rubber inevitably responded to planned contraceptive display laws, and to the pieces of regulation that followed after the war, but these responses were sometimes surprising. As will be shown, rather than viewing restrictive practices wholly as impediments, London Rubber saw regulation as a potentially protective mechanism that could freeze out competition in a way that was productive for maintaining the monopoly. So far as machine vending is concerned, it is argued that, even though this type of retailing was in demand, London

Rubber deliberately curtailed its spread as a precaution against low-cost startups, thereby limiting competition. Lastly, the question of condoms being kept 'under the counter' is addressed. Displaying condoms was contentious and many retailers chose not to keep them on open shelves, but this does not necessarily mean that shopkeepers acted out of prudery, or solely in response to cultural debates on display. I suggest that keeping condoms out of reach may have been linked to their value and potential for theft, rather than as evidence of censorship in action.

The 1939 Contraceptives (Regulation) Bill

In the 1930s, contraception was gradually becoming accepted as a reality of daily life, although many organisations and social interest groups felt that birth control should only be practised by those already married with families. The Church of England's policy on artificial family limitation, for example, had a wide-reaching influence on public life. Generally speaking, Anglican policy is decided according to the issues of the day, and ratified through resolutions made at the Lambeth Conferences, which are held every twelve years and attended by all active bishops from around the globe.[1] Resolution 41 of the 1908 conference denounced contraception, and called upon all Christian peoples to 'discountenance the use of all artificial means of restriction as demoralising to character and hostile to national welfare'.[2] Bishops at the 1920 conference still disapproved, issuing Resolution 68 as an 'emphatic warning against the use of unnatural means for the avoidance of conception'.[3] By 1930, however, the conference had conceded to the reality that most people, including Christians, had access to and used contraceptives of one sort or another. Resolution 18 of the 1930 conference therefore permitted contraceptive use, but only within the limited circumstances of marriage. The resolution read: 'Sexual intercourse between persons who are not legally married is a grievous sin. The use of contraceptives does not remove the sin. In view of the widespread and increasing use of contraceptives among the unmarried and the extension of irregular unions owing to the diminution of any fear of consequences, the Conference presses for legislation forbidding the exposure for sale and the unrestricted advertisement of contraceptives, and placing definite restrictions upon their purchase'.[4] Changing times may have meant that the Church of England was compelled to accept the use of contraceptives by Anglican Christians, but as Resolution 18 shows, it was not obliged to accept the means of supply. In light of its concern for marriage and the Christian family, the Church supported the idea of a government-run monopoly on contraceptive retailing.

By the early 1930s, this and other complementary aims were articulated by a group of campaigners as a new set of proposed laws, in the shape of the Contraceptives (Regulation) Bill, which, campaigners said, dealt with the protection of privacy rather than with preaching morality.[5] Ostensibly, the goal of the bill was to regulate the display of contraceptives on the high street,[6] thereby restricting their use to 'family planning'. This meant that contraceptives would function to support child spacing within marriage, and not any other purpose, such as sex outside of marriage. The campaign was led by Lord Dawson of Penn, physician to the Royal Family and then president of the Royal College of Physicians, who had previously addressed the Church Congress at Birmingham urging it to accept birth control and now canvassed on behalf of the Birth Prevention Accessories Committee of the Public Morality Council in respect of the bill.[7] The committee's position was that, in lieu of taking birth control off the shelves completely (which seemed impossible), contraception should be regulated by medical professionals.[8]

For campaign purposes, the chief object of the bill was to target immature youth and the displays of heavily branded birth control products that supposedly reeled them in. 'What really attracted youth', Lord Dawson said, 'was the picture, the drawing, the photograph, and glaring written descriptions. They would never be attracted by the dull appearance of the contraceptives themselves'.[9] Displays apparently were so 'dazzling' that passers-by were powerless to prevent themselves from entering shops and purchasing contraceptives spontaneously, compelled by their attraction to the gaudy birth control brands.[10] On the flip side, Dawson claimed, suburban housewives had too shy a temperament to ask for 'those things in the window', meaning that their 'relief by means of contraceptives' was inhibited by the very factors that pulled in unmarried youths.[11] Supporters of the bill believed that a far better system for contraceptive retailing would be a regulated trade reserved for responsible married adults: plain packaging and uninspiring, fact-based labels. Comparable to the later Point of Display law for cigarettes, which came into force under the 2009 Health Act and saw tobacco products covered by opaque shutters in shops, 1930s campaigners felt that attractive packaging enticed consumers into patterns of behaviour in which they would not otherwise engage. Eliminating dazzling sales promotion messages,

1   The Hygienic Stores Ltd, 24 Charing Cross Rd
2   Martin Burns Ltd, Chemists, 79 Charing Cross Rd
3   Hygienic Stores Ltd, 84a Charing Cross Rd
4   The Hygienic Stores Ltd, 95 Charing Cross Rd
5   S. Seymour, 98a Charing Cross Rd
6   Martin Burns Ltd, Chemists, 128 Charing Cross Rd
7   Hygienic Stores Ltd, 141 Charing Cross Rd
8   Wards Surgical Stores, 151 Charing Cross Rd
9   Boutalls Ltd, Chemists, 5 Green St*
10 Hygienic Stores Ltd, 8 Green St
11 W. Georges Surgical and Drug Stores Ltd, 10 Green St
12 International Pharmacy Ltd, 34 Leicester Sq
13 S. Seymour Ltd, 48 Leicester Sq
14 Heppells Ltd, Chemists, 1 Cranbourne St
15 Hygienic Stores Ltd, 48 Cranbourne St
16 W. Challice Ltd, Chemists, 3 Villiers St
17 Johnnies Rubber Stores, 37 Villiers St
18 Hygienic Stores Ltd, 39 Villiers St
19 E. Villiers, 49 Villiers St
20 Wards Hygienic Appliances, 191 Villiers St
21 J. Dawson, 19 Embankment Place, Villiers St
22 S. Seymour, 47 Bedford St
23 Ray and Co. 4 New Oxford St
24 Ltd, Chemists, 49 New Oxford St
25 Lewis and Burrows Ltd, Chemists, 108 New Oxford St

* Now Irving Street

the logic went, would allow only for premeditated birth control purchases, discouraging casual trade and thereby casual attitudes to sexual relations.

Morality crusaders hijacked the bill campaign for their own purposes, although this proved difficult for its designers. The crusaders in question included the Association for Moral and Social Hygiene, the Salvation Army, the Bristol Diocesan Association for Moral Welfare, and the British Social Hygiene Council (Birmingham Branch). Having spoken out in support of artificial birth control in 1921 and distributed a practical guide entitled *Few in the Family, Happiness at Home*, written with fellow medical students, Dawson was well known for his position on contraceptives.[12] At the time of the Birmingham speech, Dawson was physician to King

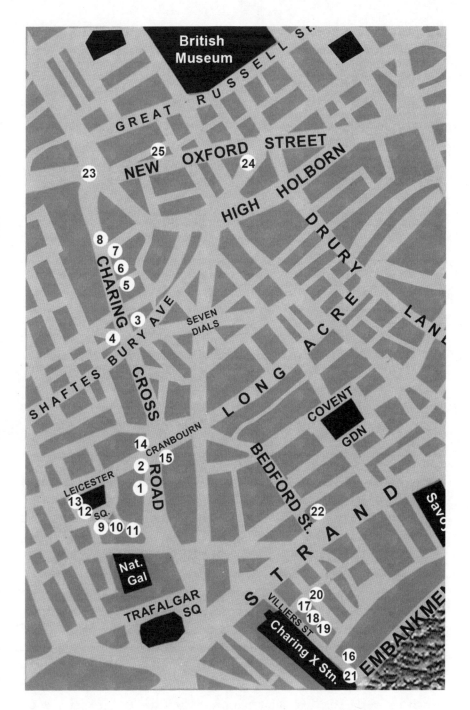

MAP 3.1   Contraceptive retailers concentrated in London's West End, 1933.
Source: Viscount Dawson of Penn Papers, Wellcome Library, London.

George V and the press pilloried him for his progressive stance, but he continued to campaign despite controversy.[13] Dawson also supported the condom as a means of contraception, commenting at the 1922 Malthusian Conference that, 'if absolute security be desired, the only way of securing it is, in my opinion, by use of the penile sheath'.[14] Rather than condemning the theoretical practice of birth control, Dawson's bill sought to control free-market commercialization and the advertisement of contraceptive availability in shops. This was articulated using the rhetoric of offences against 'public decency' committed by profit-making contraceptive manufacturers and retailers. Thus the bill sought only to circumscribe the 'worst offences against public opinion committed by those who trade in contraceptives and aggressively thrust their wares before us'.[15]

The unwanted 'thrusting' of wares really was the main issue here. Clause 1 of the bill proposed that no person would '(a) display, or cause or knowingly permit to be displayed in, upon, or outside any shop, in such manner as to be visible to persons outside the shop, any contraceptive, or any picture or written description of any contraceptive, or any box, bottle, tube or wrapper containing or purporting to contain any contraceptive; or (b) sell, hawk or offer or cause to be offered for sale, in any street or public place, or by means of any automatic machine so placed that it can be used by persons in a street or public place, any contraceptive'.[16] Support for regulation was patchy, though, even among those who regarded child spacing as a good idea. Richard Acland (Liberal MP for Barnstaple) felt that 'the bill would have no real effect on the people who made their living by exploiting the sexual fears and ignorance of poor people'.[17] In this sense, both supporters and opponents of the bill were united in their encouragement of the family planning principle, and in their dislike of visible contraceptive commerce, which was felt to abuse a pressing social need.

In the event, the bill failed to become law because of circumstance. Support in the House of Lords came too late in the 1934 parliamentary session, which was followed by a general election and change of government in 1935. The first reading of the bill passed the House of Commons in March 1938, but a second reading scheduled for March 1939 was adjourned.[18] It was put into 'cold storage' because of the Second World War,[19] but ill feeling against the for-profit industry in contraceptives lingered. The Public Morality Council's Birth Prevention Accessories Committee, which had worked on the bill for many years, watched events keenly, with a view to eventually resuming the campaign.[20]

Machine Vending

Although the Contraceptives (Regulation) Bill disappeared, fragments of the proposed law survived the war, folded into other pieces of legislation and regulation over the coming decades. The first of the derivative successes of the bill pertained to automatic machines selling condoms, specified in clause 1b. Automats had been commonplace throughout Europe at the fin de siècle, dispensing everyday items such as chocolates and postcards. They also proved a uniquely effective means of advertising and selling condoms, as they combined point-of-purchase brand promotion with out-of-hours service, negating the need for potentially embarrassing interactions with counter assistants or other customers.[21]

In Britain, there were three waves of condom automats, the first occurring in the 1920s and 1930s.[22] The social problem with these 'shilling-in-the-slot' machines was the possibility for unmonitored access to condoms at any time, for any purpose, by anyone.[23] Social organisations such as the Public Morality Council voiced anxieties that were repeated in parliamentary debates and were taken up by journalists, strengthening the case for regulation.[24] Automats provided a convenient lobbying point as they evoked the worst potential outcome of free-market contraceptives, namely their unrestricted availability to adolescents and children.[25] However, although condom automats were in use at the time of the Contraceptives Bill crusade, correspondence between the police and campaigners suggests that the aim was to forestall a likely future trend rather than kill an existing one.[26] Machines found in Leicester, Leeds, and Liverpool, which were earmarked as test cases for campaigners, turned out to be isolated incidences.[27] Campaigners also found that condom machines were not purpose-built but were, in fact, adapted from older automats. The firm Autoventors, for example, was busy converting 100 Fry's Chocolate machines in the Bradford area when campaigners caught up with them.[28] Had the contraceptive bill been successful, condom automats would have disappeared altogether around 1939 because of statutory law. Instead, the first wave of condom vending, such as it was, sputtered to a natural end along with other machine vending during the Second World War because of a straightforward scarcity of steel and other resources.[29]

The second wave of automatic condom vending came in the postwar period, during a resurgence of machines outside chemists' shops, barbershops and hairdressers, at garages, in public houses, dance halls, cinemas, amusement parks, and shopping arcades.[30] These reappearing automats once again met with opposition from Watch Committees and other public bodies.[31] Such was the concern that clause 1b of the abandoned contraceptive bill was dusted off and revived as a model bylaw, circulated by Home Secretary James Chuter Ede on 22 October 1949.[32] Ede, a former shopkeeper, suggested that condom vending through slot machines was an 'evil', but 'only in some public places', thereby maintaining the 'privacy not morality' line of the original bill campaigners.[33] In banishing vending machines from streets, the model bylaw effectively implemented the automat component of the Contraceptives (Regulation) Bill. Between 1949 and 1963, practically every local authority in the country had adopted the model bylaw, pushing condom automats out of public view and into toilets, transport cafes, and hotel cloakrooms, sending a clear message about the undesirability of the unrestricted, on-street retailing of condoms.[34]

Retail Pharmacy

The second derivative success of the abandoned Contraceptives (Regulation) Bill pertains to the Pharmaceutical Society of Great Britain, which was consulted by campaigners as the bill was being drafted.[35] The PSGB supported the view that contraceptives in shops should not be visible from the street, as per clause 1a. Prior to the 1930s, pharmacy suffered from patchy trade representation and inconsistent registration, and unqualified chemists were permitted to practise. This all changed when membership of the PSGB was made compulsory for retail chemists after the 1933 Poisons and Pharmacy Act, when the PSGB became the statutory body for poisons control.[36] Business-motivated retail chemists, who sold contraceptives and other retail items and had previously opted out of PSGB membership, were now compelled to become members. These retail chemists thereby became subject to the society's rules.[37]

Up to this point, 'sexual requisites', as they were called, were a standard item of the trade. But the PSGB felt that the open sale of sexual requisites blurred the boundaries between chemists' shops and surgical or rubber stores, thus hampering professionalization. From 1939, the rules and regulations for PSGB member pharmacies and chemists' shops were laid down in a compulsory code of practice, known as the 'Statement upon Methods of Professional Conduct'. Because the PSGB's inaugural statement was contrived when the bill was still expected to become law, it omitted direct reference to contraceptive display because this would have duplicated the expected law: the statement thereby included clauses that were on the law's periphery, filling in the blanks. The intention was that, between the PSGB statement and the new law, a visible separation would be forced between retail pharmacists and proprietors of surgical/ rubber stores, and the like. The statement explicitly decreed that chemists should not advertise all of the products they had hitherto been accustomed to advertising. The prohibition applied to medicines referring to sexual 'weakness', that is, aphrodisiacs and stimulants (clause 2). It also held that drugs used for 'abusive purposes', namely the termination of pregnancy, should not be supplied (clause 7), and that 'advertisements concerning contraceptives should not be enclosed in a package with other goods without a request from the purchaser' (clause 10).[38] But although the 1941 Pharmacy and Medicines Act recognised that the sale of contraceptives (or 'medical and surgical appliances') alongside drugs was part of the normal business of pharmacy, such activity did not meet with the professionalised image the PSGB desired.[39]

A shortfall in regulation was left when the bill unexpectedly disappeared in 1939, resulting in an unintentionally liberal period during which pharmacies and chemists' shops could continue to display contraceptive wares, even though they were no longer permitted to sell abortifacients or to give advice on sexual matters (these points being covered explicitly in the statement). Following the war, activity designed to build Britain anew, such as the 1947 National Health Service Act, necessarily absorbed the PSGB's attention, meaning that the insertion of a contraceptive display clause to replace the lost bill was not prioritised until the 1950s. By that time, however, the Family Planning Association had gained ground and was working to become the public face of respectable birth control in Britain. The FPA oversaw a national network of contraceptive clinics, and had supported the original contraceptive bill. Now that it was in a position to revise its code of conduct, the PSGB looked to the FPA for advice on the contraceptives issue. For a while, it seemed as though the association itself would be referenced in the new 1953 Statement upon Methods of Professional Conduct. A draft published in *Pharmacy Times* stated in clause 10 that chemists might only advertise contraceptives via 'an authorised notice that articles approved by the Family Planning Association or other body approved by the Council are sold'.[40] In the end, direct reference to the FPA was removed, but the association was nonetheless alluded to. The final version of clause 10 read, 'There should be no exhibition of contraceptives in a pharmacy or any reference direct or indirect by way of advertisement notice, show card or otherwise that they are sold there, other than a notice approved by the Council bearing the words "Family Planning Requisites"'.[41] After 1953, then, the PSGB's affiliation with both the FPA and contraceptives bill campaigners was writ large in clause 10, which served the aim of aligning their particular mode of contraceptive supply away from the for-profit sphere and firmly towards family planning values.

Clause 10 was unpopular among the PSGB membership. At the annual meeting on 13 May 1953, Mr C.A. Barnes from Bromley moved to delete the clause on the grounds that 'it had nothing to do with the pharmaceutical service' chemists provided. [42] Mr S.G. Bubb of Reading feared that, 'if chemists did not sell contraceptives, the business would be transferred to undesirable types of shops', which was, perhaps, the whole point.[43] As it was, the strictly sanitised line taken by the PSGB did not prevent pharmacists and chemists' shops from selling contraceptives. But after the 1953 statement, in-store partnerships with brand-led lines were strictly forbidden, and obvious promotion was outlawed. The PSGB's long-held attitude to contraceptive sales, which had been temporarily lost in a grey area, were set down in black and white.[44] From the 1950s, the retail pharmacy trade in contraceptives entered into a restrictive period.

The Benefits of Regulation

The campaign to regulate contraceptive provision, and its residual effects on vending machines and pharmacy display, provides an excellent lens for understanding London Rubber's way of business and corporate mindset. As a company, London Rubber depended on the sale of condoms and relied on the recognisability of its brands, of which Durex was the best known. However, it did not automatically follow that London Rubber would completely oppose the regulation of contraceptive visibility on the high street or in the chemists' shops. Back in 1933, Angus Reid visited and corresponded with Lord Dawson on behalf of London Rubber as Dawson was assembling the case for the bill, in order to discuss how a regulated trade might look. Reid supported the theoretical restriction of contraceptive sales to professional chemists, seemingly on the understanding that London Rubber would step up to supply a regulated trade exclusively. 'German and other foreign products of this nature can be bought very cheaply, and they are sold cheaply too', Reid wrote after meeting with Dawson. 'If you eliminate the cheap end of the trade by stopping foreign importation, at the same time you stop the supplies of all these miscellaneous traders [hairdressers, tobacconists, herbal stores

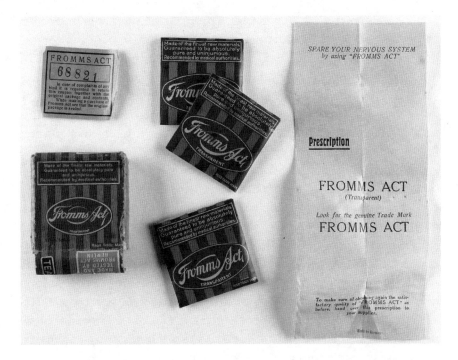

FIGURE 3.1   Fromms Act import condoms, German, 1930s–40s. Angus Reid was keen to eliminate 'the cheap end of the trade,' namely foreign imports.

etc.], as apart from chemists, who sell contraceptives today'. Of course, London Rubber did a roaring trade with the 'hairdressers, tobacconists, herbal stores etc.', thanks to its early wholesaling days. But by 1933, the company had stopped depending on imports because it was manufacturing its own condoms, via Lucian Landau's British Latex Products, in Hackney.[45] London Rubber was now an expanding concern cultivating its future monopoly in production, and seeking to dominate supply on every angle. A ban on foreign imports was wishful thinking, but it would have been helpful in hastening the company's market omnipotence (and, by extension, the control of retail outlets). In contacting contraceptive bill campaigners just as the company was getting a foothold on production and distribution, London Rubber pursued a mutually beneficial alliance with the socially concerned side of contraceptive business, envisioning an exclusive PSGB trade just for itself. Such an allegiance was purely imaginary, however, and never materialised because conspicuous commerciality stood counter to the PSGB's aims.

Where automatic vending machines were concerned, London Rubber had been among those agitating for their removal. In his 1933 correspondence with Dawson, Reid seemed unconvinced of the automats' ultimate success. 'Personally, I do not feel there is any possibility whatsoever of these machines becoming general throughout the country', he wrote. 'We did, as a matter of fact, try out one dozen a considerable time ago, although not without misgiving, and the experiment was an utter failure'. Alerted to the fact of the Leeds machine uncovered by campaigners, Reid continued, 'This was not supplied by us, it was not our intention to place any of these out at all and we have no machines in use in any part of the country'.[46] Reid's lack of enthusiasm for machine vending is puzzling. Contraceptive bill campaigners had clearly felt that these machines had the potential to be very successful, so why was this an anathema to London Rubber? The likely answer is that the company wanted to suppress machine vending as a protective measure. From a competition perspective, the risk was that automatic vending might be too successful and stray beyond London Rubber's control. That some enterprising business people were already adapting chocolate machines into condom machines is a case in point: these entrepreneurs had discovered a gap in the market whereby brand loyalty was superseded by convenience at point of purchase. A network of such machines, conceivably stocked with cheap imports, would open the floodgates of consumer choice – and, with that, opportunities for competition to establish itself.

The feasibility of this defence argument might be gleaned by examining how the company dealt with the third wave of automat vending. In 1964, London Rubber bought out Autonumis, a vending machine manufacturer in Bath, and subsequently set up a machine vending division.[47] The new venture was unprofitable, contributing just 1 per cent of total sales across the London Rubber group by the close of the 1960s, and official reports recorded that vending was simply unsuccessful.[48] The retailer's magazine *Retail Business Survey* blamed the 1949 bylaw, equating regulation with retarded sales through automats.[49] Unofficially, though, London Rubber was quietly suppressing machine vending by keeping Autonumis just successful enough in general machine vending services to keep out competition. Former sales manager John Harvey is adamant that the only reason London Rubber got into automats was to curtail their spread, the purpose being to squash competition and to protect the integrity of the Durex brand. 'We were terrified of machine vending', he says, 'because it would have opened up the market enormously! The significance of our brands was huge! If you had vending machines appearing all over the country, anyone could put whatever brand they wanted on that, where you wanted it to be … ultimately, we had to join it. It was too big, and we had to set up our own vending division. But we didn't want it'. [50]

According to Harvey, Autonumis had become a subsidiary overnight after eastern territory sales rep Joe Buxton had spotted random machines in Archway and Bethnal Green while doing his rounds. 'He phones up the office straight away and I went down … with one or two other quite senior people, to look at this vending machine and to discuss the implications of it', Harvey says. 'That day we went and had lunch at a pub just around the corner. It was so important to us, we were terrified. And it was a man running it who was not known to us at all, you see he didn't have to be: he was just a bright boy who saw an opportunity. We didn't allow bright boys like that. We would buy them out'. F.L. Davis, the long-standing London Rubber director known informally on the shop floor as 'French Letter Davis', dispatched a team of executives to Bath, where Autonumis was purchased outright. Thereafter, London Rubber was able to keep the automat trade in its pocket.[51]

The Retail Chemists' Trade and Durex

Like any business, London Rubber adapted its attitude towards supply and sales according to extrinsic changes in the market environment. This meant that views expressed by the company in one decade might conveniently disappear in the next, and that London Rubber might openly object to one set of restrictions even as it used them for its own benefit. London Rubber's doublethink is especially evident in the case of pharmacy and chemists' shops, because the latter's trade was so desirable. Retail chemists rapidly increased in number following the 1946 Health Service Act, which amplified demand for prescriptions.[52] Between 1957 and 1961, the overall rate of sales through retail chemists increased more than all other retailers, despite the PSGB's restriction on contraceptive brand advertising. Chains of retail chemists grew, and they diversified their stock to include, for example, gramophone records and 'fancy goods', attracting a varied clientele.[53] The new popularity of chemists as retailers offered London Rubber an unprecedented opportunity to expand sales. As the actual market for condoms in the mid-twentieth century was but a fraction of the potential market, hundreds of thousands (if not millions) of non-users were yet to be converted.[54] This is why high street pharmacies and chemists' shops were considered the most important contraceptive retail outlet by the early 1960s.[55]

London Rubber actively incentivised pharmacists and chemists' shops to stock its products. The premium Durex brand was made exclusive to the pharmacy trade and to herbalists.[56] Outlets that held other condom brands would be offered like-for-like substitution for London Rubber stock, a common (if underhanded) strategy in the condom business.[57] This saw shelves cleared of other brands and filled with Durex. For retailers, the attraction of stocking London Rubber products lay in the 'legendary' potential for high margins, which could be achieved through complicated bulk purchasing arrangements.[58] This was a historical feature of the trade stemming from the condom's cultural problems, where high margins served as an inducement for more wary stockists to sell them.[59] The potential distributive margin for condoms ranged from 100 to 208 per cent, with Durex offering the biggest,[60] although by some standards even this appears conscrvative. Andrea Tone, who has studied the American contraceptive retail trade, put margins for pharmacy sales of condoms as high as 300 per cent, adding that, 'price mark-ups exceeding 2,000 per cent were not unknown'.[61] Margin calculations were a closely guarded trade secret, but even the standard return on retailing at suggested prices for a packet of three (72 per cent before the Second World War, and around 62 per cent afterwards) was higher than other consumer items (appendix 3). Surgical sundries, by way of comparison, were marked up at just 25 per cent, while other small-footprint items, such as cosmetics, brought an industry standard profit of $33\frac{1}{3}$.[62] Pharmacists were nonetheless reluctant to be seen supplying condoms, and those who did were reticent about it.[63] 'They didn't want to stand up and be counted', Harvey says.

Aside from the general disapproval of the PSGB, a significant factor in resistance to stocking Durex was the increase in female customers, and the growth of the toiletries and cosmetics categories. Female consumers were especially represented among pharmacy customers, as housewives and mothers. The average housewife visited a chemist's shop once a fortnight, and younger housewives with large families and young children visited more than once a week.[64] Unlike contraceptives, pharmacists held make-up brands in high esteem. Harvey says, 'They were very, very keen on the cosmetic trade. They dominated cosmetics. That's all gone for a Burton [i.e., over] now, really. But brands like Elizabeth Arden and Yardley, names with a bit of class about them … that was where the money was for chemists. They wanted to cultivate that trade very definitely. It affected us only indirectly. I came to know these things when I studied the market a bit more. The last thing these people wanted was groups of men lurking about furtively while these rather posh women are coming in … although there was a huge profit in protectives for them, a huge profit'.[65]

Regulation notwithstanding, the retail pharmacist was already a difficult trade customer for contraceptive makers. Even as the new self-service supermarkets stole pharmacy trade in everyday product groups such as toothpaste, toilet paper, and soap,[66] they were reluctant to stock London Rubber products. Trust between proprietors and London Rubber sales reps, who travelled the country soliciting and maintaining trade custom, was necessarily established over time. 'When they got to know who you were, which they quite often did with London Rubber (we were prestigious to them as well, we brought them a big margin) they would invite you straight away through the back', Harvey recalls. 'You really made it when you were a rep and you got invited round to the dispensary. Especially if they give you a cup of tea. Which they did. The London Rubber man, even to these people who wanted to keep their trade posh, they didn't mind having the big profit they could make from Durex as long as it was all quiet and discreet'.

In-store advertising, on the other hand, was difficult to make quiet and discreet, and it was no longer permissible under the PSGB's 1953 statement. London Rubber's intention to tap into the growing success of retail pharmacy would be hampered if potential customers were not alerted to the presence of Durex in shops, because Durex was marketing-led. Display of brand names in shop windows and on display units provided the most effective overall substitute to mass media brand advertising, which was prohibited. But the 1953 statement forbade it.[67] 'In those days the only advertising (we called it advertising but of course in marketing terms it's not advertising) was point-of-sale display', says Harvey. 'It was the only thing we could do. So, we made – well, we didn't make them ourselves, but we brought them in – plastic shelf strips in particular that had 'Durex: The Best There Is' on them, in mauve with a yellow background. That was what we called advertising'. The Durex shelf strip, common enough in other places such as barbershops, was how London Rubber tried to get around PSGB rules. Harvey knew of 'a tiny number' of chemists who defiantly displayed them. But London Rubber wanted a slice of the legitimate business and solicited the PSGB with a new shelf strip loosely meeting the requirements of the 1953 statement. The strip advertised Duragel, London

Rubber's spermicidal cream, accompanied by the epithet 'Approved by the Family Planning Association'.[68] The FPA, with whom the PSGB had consulted on the matter of contraceptive display, kept a well-respected 'Approved List' constituting the only form of birth control regulation in Britain at this time. The idea was that, if the FPA approved, the PSGB could not object. But in the event, neither the FPA nor the PSGB would endorse the shelf strips. London Rubber was only permitted to supply signs that announced 'family planning requisites', *sans* brand name, as per the 1953 statement. They acquiesced and supplied the toned-down strip, albeit in the Durex colours of yellow and mauve. But the meaning of the phrase 'family planning requisites' was opaque to some people. 'In those days it could have been French or German, it wouldn't have made any difference', says Harvey. 'So, it was a complete waste of time'.

Ascertaining levels of sales to the pharmacy trade is difficult because of the historic incongruity of the figures, which put it at between 33 and 80 per cent of total condom sales in the 1960s.[69] However, while historians have noted the cultural difficulty attached to stocking and purchasing condoms,[70] what they have not supposed is London Rubber's own hand in artfully perpetuating the trade's 'mystique'.[71] Rather than impeding London Rubber, PSGB regulation actually helped the monopoly to flourish. Combined with the social stigma surrounding condoms, display restrictions in chemists' shops and pharmacies meant it was almost impossible for new competition to gain traction. London Rubber may not have been able to promote itself in-store, but at least it was already in the shop. 'It was actually in everyone's interest to maintain this stigma', says Harvey, by which he meant that the stigma was good for the whole trade, but best for London Rubber. So, although there was a hierarchy of outlets in terms of prestige, London Rubber's domination depended on its willingness to supply all types of retailer. The company's policy, therefore, was ambivalence.[72] When the groundbreaking pre-lubricated Durex Gossamer arrived in 1957, London Rubber purposefully used it as a vehicle to open up the barbershop trade, in spite of having previously made Durex exclusive to herbalists and pharmacy. This is because exclusivity in respectable stores gave Durex Gossamer a gloss of propriety that made barbershops want it more. 'Yeah this changed everything,' John Harvey says. 'This was, consumer-wise, possibly a bit mythical, but it was a lubricated protective which suited London Rubber (again this was a huge stroke of luck) because it used the same technology ... they squirted a little bit of (I think it was silicone) totally by machine and it permeated

FIGURE 3.2   Durex display sign in pink neon, 1950s/1960s.

the whole product.' The ingenuity of London Rubber's engineers meant that Gossamer could be treated with the in-house powder lubricant, Sensitol, and foil packed, all as part of the same seamless automated production process. This new and very slippery, sealed-for-freshness condom was unlike anything else on the market. The everyday dry condom was instantly outmoded, compared to the ready-to-use Gossamer, which could be deployed exactly as it was required without needing to add lubrication from a tube. For Harvey, Durex Gossamer was 'the final piece of the jigsaw puzzle' in opening up the hairdresser trade.

The chasm between barbershop and chemists' shops notwithstanding, the concept of the 'respectable' condom remained vague. From the London Rubber point of view, the best Durex outlets were pharmacies just off the main drag. 'They didn't have a flamboyant, lovely display of cosmetics', Harvey says. 'They were the sort of dregs of the chemist world in a way, but they sold a lot of protectives'. These were good outlets expressly because men could make purchases in privacy. 'It was a very furtive trade and the people who were in it before the war ... they fostered that as well', Harvey says. 'They wanted it to be that way'.[73] Mail order also remained a popular way of obtaining condoms. While the expanding pharmacy sector was undoubtedly important, the steady demand for condoms was well met by wide and varied channels of supply.

Under the Counter?

With the exception of recent work into the retail contraceptive trade conducted by medical historian Claire L. Jones, there is a popular idea that condoms were kept beneath the serving counter in shops, or in some other out-of-sight place, purely to negate the embarrassment of counter staff or customers.[74] The notion that condoms were kept hidden out of deference to the PSGB's 1953 statement has served as a culturally convenient explanation for why the oral contraceptive pill was later so successful insomuch that, unlike its shadowy counterpart, the pill was widely discussed and seen.[75] However, although the Boots chain elected not to promote condoms (and, prior to 1965, would only supply them on prescription),[76] the argument that professional prudery alone kept condoms concealed is something of a non sequitur given that, even by the 1960s, most chemists' shops still served their customers from behind the counter and had not switched over to the new self-service style of shopping.[77] In the context of service-oriented chemists' shops, comparatively few display items were available for customers to self-select up to the mid-1960s. Even though the number of British self-service outlets more than doubled between 1956 and 1961 from 3,000 to over 8,100, independent chemists' shops were especially slow to adapt. By the mid-1960s, counter sales accounted for two-thirds of the retail chemists' income, and switching to self-service seemed unnecessary.[78] At the same time, manufacturers became disenchanted with chemists as retail outlets because, retail reports said, they paid 'too much attention to their professional status, and too little to their commercial activities'.[79] Rather than moving condoms themselves under the counter in pharmacies, then, the effect of the 1953 statement was to keep condoms exactly where they were because of a pre-existing culture of counter-based service.

In any case, counter service was not necessarily an impediment to condom sales. Although Boots's resistance to stocking condoms was indeed based on fear of embarrassment (by female assistants as much as male customers), others saw service culture as a positive enhancement to the contraceptive trade.[80] 'On certain types of merchandise, such as that sold in the Surgical Department and to some extent on the Chemist Counter', *Retail Business Survey* reported, 'advice is essential and appreciated'.[81]

In Stoke-on-Trent, surgical and rubber store proprietor F. Gedge, who had been trading since 1935, used a combination of window display and a personal counter service, reporting himself to be a trusted source of advice for customers. Speaking to photographer John Londei in 1983, he reflected that 'nothing much had changed over the years', and that when it came to contraceptives, 'people have always known where to get them'. Gedge was viewed as a consultant as well as a salesman. 'They shuffle like, on the spot', he said. 'I always know when they want to talk. Mostly it's the wives. The men never talk to me about it. Although there are exceptions. But mostly it's the women. You see they'd discuss their problems with me, whereas they couldn't with their doctor. I'm regarded as an expert on the subject'. [82] Following the separation of chemists' shops and surgical stores forced by the professionalization of pharmacies, specialist retailers only became more important for consumers needing advice. Gedge reported that his counter service gave him the edge, saying that 'there will always be those who prefer to come to me rather than ask a young girl on the Boots counter'. [83]

The serving counter itself was less of an impediment to purchase than the perceived knowledgeability of the person behind it, and *Retail Business Survey* blamed the lack of training among chemists' counter staff as the real problem. [84] A case from the FPA archive would seem to support this position. In 1956, an unsuspecting Boots customer from Liverpool became pregnant after purchasing and using a spermicide: it turned out that she had in fact been supplied with a lubricant instead of a spermicidal crème because the counter assistant at Boots confused the boxes. [85] The chain would later supply staff with a training leaflet. [86]

Another reason retailers may have kept condoms from the counter-top is the simple threat of pilferage, or shoplifting. Retail theft is a notoriously difficult area to investigate because shopkeepers conceal weaknesses through the use of mysterious nomenclature such as 'wastage', 'shrinkage', and 'leakage'. [87] With the exception of T.C.N. Gibbens and Joyce Prince's study on women shoplifters in London at the cusp of the 1960s, contemporary evidence on the subject Britain is scant. [88] Yet fear of pilferage cannot be discounted as a contributory factor in keeping condoms back for counter service. In England and Wales, known incidences of larceny from shops and stalls more than doubled between 1946 and 1960. [89] This was directly due to the rise of self-service. [90] And in 1970s America, pharmacists cited fear of pilferage as one of the main reasons for not putting condoms on display. [91] Later studies would suggest that for some men, purchasing condoms from a sales clerk evoked more anxiety or apprehension than simply stealing them. [92] For retailers, then, keeping high-margin, small-footprint items out of view almost certainly served the dual purpose of also keeping them out of the reach of shoplifters. With this in mind, testimony to the effect that in some mid-century British pharmacies, 'the articles were kept, no less securely than the dangerous drugs, locked in the safe next to the cash box', reads as a description of everyday wastage prevention as much as evidence of ritual humiliation or embarrassment – useful as that might have been for the industry.

A Tricky Business

Earlier in this book, a discussion of the VD crisis explained some of the reasons why the condom was viewed with uncertainty and distrust at the start of the twentieth century. This chapter has outlined some of the key reasons why marketing condoms remained a tricky business in the interwar period and into the 1950s and 1960s. A combination of pressures from religious and moral groups, tethered to the new idea of 'family planning', led to the formulation of a set of prospective new laws aiming to curtail the commercial end of the contraceptive trade. Because of intervening events, the Contraceptives (Regulation) Bill did not become law. Interested parties therefore took elements of the bill and wove them into regulation, although this took some years. Nevertheless, rather than working against regulation, the London Rubber Company supported the idea of restricting contraceptive availability to the best products.

In practice, regulation was a double-edged sword. Retail pharmacists and chemists' shops benefitted enormously from selling condoms, and their newly professionalised status gravitated to the brands they carried, such as Durex. This was important for London Rubber, which took care to protect its brand, therefore maintaining high margins as an incentive to retailers. Indeed, it was the high value of the popular and small-footprint condom which contributed to it being kept 'under the counter'. London Rubber skilfully negotiated the threat of restrictive retailing in the 1930s, and then the implementation of aspects of these restrictions in the following decades, but the company went so far as to enact its own programme of restrictive practices by buying up vending machines as an anti-competitive measure. The next chapter continues the theme of the seen and the unseen by examining London Rubber's relationship with the British Family Planning Association, which, as will be discussed, was partially funded by the company itself, with the goal of using the association's good name for its own publicity purposes.

London Rubber and the Family Planning Association

The previous chapter showed how the for-profit retail trade in contraceptives came under public scrutiny with the proposed Contraceptives (Regulation) Bill in the 1930s. Restrictions on advertising that followed in the wake of the (abortive) bill made it difficult to publicize contraceptives via the usual channels of retail chemists, pharmacies, and vending machines. This chapter is concerned with publicity in relation to London Rubber's supply relationship with the British Family Planning Association (FPA), which was the leading non-profit advocate of planned families and child spacing, and which provided women with low-cost contraceptives and contraceptive advice. As will be shown, London Rubber targeted the FPA from the 1930s onward, in order to make itself the main supplier of rubber contraceptive goods to FPA clinics. By the 1950s, London Rubber had a clear programme to take advantage of this supply relationship as a means of obtaining publicity for itself, and improving the troubled image of the condom.

Promoting commercial contraceptives in the middle years of the twentieth century was challenging. It was perfectly legal to advertise condoms. For newspapers, contraceptive ads were an important source of revenue,[1] but advertising was periodically subject to 'social crusades' against it, meaning that promotion was approached with caution.[2] Newspaper advertising was indirect, using euphemistic ads and avoiding brand names. Respondents were encouraged to request further information from manufacturers via coupon, rather than being told about products up front. This information would be supplied in the form of catalogues or information booklets, which could be consumed in private. These materials were well illustrated, but the coupon ads placed in newspapers were necessarily implicit rather than explicit in nature; they did not incite direct action to seek out branded products.[3] This protected media vendors, manufacturers, and ad agents from criticism, but created work for mail order consumers who, in order to discover the brands on offer through the ads, had to order and wait for the catalogue, rather than order the product straight off.

So far as high street retailing was concerned, promotion in pharmacies (a highly desirable type of retail outlet) was obstructed after restrictions imposed by the Pharmaceutical Society of Great Britain in 1953 (see above), whereas traditional condom retailing – in barbershops, tobacconists' shops, and surgical stores – was not restricted in terms of promotion and display.[4] Barbershops did especially well, taking one-third of the market (equal to that of retail chemists) in the 1960s (figure 1.3). In the 1950s, however, a hierarchy of respectable retail outlets had been created when pharmacy was professionalised, meaning that, for London Rubber, there was a potential reputational advantage to be gained through association with high-end retailers. Having floated shares on the London Stock Exchange in 1950, London Rubber had a responsibility to shareholders to expand, to return a profit, and to build and protect the monopoly in condom manufacture and distribution. In other words, it needed to grow the contraceptive market.

Meanwhile, the FPA was aiming to expand its national network of contraceptive clinics.[5] London Rubber supplied the FPA with condoms, diaphragms, and creams, and was aware that the FPA favoured the controlled supply of approved products, following its discussions with pharmacists on restricting display. The Family Planning Association was the most outspoken and best-known campaigner for contraception in the postwar years (Stopes and Dawson notwithstanding), and built its reputation on a normative user base of responsible, married, female contraceptive consumers who, the FPA felt, should aspire to middle-class values.[6] If London Rubber could solicit cooperation with the FPA, then this would enhance the public image of its product, forcing public acknowledgment of the largely middle-class demographic of condom users, the middle class being well represented among FPA staff and customers.[7] Skilled working-class and middle-class consumers were more likely or willing to be tied into a cycle of contraceptive consumption than lower socioeconomic classes such as unskilled manual workers, but this ran contrary to the common perception at the time.[8] Tethering the image of Durex condoms to responsible young marrieds who were spacing their children might improve the public acceptability of the condom without trying to change sexual behaviour, force the acceptability of non-normative practices, or disrupt class boundaries. As Paul Jobling has observed, by putting forward a suggestion that consumers should conform to the same sexual practices in respect of contraceptive needs and sexual desires, London Rubber could 'disavow any real distinction between the needs and expectations of straights and gays on the one hand, or those from different class backgrounds or ethnic origins on the other'.[9] Promoting condom use as part of normal and happy family life, as exemplified by the FPA, would serve to smokescreen the less salubrious corners of London Rubber's client base (such as prostitutes and their clients), which would chug along, unaffected, as a quietly reliable income stream.

Attachment to the FPA as an organisation would also give London Rubber the opportunity to make more general claims about its product than it could ever hope to pursue through consumer advertising. This can be explained using criteria laid out by Peter Miskell in his study of toothpaste marketing between 1955 and 1985. While the happy and materially comfortable middle-class family could be presented as an 'effect' of condom use, it was also important for London Rubber to stress the therapeutic nature, or medical benefit, of their product (steering clear of disease prophylaxis). Stressing therapeutic and medical benefits would serve the function of, eventually, attracting the medical profession to the condom, thereby widening the market and reducing the need for consumer advertising, which was problematic anyway. Miskell found that toothpaste brands making appeals to cosmetic concerns were dependent on consumer advertising and promotional support, while those making therapeutic claims were less dependent on these in the longer term and also sold at a significant premium.[10] The therapeutic nature of toothpaste, Miskell says, could be stressed through (a) official endorsement, (b) allusion to the support of practitioners, and (c) functional illustration of the claims made (such as biting into an apple).[11] Clearly, functional illustration of a condom in use was not a possibility at this time, but official endorsement from the FPA would obviate the need to negotiate or rely on consumer advertising in the long term, as was the case for toothpaste brands endorsed by the American Dental Association, for example.[12] In a worst case scenario, allusion to the support of FPA practitioners in lieu of actual endorsement would go some way toward supporting the price premium on Durex-branded products already in place through pharmacy sales. London Rubber thereby solicited a partnership with the FPA that went beyond mere supply of contraceptive products for FPA clients. The FPA existed to make family planning practice more acceptable in the mainstream through lobbying and widespread clinic work. Greater awareness and acceptance of contraceptive practice, especially among women, would open the potential market for contraceptive sales. Supporting the FPA therefore made perfect sense to managing director Angus

Reid, who proclaimed, 'What is good for birth control is good for London Rubber'.[13]

The Family Planning Association

The FPA was a non-profit provider of contraceptive services well known for its focus on women.[14] It was also a pressure group 'within a lineage of pressure groups' that included the Malthusian League, the Abortion Law Reform Association, Marie Stopes's Society for Constructive Birth Control and its immediate forerunner, the National Birth Control Association.[15] As an umbrella body, the FPA supplied uniform policy-making and a scheme of collective administration to associated birth control clinics throughout Britain. As such, it supported the collective interests of clinics, and undertook the expansion and promotion of this network. In its threefold capacity as a clinic-providing body, a self-appointed contraceptive standards agency, and pressure group, the association was instrumental in devising and implementing systematic day-to-day birth control services, testing and classifying contraceptives, and providing pregnancy testing. Its membership cooperated with government initiatives on birth control and advised local authorities on the provision of contraception as a part of everyday healthcare.

The FPA was born out of the interwar birth control clinic movement, wherein five societies amalgamated as the National Birth Control Association in 1939.[16] In 1949, the Royal Commission on Population had recommended to the government that the new National Health Service include provision for family planning services, but the recommendation was not implemented, leaving the FPA to undertake the growth of clinics on a national basis. Although these would gradually be absorbed into the NHS beginning in 1974, this eventuality was not certain in the immediate post-war years, when the creation of the NHS had been politically delicate anyway. As such, one of the core stated aims of the FPA from the mid-1950s was to spread the concept of family planning and to 'influence formers of opinion'.[17] Together, these actions would work (it was hoped) to make family planning visible, and socially acceptable.

The FPA was a female-run organisation, centred on the needs of married women and their families. Its early focus was the provision of birth control for poor women, but the association had difficulty attracting and retaining them. A shift in clinic attendance occurred after the 1930s as middle-class women began to dominate the lists.[18] The majority of the FPA's medical officers, staffers, committee members, and supporters were also middle-class women. A focus on female methods of contraception was intended to ensure that women themselves had contraceptive responsibility. Unfortunately, this meant that condoms were simply underrated at the FPA,[19] which promoted the use of diaphragms, caps, and spermicides.[20] A survey undertaken by an FPA working party in 1959 found that clinics recommended the diaphragm to over 97.5 per cent of clients.[21] This was in spite of the fact that the majority of couples left contraceptive initiative to men.[22] The association nonetheless bought in product from London Rubber and other traditional contraceptive manufacturers to supply to those clients who requested male methods. From London Rubber's perspective, the surge of FPA activity in the mid-1950s presented some exciting opportunities. Rather than being financially motivated to pursue a deeper alliance with the association as some historians have suggested (because of the potential revenue available from increased contraceptive sales),[23] London Rubber's supply relationship with the FPA was based on the reputational stake it could give them. This was considered so valuable an opportunity that, as will be discussed in more detail below, London Rubber even ventured into making female contraceptives. As with vending machines, domination in this area would ultimately mean that London Rubber would be able to restrict the women's market, and limit all-round competition in rubber contraceptives. 'It was a two-edged sword', says former London Rubber sales manager John Harvey. 'We didn't want them [the FPA] to succeed because it was putting our trade at risk for one thing. If you put a woman in charge of the birth control that was the profit out of the game'.[24] The FPA was always short of funds, and this state of affairs was further impeded by a long-standing institutional dislike of the profit motive, which, in many respects, set it in opposition to for-profit manufacturers. London Rubber and the FPA would eventually meet in the middle because of a mutual need for publicity. By the mid-1950s, London Rubber was funding select aspects of the FPA's publicity campaigns, and was piggybacking on the media successes it had partially engineered. The result was a difficult relationship, marked by exploitation, dependency, and resistance on both sides.

Background: Early Courtship, Diaphragms, and Dependency, 1930s–60s

London Rubber and the FPA both came of age in the 1930s, but followed ideologically divergent paths. The FPA was a non-profit organisation distributing contraceptive advice within a social remit, while London Rubber was a commercial outfit making a business out of condoms: each sought to dominate their respective corners. From the earliest, London Rubber recognised that an alliance with the FPA would (outwardly, at least) soften the edge of its commercial intent, but found the association unwilling to cooperate. In 1938, for example, London Rubber unsuccessfully appealed to the NBCA (the FPA's earlier incarnation) for permission to use its name on 'advertisements or notices in shops', which was flatly refused.[25] In 1939 it applied (unsuccessfully) to become a subscribing member of the association, but the FPA made clear its desire to distance itself from the commercial aspect of contraceptive supply. London Rubber's cheque was returned with a note stating, 'there is no provision in our constitution for the membership of firms, or of any other organisations … membership is strictly limited to private individuals'.[26]

Resistance to commerce was ingrained at the FPA, which had previously handed over distribution rights for its in-house spermicide, Volpar, to British Drug Houses. BDH's marketing manager told the FPA's 'ladies' that they were 'throwing away a fortune', but 'the ladies refused to listen to financial reason and did not want commercial involvement', specifying that only a small profit should be returned to them. 'We were sentimental idealists', FPA pioneer Helena Wright later explained.[27] The FPA opted for free supplies for clinics, rather than royalties.[28] If London Rubber could not infiltrate the FPA through formal channels, then, the next best thing was to make itself indispensable by bartering contraceptive stock and making special deals.

As a non-profit organisation, the FPA necessarily engaged with manufacturers to keep the resale price of contraceptives affordable, which in turn obliged them to accept almost any special terms proffered. This naturally made it susceptible to overtures from manufacturers intending to service commercial interests. In the 1930s, manufacturers watched the birth control clinic movement taking shape and, keen to secure future supply contracts, vied for the FPA's attention, making tit-for-tat complaints to undermine each other in the process. For example, Mr Harrison, of Prentif, claimed that London Rubber could not possibly air-test all of the condoms it supplied, and had sacrificed quality for volume. To prove this, he air-tested twenty-eight gross of London Rubber condoms and found that 1,069 out of 3,312 units were faulty, adding that London Rubber's trading methods were 'deplorable'.[29] The veracity of this accusation would become apparent as the association's relationship with London Rubber matured, but at this point the FPA's preoccupation with female contraception gave the company their inroad. There were two main types of female barrier method at this time; the occlusive cap (also known as a 'check pessary' or 'cervical cap') which slotted over the cervix, and the diaphragm or 'Dutch cap', a larger sprung device that formed a barrier by pressing against the vaginal wall. Both were produced from rubber, although diaphragms included a sprung metal rim. Diaphragms provided the means through which London Rubber achieved early domination of the clinic market, even though they were not profitable, because they gave London Rubber the opportunity to flex its manufacturing muscles.[30]

Competitors such as Ortho, Lamberts, and Prentif supplied both cervical caps and diaphragms to the FPA, but none could match London Rubber's enviable ability to produce quickly and at great economies of scale. Diaphragms were hand tested and finished, which was labour intensive. They came in different sizes, each of which required the fabrication of individual steel moulds.[31] In the early 1930s, manufacturers competed for the FPA supply contract. Harrison Kent (which traded as Prentif brand) proactively courted the association from 1934, but was fundamentally a cap manufacturer inexperienced in sprung diaphragm production. Prentif retooled in order to produce prototypes from sheet rubber to meet the FPA's needs and also began importing American Koromex diaphragms in the hope of achieving the association's approval.[32] Prentif refused to entertain the idea of latex caps (made by London Rubber), believing 'condom rubber' to be too thin, but ran into difficulty when the Koromexes were recalled in 1935 due to sizing problems.[33]

The ability of other companies to manufacture this product was impeded by war conditions, because condoms were prioritised. By 1949, London Rubber was manufacturing diaphragms in large numbers through injection moulding, and had become the FPA's core supplier of both diaphragms and condoms.[34] The FPA continued to use diaphragms from mixed suppliers, but dropped Lamberts's sheet process product in 1951 because of the superiority of the London Rubber alternative.[35] The FPA Hackney branch clinic reported that London Rubber diaphragms just seemed 'so much better than Lamberts's'.[36] This was because the flat spring in the Lamberts's diaphragms kept poking out into the vaginal cavity during use, whereas the London Rubber injection-moulded model securely enfolded a coiled spring in the liquid latex rim as the diaphragm was formed. Lamberts's was unable to retool as quickly as London Rubber, and so lost out in the important clinic supply market early on.[37]

By 1952, London Rubber claimed three-quarters of the diaphragm market.[38] According to Harvey, London Rubber propagated the idea that its diaphragms were superior by producing more sizes than Ortho, who were by now the main competition. Whereas Ortho's (and also Lamberts's) sizing went up in 5 mm increments, London Rubber went one better by producing gradations of 2.5 mm.[39] 'We kidded the people that that was an advantage', Harvey says. 'I don't know technically enough about it, but I suspect we are talking two-and-a-half millimetres difference ... common sense says to me that's not really crucial. But some doctors used to go for these two-and-a-half gradations'.[40] The FPA fell for this trick, believing that the small difference in size would improve spring tension.[41]

The need for a doctor's prescription added what Harvey calls 'prestige' to the diaphragm. Unlike condoms, they were fitted following an internal examination and were prescribed by size. Despite this transference of 'prestige' to London Rubber, however, diaphragms were manufactured at a loss. Ernest Dichter Associates, which carried out market research for London Rubber in the early 1960s, found that, among their sample, lovemaking occurred around twice per week, or 100 times per year. On the supposition that women renewed their diaphragm annually, the sale of one would equate to 100 condoms.[42] This meant that diaphragms were not really viable as consumer products because it took too long for them to be replaced. For all intents and purposes, London Rubber was producing them just for the FPA,[43] mainly because of the gravitas and control it gave them.

Another way London Rubber made itself indispensable to the FPA was with free items, discounting, and preferential terms for stocking London Rubber product, such as six-month credit deals.[44] Although suppliers such as Lamberts and Shield Rubber Co. offered specials and discounts, London Rubber bettered all competitors, making offers that the growing association was not in a position to refuse.[45] By the 1950s, London Rubber condoms were discounted at 20 per cent, and diaphragms between 40 per cent and 50 per cent. Diaphragm fitting rings, a fundamental piece of clinic equipment, were reduced by one-third, as were finger cots (which were essential for internal examinations). Elarcreme (later Duracreme), London Rubber's spermicide for use with diaphragms, was discounted by 15 per cent.[46] These reductions allowed FPA clinics to provide low-cost contraceptives while making a profit,[47] enabling them to forecast predicted income into their financial planning. FPA clinics derived almost half of their income from sales of contraceptives and related sundries.[48] London Rubber also supplied new clinics with valuable start-up kits, gratis. When the Wigan branch opened in 1951, it requested six dozen Elarcreme and six dozen assorted Dutch caps from London Rubber, to be dispatched free of charge, as advised by FPA HQ.[49] Demonstration

FIGURE 4.1   Diaphragm testing by inflation, 1950s.

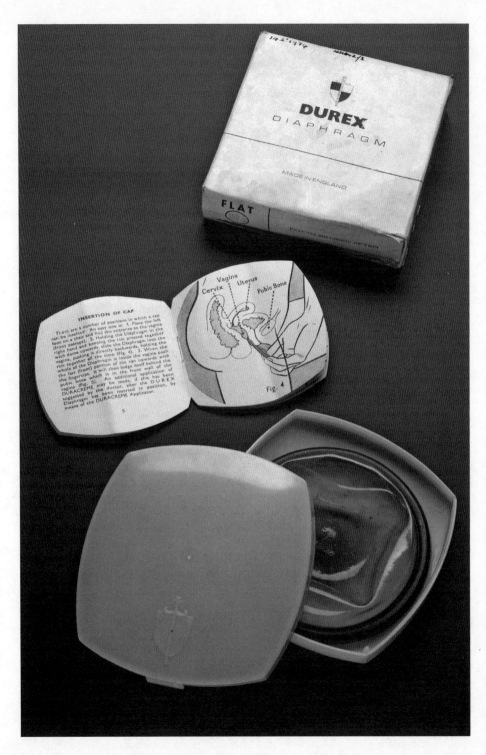

FIGURE 4.2   Durex diaphragm, England, 1955–70.

diaphragms were particularly expensive: London Rubber supplied them free to new branches from 1960.[50] By the mid-1960s, free packs for new clinics comprised five dozen Durex diaphragms, five dozen tubes of Duragel spermicide, one set of twenty practice diaphragms, three dozen packs of Durex Gossamer condoms, six dozen Gossamer samples, three dozen packs of Durex, and twelve spermicide applicators.[51] On top of all this, London Rubber also operated a lucrative cash-back scheme, paying 5 per cent rebates on quarterly sales. By 1964, London Rubber 'donations' totalled £3,500 annually, a not-inconsiderable sum.[52] Branches thereby became dependent on freebies, discounts, and cash-back schemes for meeting day-to-day running costs, making them beholden to London Rubber, at least in theory.

Resistance and Sanctions at the FPA

Dependent as it was, the FPA was not entirely without power in its relations with manufacturers. Prior to the availability of the pill, no contraceptives were listed in the *British Pharmacopoeia*. The only centralised list respected by medical persons and consumers was the FPA's own 'Approved List', which the association published regularly and made available to all for a small fee. The Approved List was begun in 1934 under the FPA's earlier incarnation as the National Birth Control Association, and was continually reviewed.[53] An early form of contraceptive regulation, the Approved List was intended to weed out products of dubious manufacture and efficacy, with the effect that the FPA became the public authority on authentic contraceptive goods and practices: only Approved List products would be sold through their clinics. Manufacturers wanting their products included on the list paid a fee for testing.[54] The Approved List promoted basic standards of safety and efficacy, which had been devised for the association, in lieu of relying on manufacturers' own testing methods.[55] As the list was distributed by consumers as well as birth controllers, it constituted a powerful form of direct advertising and was also the only way the FPA would permit its name to appear in conjunction with commercial manufacturers and their brands.

In order to maintain the integrity of the list, the association resisted commercial exploitation, but was nonetheless subject to attempts from manufacturers to segue items onto the list that had not been tested. In 1937, FPA general secretary Margaret Pyke circulated a letter to correspondents who had been contacted by London Rubber, announcing that their products were now on the Approved List. 'I am therefore writing to inform you', Pyke wrote, 'that the only goods retailed by the London Rubber Company which have been tested to date by this association and placed on the list of approved goods are Ona and Durex condoms'.[56] At this time, London Rubber distributed an array of family planning goods, including products for terminating pregnancy.[57] Prior to the 1967 Abortion Act, this procedure was illegal and there had been several attempts to prevent the advertisement of abortifacients.[58] From the FPA's perspective, stating that London Rubber products were on the Approved List erroneously suggested that the entire company catalogue enjoyed the FPA's support, including not only those products that had failed safety tests but which facilitated the illegal termination of pregnancy. The association tried to bring London Rubber in line using the Approved List, threatening to remove its condoms if the company did not date-stamp them.[59] While it is true the FPA preferred female contraceptives, the row over date-stamping made it genuinely difficult for them to approve condoms that might perish if stored for too long.[60] However, London Rubber was the number one supplier of both condoms and diaphragms, and the FPA never made good on their threats. A situation thereby existed wherein the association was obliged to supply condoms to those who wanted them, but did so without full confidence.

John Harvey recalls a troubled relationship between London Rubber and the association. 'We didn't like the FPA any more than they liked us, really', he says. 'It was pretty cold, and had arisen from their side'.[61] Cash flow was an ongoing issue for the FPA, which received limited local authority support in some areas but largely depended upon donations, subscriptions, income from services (such as pregnancy testing), and the benevolence of manufacturers. For London Rubber, special offers effectively supplanted a formal membership in the association (which it had been denied) by making the company into a pseudo-shareholder. As such, London Rubber expected a return on its investment. Limited offers of aid went some way to equalising the power held by the FPA's Approved List, and when the FPA threatened to remove London Rubber from the list, the company punished them with sanctions, ostensibly because of poor sales performance. 'The amount of business we are getting from your Clinics for ELARCO Diaphragms and ELARCREME is disappointingly small', Angus Reid wrote in 1951, notifying the FPA that the number of free diaphragms customarily given to clinics would decrease. 'We regret this', Reid said, 'but you will realise that the arrangement was made on the premise that there would be a substantial flow of trade to help offset the loss incurred with these free supplies and unfortunately this, as we say, has not materialised'. Reid made it clear that free supplies were not given out of kindness, but were contingent upon performance. 'We will, however, be pleased to reconsider the matter if and when purchases increase', he added.[62]

The FPA was continually targeted as London Rubber sought official endorsement in the hope that the respectable face of the association would gravitate to Durex and other London Rubber products. The company pushed for the FPA's official endorsement of the company, something that staffers were very much alert to. In one letter to General Secretary Margaret Pyke, a correspondent suspected ulterior motives during a meeting with Reid over a special offer. 'I do not know if my sudden thought during the interview may have been right; he happened to mention the word 'advertisement' and it struck me that their offer may have been an attempt at being able to advertise these goods to the public "as supplied by the FPA clinics" as an alternative to being on the Approved List', she wrote. 'I immediately said, "Of course if we accept this limited offer it will not entitle you to advertise to the public that these goods are the same as supplied to the clinics" and he answered, "that would not be approved, I suppose?" I wondered if this had knocked their real plan on the head'.[63] In other words, where London Rubber expressed a desire to help lift up the FPA, it also wanted to take advantage of its reputation for advertising purposes. But the association was wise to London Rubber's shenanigans.

There were other gripes. Calls to FPA clinics from pushy London Rubber salesmen were a particular, long-standing source of friction. Insiders at the FPA regarded salesmen's visits as a redundant annoyance,[64] and some of the salesmen concurred. 'Sometimes you sat in a clinic waiting to see someone in authority with all these different women', recalls John Harvey. 'You sat there with your briefcase and your suit. Most of us twigged that the only person there was any point in seeing was actually a layperson, the secretary. And we contrived to get – I don't know how we did it – but we contrived to get their addresses. We used to call on them at their private addresses, just what we called a "courtesy call". And even now, I'm not too sure what we hoped to achieve'. London Rubber reasoned that it was being forced into pushy tactics because of barriers to advertising in the mainstream.[65] Either way, the company was determined to benefit from its relationship with the FPA.

Deference to FPA Authority

Some historians have referred to the FPA as having the monopoly on British contraceptives in the post-war period, thanks to the power it wielded over manufacturers through the Approved List.[66] If it had actually been the case that the FPA provided more contraceptives on the ground than London Rubber, then the tail would have been wagging the dog. The FPA's clinic network was wide, geographically speaking, but its main impact lay in pressing for state-approved contraceptive provision, standardization of birth control preparations and devices, and wider access. These aims were supported by mass media attention, although this was initially slow. By the 1950s, however, the FPA had 'set about learning the art of public relations', and became media savvy.[67] An expansion programme was underpinned by a publicity drive, utilizing current affairs as a justification for outreach. Talking heads were supplied to radio and television programmes, making the FPA better known.[68] Still, the public's responsiveness was not perfect. In a 1959 Gallup opinion poll, 59 per cent of respondents were aware of what the FPA did and over half of the men and women surveyed were approving of contraception.[69] However, only 8 per cent ever asked the FPA for advice, indicating there was much work to be done.[70] In the interim, the association was the trusted voice of socially motivated contraceptive practice in Britain.

The 'Planned Families' Booklet

Once the association became a household name in the 1950s, cooperation was not just desirable but necessary. A case in point is the 1956 edition of London Rubber's booklet, *Planned Families*, which Reid wanted the FPA to endorse. 'We, I think, would be assisted ... because with the added prestige flowing from your organisation, well-known of as a voluntary and independent character, a number of publications now either wavering or negative might accept the advertising', he wrote.[71] He suggested adding to the booklet a statement to the effect that 'the Publication "Planned Families" has the approval of the FPA which is a voluntary, independent, non-profit making organisation, concerned with promoting family welfare'.[72] However, the FPA stuck to its guns. Permission was refused, with the committee feeling (quite rightly) that 'the true nature of the advertisement had already been sufficiently camouflaged and that further references to the FPA would only be misleading'.[73] London Rubber, the FPA believed, was always trying to appropriate the association's reputation to service its own promotional requirements. In some respects, London Rubber was forced down this route. Like other manufacturers, it had long used booklets as a form of promotion: as early as 1936, another booklet, *Happier Families and How*, was distributed to consumers for free.[74] Following the PSGB's 1953 statement against the brand advertising of contraceptives in pharmacies, print media vendors carrying publicity sought to protect themselves by requiring advertisers to carry a disclaimer from the FPA to legitimate it.[75] Newspapers did not want to lose regular advertisers, and the requirement for FPA approval looked like a good way of offsetting responsibility should any objections to the ads be voiced, and it was not unknown for editors to contact the FPA directly to request approval for ads received.[76]

In April 1955, and with the necessity for FPA approval in mind, London Rubber's advertising consultant, Dennis Blairman, asked the FPA for assistance in promoting *Planned Families*, but this appeal to the association's good nature did not succeed.[77] Nevertheless, London Rubber pushed on with the booklet, disguising the fact that it came from a commercial supplier in order to get consumers and newspapers to accept it. It is not clear if this was enough to satisfy the newspapers, but one FPA insider strongly suspected that the use of the term 'planned families', an obvious reworking of 'family planning', was chosen 'to allay the fears of the prospective customer to get them to apply for the booklet'.[78] London Rubber's courtship of the FPA, which had begun in the 1930s, was always accompanied by bits of print literature that appropriated the rhetoric of the clinic movement. And while these booklets could be obtained directly through the company via coupon advertising in the consumer press (sometimes with a free sample condom), later versions were mainly distributed on counter-tops in chemists' shops and barbershops.[79] Trade organs such as *Chemist and Druggist* and *Health and Beauty* advertised the booklets without coupons, as they were trade publications selling the booklets (and reinforcing the London Rubber name) to proprietors.[80] By 1958, *Planned Families* was being pushed aggressively through consumer newspaper coupons, cinema advertising, and pharmacy promotion. London Rubber circumvented the PSGB's display rules by applying a workaround suggested in 1940, when Postmaster General W.S. Morrison was petitioned to control the distribution of birth control literature. Major Sir Jocelyn Lucas had asked if circulars might be mailed in sealed envelopes.[81] London Rubber accordingly supplied its 1958 counter-top booklet in a sealed envelope with a warning label on the back. Visible acquiescence to public concerns provided a kind of insurance against accusations of recklessness, and a partial solution for inconvenient regulation.

FPA: Propaganda Machine

The FPA's authoritative reputation, which London Rubber so desired for itself, did not simply appear out of nowhere; it came about through a considerable effort to make the association palatable to the mass media. The FPA had not always been popular, and the first half of the 1950s was still clouded by what some viewed as the 'dark days of family planning'.[82] Catholic opposition was prominent following the pope's 1951 address to Italian midwives, and some British public figures, such as Conservative MP for Brighton Luke Teeling, considered the FPA to be highly controversial.[83] Like London Rubber, the FPA also suffered from media embargos, and newspapers had been cautious about advertising them. *News Chronicle* editor Michael Curtis explained that popular newspapers set out to be 'family newspapers' and erred on the side of caution with family planning items.[84] The BBC was also resistant.[85] Nonetheless, media acceptance was a necessity, and the FPA forced the issue as a matter of survival, taking decisive action in the shape of a calculated public relations campaign. It was the minister of health's public visit to the FPA flagship branch in North Kensington in November 1955 that marked the media's shift from silence to advocacy. As the first official, public support from a government minister, this was the pivotal moment when the FPA became publicly acceptable.[86] It became woven into FPA lore, and it happened entirely by design. Iain MacLeod, then the minister of health, had suggested a visit to FPA general secretary Margaret Pyke during a chance meeting at a luncheon, knowing that it would draw media attention to his support for the association.[87] The suggestion galvanised Pyke and the FPA's Public Relations Sub-Committee, who drew up a detailed plan to attract media attention focused on the visit.[88] For maximum exploitation, the visit was presented as being part of the FPA's own Silver Jubilee celebrations, which also explained the reason for MacLeod's attendance. The North Kensington branch clinic had just been revamped following a grant from the Eugenics Society, and was renamed the North Kensington Marriage Welfare Centre.[89] This clinic provided not only contraceptive advice, but marriage counselling and infertility treatments. These were progressive, forward-looking services (for the time), and set the tone for the publicity stunt.

Knowing that editors were resistant to publishing FPA material, Pyke solicited a private meeting with some national titles prior to the visit, presumably to suggest family-friendly angles and to put Fleet Street at ease.[90] By forging an association between MacLeod and the FPA in editors' minds in October, Pyke secured unprecedented exposure for the visit in November. The result was a burst of publicity for the FPA, and good coverage in the *Times*. Pyke was interviewed on BBC Television, and Macleod would also appear on TV defending the FPA.[91] Between 1955 and 1960, the FPA featured on at least one BBC television or radio broadcast per year.[92] As even small-print articles generated measurable impact in the 1950s,[93] the benefit of broadcast exposure for the FPA was especially significant. Media excitement only complemented this 'great period of expansion' for the FPA:[94] a new clinic for married women was opening every two weeks.[95] The association was also in a strong position to compete with the National Marriage Guidance Council in providing sex counselling.[96] Through its publicity work, then, the FPA became a consultant to the media, whereby it 'briefed journalists, supplied ideas for articles, and commissioned opinion polls with significant news value'.[97] A further publicity coup occurred when the Church of England consolidated its position on contraceptive use, which it had approved at the 1930 Lambeth Conference. Nearly three decades had passed since the church's original concession to the practice of family limitation within marriage, but whereas the earlier resolution had passed with a majority of 193 bishops to sixty-seven in 1930, in 1958 over 300 bishops from forty-six countries unanimously decided that family planning was a 'right and important factor in Christian family life'.[98] It was this unanimity that made the story newsworthy and renewed interest in the church's progressive position. Considerable publicity ensued, and this reflected well on the FPA, which had clergymen serving on its committees.[99] The Church of England's approval of family planning was widely read as approval of the FPA and its work, and supporters of the FPA ran with this idea. Lena Jeger, MP for Holborn and St Pancras South, cited the conference in the Commons debate over a 1959 BBC television screening of *This Week's Good Cause* (featuring the FPA), declaring that 'the Lambeth Conference has given its blessing not only to family planning facilities, which this Association provides, but also to its compassionate and very Christian work in helping couples to have children who are otherwise unable to do so'.[100] The BBC programme was felt by many to be 'the FPA public relations coup of the decade'.[101] However, this newly enhanced profile further pressured contraceptive manufacturers to demonstrate the association's approval in order to derive benefit for themselves and their products.

London Rubber: Sponsorship of FPA Publicity

Positive coverage for the FPA was good for the business of contraception, and created corporate sponsorship opportunities. When the FPA could not afford a full-time public relations manager to capitalise upon its media success with the 1955 Silver Jubilee event, London Rubber stepped in with financial and practical support. But the company was picky about where its money went, ultimately aiming to further its own commercial ends. For example, London Rubber sponsored a double-page spread in the tenth anniversary issue of *Family Doctor* in 1961, costing £360.[102] That year, London Rubber had been courting doctors with a series of *British Medical Journal* ads just as the new oral contraceptive pill was coming to market.[103] Earlier requests to publish London Rubber adverts in the FPA's journal, *Family Planning*, had been refused, but sponsoring FPA publicity allowed London Rubber to claim a collaboration, and to capitalise on the FPA's media successes.[104] Because the FPA had deliberately made itself into a household name before securing the resources to maintain its position in the public consciousness, opportunities for corporate sponsorship abounded. Angus Reid, for example, funded a prestigious International Planned Parenthood Federation meeting at the Hyde Park Hotel, inviting Iain Macleod in the interests of publicity.[105] On another occasion, £350 was provided for the FPA to advertise on the London Underground.[106] London Rubber also made a significant contribution of £1,000 to the production of the FPA propaganda film, *Birthright*, in 1957, and paid for a House of Commons Reception.[107]

Knowing that the FPA had neither the funds nor the expertise to fully exploit its sudden media success, London Rubber also offered the services of a contracted PR professional, Dai Hayward, free of charge. Hayward had previously been employed by the David McCaulay advertising agency, which had distributed the *Planned Families* booklet.[108] Hayward assisted the flagship FPA branch at Kensington, which 'worked very well as there were so many FPA activities for the Press to work on'.[109] London Rubber then took Hayward in-house, loaning him to national branches to help with public relations at a local level, whenever and wherever he was needed.[110] This worked well at first, and Hayward was very much valued at the FPA, but discomfort arose when the Basildon branch distributed cards detailing clinic hours reading, 'Printed by courtesy of the makers of Durex products'. Though it was happy to take London Rubber's money and services, the FPA remained unwilling to either endorse or act as a conduit for advertising London Rubber brands. Norman Berry, London Rubber's advertising manager, denied all knowledge of any scheme to hijack the cards,[111] and after the incident all material produced with the cooperation of London Rubber was cautiously filtered through the FPA head office.[112]

In any case, Hayward worked tirelessly to publicise the FPA and they were grateful to have him and his enthusiasm around. Hayward's *Family Doctor* spread had listed all 300 FPA clinics, an invaluable piece of publicity for demonstrating the association's reach and authority to the distant medical profession.[113] In 1960, Hayward arranged a press conference with refreshments for a *Birthright* screening at the Darlington branch, circulating stories to newspapers in Teesside, and partially covering the cost of invitations.[114] He also placed an advertisement in the *Times*, at the cost of £36, to publicise the good works of the FPA.[115] Still, although Hayward was effective and popular, his relationship with the association ended abruptly when he left London Rubber at the end of April 1961 for reasons unknown, and without another job arranged.[116] Brigadier R.C. Elstone, then in charge of FPA publicity, lamented that the association could not afford to employ Hayward themselves, and the free public relations service was over.[117] Such was London Rubber's ability to offer with one hand and take with the other, as it tried to keep the FPA in its debt.

A Complex Relationship

This chapter has described the complicated relationship that existed between London Rubber and the FPA from the 1930s to the early 1960s. It has been argued that London Rubber deliberately courted the association in its early days, with a view to supplying diaphragms over and above other potential suppliers. By freezing out competition, London Rubber made the FPA partially dependent on the services it was uniquely positioned to offer. The company coveted this dependent relationship from the association's earliest days, when it was clear that the clinic movement would not only expand the market for contraceptives, but would help to make it respectable. London Rubber sought to align itself with the FPA's middle-class customer base, and thereby its values, which were oriented around the family, marriage, and the controlled supply of quality contraception. This, it was hoped, would go some way to repairing the troubled image of the condom as a contraceptive.

So far as the FPA was concerned, constant financial difficulties meant that it was not in a position to turn down London Rubber's help, but its members were wise to the company's intentions and trod with caution. The FPA necessarily created publicity opportunities for itself, and accepted London Rubber's assistance in maximizing them, although it occasionally threatened to sanction the company for pushing the boundaries. The two organisations were codependent, and the relationship remained difficult to negotiate. London Rubber succeeded in enabling the association to fan the flames of its own successes, which reflected well on everyone in the contraceptive business and kept the concept of family planning in the public eye. Advertising contraceptives was a tricky business involving many stakeholders, each with their own agendas. London Rubber and the FPA were united in their desire to make contraception more acceptable in the public sphere, but were fundamentally opposed in the way they conducted their affairs. 'These are do-gooders', Harvey says. 'They are very nice people, but they are not the type of people we were used to ... they were distant'. As will be explored in the following chapters, London Rubber retained its relationship with the FPA into the 1960s, but also shifted its focus to other areas, organisations, and personalities from whom it sought to benefit as it became clear that the FPA was not for turning.

The previous four chapters have been concerned with the history of the London Rubber Company; the history of the condom; the complex intersections between these two histories with certain aspects of social and cultural life (the VD crisis, the Great War and the Second World War, publicity, retailing and morality debates); and growing tensions between the company and the Family Planning Association, which provided contraceptive services and advice without a profit motive. This chapter describes some of the organisational changes that took place within the company at the cusp of the 1960s, and discusses how these were affected by changes elsewhere – for example, London Rubber's relationship with the Admiralty, and the new British safety standard for condoms. At the beginning of the 1960s, the oral contraceptive pill (which is discussed in detail in subsequent chapters) was still very new and was not being used in large numbers. In this chapter, it is argued that the company used this time to construct a mechanism for the future protection of the condom, which was its most profitable product, and to provide for future volatility in the market by creating new revenue streams. In 1961, a new division was formed to deal with the contraceptive and latex side of the business, which was called London Rubber Industries, or LRI.[1] The company faced many new and unique challenges to its business in the 1960s. As will be shown, by using public relations techniques, London Rubber was able to turn challenges into opportunities, a skill that would only become more pertinent as the company's relationship with consumers changed. London Rubber also showed an early awareness of the oral contraceptive pill, and factored this into its strategizing for the future.

Well Protected: The Creation of London Rubber Industries

'If the 1950s had been the boom time for London Rubber', read *The Economist* in 1966, 'the 1960s was characterised by diversification, the levelling out of profits, and the end of reliance on the condom as the company's

FIGURE 5.1   The London Rubber Company (British Latex Products) Rubber Works off the North Circular Road, Chingford, 1951.

main form of income'.[2] For London Rubber's part, the need to broaden its activities had been felt for some years.[3] Britain had suffered several significant crises in the 1950s, including trouble in the Suez and the devaluation of sterling. Technologies that had been developed towards the end of the war, plus the generation of capital through a public flotation, helped the company to weather storms in the national economy (see table A2). But London Rubber remained mindful of the need to ensure future security, even amidst the 'dash for growth' driving productivity in British industry.[4] In addition to a modernisation programme, the extension of product lines into balloons and gloves, and intensive marketing activity, London Rubber had spent the previous decade building capital reserves. Careful investment in financial and material infrastructure came to fruition as London Rubber stepped into the new decade, allowing it to pursue diversity and coinciding with changes in the marketplace. The 1960s, historian David Edgerton tells us, 'was British manufacturing's moment'.[5] It was certainly London Rubber's: unemployment was low, productivity was high, and although there was always room to improve demand for rubber goods, sales of condoms tumefied. The British public might have become wrapped up in *Coronation Street*, the *Lady Chatterley* affair, the Profumo scandal, and the Beatles, but they were also having plenty of sex. London Rubber, enjoying the fruits of an increasingly sexualised popular culture, concerned itself with product development, diversification, and expansion through acquisition, which moved especially quickly in the first part of the decade.[6] The company's trading areas and company structure were reorganised, the expansion programme was amplified, and resources were deployed in several distinct directions. It branched out by creating and acquiring new business interests, forming subsidiaries abroad, and intensifying British marketing.[7] At the cusp of the 1960s, London Rubber Chingford owned and occupied approximately 250,000 square feet of modern freehold factory,[8] and was at full development by 1960–61.[9] There were 2,500 staff on the payroll, and London Rubber was the largest maker of dipped rubber goods in Europe, with 35,000 trade accounts at home and eighty agents in overseas territories.[10]

By 1960, the long-running Malayan Emergency had come to a close in favour of British interests,[11] stabilising rubber supply. London Rubber's concern, as the near-monopoly manufacturer of condoms, was to hold any market that touched upon latex rubber dipping in order to suppress competition. Being able to stockpile large volumes of raw material allowed the company to control the production of latex consumables in Britain. Each of its seven bulk storage tanks had a capacity of 25,000 gallons of liquid latex, and London Rubber used approximately 1 million gallons annually.[12] It could store more than any other user of latex in the country, maintaining this position by subsuming or discouraging the balloon, rubber glove, and condom interests of competitors.[13]

London Rubber also moved into completely unrelated goods and services, such as wines and spirits, which was prompted by extrinsic factors mirroring a general trend towards diversification in British industry.[14] Over the 1960–61 financial year, London Rubber's portfolio of business interests covered such diverse areas as investments, surgical hosiery, retail wine and spirit off-licences, adhesives and glues, and even a restaurant and cocktail bar (see appendix 4). Annual reports described a company in good health (appendix 2), and sales of condoms continued to grow (appendix 1). As part of a reorganisation that followed the expansion of latex dipping in the 1950s, London Rubber was divided into parts that would either deal with contraceptives, or were focused on other

FIGURE 5.2   Arrival of tanks for bulk storage of latex, 1950s.

FIGURE 5.3   Frontage of North Circular Road factory, 1950s.

FIGURE 5.4   Stripping gloves from moulds, 1950s.

products and services. The new division dealing with contraceptives and dipped latex goods was christened London Rubber Industries, or LRI, consolidating and sectioning off the contraceptive side of the business as the major subsidiary of the parent company, London Rubber Group, which was now established as a non-trading holding company.[15] Disparate divisions (such as wine merchandising) were compartmentalised under the 'Group' umbrella, so that non-contraceptive and non-rubber interests might operate independently. Henceforth, LRI constituted

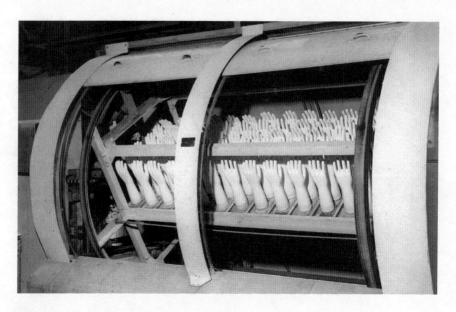

FIGURE 5.5   Gloves in vulcanizing oven, 1940s–50s.

the major, wholly owned subsidiary, bringing in the biggest proportion of profits within the group,[16] with condoms accounting for 40 per cent of group sales in the early 1960s.[17] Although the 1960s marked the beginning of diversification, condoms secured the group's on-going prosperity for the time being.[18] For the sake of simplicity, I shall continue to refer to 'London Rubber' up until chapter 9, although readers should henceforth take this to mean the new LRI division of the company.

Condoms at Home and Abroad

London Rubber had spent decades building the brand equity of its Durex line, to which it added Gossamer, the first pre-lubricated condom, in 1957.[19] While its predecessors were packed in paper envelopes, lubricated Gossamer condoms were sealed in foil pockets, using London Rubber's own Rotoseal foil packaging machine.[20] Durex Gossamer rapidly became the best-selling and most profitable product, making it London Rubber's flagship brand for the 1960s. 'That was by far our most important product', John Harvey says. 'It changed everything'. Harvey was on the front line selling Gossamer to trade customers, and had first-hand experience of its popularity. 'We were able to introduce it that it would transform the sexual experience, really', he recalls. 'That was a bit of an exaggeration really, but you know it's a bit of a difficult subject, this. Because you then come into people's sexuality and the sexual techniques that they use which is so important to the method really. But people thought it was a far superior product and we upped the price by a huge amount which must have been out of all proportion to its cost, but we pushed it up I think from 2/6d for three for the dry [unlubricated] protective, we marketed this at, I think, 3/9d'. Gossamer's unprecedented premium (3/9d was a hefty price tag in the 1960s), coupled with the brand's prestige, made it irresistibly attractive to retailers. Whereas only pharmacists and herbalists had been privileged to stock the original Durex brand, Durex Gossamer was also offered to barbershops, who suffered no restrictions on promotion. The average heterosexual man having sex around 90 times per year, London Rubber said, might spend 10d per week on the cheapest branded condom, Velsan, but 1/9d weekly on Gossamer.[21] Such was the opportunity for barbershops to enhance their status as retailers that they were prepared to take less money. 'The ridiculous thing when I tell you now', Harvey says, 'is that not only did we up the price, but we reduced the margin to the trade. So, we pushed that button ... they sold like hot cakes'.[22] Harvey's claim of a falling distributive margin is borne out by figures reported by London Rubber, who gradually reduced margins (appendix 3) while heavily promoting Gossamer to the trade to increase volume sales.[23] Following the 1964 Resale Prices Act, London Rubber could not legally continue to enforce these selling prices: all it could do was recommend a retail price to consumers. However, the company's dominance of the sector meant that even after 1964, it retained 'a considerable power to influence' the prices offered by retailers.[24]

London Rubber was concerned with improving the profile of condoms in order to attract a broader demographic of users, and aimed for tasteful discretion. 'Durex Gossamer', a trade advertisement proclaimed, 'has created an entirely new class of protective user ... people who had never used a protective before ... Not only has it held existing customers at a higher rate of turnover, but *it has created an enormous new market with previous non-users to whom the ordinary protective is unacceptable*'.[25] The creation of new condom users was the goal for the 1960s, and this was reflected in an image change for Durex Gossamer's packaging. Matchbook packs and paper envelopes were out, and the brand was now presented in slim line 'Pocket Packs' in French grey and burgundy that were strikingly modern, pleasant to touch, and elegantly mobile. Pocket Packs were undetectable inside, for example, the breast pocket of a sports jacket.[26] They were composed of a slim cardboard envelope containing three loose

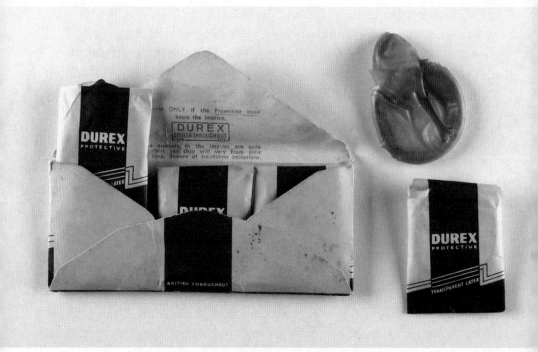

FIGURE 5.6   Durex in paper envelopes, 1950s.

condoms in rectangular foils, which took up little space and facilitated easy removal. With its curved edges and overall fine appearance evoking the ultra-thin condom itself, the new Durex Gossamer was confident, understated, tactile, and masculine. This stylish and user-friendly packaging invoked the professionalism and modernisation of a newly organised company primed for the coming decade.

In terms of its supply to Family Planning Association clinics, the old ONA clinic brand was wound down in 1960 to focus on Gossamer. These were now given away with cervical caps in FPA clinics, under the name Atlas Gossamer.[27] By 1963, British condom sales amounted to 100 million units per year (appendix 1), and the eight brands of condom most frequently found in British shops (Durex Gossamer, Durapac, Durex Coral Supertrans, Durex Nu-Pac, Durex Protectives, Ona Protectives, Ona Coral Supertrans, and Velsan) were London Rubber products.[28] In 1964, a *Retail Business Survey* estimate put the value of the British rubber contraceptive trade at 5 million pounds (figure 6.1, below).[29] Durex Gossamer was the up-to-date, technically innovative, lifestyle condom for the new decade,

FIGURE 5.7   Packing into paper envelopes by hand, North Circular Road, 1950.

and it led the way for London Rubber, accounting for a whopping 71 per cent of its overall condom sales by 1965.[30]

Overseas, London Rubber Group adopted a different tactic and gambled on the much-talked-about world population problem fuelling international family planning schemes in Global South countries. It sought to install subsidiaries so as to take early advantage of anticipated interventions in population by non-profit organisations. This was not always successful, however, and London Rubber Group was very much let down by a venture in Pallavaram, Madras. London Rubber Company (India) Private Ltd was established in 1963, with a view to supplying family planning clinics there.[31] India was the first country to integrate family planning into governmental policy in 1952, but developing the infrastructure for these clinics took years longer than expected.[32] The intention had been to have a London Rubber factory in Pallavaram ready to supply the Indian government when its clinic plans reached fruition, but by 1970 a supply contract had still not materialised and the factory had been sitting empty for years. To add insult to injury, India was flooded with free condoms

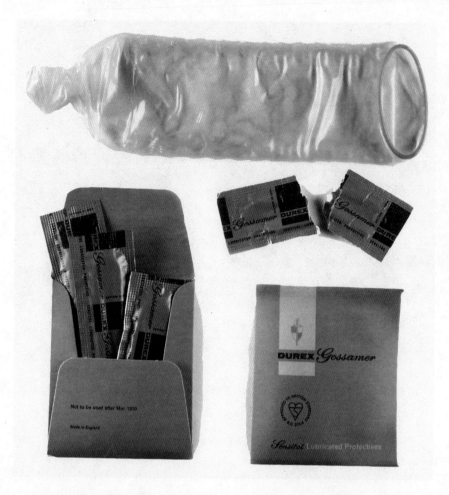

FIGURE 5.8   Durex Gossamer in foiled envelopes and (outer) paper 'pocket pack', 1960s.

from international family planning organisations, which had been produced elsewhere.[33]

London Rubber Group also looked to Europe, where it developed interests in future European Common Market countries.[34] It sought to take advantage in areas where post-war condom production had declined (as in Germany), and in other countries where condoms were becoming popular. For example, London Rubber A.B., Stockholm, was established in light of progressive family values propagated by the Swedish Association for Sex Education, the RFSU (Riksforbundet for Sexuell Upplysning). This organisation raised money through the sale of contraceptives, and

FIGURE 5.9   Rotoseal packing line, North Circular Road, 1950s.

retailed condoms through dealers, mail order, machine vending, and at RFSU-operated shops and sales centres throughout Sweden.[35] London Rubber would go on to become an RFSU supplier.[36] The progress of these international ventures was initially sluggish, with the new condom subsidiaries in West Germany, the Netherlands, Sweden, and Austria, underperforming at first. Nonetheless, London Rubber Group was undeterred. In 1963 it negotiated the friendly acquisition of the two Julius

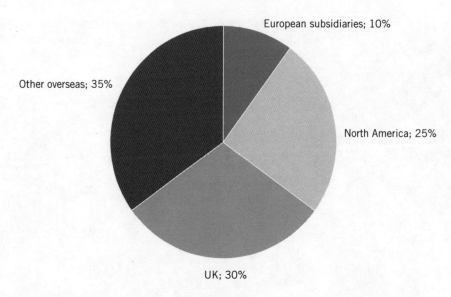

European subsidiaries; 10%

Other overseas; 35%

North America; 25%

UK; 30%

FIGURE 5.10   London Rubber Group total sales distribution 1965–66. Source: London Rubber Company papers, Waltham Forest Local Studies Centre, London. © J. Borge 2019.

Schmid condom companies in New York and Toronto.[37] Despite producing old-fashioned condoms, Schmid held one-third of the North American market for contraceptives.[38] Together with the Madras outfit, London Rubber Group now had the biggest production capacity in the world, even if it wasn't being fully utilized.[39] As with the European subsidiaries, American interests made no contribution to Group profits immediately following acquisition, but greatly expanded global market share.[40] By 1965, the London Rubber Group's North American, European, and other global interests (including India) would together exceed the contribution made by the British sector (figure 5.10), although much of its non-British business was supported by exports from Chingford, including (according to differing reports) 40 to 50 per cent of condoms.[41]

The Rocky Road

As the cornerstone of its prosperity, the company invested in condoms in the 1960s as it always had done, but the need to broaden its activities and gradually reduce dependency was crystalized by a number of extraneous factors at the beginning of the decade. In addition to slow movement in international subsidiaries, there was a drop in Admiralty business, negative publicity from the Consumers' Association, and voluntary regulation through the British Standards Institution. In the case of the Admiralty, London Rubber had enjoyed an ongoing contract to supply the armed forces through the government, which purchased condoms at 16/- per 144 units. This was well below cost, but the supply contract offered security and prestige, and (more importantly) it constituted a significant barrier to would-be competitors.[42] However, the arrangement with the Admiralty was impacted by the gradual diminution of the Royal Navy. Back in 1939, five years after condom issue had become standard across the fleet, the Navy had 300 ships and 161,000 men.[43] Individual ships carried an average of 864 condoms (6 gross), which were also supplied onshore at air stations and medical units, meaning that a continuously replenished stock across the Navy would have amounted to hundreds of thousands.[44] By 1961, the fleet had reduced to 188 ships and the Navy had gone from being the first to the third largest in the world — a decline symbolized by the 1960 scrapping of its flagship vessel, the poignantly named HMS *Vanguard*.[45]

The original decision to issue naval condoms in 1933 was to prevent VD on the basis that naval personnel travelled frequently to numerous international ports, with the potential for sexual entertainment each time they landed.[46] By the 1960s, fewer men were travelling to foreign ports as headquarters staff increased, and sailors were also away from shore for longer.[47] A 1960 policy review reported that infected sailors would no longer have to be segregated onboard due to advances in pharmaceutical treatment for VD. Segregation had been an original justification for introducing condoms because treatment took many months, causing operational problems at sea. This was no longer the case. It was decided to restrict the issue of condoms to men serving overseas in the RAF and the Army, mirroring a system that had been in place for these parts of the armed forces since the end of the Second World War.[48] Naval issue of condoms on home territory ceased from 14 December 1960. Ships at home would carry dramatically reduced stocks, which were issued only when visiting foreign ports. In January 1961, ships returned their stock to the chief pharmacist's medical store in Greenock, following a confidential order.[49] Between 20 January and 10 February 1961, 11,376 condoms were returned to Greenock from ships, air stations, and onshore sick facilities.[50] In terms of London Rubber's gross annual product, a few thousand condoms were but a drop in the ocean. But the reduction in Naval stock signalled a wider shift in practices and attitudes.

On the retail consumer side, although overall sales grew throughout the 1960s, the condom's public image remained troubled. In particular, London Rubber received damning negative publicity from the Consumers' Association magazine, *Which?*, over the winter of 1963–64. As well as attacking the reliability of London Rubber products, the *Which? Special Report on Contraceptives* stirred up old animosity felt by social organisations (such as the Family Planning Association) toward the commercial sale of branded contraceptive goods. London Rubber's star brand, Durex Gossamer, was painted as especially unreliable.[51] Prior to the *Which?* report, the FPA and the London-based International Planned Parenthood Federation (IPPF) were the only organisations conducting the regular, systematic testing of widely available contraceptives. The FPA's in-house regulation through the Approved List had begun in 1937, and was well established as the only testing body in Britain.[52] The IPPF's Evaluation Sub-Committee was founded in 1955 with a view to setting international standards in conjunction with the FPA and University College Hospital Medical School in London, where the Rubber Group Sub-Committee oversaw condom testing.[53] Rather than conducting independent experiments, then, it made sense for the Consumers' Association to join forces with the IPPF and the FPA and to use their resources in conducting experiments for the special *Which?* report, and tests were carried out in conjunction with them, using their own standardised methods. In addition, a draft British Standard for condoms, which is to say a proposed method of quality testing which had been used by the FPA since 1960, was incorporated into the *Which?* testing scheme.[54]

The downside for London Rubber was that neither the IPPF nor the FPA especially favoured condom use at the time of the special *Which?* report. The IPPF, for example, stated that 'the sheath' at first appeared to be a safe method for preventing conception but frequently failed in use.[55] So far as *Which?* was concerned, the Consumers' Association existed to protect the interests of end-users rather than businesses. The *Which?* report therefore served as a joint propaganda project between non-profit family planning collaborators and their supporters, who were united in publicly attacking for-profit contraceptive commerce. In addition, and perhaps even more cynically, the report also served as an apparatus for boosting Consumers' Association membership. Although *Which?* was a subscription journal catering mostly to *Telegraph* readers,[56] family planning was a topical trend in the British press in the early 1960s,[57] and a timely and relevant report on contraceptives would attract attention and entice new paying members to join the association. The special supplement was publicised in a flurry of national press coverage in conjunction with the FPA, some two months ahead of launch.[58] A six-page press release on Friday 15 November 1963 tempted media vendors into circulating juicy snippets over the weekend, under the proviso that readers wanting more would have to join the Consumers' Association in order to purchase the full report at 10/-.[59] The report was referenced widely well into 1964 and the joint pre-sale public relations efforts of the Consumers' Association and the FPA ensured that it was hotly anticipated when it was finally published.[60]

One of the special attractions of the *Which?* report was the detailed information it contained on methods and brands, which was novel at the time. With standard IPPF/FPA testing, individual results were not made generally available to the public. In the case of the FPA's long-standing Approved List, failed products were simply omitted: it contained only details of those products deemed acceptable. By contrast, the *Which?* report offered up grisly details of comparative tests in which brand was pitted against brand, and different contraceptive methods went head to head. Failures were especially vilified. Durex Gossamer failed miserably in the examinations in which twenty-seven makes, including thirteen London Rubber brands, were tested. Lesser-known brands that were produced by London Rubber for other companies (a fact not widely known) were also listed in the report, and many did badly. By contrast, although five brands of oral contraceptive pill were available at the time, these were not tested by the Consumers' Association under deference to the FPA's own testing body for oral contraceptives, the Council for the Investigation of Fertility Control (see chapter 8).[61]

For all intents and purposes, the *Which?* report amounted to a direct attack on London Rubber products, if only because the products fared so badly. For the condom tests, *Which?* panelists filled them with 300 ml of water to look for holes. Durex Gossamer's failure rate was between 8 and 10 per cent, worse even than Lloyd's Grade B which was marketed as a second-class product.[62] In strength tests, where 100 samples of the top eight brands were filled with 5 pints of water, Gossamer burst more often than any other condom.[63] London Rubber publicly responded that the *Which?* tests 'should not be taken too seriously'.[64] This was probably because the methods used did not align with the electronic testing techniques conducted in the factory. In fact, London Rubber had long claimed that the very tests devised by the FPA and BSI in preparation for the British

Standard (and used by *Which?*) exerted pressures on condoms that they would never be subjected to in use, and actually compromised the integrity of each unit.[65] This could well have accounted for the test failures. But public opinion was against London Rubber following the press release by the Consumers' Association, which had built up a great anticipation for the results. On 22 November the *Lancet* spoke out in support of the *Which?* tests, calling them 'fair and apposite', and adding that 'the findings should stimulate manufacturers to do better and would-be birth controllers to choose more wisely'. Reporting on the same day, the *Yorkshire Post* concurred that the tests were 'drastic but fair'. The *Which?* report effectively undermined London Rubber's own quality control measures, which in turn attacked its credibility.

The report also dealt with the qualitative experience of condom use, downplaying the significance of Durex Gossamer's self-contained lubrication. London Rubber's claims for an increased level of sensitivity during sex – a unique selling point for Gossamer – were written off as 'optimistic'.[66] Space was given over to the FPA to critique London Rubber's in-pack advertising, catalogue coupons, and promotional booklets, which were seen as 'undesirable advertising'.[67] Newspapers such as the *Birmingham Post* evidently shared this position. On 15 November, it reported that 'contraceptives are often sold irresponsibly', and, quoting directly from the *Which?* report, objected that 'advertising – often misleading – was disguised to look like disinterested advice'.[68] As discussed above, London Rubber's cashing in on family planning as a social cause had been a long-standing issue between them and the FPA ever since the *Planned Families* booklet. Disinterested advice, which was designed to appear impartial but was really a device for pushing London Rubber products, was viewed with distaste. The left-leaning Consumers' Association had a notoriously recalcitrant relationship with business and, for that matter, consumerism itself.[69] Its *Which?* report was clear in favouring the social, clinical provision of birth control over brand-led, for-profit sales of commercial contraceptives, and the cumulative effect of this criticism made London Rubber appear tawdry and callous: a profiteer shamelessly pushing sub-standard product onto an unwitting public. London Rubber was the only manufacturer named in the *Which?* press release,[70] and condemnation was parroted in the *British Medical Journal*, *Medical Officer*, and *Daily Mirror*.[71] Surprisingly, however, London Rubber came through the episode largely unscathed, despite the joint attack. According to Diana Mallory, reporting in *Queen* on 4 December 1963, London Rubber's shares

shot up by 1/6. 'The *Which?* report', she said, 'although it condemned —
and perhaps *because* it condemned — did more to emphasise London Rubber's share of this profitable market than any uncritical report could have
done'. The *Which?* press release gave newspapers and magazines a legitimate opportunity to mention London Rubber, feeding into the trend of
discussing family planning in the press. On the reverse side, the *Which?*
report resulted in over fifty national press stories referring to the pill as
the only 'safe' method of contraception, to the detriment of the condom.[72]

'A Huge Marketing Ploy': British Standard 3704

During the period in which the Consumers' Association undertook contraceptive testing for the *Which?* report, London Rubber collaborated
with the FPA and the British Standards Institution over the new specification for rubber condoms, but not all of its suggestions were implemented
into British Standard BS3704, which was published shortly after *Which?*
in April 1964.[73] The most important of these suggestions was electronic
testing which London Rubber had introduced as part of its modernisation
programme in 1953.[74] In the electronic test, each condom was placed over
a probe and a charge was sent through it. Condoms were rejected from
the production line when a charge was detected outside of the condom,
indicating a fault. As with the lubrication on Gossamer, electronic testing gave London Rubber a unique selling point that was important for its
marketing pitch prior to the ratification of BS3704. The Ministry of Health
had eschewed involvement with contraceptive testing and approval,[75]
meaning that the eventual establishment of a British Standard was necessarily a collaborative process between non-governmental stakeholders.
The British Standards Institution (BSI), the IPPF, the FPA, and London
Rubber all ensured that they were represented on the BSI's Technical
Committee. But much to London Rubber's chagrin, electronic testing —
which was unique to the company and not practised by the FPA or IPPF
in their own tests — was not deemed a suitable barometer of condom reliability. Instead, BS3704 depended on air inflation and filling condoms
with water, as *Which?* had done. But although the BSI was, to use John
Harvey's term, a 'nightmare' to London Rubber, the company's response
to BS3704 was simply to take ownership of the situation. After all, even
if it was vetoed on some aspects, London Rubber and its representatives
had helped to prepare the standard.[76] And once BS3704 was published,
London Rubber was the only manufacturer licensed to manufacture
under it, and to bear the coveted BSI kite mark (a kite-shaped symbol

denoting the BSI's approval) on its products.[77] Evidently, close cooperation with the BSI had meant that London Rubber was in a position to negotiate, based on its expertise in the field, a standard that was achievable using its existing technology. This may have ruffled feathers at the FPA (which had lobbied the BSI to regulate condoms in the first place), but London Rubber's exclusive right to bear the BSI kite mark nonetheless resulted in the rapid improvement of condom quality,[78] which was, after all, what everyone wanted.

London Rubber would retain the kite mark under the proviso that one condom in every 100 would be tested for compliance, and that this random testing detected a failure rate of no more than 1 per cent.[79] BS3704 also resolved a long-standing date-stamping issue by requiring that every pack be marked with a use-by date.[80] Back in the late 1930s, London Rubber had tussled with the FPA's forerunner, the National Birth Control Association, over the date-stamping of condoms, claiming that its products would last from three to five years, while the NBCA felt two years was closer to the mark. They rationalised that one could not know how old a condom was unless there was an indication of the date of manufacture upon the product. London Rubber told them that this would contradict the five-year storage guarantee they had been making to their customers for years, and that date-stamping would also involve impracticable retooling. The FPA threatened to take London Rubber off the Approved List, but to no effect: Durex remained both on the list and un-stamped, thanks to the many discounted products London Rubber supplied to FPA clinics.[81] In 1964, however, rather than impeding London Rubber, date-stamping under the terms of BS3704 turned out to be an advantage. 'I mean, I think in general sales, this business of putting the sell-by date or use-by date was a huge marketing ploy', Harvey says, suggesting that consumers would have to exhaust or replace their condoms more quickly with a use-by date made clear. 'It sells a lot more but for the most part, you don't need to throw these products away when they reach that date'.[82] During my research for this book, I opened a foil-sealed, lubricated Durex Gossamer manufactured in the mid-1960s and was astonished to find it moist, pliant, strong, and easy to unroll onto my fingers, after more than fifty years of inconsistent storage conditions. While this test was in no way a measure of its current reliability if used as intended, the durability of this condom as an object, which showed no outward signs of deterioration, was very impressive. BS3704 also laid down the first standardized rules on condom size: overall length was to be no less than 175 mm (or just under 7"), and the width when laid flat no less than 49 mm (just under 2", meaning a circumference of around 4").[83]

In spite of the *Which?* report's attack on London Rubber, its marketing methods, and its products, BS3704 provided for a new era of reliability and cooperation. It also marked the end of London Rubber's piggybacking off the FPA's reputation. The association, as the recognised testing body for British contraceptives up until BS3704, had never been complete in its support for London Rubber. Any official endorsement it might have given was now supplanted by the BSI's seal of approval. The new kite mark was the gold standard of official endorsement, which reinforced the price premium on Durex and meant London Rubber could go on without consumer promotion for the time being.[84] Following the publication of the British Standard, the FPA stopped concerning itself with the testing or approval of rubber contraceptives.[85]

For London Rubber's part, the company wielded its cooperation with the BSI committee and exclusive use of the kite mark to counter the negative publicity generated by *Which?* BS3704 offered an opportunity to both reclaim and proclaim the public safety of London Rubber products: the potential impediment of the British Standard was thereby appropriated by London Rubber as though it had been their idea all along, and publicly dressed up as a victory. The company funded a special press conference and awards ceremony at the Waldorf Hotel to mark the handing over of its kite mark licence, followed by a tour of the Chingford plant for maximum exploitation.[86] The BSI's press release smoothed over previous bad publicity for the condom in the interests of upholding the institute's own standard. 'In a mass-produced product of this kind it is difficult – unless the price is made prohibitive – to preclude altogether a small number of sub-standard items', it read. 'The British Standard ... by demanding an extremely high degree of quality control in the factory, will obviate this risk as far as possible'. London Rubber ran publicity in the medical press, seizing the opportunity to limit the damage done by *Which?* On 19 June 1964, for example, it ran an advert in *Nursing Mirror* announcing 'Durex. The First Protectives to Receive BSI Approval'. Lastly, BS3704 officially acknowledged the condom's place in medicine, because the specification was authorised by the Surgical Instruments and Medical Appliances Standards Committee of the BSI.[87] This was especially important at the beginning of the 1960s when the oral contraceptive pill – a medical product – encroached upon the traditional, non-medical contraceptive marketplace.

FIGURE 5.11   Syntex scientists with a barbasco giant yam, which was used to produce the oral contraceptive pill. Syntex S.A., Mexico City, 1951.

The Pill: Early Awareness

From the late 1940s, Syntex S.A., a small Mexico City operation working with American scientist Dr Russell E. Marker, developed a high-yielding and cost-effective progesterone production method that would revolutionise the hormone industry. Syntex and Marker mechanised a process for extracting 'diosgenin' from local yams.[88] This substance was then employed to synthesise hormones (which were used in a broad range of therapies) instead of extracting them from animal products, a time-consuming and costly process.[89] Following Syntex's entry to the hormone market, world production of progesterone jumped from a few pounds annually in the post-war period to around one ton per month by the early 1950s.[90] The acceleration of Syntex's diosgenin extraction from the barbasco yam broke the pre-existing European monopoly on animal hormones, which resulted in dramatic price reductions and an unparalleled yield from abundant natural sources.[91] In May 1951, *Fortune* reported that the basic female hormone estrone cost $40 per gram to make when extracted from a mare's urine, but cost only $10 when synthesised through yams. Easy and inexpensive availability led to the development of a mass-produced product that was first marketed as a gynaecological therapeutic agent, and which would be repackaged as the pill in the 1960s.[92]

It was the Searle company which first made the transition from marketing synthesized progesterone as a hormonal therapeutic to selling it as an agent expressly for contraceptive use, using norethynodrel (its own 'star molecule' synthesised progestin).[93] The therapeutic version of norethynodrel first appeared as Enovid in America and Enavid in Britain from 1957, 'for use in certain menstrual disorders'.[94] Launching as a therapeutic instead of a contraceptive allowed Searle to test market receptiveness while establishing its practical ability to produce the hormone. Rather than use the Syntex progestin norethisterone, Searle secured its own supplies of diosgenin through the acquisition of the Mexican company Root Chemicals, Inc. and its subsidiary, Productos Esteroides, S.A. in 1958.[95] Following this, Searle added a supplement to Enovid's American license, enabling the therapeutic to be marketed for conception control from 1960, which marked the arrival of the pill in Western markets.[96] Searle reported that Enovid was widely accepted by the medical profession, predicting that it would become 'internationally recognised as the first orally active drug for effective physiological control of human ovulation'.[97] As the Syntex company would later observe, 'The stage was set for the drama of oral contraceptives'.[98]

The future contraceptive pill came to London Rubber's attention in the 1950s, in the context of corporate competition, the 'treasure hunt' for steroids, anticipation of a new contraceptive trade for pharmaceutical houses, and rumours of a simple, low-cost solution for world overpopulation.[99] From 1955 onward, London Rubber 'became increasingly aware of the threat posed by the contraceptive pill to the sheath business'.[100] This is consistent with the first public announcement of the possibility of creating an oral contraceptive at the Fifth International Conference on Planned Parenthood, Tokyo, in October that year, although British newspapers such as the *Manchester Guardian* had already reported hopeful rumours of a pharmaceutical solution to world overpopulation in 1954.[101] On 22 January, for example, an unnamed Indian birth control advocate was quoted as saying, 'In America they are experimenting with a pill … the whole world is waiting for the results'. On 12 July 1954, the World Population Study Group's report for the World Population Conference in Rome was quoted in the *Times* as making a 'strong plea for intensive research into oral methods – such as a pill that would ensure sterility'. The world population control movement, which was active at the time, provided the means for birth control campaigns to gain traction and legitimacy, 'creating a context wherein the marketing of the oral contraceptive was appropriate and viable'.[102] For the purposes of the printed press, recourse to a probable future pill to curb fertility anchored overpopulation stories within a simple and familiar conceptual framework that translated to a mass audience, and the pill became big news.

Press rumours of a future oral contraceptive were further provoked when Enovid/Enavid hit the market. In 1957, Searle wrote to American physicians informing them that it was safe to prescribe Enovid as an anti-ovulant, as well as a therapeutic, meaning that its contraceptive facility, in some respects, got in under the radar.[103] Others were not fooled. On 12 July 1957 the *Times* reported that Enavid (the British version) 'definitely inhibits ovulation'. One year later, on 19 October 1958, the *Sunday Pictorial* would report on 'X-Pills' being sold in British pharmacies for the same purpose.[104] In 1959, the oral contraceptive pill got its British television premiere on a discussion programme called *Go Forth and Multiply*, which announced a 'new method of birth control where a woman takes a pill by mouth', discussed in the context of overpopulation.[105] The programme, which was shown on ITV (the commercial channel) at 10:15 p.m. following the evening news, generated great excitement, especially within the FPA and among their international colleagues. 'All of us here in the New York office have been absolutely drooling at the thought of the discussion', wrote an IPPF colleague. 'I wish we might have seen and heard it'.[106] Mass media discussion of contraceptives had hitherto been restricted to print media and radio programming, so reference to the pill on television was a watershed moment. By the late 1950s, the cat was out of the bag and it was clear that at least some women were already using orally active steroid hormones for birth control.

Looking back on the period, John Harvey says that, realistically, machine vending posed a far bigger threat to London Rubber than the pill.[107] Indeed, even as oral contraception increased in popularity, British users of condoms would outnumber pill users three to two well in the 1960s.[108] However, the problem was that the pharmaceutical development of oral contraceptives, which was undertaken by several companies simultaneously in distant lands, could not simply be subsumed or purchased by London Rubber in the same way that it had acquired vending machine makers. An additional problem was that the testing and development of the pill was led by the Family Planning Association. British oral contraceptive trials began in 1957 in Slough and Birmingham. These were run under the auspices of the Council for the Investigation of Fertility Control (CIFC), the regulatory arm of the FPA.[109] Trialling the pill made clear the

FPA's intention to embrace new contraceptive technologies and use them in its own clinics. London Rubber appealed to the FPA for news of (and involvement in) the pill development process, but was brushed off.[110] Thus, in order to get on the inside of developments, the company found reasons to engage the CIFC/FPA in other ways. It offered up non-pharmaceutical products for testing alongside the new oral contraceptives, so that the company might fall within the newly established CIFC's purview. After Durex Gossamer was launched in 1957, for example, London Rubber offered to supply 500 CIFC testers with six months' worth of the condoms free of charge.[111] In 1958, London Rubber proposed to give 2,000 free tubes of Duracreme spermicide for distribution among clinic users, to which the CIFC was initially receptive.[112] Duracreme customers had previously reported curdling, which justified testing a new formulation, and London Rubber used the opportunity to publicise Duracreme's new bigger tubes, which were rolled out to compete against Ortho's large tubes of Orthocreme.[113] After the false start, however, the CIFC elected not to trial Duracreme, deciding that 'the Council exists to undertake clinic trials of new contraceptives only'.[114] This was the crux of the matter, as the CIFC's main remit was to oversee testing of oral contraceptives: Duracreme — and all other Durex products — were simply cuckoos in the nest.

As the FPA built up to releasing Searle's Conovid, the first pill marketed expressly for conception control in Britain, relations between London Rubber and the association cooled. London Rubber continued to support the FPA with discounts and special offers into the 1960s, but big project support was withheld, as in the case of the never-made sequel to *Birthright*.[115] In overseeing the British testing of oral contraceptives such as Conovid with Searle, and then Anovlar with the German firm Schering AG, the FPA developed new working relationships with companies completely outside of traditional contraceptive trading. This cooperation, as much as the pill itself, marked the FPA's shift away from mechanical contraceptives, at least for the time being.

In America, and in the build-up to the oral contraceptive being fully marketed, long-standing condom manufacturer Julius Schmid (of West Paterson, New Jersey) suddenly hit hard times. Along with Young's Rubber Company, Schmid was a leading US manufacturer whose condoms were sold in drug stores throughout the country.[116] According to the medical historian Andrea Tone, condoms (which had, for a time, played second fiddle to female contraceptive devices) had enjoyed a renaissance in America in the 1950s, becoming the most frequently used contraceptive.[117] At the time Enovid became available, condoms took two-thirds of the $200 million American contraceptive market,[118] and Schmid had a powerful nation-wide selling organisation with strongly entrenched trademarks, Ramses and Sheik. The company was attractively set up with a 200,000 square foot freehold factory on 15.5 acres of freehold land, and 19,000 square foot of leased office and storage space on West 55th Street in New York City.[119] But following a profits peak of $738,383 in 1956, Schmid experienced a sudden and rapid decline. Eddis & Associates, Schmid's accountants, reported a profit drop to $686,172 in 1957, then to $593,125 in 1958, reaching a low of $568,173 in 1960.[120] At this time, Enovid's trial as a contraceptive in Puerto Rico was being covered in a diverse range of American consumer periodicals including *Time*, *Business Week*, *Consumer Reports*, *Fortune*, *Nation*, *Reader's Digest*, *True Story*, and the *New York Times*.[121] By 1959, the proto-oral contraceptive was being used by 500,000 American women.[122] While it is impossible to draw a certain correlation between Schmid's deterioration and Enovid's uptake, it is reasonable to suppose that London Rubber might have made the tangential connection for themselves, firstly as an interested competitor, and secondly as Schmid's prospective buyer. According to Andrea Tone, 'by the mid-1960s, the Pill's popularity had proven that the over-the-counter condom had finally met its match, at least in the United States'.[123] It was only in the build-up to London Rubber Group's takeover of Julius Schmid (US and Canada) in the summer of 1963 that profits would begin to recover, helped by the fact that Schmid finally dropped its naphtha-based cement dipping process the same year.[124]

Being that Schmid operated out of New York City, the acquisition was also beneficial for London Rubber in setting up to challenge 'Durex Products Inc.', a New York firm that had been selling contraceptives under the same name since 1946.[125] In the months prior to the Schmid acquisition, London Rubber had lost a trademark appeal against Durex Products Inc. at India's Supreme Court, which had ruled in favour of the respondent in respect of 'special circumstances'. The first circumstance was that, in the view of the Deputy Registrar of Trade Marks, contraceptives were 'necessary in the Indian context for the welfare of the nation', insomuch that they were considered a socioeconomic necessity in India at the time.[126] Indeed, this positive attitude towards contraception in the wake of the 'population bomb' was the very reason London Rubber sought to secure a presence in the Indian market with its venture in Pallavaram (above). The other special circumstance pertained to 'the fact that the applicant's mark is largely confined to contraceptives for use by women'.[127] This assertion that Durex Products Inc. was not in direct competition with London Rubber because of a fundamental difference in market is supported by listings of wholesale contraceptives detailed in American pharmacy trade publications, which suggest that the main business of Durex Products Inc. was caps, diaphragms, douching powders, and foams (such as Durafoam).[128] Although London Rubber manufactured women's contraceptives at home, including creams, diaphragms, and an oral contraceptive pill (below), these interests appear to have been confined to Britain, where they were deployed expressly to counter competition by controlling or otherwise infiltrating the local women's market, and to supply the FPA. Nonetheless, the purchase of Schmid, which had been producing diaphragms for the woman-centred American market under the Ramses brand since around 1940,[129] would have put London Rubber in a position to challenge Durex Products Inc. on its home turf. By 1972, the company had disappeared from American pharmacy trade publications.[130]

Into the 1960s

For London Rubber, the early part of the 1960s was marked by change in the contraceptive marketplace, diversification, and structural reorganisation. The subsidiary London Rubber Industries was separated from the wider London Rubber Group, taking charge of dipped latex products and supporting new ventures that, it was hoped, would make London Rubber Group less dependent on the condom in the long term, in case oral contraceptives became popular. Since the 1960s, the pill has come to be regarded as a 'disruptive technology' by contraceptive historians,[131] following from the theory of 'disruptive innovation' forwarded by the American academic and business consultant Clayton M. Christensen in the 1990s.[132] A 'disruptor' in this sense would be an innovation providing a new set of values, creating a new market, and overtaking an existing one.[133] Whereas Durex Gossamer, as the first lubricated condom, was an 'evolutionary' innovation (insofar as it improved an existing product within an existing market), 'disruption' was certainly a possible outcome of the new-type contraception. The pill looked poised to carve a new market for women's contraception, with the possibility of supplanting the condom, imbued with the values of a family doctor instead of a barber.

In later decades, London Rubber would come to refer to the pill as the factor that prompted it to begin its diversification programme.[134] At this point in the early 1960s, however, the company could only guess at the

FIGURE 5.12   Elkan Jackson and Angus Reid, 1951.

future ramifications of the new contraceptive on the block. Reading the pill's emergence as a warning, London Rubber moved to protect its interests. Consequently, when Conovid appeared on the British market in January 1961 and in FPA clinics one year later, London Rubber had already begun a programme of structural change, anticipating both positive and negative effects resulting from the pill. On the positive side was the wider global acceptance of contraceptive practice linked to population worries, which London Rubber set out to turn to its advantage. The negative implication lay in not knowing how the market would develop. By staying aware of developments in contraceptive technology, London Rubber was forewarned to modify its business areas as insurance against possible crises, even though it was not always clear how these might materialise. One area that could not be guaranteed was consumer behaviour and attitudes towards changing contraceptive practices. It was here that 'disruption' arising from the pill was most likely to manifest, although traditional contraceptive companies could only plan for possible outcomes. 'We live in a changing world', London Rubber chair Elkan Jackson stated cautiously in 1959, 'and one hesitates to forecast'.[135]

6

The Consumer Speaks

'I don't think they're very go ahead otherwise they wouldn't still be making French letters ... they'd think of something better'.
A twenty-six-year-old working-class male to Ernest Dichter Associates, 1961

This chapter discusses the biggest long-standing sales problem that London Rubber faced at the beginning of the 1960s, which is to say communicating the desirability and availability of condoms to potential new customers through consumer advertising.[1] As will be argued, the pill and its stakeholders redefined the parameters of the contraceptive marketplace, and in so doing engineered a culture of acceptance in order to 'establish oral contraception in the national consciousness'.[2] Unfortunately for London Rubber, this reinforced age-old barriers to the cultural acceptance of condoms as embodied by impediments to consumer advertising. The company had attempted to circumvent the need for direct-to-consumer advertising by securing official endorsement from the FPA, but this had limited success. Although it would eventually achieve endorsement from the BSI in 1964, the interim period required action and a better understanding of the consumer, if only because of potential market disruption threatened by the emergence of the pill. As this chapter will show, London Rubber proactively tackled the pill as early as 1961 by producing a booklet containing warnings about oral contraceptive safety aimed at contraceptive consumers. In order to test whether these warnings were effective, London Rubber commissioned market research, but was unhappy with the results. A second market research study only confirmed the negative attitude consumers had towards condoms, and to the specific concept of condom advertising. Examining these market research reports in detail, this chapter finds that London Rubber's options for advertising its product remained frustratingly limited.

Pills Take the Stage
In 1961, condoms enjoyed an existing consumer base of around 49 per cent of married couples.[3] Customer

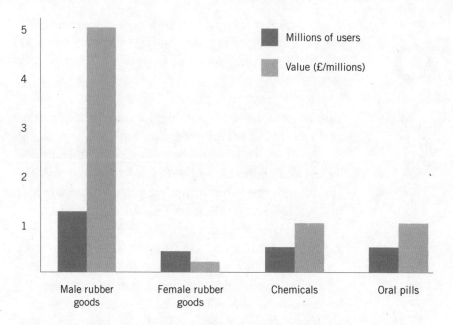

FIGURE 6.1   Estimated value of contraceptive market by theoretical consumer buying prices, 1964. Source: Economist Intelligence Unit, 'Contraceptive Products,' *Retail Business Survey* 92 (1965): 12, table 2 (Trade and EIU estimates). © J. Borge 2019.

retention was not a problem because users who were already loyal to the Durex brand were unlikely to switch, and London Rubber products dominated the market in any case.[4] The issue, rather, was attracting difficult-to-reach non-users who might be converted to condom use, namely those who used chemical contraceptives (12 per cent of married couples) or *coitus interruptus*/withdrawal (44 per cent).[5] The 1961 contraceptive market consisted of 2.25 million users, half of the potential market of 4.5 million, meaning that, had the pill not existed, London Rubber would have had the scope to double its trade. The pill, so it was thought at the time, added around half a million new users (from previous non-users) to this (figure 6.1). The condom and the pill were therefore vying for possible shares of an expanding market, rather than simply snatching existing business away from each other.[6] In this respect, the general popularity of the concept of oral contraception helped the case of the condom, by making consumers more receptive to the idea of using contraceptives. On the downside, condoms were not as publicly foregrounded as the pill, which was discussed widely in print, on radio, and on screen. To be sure, there were many stakeholders in oral contraception, including international family planning movements and social reformers, manufacturers and their associates (such as advertisers and wholesalers), journalists and media vendors, and women users, their partners, and their children, at home and abroad. However, most of what manufacturers knew about actual usage patterns was derived from sociological studies conducted before the arrival of oral contraceptives.[7] It was in the effervescent and lasting media discourse that events and attitudes converged.

An early place where the oral contraceptive gained traction was in the doctor's office. Discussion of oral contraceptives in medical circles was natural and necessary, the pill being a prescribed medicine. However, this had never been the case for condoms, and it left them at an early disadvantage when the pill came onto the scene. Given that the medical profession had hitherto resisted contraception as part of its remit, inclusion of the pill into the everyday practice of GPs and gynaecologists was relatively new, and for this reason it generated debate.[8] The need to inform and educate future prescribers also opened up advertising to oral contraceptive manufacturers. This was necessarily restricted to the medical press, because pharmaceutical houses were bound by a voluntary agreement not to advertise prescription medicine to consumers, meaning that advertising was only directed at pharmacists and doctors.[9] Significantly, however, the manufacturers of traditional, non-prescription contraceptives (such as London Rubber) were still excluded from the conversation, which was a throwback to the long-standing social discomfiture surrounding condoms and what they were understood to represent culturally.

It was in the final quarter of 1961 that events converged to platform the mass rollout of oral contraceptives in Britain. In September the *British Medical Journal* ran a full-page article on Searle's pill, Conovid, alerting the medical profession to its existence.[10] Conovid was made available at FPA clinics in October,[11] which coincided with several relevant events. In November, the second part of the Population Investigation Committee's research into marital contraceptive practices was released and widely publicised,[12] and a conference on population was held at the University of Birmingham.[13] On 4 December, Conovid became available through subsidised NHS prescription. Although it had been available for the whole of 1961, it was only in the autumn that Searle began to actively market it in Britain. Searle encouraged early adoption by GPs, publishing full-page ads in the *Monthly Index of Medical Specialties* and the *British Medical*

Journal in October 1961, and the *Practitioner* in January 1962. It also timed publicity for maximum effect: having drip-fed news through the medical press, full marketing was pursued once Conovid had received positive results in clinical trials though the Council for the Investigation of Fertility Control (CIFC). This was important because other companies were also in the process of getting approval for their own-brand pills. In 1962, Conovid was joined by Conovid-E (Searle's own variation), Roussel's Pre-vision, and Schering's Anovlar. Market competition increased year-on-year: by 1965, there would be twelve oral contraceptive brands available in Britain, and pharmacy sales value had jumped to £1,105,000 (from £96,000 in 1962).[14] Meanwhile, London Rubber was a specialist manu-facturer of latex contraceptives and could not match the long-established relationships that pharmaceutical houses had nurtured with physicians through many years of providing medicines. Unlike the condom, the pill received an automatic audience with doctors, creating an extension of the contraceptives market from which London Rubber was excluded by default.

In theory, the consumer advertising of condoms was permissible in the 1960s, but custom and practice varied according to claims made by the advertisements, and the medium through which these messages were transmitted. Media vendors could accept, reject, or withdraw campaigns according to editorial or other policies. One particular issue was the Durex trademark's synonymy with condoms, which made display of the name itself very difficult outside of certain retail environments or catalogues.[15] For example, and according to John Peel, when London Rubber placed an innocent ad for Durex rubber gloves on the London Underground in 1960, the British Transport Commission withdrew the poster even though the advert did not contravene guidelines.[16] In print, then, con-traceptive advertising was fairly arbitrary according to the requirements and preferences of editors: generally speaking, provincial papers tended to take ads, needing the regular revenue more than bigger papers, while the nationals tended not to.[17] The pill, on the other hand, with its back-ground as a gynaecological therapy and its controlled distribution, did not evoke a historic connection to prostitution, disease, or extramarital sex, as the condom did. Furthermore, pictures of the pill itself were inoffen-sive because it was just a tablet. On top of all this, condoms just seemed 'traditional' and old-fashioned when set against the technologically so-phisticated pill,[18] so much so that reporting on oral contraceptives made media vendors appear up-to-the-minute, and oftentimes progressive.

In short, oral contraceptives were a glamorous, topical story that could present sex, sexuality, and plentiful images of women under the label of the public interest. After all, the pill was still in development in the 1960s, and changes to the technology were necessarily reported for the public record, whereas the mechanism of action for condoms, fundamentally, had not changed. Oral contraceptives dramatically increased the public appetite for contraceptive information more generally.[19] Images of the oral contraceptives and their branded packaging were widely circulated to accompany news stories, helped by the willingness of manufacturers to provide press stills and samples.[20] London Rubber was ready to contribute to the conversation, but was not invited to the party: its participation in debate was restricted because of the long-standing cultural aversion to the public discussion of condoms. TV producers simply preferred to stage discussions of the pill in place of other contraceptives because it was brand new, and because its medical status offset their own responsibility for tackling the subject. The pill also worked as shorthand for sex without directly evoking the body.[21] Condoms, on the other hand, were undeniably penis-shaped and dealt directly with the private messiness of sex. In short, condoms were the very antonym of glamour. Like toilet paper, marketers considered them to be simply 'unmentionable',[22] and they did not surface in the mainstream. Given that most media vendors were ostensibly free to elect whether or not to bring condoms into the public discussion of contraception, however, the ultimate decision as to what was deemed acceptable lay not with regulators, but with consumers.

In 1961, as the pill became available, two important contraceptive use surveys came to fruition. These were the Population Investigation Committee's 'Birth Control in Britain', produced by Rachel M. Pearce and Griselda Rowntree (above), and Francois Lafitte's 'The Users of Birth Control Clinics', a survey undertaken for the FPA.[23] Both reported that withdrawal ('pulling out') was the most widely used contraceptive method at the time, and that the condom was the most frequently employed method where an appliance was used. Both surveys were fairly well publicised. So far as London Rubber was concerned, the fact that condoms were used extensively was not new information: what the company needed to know was what consumers really felt about them, and about condoms being advertised, in order that these feeling might be targeted and redirected to better suit London Rubber's aims. The Pearce/Rowntree and Lafitte reports outlined what types of birth control were practised and how users managed the concept of family planning, but did little

FIGURE 6.2   Inflation testing of condoms, North Circular Road, 1950.

to reveal the complex emotions consumers held about specific products, and the idea of having these products sold to them. And so, in 1961, London Rubber commissioned two pieces of private market research for its own use, firstly from The Pulse, London, and then from Ernest Dichter Associates. The purpose was to better understand contraceptive users,

FIGURE 6.3   Electronic testing of condoms on Automated Protective line, North Circular Road, 1950s.

and to strategize for both the retention and expansion of condom customers with a view to assessing (and perhaps changing) deep-seated attitudes towards condom advertising.

The Pulse, London

Under commission from London Rubber, market research consultants The Pulse, London (TPL) produced a quantitative research survey of 109 married women interviewed over January and February 1961, entitled 'Family Planning Enquiry'.[24] TPL had carried out sophisticated and large-scale quantified research studies before, such as a viewership survey for Associated Rediffusion Television.[25] For London Rubber's purposes, TPL was tasked with finding out about the public's attitude toward advertising for contraceptive products.[26] Specifically, it tested responses to the company's *Modern Family Planning* booklet, which was the latest incarnation of *Planned Families*.[27] At the time, *Modern Family Planning* was London

Rubber's main tool for attracting new consumers, explaining the theory of contraceptive practice, outlining techniques, and promoting London Rubber's range of products. Its most important function, however, was to undermine products and techniques that did not reflect the company's commercial interest. This was achieved by explaining each rival method and then discouraging its use, thus creating a hierarchy of methods with condoms at the top. For example, diaphragms were portrayed as messy, bothersome, and characterised by a long preparatory procedure involving repeated medical check-ups, smearing with spermicide, laborious insertion and aftercare, and all with no guarantee of success. 'It is hardly surprising', the booklet read, 'that many women eventually give up on the diaphragm method and change to a method that is simpler and aesthetically more acceptable – the protective'.[28]

This edition of *Modern Family Planning* undermined the new oral contraceptive over four dedicated pages. It characterised the pill as an incomplete technology in the experimental stage, rather than a perfected method that was safe to use at the beginning of the 1960s. This might seem prescient of the company at first glance. London Rubber's tentative, early attack on the pill predated the first big oral contraceptive health scare in August 1962, when the pill was linked with thromboembolism.[29] However, London Rubber was merely picking up on the fact that some doctors had already become concerned about oral contraceptives.[30] For example, Dr Robert J. Hetherington, a specialist in geriatrics from Birmingham, began collecting promotional material related to the pill early in 1961.[31] Like many others, Hetherington was concerned about possible long-term implications of oral contraceptive use.[32] London Rubber simply latched onto such doubts, emphasising the side effects and the unknown long-term dangers. 'Eventually, a safe and satisfactory contraceptive tablet may take its place with other accepted contraceptive methods', *Modern Family Planning* magnanimously conceded. 'In the mean-time, the protective has been proved as a simple and highly reliable method of contraception'.[33] London Rubber's claims about safety were made with a view to discouraging oral contraceptive use, but they also predated the Dunlop Committee's investigation into the safety of drugs (including the pill), which began in 1965.[34] This is important because it shows that London Rubber was not so much inventing problems with the pill, but rather was fanning the flames of pre-existing uncertainties in the medical world. Anti-pill claims were also a useful sideways swipe at the FPA, under whose auspices (via the CIFC) all oral contraceptives on the market were cleared for use.

The TPL study of consumer responses to *Modern Family Planning* ostensibly served as way of gauging the consumer position to general contraceptive advertising, but it was also a stealthy means of surveying early attitudes to the concept of the oral pill among then-current contraceptive users. Specifically, London Rubber was curious to know if discouraging enthusiasm about the pill actually worked. Following the trend set by social surveys on contraception, TPL's study was designed to survey 330 women, a third of whom agreed to answer questions about family planning. No correlation between age, social class, and willingness to be interviewed was discovered, although mothers were found more likely to cooperate than non-mothers.[35] The booklet was left with respondents for one week, after which time interviewees were telephoned and asked seventeen questions ranging from abstract opinions about the concept of family planning, to world population, to the advertising of contraceptive products. Respondents were also probed about their general awareness of the contraceptive marketplace and their personal response to it. The research also enquired about the nascent contraceptive pill. Results were tabulated, with verbatim quotes referencing the booklet cited in the final report. In this way, TPL's survey was designed to assess the effectiveness of anti-pill propaganda included in the *Modern Family Planning* booklet and London Rubber's attempts to push its own products, rather than assess respondents' general feeling about contraception.

Having read the booklet, 76 per cent of women reported having had heard about the pill's existence.[36] Asked what they knew, 28 per cent said that 'it is still in the experimental stage'; 17 per cent knew that it had to be taken every day; 14 per cent had heard that 'it can have a bad effect/make you ill'; and 8 per cent felt that it would not be completely effective. These were all negative angles on the pill that had been pushed in *Modern Family Planning*, so it looked as though this type of anti-pill propaganda could be effective. However, over half of women respondents felt that the pill was a good idea and the majority had not yet caught wind of the possible side effects.[37] This was in spite of the booklet placing a strong emphasis on nausea, tiredness, headaches, sore breasts, and abdominal pain, all of which were consistent with early therapeutic and contraceptive pill use.[38] This result suggested that the company would have to try harder to convey the negative aspects of the pill.

TPL's research also suggested room for improvement in London Rubber's communication efforts more generally. The question of 'what method of family planning informants would advise a person to use' posed particular difficulty for TPL's respondents. Although a small percentile said that they would recommend the cervical cap, or 'contraceptives' in general, the survey did not record any respondents who actually said 'condom' in their telephone interviews. The word, it seemed, was unspeakable, which is probably why London Rubber preferred to use the word 'protective' instead. This reluctance to refer to the condom directly only corroborated its problematic cultural status. By contrast, the study confirmed that the pill was completely immune to any cultural prohibition, as it was freely discussed. Furthermore, when pressed to think about recommending a contraceptive, 68 per cent of respondents defaulted to recommending a clinic or a doctor rather than a specific method or brand.[39] In other words, both medical opinion and FPA clinics – both of which worked in conjunction with the pill but against London Rubber and the condom – served as cultural synonyms for contraception among London Rubber's target market. This was in spite of the fact that clinics and doctors were among the smallest retailers of contraceptives at the time (figure 1.3).[40]

A more positive result was that 51 per cent of women named Durex as a contraceptive, a high level of awareness among a group who did not necessarily buy condoms for themselves. Ten per cent mentioned Rendells soluble pessaries, which was the next leading British contraceptive brand, and which was administered through the vagina – meaning that women had direct experience of purchasing and using it themselves.[41] Both Durex and Rendells were well known to social classes A–D under the system used by marketers, namely: (A) higher managerial and administrative; (B) intermediate managerial and administrative; (C) junior level managerial or administrative and skilled manual workers; and (D) semi-skilled and unskilled manual workers. Of these, the ABCs were slightly more forthcoming with brand names for contraceptives in general, which corroborates other research suggesting that the unskilled working classes were less likely to make routine use of condoms (see above).[42] Over half of the respondents were aware of family planning advertisements in the press, and were responsive to coupon ads.[43] Those who would not send off a coupon claimed to prefer professional medical advice from a clinic or doctor,[44] suggesting the existence of a large group of swing consumers who might be pulled away from clinics if their concerns about medical authority were otherwise satisfied.

The *Modern Family Planning* booklet, which was supplied one week before questioning, was generally found to be 'very good', 'interesting', and 'informative'.[45] All respondents found it clear, and only around 2 per cent of respondents thought any of its content objectionable.[46] Verbatim quotes on the booklet were generally favourable, but TPL reported an uncomfortable response to its underlying commercial nature, which stood out to the cohort. The dichotomy, as revealed by the survey, was that Durex served as the most useful cultural shorthand for referring to condoms, but was, at the same time, resented for being too commercial. A sizable number of women begrudged attempts to dupe them with *Modern Family Planning*, which pretended it was an educational tool instead of a piece of advertising.[47] 'Didn't like it as commercial, not convincing as pushing own product', or 'advertising and not really family planning', were typical responses quoted in the verbatim dataset.[48] Clearly, the resistance to commercial contraception whipped up by contraceptive bill supporters in the 1930s had not gone away.

London Rubber was displeased with TPL's research in any case. 'There was, unfortunately, a high percentage of women who declined to answer the questions', wrote the company's PR officer Dai Hayward. 'This was because the briefing of the investigators was badly done ... Somehow the investigators got the idea that if a housewife already had children, she would not be interested in planning their family, and didn't pursue questioning if there was the slightest reluctance to answer'.[49] Either way, the report indicated a general reluctance among women to discuss contraception, or at least to discuss it with strangers. Only one-third of those originally approached were receptive, and these respondents, TPL said, were almost certainly more sympathetic in the first place and did not reflect a cross section of the general populace.[50] As the basis of all market research technique is the careful selection of persons from whom the information is to be obtained, a sample group must represent the potential consumers of the product being investigated.[51] The problem with TPL's research was that the final sample did not match the target of potential contraceptive consumers – which is to say, non-users who might be converted – since the cohort questioned was already receptive to the concept of family planning. Although the research was useful in may respects, it did not quite hit the mark.

London Rubber nonetheless extracted value from its investment, using findings from the survey in print campaigns and pressing on with *Modern Family Planning*. Rather than advertising condoms, the print campaigns communicated the availability of the booklet. It was also given free to doctors and retailers in the hope that they would distribute it to potential customers. Counter-top display kits were promoted in trade journals, and a full-page advertisement appeared in the *Lancet* pitching London Rubber print booklets as a time-saving device for physicians.[52] *Modern Family Planning* was deployed to preempt contraceptive inquiries to doctors as the pill grew popular, since TPL's respondents preferred to approach doctors for contraceptive advice.[53] In December 1961 London Rubber produced a modified edition of the booklet, which was less damning of rival contraceptives and was, consequently, accepted by the FPA.[54] By toning down its anti-pill message and incorporating statistics from the research, *Modern Family Planning* better disguised its commercial intent for the time being.

Ernest Dichter Associates

The second known piece of research commissioned by London Rubber in 1961 was a motivational study from Ernest Dichter Associates. Rather than using quantitative methods, this particular consultancy used 'motivation research' to assess and define the needs and attitudes behind the purchase of a product, a method that combined psychoanalysis with 'depth interviews' in order to uncover consumers' unconscious wants and desires. The 'depth interview' was a form of non-directive discussion, which allowed the interviewer to pick up on the interviewee's chance comments about a product.[55] Commissioning a study from the newly opened EDA London was a bold move, given that the consultancy was coldly received when it opened, and was only moderately successful in Britain.[56] In America, however, Dichter's Institute for Motivational Research, Inc., was developing a track record in birth control research. In 1958, for example, the IMR undertook work for Ortho to look at the advertising problems of Preceptin and Delfen spermicides,[57] recommending that young medics might be targeted for advertising because they were more receptive to 'new techniques' than older MDs.[58] According to IMR, Ortho might also help younger MDs to understand the woman end-user's 'great needs in the area of contraceptive decisions: the warmth, and tangible sympathy and understanding of her doctor'.[59] IMR also worked with Young's, who made Trojan condoms, in a study completed in 1962.[60] In this case, the research indicated 'a need to take bold steps to show that the condom manufacturer is not capitalising on vice'.[61] Packaging, it was suggested, was one such way to imbue Young's condoms with a sense of solidity in place of sexual transience. For example, users showed a marked preference for secure foiling and modern plastic containers, as opposed to semi-open paper wrappings and old-fashioned tins.[62] This pre-existing experience in the contraceptives field meant that the IMR organisation was already well versed in the problems of traditional contraceptive manufacturers. In addition, IMR was also experienced in advising the very pharmaceutical companies who would become London Rubber's rivals in the oral contraceptive field, such as Schering.[63] EDA London therefore pitched to London Rubber on the back of its existing contraceptive expertise, and was successful.

The surviving EDA research documents for London Rubber comprise their original proposal,[64] pilot research,[65] and a progress report.[66] EDA was commissioned in the spring of 1961 through London Rubber's advertising contractor, Crane, a publicity agency specialising in female consumers. The cost was £1,750, and work was completed during or just after July 1961.[67] Overall, and in conclusion, EDA proposed the development of a 'practical advertising, public relations and marketing policy which would contribute to the expansion of protective contraceptive usage generally, and the Durex brand specifically'.[68] This aim was much clearer than it had been in the TPL research: London Rubber wanted to know how to get non-users of condoms, including women, to start buying Durex, and how to induce existing users to buy more. EDA sought to answer these questions by discovering factors that motivated and inhibited people in their contraceptive habits.[69] Unlike the TPL, EDA wanted to capture a cross section of the contraceptive-buying public rather than sampling married women consumers already familiar with contraception they obtained from clinics. This was important because London Rubber's future goal was to capture potential contraceptive consumers who might get their birth control from retailers, who were the biggest outlet. EDA thereby used a mixed cohort, composed of 129 married, single, and divorced men and women from the middle, lower-middle, and working classes, with children and without, aged between 18 and 50, and of mixed religious affiliation, although mainly Christian.[70]

Consumers Resist Condom Advertising

EDA's pilot study corroborated several known factors about British birth control habits. It found the most common birth control practice employed by non-users of contraception was withdrawal. Even with a mixed cohort, this finding is consistent with available survey data taken from married couples, such as Moya Woodside's 1943–46 study, and, more pertinently, Pierce and Rowntree's PIC research, which was being publicised just as the

EDA research was conducted. All found withdrawal to be the most widely used technique, followed by the condom, which was the most commonly used artificial contraceptive.[71] EDA also corroborated the existence of a deep-set consumer resistance to branded condom advertising, as flagged by TPL. The added value that EDA gave to this finding was an explanation of the emotional reasoning behind it. Direct consumer advertising of contraceptives, EDA said, would 'run the risk of associating these products with promiscuity and immorality' and 'might arouse a good deal of moral indignation'.[72] Clearly, condom consumers still did not wish to associate their use of the product, or themselves, with the seedier aspects of illegitimate sex. On a related point, EDA also confirmed the importance of medical authorities as legitimate sources of contraceptive information in the minds of consumers.[73] These facts were not news to London Rubber, which had tried to rope the FPA into its advertising scheme and increasingly appealed to doctors through medical advertising and sampling.

More worrying, however, was EDA's roundabout indication that the condom's image would only deteriorate further as the pill's reputation inevitably improved in the 1960s.[74] The sleek new brand identity of Durex Gossamer would have limited effectiveness, EDA said, because 'the image of the condom derives almost entirely from the history of the product, the context in which it is seen to be used, and the actual nature and structure of the product itself'.[75] In other words, the public imagination still conflated the condom with extramarital sex, VD, and prostitution, and associated its physical use with what historian Hera Cook calls 'the red and pink, slime and rubber, of condoms and caps, sex and genitals'.[76] EDA's findings also concurred with the idea that, for some wives, 'the use of a condom may symbolise their own degradation to the status of prostitute'.[77] Using birth control in the pursuit of pleasure, EDA said, 'symbolise[d] a permissiveness towards sexuality which arouses guilt'.[78] Respondents revealed either directly or indirectly that they thought contraceptives indecent, or 'have a cheapening effect on one, or make one feel like a prostitute, in the case of women'.[79] According to historian Julia Laite, the immediate postwar years had seen street prostitution skyrocket, following the departure of troops.[80] Police activity on soliciting also increased.[81] In the 1950s, a wave of 'prostitution panic' swept through the British press, following sensational stories on 'emperors of vice' such as the Messina brothers,[82] while the 1957 Wolfenden committee report tethered street prostitution to homosexuality (the two areas the committee was charged with investigating), keeping both in the public eye.[83] This meant that, for the general public and wives who might be considering planning their families, the idea that prostitution was immoral and undesirable was fresh in their minds when considering the condom as a contraceptive option.

The above observations notwithstanding, EDA's original contribution lay in the evidence-based qualitative conceptualisation of what contraceptives meant to customers socially and psychologically, a path that was not pursued by the largely quantitative social surveys at the time. In EDA's words, contraceptives (i.e., condoms, diaphragms, and pessaries) 'were felt to be used by progressive, responsible people, but also lustful, selfish types' and 'aroused feelings of guilt (meaning their use needed to be justified)'. Contraceptives 'caused anxiety', 'aroused feelings of disgust (being dirty and messy, almost indecent/obscene)', 'were frustrating (interfered with spontaneity)', and 'were felt to lower moral standards (because contraception has made chastity an anachronism)'.[84] By contrast, the 'ideal' birth control method (which did not provoke such negative connotations) was 'very definitely' the oral pill.[85] 'Eighty per cent of the respondents felt that this method would do away with the 'interference', 'messiness', and the 'complication' of the existing methods'.[86] Obviously this was not good news for a company whose thousands of employees depended on the popularity of condoms. With that said, however, EDA did reinforce the sentiment propagated by *Modern Family Planning* rhetoric that the pill was a 'future' contraceptive – a 'dream' or 'ideal' rather than a viable option in 1961.[87] The problem, EDA warned, was that current condom users, though partially leaning towards the diaphragm, were 'dreaming about oral pills'.[88] Even with the potential for dangerous side effects, 'such as cancer, illness, loss of fertility, development of secondary male characteristics in the female etc.', the pill was still 'definitely felt to be the ideal' by EDA.[89] For London Rubber, the question was how to overcome the looming threat of the pill while creating a positive image for Durex in the minds of consumers.

Corroborating 'Unmentionableness'

London Rubber had already tried, and failed, to achieve official endorsement of its products from the FPA in lieu of open consumer promotion. At this point in the 1960s, which is to say the window of four or five years when the pill was just becoming known and the British Standard for condoms had not yet arrived, the company needed to decide whether or not to pursue open consumer advertising. EDA pointedly advised London Rubber against consumer advertising because the customers simply did not like it. 'We are aware that the media are closed to brand advertising', EDA said. 'However, respondents are also opposed to brand advertising'.[90] There was no two ways about it: consumers used condoms, but did not want to be personally associated with the Durex brand. Nor did they want their families to be exposed to condoms and their purpose through brand awareness. Generally speaking, the research reported, 'it was felt that advertising contraceptives through newspapers, radio and television might have harmful effects on children'; would incite children and adolescents to 'experiment' and therefore lower 'moral standards'; and would 'cause embarrassment' and therefore be 'distasteful and indiscreet'.[91] Even in 1961, then, the concerns that contraceptive bill supporters had extolled in the 1930s lingered on in the minds of EDA's respondents. Historians and others have readily accepted overzealous regulation as an explanation for why condoms were purportedly hidden in mass media advertising in the mid-twentieth century.[92] This supports the popular power-driven thesis that regulators wielded top-down control over consumers and their habits. But approval of the family planning principle in the abstract was not tantamount to approval of the commercial advertising of for-profit brands, as some researchers have reported.[93] The difference is borne out clearly by the market research undertaken at the time. TPL's study found that 92 per cent of women saw family planning as important, and 84 per cent thought there was a need for advertising it, but both TPL and EDA showed that favourable attitudes dropped off once the commercial element was introduced. For example, given the choice of three types of marketing, 93 per cent of TPL's respondents favoured ads for clinics, and also general advice booklets, but 58 per cent were opposed to the direct advertising of 'family planning goods', which is to say branded contraceptive products like Durex.[94] Rather than changing alongside regulation in later decades, consumer opinion remained remarkably consistent: consumers did not like to see branded condoms advertised.[95]

During the period in which London Rubber commissioned its market research, dislike of commercial contraceptive promotion was widespread. Towards the end of the 1960s, social marketers struggling to encourage contraceptive use in Global South countries would avoid using obviously commercial marketing techniques not because they were ineffective, but because they were ideologically incompatible with the aims of socially motivated population controllers. 'Many social scientists', said social marketing pioneers John Farley and Harold Leavitt, 'seem to feel either uncomfortable with or vaguely hostile to the notion of mass marketing (for profit) of things in general and contraceptives in particular'.[96] As notions of family planning and population control strengthened their hold in the mid-twentieth century, for-profit contraceptive houses were construed as the very enemy of social family planning policy both globally and nationally. During the 1967 House of Commons debate on the Family Planning Bill, for example, the MP Leo Abse said, 'What is certain in this country, however, is that it cannot be left to competition between rival manufacturers to ensure that local authorities will obtain contraceptives for their clinics at realistic and reasonable prices, because a sinister monopoly dominates the whole contraceptive manufacturing industry'.[97] The 'sinister monopoly' referred to was, of course, London Rubber, whom Abse painted as nothing less than a profiteer.[98]

Looking back over London Rubber's marketing problems, business historians Aubrey Wilson and Christopher West would later articulate the troubled commercial condom as a 'classic unmentionable product'.[99] 'Unmentionables', they explain, 'are products, services, or concepts that for reasons of delicacy, decency, morality, or even fear tend to elicit reactions of distaste, disgust, offense, or outrage when mentioned or when openly presented'.[100] As 'unmentionables', condoms were universally aligned with 'weaponry, hard and soft drugs, hygiene products, prostitution, abnormal or even moderately unusual sexual practices, and sanitation services'.[101] This meant that even though condoms were the most widely used form of appliance contraceptive at the cusp of the 1960s, they were also the most untenable marketing entity because of the guilt and distaste they evoked in consumers. Wilson and West include the broad category of 'birth control' in their list of 'unmentionables', although a distinction is made between the condom and the pill, which 'in contrast to the sheath became the modern, clean, reliable, and unobtrusive method'.[102] The pill was eminently 'mentionable', and was the only birth control technology that could be (and was) talked about in public.[103] The FPA's Dilys Cossey agreed. 'The pill made contraception an item of talk – of dinner-table talk', she told oral contraceptive biographer Bernard Asbell. 'You could say to somebody, "What kind of pill are you taking?" Whereas you couldn't say to somebody, "What brand of sheath are you using?"'[104] This sums up the dichotomy of the condom trade. London Rubber's strategic position in the early 1960s was and remained ambiguous, because it had to be. On the one hand, it was not in the company's interest to acknowledge consumers' dislike of contraceptive advertising, because this might corroborate pre-existing negative opinion, as well as colour the opinion of existing customers. On the other hand, allowing social stigma to remain unchallenged served as a useful deterrent to competition from rival condom manufacturers.[105]

Appropriating the Pill

EDA felt that consumer resistance to the brand advertising of condoms would only be changed through a process of education over time. If London Rubber wanted to advertise condoms in the interim, this would be best done by treating the pill as a 'contraceptive of the future' rather than of the present. [106] London Rubber, EDA inferred, might ride upon the pill's coat-tails and use public interest to the condom's advantage. In lieu of open consumer advertising, and in order to attach itself to the pill's publicity, EDA advised London Rubber to promote using public relations techniques and press releases. According to EDA, these would be 'far more effective than straightforward advertising', and would have 'a more authoritative and less commercial connotation'.[107] EDA regarded PR and press releases as more suitable for the condom than open consumer advertising as a means of spreading 'education and general enlightenment',[108] because the former methods could appear as though they were coming from somewhere else. The pedagogic process was also thought to be important in terms of preparing audiences for any condom advertising that might take place in the future: pushing an already hostile audience at this point in time would further associate condoms with 'promiscuity and immorality'.[109] PR and press releases, on the other hand, with their inherent function of dispersing information using the characteristics of the media vendor (for example, op-eds in newspapers), could 'help reduce guilt feelings on the subject of sex and contraception' as part of an 'enlightenment' programme. The future goal, then, would be to bring consumers around by changing the attitude of mass-media directors 'towards the promotion of contraceptives'.[110]

As TPL and EDA had both found that consumers were more likely to trust medical voices as the conveyors of family planning advice, it was felt that this should be fully utilized.[111] EDA had found that a 'medical authority' was seen as the ideal and most appropriate source of contraceptive information.[112] Although doctors did not universally endorse oral contraceptives, medical authorities were already its developers, stakeholders, and gatekeepers.[113] In the public imagination, the pill and doctors were interlinked, irrespective of the nuanced debates taking place in medical circles. 'However', EDA said, 'we feel that people do not just want a clinical discussion of the facts of life or the facts of contraception; they also want emotional support and a certain degree of 'understanding' when they seek contraceptive advice'.[114] This observation offered a potential lifeline to London Rubber. The company would have to lobby doctors for support, but an emotional framework for marketing output could be easily created using EDA's research findings and counsel. To this end, current or potential contraceptive users might be 'absolved' from contraceptive-induced guilt by blending medical authority with real-world facts and moral reasoning.[115] The application of this 'insurance' or 'negligence' model might also be applied to class differences, EDA said.[116] In particular, it was suggested that London Rubber could seek to emasculate the unskilled working-class male – reportedly the least likely demographic to use condoms – by shaming him for his sexual profligacy, then offering absolution through Durex. EDA felt this to be reasonable because, according to the research, non-users of contraceptives were prevalent in the 'lower income groups and cultural groups' that favoured male responsibility for birth control anyway. Peer pressure might therefore be harnessed and manipulated to obtain results.[117] EDA also suggested pushing the envelope on controversial issues so that London Rubber might be presented as a progressive element in family planning, thereby forcing the future acceptance of brand advertising. For example, it was suggested that London Rubber might target pre-marital couples, which might pave the way towards acceptability, but London Rubber was reportedly unhappy at this suggestion.[118] It ran the risk of reinforcing the old associations with adultery and vice, just as marriage was becoming more popular.[119] In the end, however, London Rubber elected not to target the groups EDA had suggested, such as the unmarried or the diseased. It also decided against EDA's suggestion to target the working-class male by slanting him, aiming instead for the same target group as the pill, namely middle-class marrieds.

Ways Forward

In this chapter, it has been shown that, as well as being actively marketed, the oral contraceptive pill was widely covered by the mass media. This worked to the detriment of traditional contraceptives, which were already difficult to advertise because of a long-standing cultural resistance. Aware of this problem, London Rubber undertook market research through TPL, ostensibly to test how women consumers viewed the idea of contraceptive advertising, but what they were really testing for was the effectiveness of anti-pill messages contained within their new booklet,

Modern Family Planning, which was given to the cohort before they were interviewed. This booklet deliberately drew attention to uncertainty about the pill's long-term safety, pre-dating the big oral contraceptive health scares of the 1960s. But it was difficult to see if these messages actually worked on the intended audience, both because of problems with the technique used by TPL, and because of issues with the cohort, which did not represent the condom-buying public. What the study did suggest was an antipathy towards commercial sales messages, and receptiveness towards medical authorities when seeking advice on contraception. Both of these findings underpinned London Rubber's problem of the present moment, which was that the pill was prescribed by the trusted medical authorities, and received publicity in a way that resembled news coverage or the discussion of current affairs – coverage that the condom was never likely to get.

London Rubber commissioned a second study by EDA, which surveyed a bigger, mixed cohort and returned similar findings to the first. But unlike the TPL study, the EDA research discovered emotional motivations for consumer attitudes. The oral contraceptive was viewed as an ideal that consumers dreamed about, whereas traditional contraceptives conjured up images of selfishness, lust, guilt, and vice: negative feelings even in the minds of those who used them. EDA warned London Rubber against trying to push advertising onto consumers because they would continue to reject it. Instead, London Rubber was urged to use indirect public relations techniques to undermine the pill as the 'contraceptive of the future'. The next chapter details how London Rubber set about exploiting the progress that was being made by pill manufacturers while quietly aiming to sabotage it from within, seeking to undermine the cultural phenomenon of the pill in the public sphere.

7

The Public Relations Game

I got involved in misrepresentation all round.
Timothy Grey, London Rubber PR *agent*

This chapter describes how, between 1961 and 1965, London Rubber waged a below-the-line disinformation campaign against oral contraceptives using public relations techniques to communicate with doctors, consumers, and the general public. The purpose of this activity was to undermine what London Rubber bitterly referred to as 'the glamour of publicity that surrounded oral contraception'.[1] At no point in London Rubber's history was it more important to assert the primacy of condoms than in the 1960s, when the pill dominated the news and contraceptive futures were uncertain.[2] The campaign was first exposed in a *Sunday Times* article in June 1965, revealing a culture of responsive, scattergun PR activity among London Rubber's agents and representatives.[3] The *Daily Mail* uncovered further details that September.[4] Far from being complacent, as some historians have suggested, London Rubber used every tool at its disposal to protect its interests once the pill had become available in Britain.[5] In a difficult media climate that rejected London Rubber's appeal to balance the birth control debate,[6] underground PR techniques enabled the company to penetrate discussion through the stealthy use of booklets, journals, films, front organisations, and spokespeople. These deliberately 'obscured processes' were a hidden part of London Rubber's modus operandi.[7] The company also planned to snatch market share from the pill by presenting condoms as being complementary to the oral contraceptive pill. It cultivated receptivity to the London Rubber brand by presenting itself and its proxy agents as authorities on new reproductive technologies. Perhaps the most surprising outcome of this activity is the fact that, even when its questionable behaviour was uncovered, London Rubber benefitted from the resultant publicity.

Motivation to Action

Market research commissioned by London Rubber had predicted that the pill would become better known and accepted as the 1960s progressed, and that it would likely supersede the condom as the most used contraceptive in Britain. 'We do, almost without doubt, feel that the oral pill will replace the condom in the long run', reported Ernest Dichter Associates.[8] Research also indicated that brand-name condom advertising would remain unpopular.[9] Both TPL and EDA advised London Rubber that consumers were more receptive to contraceptive information from medical authorities than from commercial manufacturers.[10] In particular, EDA identified a trend towards female responsibility for contraception, and found women especially likely to be influenced by authority figures, such as doctors.[11] Women made up an important part of London Rubber's targeting for the 1960s because they possessed the swing vote. As potential new users of contraceptives who were inspired by the acceptability and easy availability of the pill, women might be swayed towards condoms. However, medical advocacy for London Rubber would not be possible while condoms were still being pushed aside by prescribers who had not traditionally dealt with them, largely because contraception had hitherto been outside of the doctor's purview.[12]

London Rubber's multifaceted, clandestine PR programme sowed uncertainty and confusion about the pill, following in the footsteps of, for example, British American Tobacco (BAT). Back in the 1950s, BAT had engaged PR firm Hill and Knowlton to undermine research showing that cigarettes caused cancer, calling out controversy, contradictions, and unknowns in order to make the research sound unreliable.[13] London Rubber similarly embraced 'doubt as a means of establishing controversy' by stirring the debate on oral contraceptive safety using simple subterfuge.[14] At the time, the pill was linked to cancer, thromboembolism, and, among other less life-threatening things, 'women with beards'.[15] Medical uncertainty was also in the news for other reasons. The thalidomide tragedy in 1961 prompted an impassioned debate about how drugs were trialled and tested in Britain. Thalidomide was a sedative prescribed to expectant mothers, which was found to cause babies to be born malformed, or with absent limbs. On top of this, there was further controversy about the cost of patented drugs, such as antibiotics, to the NHS.[16] The overall aim of London Rubber and its PR agents, then, was to massage pre-existing doubts about the use of medicines, and to turn public opinion against the pill. This was alongside a concurrent image programme that presented condoms as the informed choice for informed couples.

Front Organisations

PR officers working on behalf of London Rubber established 'front organisations' under various *noms de plume*, which disseminated negative rhetoric intended to damage confidence in the pill and recruited (sometimes unwitting) supporters to champion them. Working in the lobby group tradition (and on occasion pretending to be legitimate lobby groups themselves), London Rubber's front organisations were designed to agitate in the hope of raising parliamentary questions.[17] Front organisations were the thorn in the side of the PR industry, which was widely disliked and was trying to reform itself. But even though the Institute of Public Relations (IPR) understood PR to be *'the deliberate, planned and sustained effort to establish and maintain mutual understanding between an organisation and its public'*,[18] the popular conceptualisation was that it was characterised by one-sidedness and stealth. 'The whole point of many PR campaigns', Samuel Finer wrote in 1966, 'is to conceal the fact that they are campaigns. The press is fed with articles, true as far as they go, which favour the client; but the public is not made aware that there is a client who is paying for such selective self-advertisement'.[19] Many personalities in the public eye held similarly negative views. Harold Wilson thought PR 'a most degrading profession', and Malcolm Muggeridge simply called it 'organised lying'.[20] Others referred to public relations professionals as 'creepers', 'nasty people', and 'prostitutes'.[21] It was in this hostile atmosphere that the IPR launched the 1963 Code of Practice, which outlawed, along with the dissemination of false or misleading information, front organsations. IPR president Colin Mann described such organisations as groups whose mechanism of action was deception, insofar as their titles 'suggested an impartiality they did not, in reality, possess'.[22]

Mann may have sought to distance the PR industry from such groups, but they did not disappear. In London Rubber's case, use of front organisations meant that anti-pill messages could be attributed to benevolent-sounding parties such as medical and social concern groups, concealing commercial intent and giving them legitimacy. To this end, the 'Genetic Studies Unit' was invented by London Rubber's PR agent, Marc Quinn Associates, in 1964. Historians have largely overlooked this strange episode in British contraceptive history, although contemporary sources seem to have been aware of its existence.[23] Following the *Sunday Times* exposé, the GSU became the best known of London Rubber's undercover organisations. Its primary activity was the production of the *GSU Bulletin*, which circulated ready-made stories and quotable material to journalists, ostensibly as part of a campaign to safeguard against the introduction of new drugs.[24] The GSU provided a simple means of circulating anti-pill rhetoric under the guise of this broader 'anti-drug' message. Newspapers such as the *Daily Mail* had already linked thalidomide and oral contraceptive safety concerns, and despite the former disaster being a 'watershed moment in the history of medicine safety' that 'caused a complete rethink about drugs and their control', new legislation on manufacture and distribution did not come into force until the 1968 Medicines Act.[25]

Meanwhile, the Association of the British Pharmaceutical Industry was running its own PR defence campaign.[26] The GSU's communications therefore struck at the height of public debate over medicine. The *GSU Bulletin*'s job was to feed the news media's appetite for outrage over the thalidomide tragedy and drug pricing, and then spread this outrage to the pill. The unit even promised to convene its own medical panel, in competition with the government's well-publicised Committee on the Safety of Drugs.[27] Unlike news items that came directly from London Rubber (and which were rejected by media vendors, especially newspapers), stories disseminated by the GSU did not have to circumnavigate barriers to marketing because the unit was not ostensibly linked to commercial interest.[28] British journalists were already used to being papered with material from public relations officers, who had themselves 'become part of the daily machine for manufacturing news'.[29] The *GSU Bulletin* contained genuine material culled from bona fide (though sometimes obscure) periodicals, and quotable factoids from unnamed medical professionals. For example, *GSU Bulletin* no. 2 (December 1964) reprinted a letter written by Dr Peter H. Blackiston to the *Ampleforth Journal*, questioning oral contraceptive safety.[30] 'It is felt that after reading this', the *Bulletin*'s editor added, 'many worried and uncertain women will be able to make their minds up once and for all'.[31] Women may or may not have been 'making their minds up' when reading a newspaper: the job of the *Bulletin* was therefore to notify women of the doubts they should be having, and to nurture and nudge them along with various, selective bits of evidence.

In the event, the GSU was a short-lived and clumsy affair, the *Bulletin* only running to a handful of editions because Enid Duncan, a medical liaison recruited to the unit, realised she had been engaged under false pretences.[32] The end came when Duncan approached the *Sunday Times* with concerns that the operation might result in 'bad social consequences', of which she wanted no part.[33] The newspaper's exposé also implicated Patricia McLaughlin, Ulster Unionist MP for Belfast West and former director of Westbourne Press Bureau, a PR outfit that was connected to other parts of London Rubber's anti-pill campaign. Timothy Grey, head of a PR firm named Customer Relations Ltd, and Marc Quinn, were also implicated. According to the newspaper, McLaughlin admitted knowledge but not involvement in the GSU, while the portrait of Grey presented by the newspaper was painted for laughs. Grey, a former doughnut franchise promoter, protested that he had a philanthropic motivation for organising the GSU, so moved was he by the tragedy of 'theodolite babies (sic)'. To his credit, Grey made no attempt to refute the charge of orchestrating the London Rubber scheme, admitting, 'I got involved in misrepresentation all round'.[34]

However, philanthropic motivation shouldn't be entirely ruled out on London Rubber's part. Although it was unlikely to have been the primary motivation for establishing the GSU, the company did have a reputation for offering its technical expertise to the community. For example, London Rubber's experimental laboratories provided a free service to surgeons, developing latex products for use in their work, upon request.[35] In the early 1960s, as the problems with thalidomide births were becoming apparent, London Rubber also collaborated with Chingford businessman Burt Lyon to engineer life-like, electrically powered artificial limbs for children. An experimental London Rubber limb used a dipped latex 'skin' cast from the arm of Ann Richards, a daughter of one of the directors.[36] In the long term, these experiments might possibly have led to business opportunities (and highlighted the danger of some prescription drugs), but they were also intended to improve the quality of life for the needy or the disadvantaged, and depended entirely upon the good will of chemists and engineers at London Rubber.[37]

It should also be noted that the GSU was partially successful because some publications did, in fact, reuse the unit's scare stories. On 10 March 1965, for example, *Queen* magazine repeated 'possible side-effects' of oral contraceptives described in the GSU *Bulletin*, including 'excessive weight, liver damage, breast cancer — even a risk of geriatric childbirth'.[38] On 12 April the *Northern Echo* warned of 'possible effects [that] long-term use of the pill might have in the field of genetics', in a story entitled 'Facts about "the Pill"' that also used *Bulletin* material. The article conceded that there wasn't much evidence that the pill was dangerous, but that 'only time would tell'.[39] Though haphazardly assembled, GSU *Bulletin* raised valid concerns about the use of the pill that would be repeated by campaigners for women's health well into the 1970s. The GSU *Bulletin* also warned about the abuse of tranquilizers and Drinamyl (also known as 'Purple Hearts'), an amphetamine prescribed to tired housewives that became a popular (and problematic) recreational drug in the British Mod scene.[40]

Because of the *Sunday Times* story, the GSU became the best known of London Rubber's undercover operations, although several of its front organisations predated the unit. In 1963, Patricia McLaughlin had set up the London Foundation for Marriage Education trust through the Westbourne Press Bureau. The foundation operated on a budget of £10,000 with a remit to 'disseminate information on family planning',[41] mainly in the form of films.[42] Prior to this, on 11 December 1961, London Rubber opened an ambitious contraceptive clinic in London's West End called the Family Centre.[43] The foundation and the centre shared premises. According to London Rubber, the GSU was opened to take over anti-pill campaigning from these organisations, but they each made significant contributions in their own right. In the first place, London Rubber, wanting to enter the pill market, produced its own oral contraceptive, Feminor. (This London Rubber pill was trialled at the Family Centre and is discussed in detail in the following chapter.) In the second place, the foundation served as a cover through which London Rubber's agents, such as Patricia McLaughlin, could gather market intelligence. For example, McLaughlin gained entry to the International Planned Parenthood Federation's Seventh International Conference in Singapore in 1963.[44] Not being a 'responsible national organisation' but, rather, a profit-motivated commercial outfit, London Rubber had previously been prevented from joining the IPPF and was therefore excluded from its meetings. [45] The foundation, however, was included, and McLaughlin was sent as its delegate. As the theme of the 1963 conference was 'Changing Patterns in Fertility', encompassing several discussions relating to oral contraceptive and the nascent IUD,[46] its utility to London Rubber was significant, and allowed for the gathering of data on stakeholders who might be of future use to the company. London Rubber would go on to use its connections to collaborate with the IPPF on condom production in India.[47]

Fertility Abstracts
Shortly after its official opening, London Rubber's contraceptive clinic, the Family Centre, launched a medical abstracting journal, *Fertility Ab-*

stracts.[48] Market research suggested that medical authorities should be responsible for distributing London Rubber's sales messages.[49] This meant working harder to place the condom in the mindset of physicians. As the debate around oral contraception gathered pace, doctors hankered after accessible, up-to-date information on developments in contraceptive technology. At the beginning of the 1960s, the only relevant English language journals fulfilling this function were *Reproduction and Fertility* and *Fertility and Sterility*. Donn Casey, a fertility professional who worked for the highly influential Population Council in New York, was concerned that collecting and navigating new information surrounding the pill was difficult as the field was so new. Publications, Casey said, 'usually have to be ferreted out of the literature of other branches, such as endocrinology, pharmacology, physiology, biochemistry, enzymology etc'.[50] Casey suggested that an international Research Information Service might serve as a comprehensive indexing and abstracting facility, collecting information on relevant publications.[51] Early in 1961, he drew up a prospectus, canvassed support, and applied for a Ford Foundation grant to establish the service in association with the *Journal of Reproduction and Fertility* in Cambridge.[52] However, before Casey's vision had gotten off the ground, London Rubber had picked up on this gap in the market, and beat him to it with their own abstracting journal.

Fertility Abstracts ran monthly from January 1962 until December 1965, as a centralised source for abstracts from over 200 international journals.[53] It was founded and edited by the Family Centre's Dr Barry Carruthers, ostensibly to centralise précised information on fertility research for the benefit of the wider research community.[54] As such, it presented a quarterly roundup of British and American patents relating to progestational and anabolic steroids, with abstracts relating to clinical, chemical, and experimental research into fertility, sterility, and contraception.[55] It recognised the wide range of fields that came under the broad heading of 'fertility, sterility and contraception', such as the psychosexual aspects of fertility and sexuality, sociology, and venereology. As such, it aimed to be indispensable to those working in fertility: the FPA even solicited London Rubber for a discounted order on the IPPF's behalf.[56] *Fertility Abstracts* rapidly became the main source of information for literature on oral contraceptives and fertility.[57]

Fertility Abstracts attempted to appear neutral. Internally, London Rubber stressed that the journal (and its 'first class' reference library at the Family Centre) was intended to be self-supporting via an annual subscription of £6 6s.[58] This was important because subscription funding made it appear impartial. In September 1964 the journal briefly came clean about its backing, bearing the legend 'Produced by London Rubber Industries' on the front cover,[59] but the attribution was soon restored to 'The Family Centre', and the London Rubber connection was moved to small print. It is possible that, under Carruthers, the journal was genuinely intended to be neutral at the outset but that this became unsustainable. Either way, by 1964–65, readership had been baited and editorial content was switched from the benign to the calculated. *Fertility Abstracts* became a vehicle for publishing anti-pill rhetoric, such as a front-page 'Obituary to the Pill' in 1965, and for carrying London Rubber's own trial data.[60] This shift occurred as attention to the pill intensified in the lay and medical press, and as more pill brands became available (table 8.1).

Small Publications

In addition to the front organisations detailed above, London Rubber used the name 'Counsel Publications' as a cover for distributing information booklets to consumers, via coupon ads. Like the London Foundation for Marriage Education, Counsel Publications shared its mailing address with the Family Centre, although literature was dispatched directly from London Rubber HQ in Chingford. The use of subterfuge for the distribution of London Rubber commercial literature was a long-standing device used to circumvent barriers to brand advertising. Counsel Publications was merely the new name for London Rubber's protean publishing arm based at Oval Road, NW1 (its first incarnation, 'Planned Families Publications', had operated from at least 1955[61]). This setup was well known to the Family Planning Association, and, the names being deliberately similar,[62] the FPA justifiably feared that such London Rubber booklets as *Modern Family Planning* and *Planned Families* might be attributed to them instead of to their true manufacturer.[63] London Rubber deliberately created this confusion, and although the FPA persuaded them to change the name in 1959, the change was not properly effected until 1960 when it became 'London Publications Ltd', then 'H.F. Booklets'.[64] In 1961 it became 'Counsel', then 'Family Counsel'.[65] All of these name changes served to distance the consumer from the purpose of the booklet when they first picked it up and took it home, where they would discover coupons for Durex products when they reached the end pages. The intention behind such booklets was to disguise their obvious commercial nature, and, to use managing director Angus Reid's words, to 'protect the susceptibilities of shareholders' – in other words, practice consumer advertising obliquely and thereby avoid reputational damage.[66] By purporting to be produced by some vague social organisation, the booklets were made more acceptable both to consumers and to the media vendors who advertised them, such as *Reader's Digest*.[67] As such, the names of the booklets also changed. *Modern Contraceptive Technique* ran to five editions in the 1950s, replaced by *Planning Your Family* in 1957 and *Planned Families* in 1958. Other contraceptive manufacturers, such as Lloyd's Surgical, produced booklets along similar lines. In the 1960s, and with the pill on the market, London Rubber expanded its literature range, creating a suite of beautifully presented, full-colour leaflets that were actively marketed to doctors. These were more direct in attacking alternative methods, and discouraged all contraceptive techniques except condoms, including such titles as *Diaphragm or Protective?* and *The Case against Coitus Interruptus*.[68] Unlike consumer booklets attributed to Counsel Publications, these were directly credited to London Rubber and were advertised in medical journals such as the *Lancet*, although consumer booklets were also advertised for doctors to give to their patients.[69]

By offering both trade and consumer material, London Rubber exploited the new medical participation in contraceptive provision engendered by the pill. To this end, both medical and consumer publications responded to market research recommendations that 'contraceptive information should be de-commercialized and put into an emotional context'.[70] While oral contraceptives were already removing material barriers to intimacy, London Rubber got to the heart of the matter by positing the very physicality of condoms as a means of emotional closeness and psychological reassurance during lovemaking, as communicated through booklets. According to *The Plain Facts* (1961), condoms enabled 'both husband and wife to relax completely and enjoy full satisfaction without worry or strain'.[71] Here and elsewhere, the condom was presented as being uniquely qualified to resolve common sexual problems, not in spite of, but expressly *because* of, its physical nature. Premature ejaculation, for example, might be easily circumvented by using a condom. Anxiety over pregnancy as an inhibition to sexual enjoyment could also be avoided through condom use. 'Wearing a protective', read *Marriages Are Made* (1965), 'provides both husband and wife with visible reassurance, freeing them from the original cause of their anxiety'.[72] In effect, this meant that couples could instantly see if the method had worked after sex, which they couldn't with the pill. Also unlike the pill, condoms were portrayed as a 'joint method' in which both husband and wife could participate.[73] This particular claim related to London Rubber's use of pleasure as a device for persuading consumers, albeit in booklets rather than in magazine adverts.

The presentation of the condom as the facilitator of pleasure was designed to directly counteract the qualitative differences between the condom and the pill thought to carry negative connotations, as highlighted by the market research. 'One of the most frequent complaints about condoms is the fact that they are not natural, that they take some of the pleasure away', Ernest Dichter Associates said. 'Thinness, naturalness, and technical perfection, all these are aspects that may have to be stressed in a new fashion in order to be able to compete in the minds of the people with the image that condoms are rather old-fashioned'.[74] Accordingly, *Marriages Are Made* extolled the condom's unique sensual qualities. 'Some couples', it read, 'have found that its application can be shared by the man and his wife and incorporated in love-play as a pleasurable, intimate, and reassuring gesture. Their shared sensual excitement is heightened, and both husband and wife can relax even more in the certain knowledge that she is to be protected from pregnancy'.[75] According to the booklet, almost every other method of contraception was 'either a messy or secretive affair'.[76] In this way, the unwelcome interference of the condom during sex was re-drawn as a benefit for both parties, unlike the woman-controlled pill.

London Rubber also produced a detailed booklet on the intersection of birth control and faith. *Some Religious Views on Contraception* (1965) purported to summarize the attitudes of the major Christian denominations, and Orthodox and progressive Jews. According to Father Thomas Corbishley, writing in the 'Catholic' section, theologians had recently begun to explore the subject of contraception 'with more understanding' than they had done previously.[77] The booklet attributed this shift to the abstract concept of the 'population bomb' (so often the case at the time), although it was the popularity of the pill that sparked debate among Catholics.[78] In Britain, debates were kept alive by home-grown activity. Dr Anne Bieżanek's Catholic contraceptive clinic, for example, was widely covered in the mass media over 1964–65, suggesting that London Rubber's underground propaganda responded to immediate, local headlines rather than global contraceptive debates.[79] *Some Religious Views on Contraception* was not reprinted, but its existence exemplifies London Rubber's attempt to make use of of every possible angle to the degree that even Catholicism, it was thought, could be hijacked for the condom's benefit!

Educational Films

Given that sponsored documentary shorts produced for government and trade bodies proliferated in post-war Britain, it was logical that market research had recommended the use of films for condom promotion.[80] London Rubber had dabbled in films prior to its anti-pill offensive, having produced a ten-minute cinema 'filmlet' to promote the *Planned Families* booklet in 1958.[81] The year before, it had contributed £1000 to the Family Planning Association's *Birthright*, which was shown at the House of Commons and at international conferences.[82] It was when the FPA decided to make a sequel, including reference to the new pill, that London Rubber decided to make its own films via the London Foundation for Marriage Education.[83] Five high-quality films were produced between 1964 and 1965, which were toured by a team of female explainers and featured discussions, refreshments, and product sampling.[84] The foundation's films were in direct competition with oral contraceptive trade shorts such as Searle's *Peace of Mind*, which was vigorously promoted around the country in March 1965 accompanied by a nurse, and was advertised via placed PR in regional newspapers.[85] In order to differentiate themselves, London Rubber's films aimed for younger, mixed audiences (such as children, teenagers, and pre-marital couples), going along with market research recommendations to pitch condoms to pre-marrieds.[86] Most teenagers had some limited knowledge of contraceptives at this time, but the majority of those with sexual experience did not use them.[87] They nonetheless wanted to learn.[88] Furthermore, teenagers had the money to spend: a reduction in adult/juvenile wage differentials following war meant that teenagers might feasibly dispose of their incomes on condoms, as well as records, clothes, and dances.[89] London Rubber thereby designed films that met the needs of young people, and also primed future contraceptive users for condom consumption. For example, *Learning to Live* (1964) dealt with sex education for older children and teens, while *According to Plan* (1964) outlined the different contraceptive methods for pre-marital or newly married youngsters. In a new and unique move, *According to Plan* (which is available to watch online via Wellcome Collection) made a point of showing contraceptives being handled.[90] This was especially important for the normalisation of rubber contraceptives for women, who were not necessarily experienced with obtaining or touching condoms, and sometimes objected to touching even their own genitals.[91] In this way, *According to Plan* aimed to demystify appliance contraceptives by showing them being unwrapped and touched in order to stress how 'simple' condoms were in comparison to other methods, just as the market research had suggested.[92] To bring this point home, female contraceptives were depicted as especially laborious and far less simple than condoms. The ideal of being able 'to swallow a pill' so as to 'have sex at any time' (as described by the market research respondents) was deliberately dismantled by showing the many steps necessary to use oral contraceptives, including invasive pelvic examinations, a long discussion with doctors, keeping a daily record of pill administration, and, most importantly, not being able to see that it had worked after sex.[93]

According to Plan was also an important vehicle for raising awareness of the condom's technical sophistication. Worryingly for London Rubber, market research had shown that respondents were unaware of the great strides that had been made in condom manufacturing.[94] Lubrication, packaging, and electronic testing were significant changes that made condoms easier and safer to use, yet they had no discernable impact on the research cohort.[95] Ernest Dichter Associates found 'very little, if any, knowledge about modern forms of condoms such as pre-lubricated types of condoms, different and new storage and packaging facilities, new developments of safer and more convenient types of condoms'.[96] London Rubber was therefore advised to 'present condoms as a modern product' and to stress the existence of new developments in order to change the condom's image.[97] In print, London Rubber simply declared that the pill was dead (above),[98] but on film, the company showcased its state-of-the-art automated dipping plant in a dramatic two-minute montage, with an original, orchestral soundtrack.[99] In this way, manufacture was depicted as advanced, impressive, and scientifically controlled. By showing the different states of the condom inside and outside of branded packaging, *According to Plan* followed EDA's recommendations in 'discussing more freely the existence of condoms ... and abandoning, to a large extent, the secretive way of discussing and displaying them' in order that 'negative connotations might be eliminated'.[100]

Paper Bombing at the Family Planning Association
As well as working the medical and consumer markets, London Rubber's attempts to sabotage the pill responded to events at the Family Planning

Association, under whose auspices the Council for the Investigation of Fertility Control conducted oral contraceptive trials. Following the announcement in December 1961 that select FPA clinics would supply the pill from January 1962, London Rubber distributed a *Woman's Hour* radio transcript (produced in 1960) in which a female doctor questioned pill safety. The unnamed doctor spoke of the 'public' test of the pill, its 'interference' with 'the natural rhythm of a woman's sexual and reproductive life', and the possibilities of long-term harm if taken 'during the long reproductive years stretching ahead of many women'.[101] In January 1962, as the FPA was rolling the pill out, London Rubber convinced clinics to distribute free Durex Gossamer samples, via the Family Centre. The samples proved popular, and the FPA placed many repeat orders.[102] In this way, London Rubber was able to access contraceptive users approaching the FPA for the pill, just at the point when they were receptive to learning about new methods. However, in an underhanded move that surprised even the FPA, London Rubber placed an anti-pill insert into Atlas condom wrappers, the association's own clinic brand.[103] 'The fact of the matter is that at present nobody knows for certain what will be the result of years of interference with the delicately balanced hormonal chemistry of the female body, either to the woman herself, or to the future generation', the slip read. 'Time alone will tell'.[104] Once discovered, this antic put London Rubber firmly in the FPA's doghouse. The Barrow-in-Furness branch, which was preparing to issue the pill, was 'horrified' by the insert.[105] London Rubber dismissed the incident as a 'mistake', but inserts were still being discovered into May 1962.[106]

London Rubber was also accused of dumping unsolicited literature at clinics up and down the country, and monitoring the activities of the clinics, to the degree that staff felt they were being 'constantly watched by a vigilant minority'.[107] Many clinics, such as Welwyn, were located in child welfare centres where local authority health visitors were targets for London Rubber sales reps and materials, as were FPA clinics themselves.[108] Local authority health visitors were important in disseminating London Rubber materials as they gave contraceptive advice to new mothers, while the FPA's importance as a distributor started to wane as it became increasingly preoccupied with the pill. For this reason, it was in London Rubber's interest to establish non-FPA distribution streams that nonetheless possessed medical authority and access to potential new consumers.[109] According to a survey undertaken by Ann Cartwright, one-third of health visitors questioned between October 1967 and May 1968 distributed leaflets on birth control – half from the FPA, and half from manufacturers. London Rubber's *Marriages Are Made* was one of the booklets most commonly given to health visitors to pass on, alongside the FPA's *Methods of Family Planning*. Here, at last, was some form of official endorsement. Half of Cartwright's national sample was 'critical or at least aware of the limitations of commercial literature', but an equal number of health visitors displayed or distributed it nonetheless, presumably because it was both free and useful.[110] London Rubber's agitprop, while deliberately pitched to undermine all contraceptive methods except the condom, was full of instructive information and didn't say anything that was untrue.

Co-opting of Experts and Personalities

Early marketing for the pill showcased named personalities such as Gregory Pincus, who was publicly toured as part of Searle's early PR drive for Enovid (Conovid in Britain).[111] Named personalities stood as advocates, who imbued contraceptive products with desirable values, such as authority and reliability. London Rubber's anti-pill programme was no different, and its various front organisations platformed co-opted experts and personalities for the condom's benefit. *Fertility Abstracts* was used for soliciting papers from academics, as well as doctors, to air the company's grievances with the pill in the guise of legitimate articles. An academic article series, running in tandem with anti-pill editorial, was begun in 1965 to present essays by sociologist John Peel, an investigator of the sociological effects of contraceptive practice.[112] It was the FPA laboratory secretary, Mrs A.D. Simpson, who arranged for Peel to visit Chingford HQ early in 1962.[113] Peel was planning to write a history of the FPA, and wanted to speak to London Rubber because of its long relationship with the association.[114] The 1963 article that resulted from this meeting, 'The Manufacturing and Retailing of Contraceptives in England', has become a key source for historians. However, until now historians have failed to make the connection between Peel and London Rubber, which sponsored his work and co-opted him to produce papers, give seminars, and generally represent the sociological research side of contraceptives on the company's behalf.[115]

Peel's *Fertility Abstracts* articles, which were published in 1965, made the case for the IUD, the condom, and for future abortion law reform, all with the effect of slating the pill.[116] For example, in 'Abortion and Family Planning in England', Peel argued that abortion had an important social function, not because contraceptive technology was inherently imperfect, but because of the 'inadequate usage' of contraceptives, including orals.[117] The pill was thereby tethered to the (then) illegal practice of abortion, and was painted as the very antithesis of mindful family spacing. Being targeted at doctors, *Fertility Abstracts* was also the ideal vehicle for setting out medical indications for condom use via Peel's articles. Clinical indications for condom use included cases of trichomoniasis, vaginal problems with diaphragm use, psychological issues of contraceptive control (where men are given responsibility), premature ejaculation, and contraceptive anxiety.[118] This canon was repeated concurrently in consumer booklets (such as *Marriages Are Made*) and in the medical press (such as the *British Medical Journal*), as London Rubber pushed for the viability of the condom as a medical device, and one that was only more relevant with the ascent of the pill.[119] Peel's article therefore corroborated information that London Rubber circulated widely while making the case for medical recognition of the condom: 'The modern protective has been shown to be a popular, effective and harmless method of contraception, with a high acceptance rate at all socio-economic levels'.[120]

It is difficult to speculate to what degree other co-opted experts and personalities were complicit with or aware of London Rubber's anti-pill campaigning. The *Sunday Times* reported that some contributors to the GSU *Bulletin* were oblivious to the true nature of the project, believing it purely philanthropic and non-profitmaking, but frequent contributors like Peel are less easy to dismiss as patsies. 'Pressure-group enthusiasts have been known to form several different organisations, staffed and funded by the same members, in order to boost their campaign image', the academic and journalist Geoffrey Alderman wrote in reference to the London Foundation for Marriage Education. 'The letterhead is different in each case, but the membership is identical'.[121] This is a fair summation of London Rubber's below-the-line PR activities, and describes the movement of co-opted personalities from one front organisation to another, even if they were not aware of the connection themselves. In the case of Patricia McLaughlin, involvement can be traced to the Family Centre, the London Foundation for Marriage Education, the GSU, Counsel Publications, and Westbourne Press Bureau. McLaughlin's usefulness related to her position as Northern Ireland's second female MP,[122] which might help London Rubber to appear more woman-aware, as well as accepted by those self-determined women who were so often targeted for the pill. In addition, members of Parliament were increasingly involved in corporate public relations in the early 1960s. The *Financial Times* estimated that there were about twenty Conservative MPs working in some sort of advertising and PR work by 1962.[123] So far as the London Rubber programme was concerned, McLaughlin's status as a consumer champion was the cherry on the cake.

The *Sunday Times* reported that McLaughlin gave up her directorship at Westbourne Press Bureau, and that the bureau stopped working for London Rubber in late 1963, but McLaughlin's own involvement had not ended. Indeed, McLaughlin was forced to discontinue in this capacity because Northern Ireland prime minister Terence O'Neil had introduced a cabinet code of conduct that discouraged simultaneously holding directorships and public office. McLaughlin was MP for Belfast West at the time, and had been involved in the Seenozip invisible zipper scandal in 1964, in which the Northern Ireland Ministry of Commerce was defrauded of £30,000. McLaughlin had been a director at Seenozip, from which she resigned in 1962. She was criticised for failing to declare her free shares, and the incident tarnished her reputation.[124] Anecdotally, McLaughlin's involvement with the London Foundation for Marriage Education has been taken for one of her philanthropic activities, and it could be that that she saw her involvement as redemptive at the time. McLaughlin became more publicly connected to her PR work as her political career waned. Later in the sixties, she would become public relations officer to the Mushroom Grower's Association, and a professional parliamentary lobbyist.[125]

So far as other co-opted persons are concerned, the sympathy of willing FPA members also added weight to London Rubber's public activities by making it appear as though the association and the company had shared aims. Sylvia Dawkins and Barbara Law (both FPA doctors), as well as Professor W.C.W. Nixon of the University College Hospital Obstetrics Department, all participated in the production of London Rubber films. The Family Centre employed ex-FPA staffers, such as Dr Barry Carruthers and secretary Beryl Northage. This overlapping of loyalties, particularly in light of the association's difficult relationship with London Rubber, was nothing short of a humiliation for the FPA. When Carruthers penned an anti-pill article in *Western Mail* on 1 October 1964, FPA insiders felt it represented a 'serious embarrassment' to the association, its members, and its aims.[126] The FPA had closed the door on London Rubber's attempts to piggyback on their good name in the 1950s, but it would appear that the company got around this by simply poaching FPA supporters and hoping that their reputations and connection with the association would gravitate toward the main goal: to get condoms taken seriously in family planning.

Aftermath

The use of front organisations by corporate (rather than political) bodies was only just beginning to be uncovered in the mid-1960s.[127] By this time, the below-the-line work of the PR industry was becoming better known through several muckraking titles, such as Vance Packard's *Hidden Persuaders* (1957) and John Pearson and Graham Turner's *Persuasion Industry* (1965).[128] As the IPR was trying to improve the image of public relations, it served its purpose to visibly admonish violations of its brand new code of professional conduct by 'naming and shaming' members who behaved badly.[129] The timing of the GSU affair converged unfavourably with a reactive drive towards openness in public relations, when the young institute needed to assert its professional status. When their connection to underground PR on behalf of London Rubber were exposed, Timothy Grey's firm Customer Relations was disciplined by the institute, alongside Marc Quinn Associates, and Quinn himself was suspended.[130] The climactic unveiling of the GSU also affected London Rubber in other ways. Public conflation of two industries that were widely viewed as distasteful, namely commercial contraceptive retailing and PR, created a platform for those with an axe to grind, and the *Sunday Times* story paved the way for future attacks on London Rubber, which became fair game in the press.[131]

What is surprising is that, in an echo of the *Which?* episode in 1963–64, consumer confidence in Durex was not damaged, even after the *Sunday Times* exposé. London Rubber group profits continued to grow (appendix 1). A possible explanation for this is the damage-limitation work the company was able to undertake through the *Sunday Times* itself. Investigators gave London Rubber the right of reply within the context of the original article, and this afforded the chance for the free and open discussion that the company had wanted all along. London Rubber's advertising director, Norman Berry, took the honest approach to explaining the company's actions. 'We have been concerned for a long time about the one-sided publicity in favour of oral contraceptives. When an idea such as this takes hold, it is very hard to resist it, no matter what the dangers of the pills may be', he said in the *Sunday Times* article. 'We therefore took expert advice, and arranged to set up an organisation to counter-balance this practice by making available all the known evidence against the use of oral contraceptives. We now realise that the method we chose, the Genetic Study Unit was, in fact, not launched on a proper scientific basis, and we therefore decided to disband it in the early part of this year, and that we would not use the technique again'.

Both London Rubber and the *Sunday Times* laid the blame at the feet of the public relations industry, and the company's decision to present its case turned a PR crisis into an opportunity: London Rubber was in a position to quickly assess and resolve the potential crisis situation before it escalated.[132] This method became a tried and tested response to corporate crisis. In 1986, for example, Johnson & Johnson faced catastrophe when an unknown party deliberately spiked Tylenol capsules with cyanide, causing seven deaths in America. Johnson & Johnson acted immediately by publicly acknowledging the seriousness of the situation and taking measures to recall and redesign the bottles. In the words of PR expert Steven R. Van Hook, 'They used the media to demonstrate their concern and their determination to resolve the crisis. It was a message of courage and leadership through effective public relations'.[133] In London Rubber's case, the company minimised potential damage to consumer confidence by quickly acknowledging the accusations against it.[134] John Peel, along with Robert Dowse, intervened to minimise reputational harm by publishing an academic paper discussing birth control societies and pressure groups, the month before the *Sunday Times* reported.[135] In 'The Politics of Birth Control', pressure group activity was shown to have had a long alliance with benevolent contraceptive provision, dating back to the Bradlaugh-Besant trials of 1877–88 (which had resulted in the formation of the Malthusian League).[136] In the 1920s and 1930s the birth control movement depended on stakeholders' powers of persuasion, Peel and Dowse wrote.[137] Their message was that contraceptive provision and public relations went hand in hand, and always had done, suggesting that London Rubber's use of PR had precedents going back to the beginning of modern birth control history.

In this chapter, we have seen how London Rubber undertook to systematically undermine the popular idea of the pill as the ideal contraceptive, using front organisations to cast doubt on its safety, its novelty, its longevity, and its ease of use. Between 1961 and 1965, the company and its agents ran overlapping campaigns of films, journal articles, news bulletins, and booklets, produced and disseminated by a small network of interconnected front organisations and spokespeople. It was necessary for London Rubber to disguise its involvement in this below-the-line PR activity, because of the sensitivity of its consumers and its product, and because its messages might not otherwise have been taken seriously. It is nonetheless difficult to see if and when any of this activity was effective in achieving London Rubber's aims, although some of the *GSU Bulletin*'s stories did result in newspaper items, and the safety of oral contraceptives continued to be questioned. London Rubber appears to have come through the affair unscathed, at least in the short term. Indeed, it benefitted from the legitimate publicity the affair received, possibly because of Norman Berry's contrite damage limitation statement to the *Sunday Times*. The story also advertised the fact that London Rubber was a successful and resourceful company, with well-performing stock, which served to advertise London Rubber as a good investment opportunity. The following chapter of this book looks at the last surprising twist in London Rubber's anti-pill programme, wherein it commissioned the creation of its own in-house pill, Feminor. As will be shown, Feminor was a fully realised project, resulting in a marketed pill that was available to the general public, although it was not especially successful.

Our sales director Roy Reid, I remember him saying at one conference, he said when we first opened up, "the theme of our conference today, gentlemen, is what we have not got. We know we've got 97–98 per cent of the trade. We wanted that 2 per cent as well (that we had not got)". And it's hard to imagine this, but everything was defensive, to protect ourselves. That explains what I was going to say to you about the pill. The only reason they ever got involved in the pill was so they knew what was going on.

John Harvey, Former London Rubber sales manager, Chingford,
8 December 2016

In this chapter, we unravel how London Rubber came to produce and market its own in-house contraceptive pill, Feminor Sequential, between 1960, when it first began looking for a unique formulation, and 1965, when it stopped development on work oral contraceptives in Britain. Feminor was officially launched in medical journals from September 1964, following clinical trials. By this time, the British oral contraceptive market comprised a half-million users and was valued at £1.5 million.[1] London Rubber spotted a gap for an all-British pill, and took the opportunity to produce one. This was partially a response to the findings of market research from EDA, which had recommended that London Rubber promote condoms in association with the pill. EDA said, 'if one wants to advertise say condoms or diaphragms (via booklets, films etc.) one might do this in_associ-ation with the oral tablet. That is, the oral tablet has been widely publicised in mass media and is a less "embarrassing" contraceptive than are the others, as it is dissociated from genital contact and therefore dissociated from sexual problems and anxieties. One might therefore acknowledge the oral tablet as the "contraceptive of the future", and bring in the condom as something which is a good substitute for the meantime'.[2] By doing this, EDA said, 'the prestige, modernity, and acceptability of the oral tablet may generalise to that of the condom. The condom would be sold under the umbrella of the oral tablet, so to speak'.[3] This advice reinforced a scheme that

FIGURE 8.1   Factory frontage, North Circular Road, 1960s.

London Rubber had already embarked upon, wherein it would become a direct stakeholder in oral contraception. In this way, it is argued, London Rubber was able to penetrate discussions about the future of the pill with the legitimate voice of a producer. Feminor gave London Rubber license to discredit oral contraception in a targeted way, allowing it to channel negative rhetoric directly to prescribers and end-users. More so, Feminor stood as a placeholder, giving London Rubber a visible stake in the brave new world of pharmaceutical contraception, however it might unfold, from the outset.[4] 'The one thing you've got to remember is our monopolistic aspect', former London Rubber sales manager John Harvey says. 'That is so important. The whole policy … was to retain the monopoly. That was more important than the actual level of sales we achieved'.[5]

As has been shown in other chapters, London Rubber's participation in the contraceptive market for women was never profitable, but it allowed the company to freeze out competition and to control areas connected to its core business of condom manufacturing and supply. Dabbling in diaphragms enabled it to strangulate rivals, and to stay abreast of developments. By the 1950s, the company controlled the market for both condoms and diaphragms, making new entry into either area formidable.[6] This kind of domination was not a possibility with oral contraception, because it came from an industry outside of London Rubber's purview. Nonetheless, the Feminor project gave London Rubber a window onto oral contraceptive developments, making it an insider. This was of crucial importance at the beginning of the 1960s, when the company needed to prepare for the possible future reduction of the condom's relevance.[7] When the pill entered the contraceptive market, condoms had just reached their apex of technical sophistication. Most importantly, the marketplace now included a larger pool of possible consumers, namely married women, who had historically been outside of the target market for condoms, even though they may have bought them.[8] While the advent of hormonal contraception seemed inevitable, its impact on the condom market would only become known over time. So far as London Rubber was concerned, to be forewarned was to be forearmed. As the medical historian Claire L. Jones says of the contraceptives business, 'success was not inevitable, nor was it wholesale'.[9]

The Search for the All-British Pill

It was only after dramatically declaring on television its intention to produce an affordable oral contraceptive pill that British Drug Houses hurriedly developed what was claimed to be the first British pill, Volidan.[10] As medical historian Sue Hawkins has pointed out, 'Britishness' was a unique and important selling point for contraceptives.[11] At a time when people were being encouraged to 'Buy British', Volidan was widely construed as a symbolic defence against a perceived takeover by American drug giants, who at the time claimed one-third of the drugs market in Britain.[12] British Drug Houses, an established producer of pharmaceuticals and chemicals with a reputation for research into steroids and chemical birth control, produced Volidan using its in-house progestogen, MGA.[13] London Rubber, on the other hand, had no history of experimentation in hormones and did not possess the research capability to produce its own progestogen. Nevertheless – and realising that British Drug Houses was in fact less British than it claimed after the American company Mead Johnson purchased a controlling share of its stock in 1961 – London Rubber decided to step forward and claim the mantle of Britishness for itself.[14]

Initially, the idea was to produce a non-hormonal alternative to the pill via the Nutrition Department of Queen Elizabeth College, London.[15] The search for an oral contraceptive had been an official part of the department's research agenda since 1955, following Professor John Yudkin's experiments on freeze-dried extract of flowering gromwell plants.[16] Gromwell made a liquid 'tasting like medium sherry' that rendered women temporarily sterile.[17] Yudkin felt that his work could result in a contraceptive method 'which might achieve its purpose with no effects at all on the Mother', thereby finding a nutritional solution to fertility control.[18] Funding for this research had been denied by the Nuffield Foundation and Medical Research Council, organisations that were disposed to 'walk warily' in the field of family planning at the time.[19] There were also fears that lithospermum therapy might result in permanent sterility.[20] So, in May 1960, London Rubber stepped up with an annual gift of £8000, made in instalments over seven years, in order for Yudkin to establish a research team to work expressly on fertility.[21] Unfortunately, the collaboration failed. In the first instance, the Inland Revenue delayed the approval of London Rubber's grant. This meant that research did not begin until March 1961, when Conovid was already making waves. In a sign of things to come, London Rubber was obliged to set up the 'London Research Foundation' as a conduit for channelling payments under section 355 of the Income Tax Act.[22] In the second instance, the Nutrition Department came up with nothing useful related to fertility, leaving London Rubber feeling that 'there was no sign of any real direction of the research'.[23] By the end of its relationship with the Nutrition Department, London Rubber's grant had resulted in a single published paper and no non-hormonal oral contraceptive.[24] By this time, other interests such as 'social nutrition' were absorbing Yudkin's department, and fertility had dropped off of the agenda.[25] London Rubber viewed its investment as 'money down the drain', and withdrew the grant early in March 1964.[26]

But luckily, London Rubber had also been trialling a hormonal pill at a London teaching hospital as a contingency.[27] This was the formula that became Feminor, the company's in-house pill. It had also been busy assembling the apparatus necessary for conducting clinical trials, publishing the results, and rolling out medical marketing while the research at

Queen Elizabeth College was taking place. In this sense, the invention of a house pill was only the beginning of London Rubber's oral contraceptive programme: just as important was the infrastructure via which Feminor (and the messages it carried about oral contraception) would reach medical audiences and end-users. With this in mind, and in order to smooth Feminor's path, London Rubber set itself up with a birth control clinic, an abstracting journal, and a stable of recognised experts.

The company's birth control clinic, the Family Centre, opened on Duke Street, London, in December 1961.[28] It functioned as a centralised hub for the Feminor programme, and as a means of attracting publicity in lieu of mainstream condom advertising. The official opening ceremony, on 30 January 1962, was led by TV *Panorama* personality Ludovic Kennedy, accompanied by his actress wife, Moira Shearer, and a gaggle of reporters.[29] Corporate sponsorship of the centre was declared early on in the *British Medical Journal*, and the connection was an open secret at the Family Planning Association; but, once it had opened, London Rubber's relationship to the Family Centre was kept low-key.[30]

Although manufacturer's clinics were rare, there were precedents. Lamberts of Dalston ran the former Marie Stopes Mothers' Clinic at 61 Marlborough Road, Upper Holloway. This was the first dedicated birth control centre in Britain, running from 1921–25. The Birth Control Advisory Bureau, as Lamberts renamed it, served middle-class women and was still running by the 1960s.[31] Lloyd's Surgical Department Ltd also offered a free advice service from its Portsmouth centre, although this was via mail only.[32] The Family Centre, by contrast, was a plush affair, offering private advice to engaged and married couples by appointment.[33] On 29 January 1962 the *Telegraph* reported that consultations cost three guineas in the first instance, and two guineas thereafter, making the clinic an exclusive option for the wealthy. Unlike the FPA clinics, which operated part time in largely makeshift premises and saw patients as walk-ins, the Family Centre had a full-time doctor and was luxuriously spread over nine red-carpeted rooms near Selfridges.[34] It supplied a comprehensive menu of private contraceptive and fertility services, rivalling similar services offered by the FPA's flagship North Kensington Marriage Welfare Centre.[35] The Family Centre's services included, for example, a replacement for the then-current 'toad test' pregnancy testing service provided by the FPA's laboratories in the basement of 64 Sloane Street. In the toad test, a patient's urine was injected into a *Xenopus laevis* toad. If the toad laid eggs, usually within twenty-four hours, then the patient was

FIGURE 8.2   78 Duke Street, London, site of The Family Centre.

pregnant.[36] Not wishing to keep its own supply of live toads, nor use the FPA's, the Family Centre instead offered a progressive chorionic gonado-tropin pregnancy testing system from Denver Laboratories, Connecticut, which gave results in two hours without the use of toads or other animals.[37] The Family Centre also offered semen analysis for fertility, pap smears, and liver function tests, 'liver disease' being one of the possible oral contraceptive side effects that London Rubber and others were concerned about.[38]

Being a fully functioning birth control and fertility clinic, the Family Centre had a legitimate clinical function in trialling Feminor.[39] 'The principal reason for these clinical trials', London Rubber said, 'is to perfect the technique of administration'.[40] Trials were overseen by endocrinologist Dr Gerald Swyer (who also chaired the FPA's oral contraceptive trials committee), along with ex-FPA staffer Dr Barry Carruthers, who served as the clinic medical advisor.[41] The medical secretary, Mrs Beryl Northage (who fielded enquiries, took charge of refurbishments, and called herself 'Aunt Mary'), was also poached from the FPA.[42] In creating a research centre run by experts linked to the progressive FPA, which was the leading authority on oral contraceptive testing and safety at the time, London Rubber gave itself the credibility of a medical research institution at the cutting edge of fertility. To this end, the centre provided an ideal base for the publication of London Rubber's medical abstracting journal, *Fertility Abstracts* (above), which itself provided a vehicle for disseminating Feminor trial data.[43] From the beginning of 1962, then, London Rubber's shop window was stuffed with legitimising activities justifying its diversification into pharmaceutical contraceptives, supported by a visible infrastructure for presenting Feminor. The next challenge was to clear Feminor for medical marketing.

Clinical Trials and Medical Marketing of Feminor

Because modern drug regulation did not begin until after the 1968 Medical Act was implemented in 1971, oral contraceptive manufacturers of the 1960s were ostensibly free to sell new drugs following the publication of trial data.[44] Compared to today, where devising and trialling a drug might take many years, getting a new drug to market in the early 1960s might take as little as eighteen months. So far as oral contraception was concerned, only the FPA's Council for the Investigation of Fertility Control (CIFC) existed to ensure, 'even in the absence of formal regulation, that all products and clinical trials with the pill were centralized and carefully

TABLE 8.1   Oral contraceptives on the British market 1961–65.

Product	Maker	Where developed	When marketed	Tablets	CIFC/ FPA approved	Market share (%) 1964	Market share (%) 1965
Conovid	GD Searle	USA	'61	20	Y	42	36
Conovid E			'62	20	Y		
Ovulen			'63	20	Y		
Gynovlar	Schering	Germany	'62	20	Y	30	34
				21			
Anovlar			'64	21	Y		
Prevision	Roussel	France	'62	20	Y	No data	No data
Lyndiol	Organon	Netherlands	'63	20	Y	4	6
Lyndiol 2.5			'65	22	Y		
Ortho Novin	Ortho	USA	'63	20	Y	4	5
Norlestrin	Parke Davis	USA	'64	20	Y	No data	No data
Volidan	BDH	UK	'63	20	Y	16	14
				21			
Feminor Sequential	LR	UK	'64	20	N	No data	No data

Source: Economist Intelligence Unit, 'Contraceptive Products', *Retail Business Survey*, 1965; 'Contraceptive Products', *Retail Business Survey*, 1969; Family Planning Association Approved List 1965.

scrutinised in Britain'.[45] The CIFC was set up in 1957 as a private limited company reporting to the FPA in order to trial oral contraception.[46] The conjoined FPA/CIFC thereby established itself as the regulatory conduit through which contraceptive pills were made available to consumers.[47] However, there was no statutory or otherwise mandatory requirement for oral contraceptives to be tested by them.[48] Trialling new pills through the FPA/CIFC delayed their release and diminished manufacturer's control at a time when oral contraceptive brands were extremely time-sensitive because of increasing competition. London Rubber would have been free to put Feminor to market without FPA/CIFC trials but for the fact that, by 1965, the seven other brands available carried the council's approval.[49] London Rubber therefore required the council's go-ahead as a basic prerequisite of oral contraceptive marketing, if only because other pills had it (table 8.1).

Not wishing further delays, London Rubber devised a plan to circumvent FPA/CIFC procedure while still getting Feminor approved. The idea was to conduct trials in-house at the Family Centre, publish the trial data in *Fertility Abstracts*, market Feminor in the medical press, and *then* present paperwork to the council after the fact.[50] Clinical trials began in May 1964 and lasted for six months, by which time Feminor had been announced in the medical press.[51] Trials were conducted under Dr Barbara Schooling and Peter Jackson. According to Carruthers, trials consisted of 100 patients, followed at intervals of between one and three years. Eighteen women withdrew after the first year because of 'adverse effects or dissatisfaction with the preparation', but Carruthers felt the group responded well overall. Two pregnancies occurred, giving a failure rate of two per 100 'woman years', although one failure was attributed to incorrect administration.[52] In summation, Feminor was felt to show 'a high level of acceptability with a relatively low incidence of side effects, compared with oral contraceptives in general'.[53] Trial data appeared in the *British Journal of Clinical Practice* and *Fertility Abstracts* the following spring.[54]

A package of Feminor consisted of fifteen pink tablets containing 0.1 mg of mestranol (oestrogen) and five white tablets containing 0.075 mg of 5 mg of norethynodrel (progesterone). Given that these hormones were already used by other pills such as Conovid and Ortho Novin, and added to this the fact that Gerald Swyer (who oversaw the Family Centre) also sat in the CIFC chair, it would seem that London Rubber presumed Feminor would be passed without the need for further trials. However, the FPA/CIFC proved obstructive. As it turned out, the council was only willing to approve formulations tested by itself.[55] It further decided that sequential pills (where hormones were separated out over the month instead of being taken in a combined pill every day) required an extra layer of scrutiny not previously advertised. For sequentials, the FPA/CIFC 'would require data from a minimum of 100 patients over a period of 18 months', an extension to London Rubber's scheme that simply hadn't been anticipated.[56]

With little choice in the matter, London Rubber begrudgingly agreed to join the queue of manufacturers, namely Stayne Laboratories, ICI, Upjohn, and Schering, who were waiting to undergo sequentials testing.[57] On the up-side, the company escaped even more testing by the newly formed Dunlop Committee for the Safety of Drugs because Feminor had been available prior to the committee's formation, thus falling outside of its remit.[58] But although this put London Rubber at an advantage over the other companies, by September 1965 it was still waiting for the CIFC/FPA to organise the trials it had promised.[59] By this time, twelve formulations

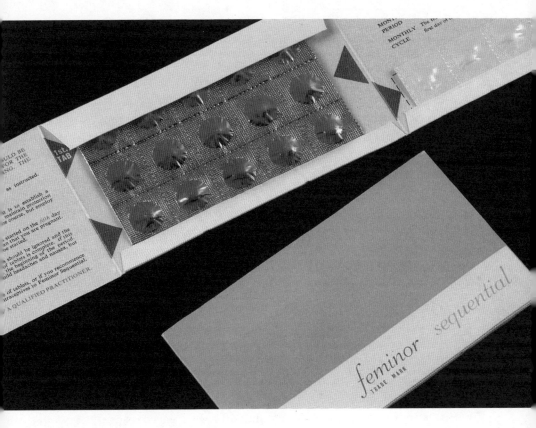

FIGURE 8.3   Feminor oral contraceptive pills, c. 1964.

of pill were available to prescribers on the British market (table 8.1), so competition was growing – and fast. Under pressure to fully roll out Feminor at this timely point in the mid-1960s, London Rubber chose to withdraw from the CIFC/FPA trial queue and go to market without waiting, on the basis of testing conducted at the Family Centre. Any future trials would be sent out to Ceylon.[60]

Although London Rubber's initial attempt to circumvent FPA/CIFC trials had backfired by slowing down efforts to fully market its house pill, the company's decision to produce a sequential rather than a combined pill also complicated Feminor's success. The future viability of oral contraception was unknown in the mid-1960s. Sequentials had been introduced in response to problems with early combined pills (namely side effects tethered to large doses of hormones administered through the month), but they had failed to provide a long-term solution as they were known to be less reliable than combined pills. The FPA/CIFC put the failure rate at four to six per 100 woman years for sequentials, compared to 0.8 for combined pills on the FPA's Approved List.[61] Manufacturers gradually reduced hormone levels in combined pills through the 1960s, undoing the unique sales angle of sequentials.[62] Lower hormone content meant that the cost of producing oral contraceptives was also reduced across the board.[63] However, special packaging for sequential pills, being a crucial part of the administration scheme to separate dosages, increased the overall cost per unit.[64]

In addition, and much to the chagrin of manufacturers with sequentials in the pipeline, the FPA/CIFC introduced a three-year cap on sequential use by women, which would limit future cycles of consumption.[65] Council member Professor N. Morris 'felt unhappy about sequential therapy with oestrogen administered alone for so long', and suggested a time cap on their use in 1963, after which a two-year limit (later increased to three) was introduced.[66] In other words, under the FPA/CIFC's guidance, women would only use sequential therapy as a stopgap, not as a contraceptive for life. Manufacturers who had already invested in the new-style pill tried to kick-start the market themselves by following London Rubber's wildcat example, withdrawing from FPA/CIFC trials in order to save time.[67] Ultimately, though, sequentials were only useful as placeholders as other novel formulations of oral contraceptive were being developed. ICI, for example, abandoned research on sequentials in 1965 in favour of the single-hormone 'mini pill'.[68] Despite success in Australia and South Africa, the British sequentials market was quickly 'doomed'.[69]

The Value of a Flop

As a commercial product, Feminor bombed. Market share was so negligible that *Retail Business* never bothered to record it.[70] Save for £32,000 spent on grants for a non-hormonal pill that did not materialise, figures detailing London Rubber's outsourced R&D outlay for Feminor are unavailable.[71] But, as the development and testing of drugs is notoriously expensive, total expenditure is likely to have been considerably more. (In the years 1963, 1964, and 1965, total R&D expenditure on all pharmaceutical products in the Britain was £13.9 million, £16 million, and £18.5 million respectively. BDH spent £500,000 perfecting Volidan, equating to around £11 million today.[72]) One area where London Rubber's investment *can* be quantified is marketing, which is especially interesting given Feminor's distinct lack of impact. Thanks to the success of condoms, London Rubber possessed considerable spending power with which to market Feminor (appendix 2). 'The money was always there and we always thought that we could buy anything or anyone really', John Harvey recalls. 'Bearing in mind that money was a bottomless pit to us. We had tons of it. The profitability was pretty huge'. London Rubber's marketing spend for Feminor was particularly concentrated in the last quarter of 1964, following the Family Centre trials, and in anticipation of successfully sailing through FPA/CIFC tests. In this quarter, London Rubber spent £1,626. Compared to Parke Davis, which spent £1,664 on Norlestrin, and BDH, which spent £1,887 on Volidan (both for the whole year), London Rubber's action can be read either as optimistic or fool-hardy. John Harvey is dubious that London Rubber's investment in Feminor was recouped.[73]

But if profit wasn't the point of Feminor, what was? And why is Feminor worthy of inclusion in the London Rubber story? One explanation is that Feminor served as a 'sleeper' brand in an uncertain contraceptive landscape, planting London Rubber's flag in an evolving market that increasingly included female contraceptive users, as well as sympathetic prescribing doctors. This may well have been part of the intention: the investment, after all, had been substantial in some respects. But as Harvey says, London Rubber had a competitive habit of 'jumping on' new contraceptives in which it had no financial interest, in order to protect the condom monopoly.[74] Could it be that Feminor was never intended to provide a realistic replacement for the combined pill? Such a supposition would comport with the sentiments of London Rubber chair Angus Reid, who said, 'We do not think ... that oral contraceptives will ever replace the traditional and still by far the most widely used method of family planning, i.e., the protective'.[75] London Rubber spent a lot on launching Feminor, relative to others, but it might certainly have spent a lot more: the company was consistently the biggest spender on contraceptive advertising, in all categories, in the 1960s.[76] Was Feminor, then, a mere component of London Rubber's bigger strategy to hijack nation-wide publicity for oral contraceptives, with the aim of getting London Rubber (and the condom) noticed? 'At no time ... do we intend to lessen our efforts to continue developing the vast market we have here and all over the world for the protective', Reid assured his staff. 'We see plenty of opportunities for further expansion in this vitally important field and we shall not fail to press them home'.[77]

London Rubber was virtually omnipotent in the contraceptive market-place, producing condoms, creams, diaphragms, and now, a pill. This made it an authority on every major commercial contraceptive available. Feminor allowed London Rubber to appear magnanimous in giving consumers the type of fertility control they apparently desired. 'We would be failing in our duty if we ignored this demand', Reid wrote.[78] But participation in the development of new reproductive technologies meant that the company understood the strengths and weaknesses of those products it sought to undermine. Oral contraception was a unique case, particularly as it made the medical profession, generally speaking, more receptive to birth control than it had been before.[79] Prior to the pill, birth control had received minimal attention from doctors, and the condom was especially overlooked as both a contraceptive and a prophylactic.[80] But the ascent of the pill led directly to the opening of potential new markets for condoms, such as family doctors and their women patients. London Rubber tried unsuccessfully to promote Durex for post-partum use during the early 1960s, but it was Feminor that provided London Rubber's passport to prescribers. It also allowed for the company to sabotage the idea of the pill from within.

Feminor: London Rubber's Legitimate Voice in the Pill Debate

London Rubber's intentions for its house pill were manifold: the company was materially invested in Feminor in the 1960s, but also stood to benefit in the longer term if Feminor could help turn public opinion against orals in the abstract. Thereby, a primary function of Feminor was the protection of London Rubber's core business of making and selling condoms. 'We had a certain amount of credit', Harvey says, 'because we poured tons of money into experts who really knew how to create a pill properly, you know ... there was the sequential method and the other [combined] method ... but basically we wanted to be having a stake in it'.[81] As a pill-making stakeholder, London Rubber contributed authoritative criticisms of oral contraception targeted at doctors, using Feminor as the conduit. In this way, the company aimed to colour the pill as the imperfect 'contraceptive of the future', as Ernest Dichter Associates had suggested during the market research.[82]

London Rubber's method was to fuel accusations against oral contraceptives centred on existing discourses on drug safety and regulation. This was especially pertinent in 1965, when the Committee on the Safety of Drugs began to investigate the pill, sustaining popular concerns about long-term harm.[83] Health risks that were widely discussed included thrombotic disorders and cancer related to high doses of oestrogen.[84]

For a company interested in discrediting oral contraceptives, anxious discussions generated by the Dunlop Committee were a gift.[85] Headlines signalling 'alarm' over the pill enabled London Rubber to easily fan the flames from a position of authority.[86] After all, why else would a cutthroat company like London Rubber wish to harm its own product? A medical division was created to sell Feminor to doctors, using medical (sales) representatives in the manner of the established pharmaceutical houses.[87] But rather than simply selling Feminor, the sales rep served as a delivery channel for anti-pill scare tactics, such as the suggestion that osteoporosis was a possible future side effect of extended oral contraceptive use.[88] John Harvey gives this specific example to illustrate how London Rubber salesmen disparaged the pill in doctor's offices. 'It was a risk and we blew it up out of all proportion, we exaggerated it', he says. Feminor gave London Rubber sales reps an audience with prescribers, and a legitimate voice in criticising the pill overall. 'We used to say, when we were talking to customers about it, we would say, "well of course this is never going to take off, this is not going to be satisfactory because the doctors are against it", and we magnified that; the doctors weren't really against it, but some of them did exaggerate all of the doubts about it'.[89] London Rubber sales reps were first briefed on Feminor's technical aspects at the half-yearly regional sales conference in autumn 1964.[90] Once inside the doctor's office, reps also incorporated condoms into the sales pitch. 'That's what the rep was for: a parley', Harvey says. 'He may not have realised it all of the time but his whole job was, in a way, protecting the monopoly'.

London Rubber's range of gynaecological products facilitated the parley, and the eventual drift toward the topic of condoms during sales conversations. For example, Candeptin vaginal ointment, a candida treatment, was developed as Feminor was being prepped for market, and was launched in 1966.[91] Vaginal ointments were a convenient vehicle promoting medical use of condoms even where the pill was being used, for cases where cross-contamination of genital infections was indicated. By focusing on gynaecology and conflating sexually transmitted infections with yeast infections, London Rubber conveyed the medical usefulness of condom prophylaxis without addressing the problematic cultural association of condoms with VD.[92] This meant that London Rubber sales reps could present the condom's dual functionality (as a contraceptive and a prophylactic) to medical customers interested in Feminor, via a portfolio of gynaecological therapies that incorporated the condom into patterns of feminine care.[93]

London Rubber also used Feminor advertising and product literature as a vehicle for agitating doctors over the pill itself, and gave them booklets and suchlike that agitated pre-existing doubts about hormone use.[94] The product literature disseminated with Feminor tablets was required reading for prescribing doctors, and London Rubber utilised it to highlight unknown future implications of prolonged hormone exposure by constantly stressing a rhetoric of uncertainty and harm. 'FEMINOR SEQUENTIAL is the latest approach to oral contraception', the 1965 Feminor booklet read. 'Its formulation is based on the rationale that it is advisable to restrict medication to the essential hormones in their natural sequence, so reducing the likelihood of long-term harmful effects to a minimum'.[95] Feminor literature made no claims for long-term safety, cleverly maintaining the sense that orals were still highly experimental, which in turn implied that women patients were little more than guinea pigs. 'Confirmation for the safety of the continued use of steroids for oral contraception will only be obtained by long experience', the booklet said. 'It should be noted that some authorities have expressed doubts about dangers that might emerge after prolonged use'.[96] In this way, doctors interested in prescribing Feminor would do so under the proviso that oral contraception was still being perfected, may or may not be harmful in the long term, and might not even provide a permanent solution to conception control. Contra-indications were also a useful means of dispensing negative rhetoric, even where side effects were not Feminor-specific. 'Tiredness, depression and headache are rarely noted during therapy', the manual read. 'Libido is not affected. *Notably there is no significant weight change during therapy*'. The latter statement – emphasis in the original – actually served to remind doctors and patients of existing concerns about weight and libido that had been discussed in the printed press, despite such problems not applying to Feminor.[97]

Other side effects, which might be found across all pill brands, were similarly itemised in product information in order to keep doubts fresh. These included: allergic states, carcinoma, cervical erosion and vaginitis, diabetes, emotional disturbance, fibroids, liver disease, ocular disturbance, thrombophlebitis, and pulmonary embolism.[98] Negative rhetoric was specifically targeted to revive reservations over pill use at the very point of prescription. While literature for other brands minimised such discussion so as not to cast doubt on the oral contraceptive project overall, Feminor literature stressed a litany of unknown quantities deliberately provoking doubt, in line with advice from the company's market research.[99] The literature read, 'Although FEMINOR SEQUENTIAL maintains a more normal hormone sequence and permits overall dosage to be reduced to a minimal level compatible with reliability, it should be appreciated that the use of steroid hormones for the prolonged inhibition of ovulation has been criticised, particularly for younger women ... The final answer to the problem of their long-term safety for such purposes as oral contraception can only be established after many years, and possibly a generation, of use'.[100] Negative rhetoric was spread evenly across Feminor promotional collateral, including stands at gynaecological conferences, film shows, advertising in the medical press, and reminder notices mailed to physicians.[101] Elsewhere, London Rubber launched a more explicit attack in sync with the product literature, namely its three-page 'obituary' to the pill which, it declared in *Fertility Abstracts*, was dead.[102] Ostensibly, London Rubber was beyond reproach because the information provided alongside Feminor was representative of ongoing safety debates, and the company was a named stakeholder invested in the oral contraceptive market.[103] By the same token, London Rubber's declared interest in the pill lent authority and weight to the pernicious doubts it propagated.

Flying the Feminor Flag?

In many ways, London Rubber's oral contraceptive project was characterised by defeat; firstly by the failure to develop a viable non-hormonal pill, then resistance from the FPA/CIFC, followed by a disappointing market share and limitations on sequentials as an oral contraceptive class. This chapter has argued that London Rubber's pill nonetheless succeeded in flying a flag for the continued relevance of traditional contraceptive houses, serving as a professional declaration of commitment to the principle of family planning, just as the pill was gaining traction in the mid-1960s. Rather than being recalcitrant about the pill, London Rubber's active participation in a changing market kept their offering on the table as part of the contraceptive futures debate. In a climate where condoms were seldom advertised or discussed in mass media, Feminor afforded London Rubber the means of piggybacking on a discussion from which it would otherwise be excluded.

9

Later Years
1965–2001 (AND BEYOND)

In the preceding chapters, I have attempted to map a very particular, previously uncharted gap in British contraceptive history by describing the first fifty years of the London Rubber Company and the condom up to 1965. This is the point at which the oral contraceptive pill began to take off in Britain, and steady, annual growth in the condom market came to an end (table A1).[1] In this detailed account of the company's first five decades, we have seen that London Rubber was far from being complacent about its own success: on the contrary, it was always strategically active and looking for opportunities. London Rubber was also forward-thinking and technologically innovative, continuing to to develop its products and widen its range of offerings. Contrary to the popular history of the pill, which suggests that its effect on wider culture – and women especially – was felt at the very moment it became available, the ramifications of oral contraception for the birth control market were not immediately apparent, at least not in terms of condom sales (table A2). Even so, London Rubber was prepared for the challenges ahead and faced them boldly. By the mid-1960s, however, the company itself was maturing. This meant, on the one hand, that its essential intrastructure and technology were solidly in place, the company being long established and well known: London Rubber held on to its first-mover advantage as the dominant, near-monopoly player in condom manufacture and supply. On the other hand, a younger and more diverse staff was replenishing the company's long-serving workforce. The board – including such leading lights as Angus Reid – was preparing for retirement. With diversification into new product areas came ambitious new personnel with wide-ranging business experience, and London Rubber continued to change with the times. During the late 1960s, 70s, 80s, and 90s, the company went through several incarnations, and several changes of senior management. It branched out into some counterintuitive product areas, such as fine china, and while the 1980s AIDS crisis reinvigorated enthusiasm for the condom more broadly, London Rubber was eventually let down by bad ventures into disparate products and services. It left Chingford for good in 1994 following an ill-fated move into photographic processing, sacking most of its British workforce. What follows in this final chapter is a précis of the main events and developments concerning London Rubber during 1965–2001. Time and space limitations have prevented me from offering as detailed or analytic account as I would like: indeed, that would take another book. It is hoped that, as well as being interesting to readers of this book, the following will serve as a framework for future research.

1965–1970

As the contraceptive market broadened in the mid-1960s, and the Dunlop committee convened to investigate oral contraceptive safety, so the debate over birth control profiteering intensified. In 1966, Aberdeen gynaecologist Sir Dugald Baird called for contraceptives to be made free on the National Health Service,[2] pressing home the need for London Rubber to protect the monopoly, and its premium lines, against future competition in the shape of other possible NHS suppliers. London Rubber began a reshuffle of its brands, introducing an innovative new thin-walled condom, the Durex Fetherlite.[3] Having attained the BSI kite mark and therefore secured a form of official approval that could actually be displayed in print advertising and on packs, the company continued to break away from the FPA, withdrawing the Atlas clinic brand in 1967. Atlas was replaced with Durex Gossamer,[4] which was actually the same product, but stocking this premium brand reduced margins to 770 FPA branches that had come to depend on large profits derived from Atlas, as well as London Rubber's generous discounts.[5] Together with Leo Abse, MP, the FPA publicly protested against London Rubber's prices and profits, dusting off and revitalising a call for a monopolies investigation that had originally been made to the Board of Trade in 1963.[6] In other respects, the FPA took a more liberal attitude to the promotional endeavours of suppliers on its Approved List in the latter half of the 1960s, no longer requiring checks on third party publicity such as booklets, further cementing the separation.[7] Having turned its efforts to changing public opinion with its underground anti-pill campaign, London Rubber began to reap the rewards of more favourable attitudes towards condoms among pharmacists, which were undoubtedly tied with the realisation that the margins on oral contraceptives could not compare with the ever-flexible potential for profit with London Rubber condoms.[8] Boots, the dominant chain of retail chemists, finally began to stock non-prescription condoms in 1965, a sign of improved acceptance among both retailers and consumers.[9]

In 1969, London Rubber introduced yet another revolutionary product, Durex Nu-Form, the world's first anatomically shaped latex condom that fitted around the glans. This was the result of years of clinical research into increasing sensitivity in condom use for men. Nu-Form also represented the culmination of London Rubber's long-running efforts to draw positive attention, as embodied in an aggressive, big-budget national print advertising campaign. Sweeping away the era of coupon and booklet advertising, and marking a new willingness of print media vendors to carry condom advertising, the Nu-Form marketing campaign directly referenced condoms for the first time.[10] Heavy mass exposure was part of a holistic scheme that included a high-quality product, top-grade packaging, and premium pricing. Like Fetherlite, Nu-Form was almost double the trade price of Gossamer. Combined, these elements worked to address the long-felt perception that condoms were cheap and distasteful, which had been corroborated by EDA's research in 1961. At this time, advances made in condom technology had gone unrecognised only to be usurped by the sophisticated, futuristic oral contraceptive pill: London Rubber had struggled to alert potential users to Gossamer's game-changing properties long after its release, instead resorting to cloak-and-dagger public relations schemes, dirty tricks, and front organisations used to undermine the competition. By 1969, however, London Rubber was poised to take advantage of an increasingly sexually permissive society (encompassing, among other societal changes, the 1967 Abortion Act that legalised the termination of pregnancy under some circumstances, and the Sexual Offences Act, which permitted homosexual acts between consenting adults in private). The Nu-Form experience was fine-tuned to give 'not only physical satisfaction … but also the satisfaction that this was not a cheap product', London Rubber explained. 'Price, quality, and packaging were important for the image of the product in fact of competition from the pill'.[11]

So far as London Rubber's Feminor project was concerned, this was strung out until 1970 and never realised any great success. British testing stopped in 1965, and Feminor was replaced in November 1968 by Feminor 21, a reconfigured version using a twenty-one-day regimen following a trend for easier self-administration.[12] This was the company's last attempt to get value from its investment in oral contraceptive research. From 1966, oral contraceptives were the only drug for which doctors were able to charge NHS patients a fee,[13] so Feminor 21 was pitched for this low-cost market, still trying to attract the attention of prescribing doctors, and to find its niche.[14] The formulation was also briefly made available as a 'menstrual regulator', Femetra, in July 1968, just in time for the *Humanae Vitae* encyclical from the Catholic Church, which prohibited the use of artificial contraception.[15] Like Tova, a menstrual regulator made by British Drug Houses, Femetra seems to have served as an undercover contraceptive for the Catholic market.[16] In the event, however, oral contraceptives more generally turned out not to be the panacea that many had hoped for.[17] Even in countries where use of the pill was highest (Sweden, Australia, and America), the remaining empty capacity for women users was enough to potentially double levels of market penetration, meaning that eligible women were not taking up the pill as much as they could.[18] London Rubber cast its contraceptive net once again, and began to produce the 'Saf-t-coil' intrauterine device under licence from its American subsidiary, Julius Schmid,[19] although it stopped making diaphragms in 1967.[20] Feminor 21 and Femetra were recalled in January 1970 following the Dunlop Committee's recommendation to stop prescribing high-oestrogen pills.[21] Given that over half of the pills on the market were recalled by their manufacturers, however, the Dunlop recommendation allowed London Rubber to make a quiet, dignified, and virtually unnoticed exit from the orals scene under cover of more successful brands, such as the original Conovid. Although the company would continue to experiment with contraceptives for women in later decades (for example, with a silicone intravaginal ring), London Rubber would not make another oral contraceptive.[22]

Following the public exposé of London Rubber's front organisations (which had been disbanded along with the Family Centre by 1966), London Rubber diverted funds into academic research in order to influence opinion, endowing the Sociological Research Foundation at the University of Hull, under the directorship of John Peel, with a grant of £50,000.[23] Ostensibly, the purpose of the SRF was to examine the 'family intentions' of couples married since 1965, while gathering and publishing new data on contraceptive use. This gave London Rubber a credible means of consolidating the continued success of the condom in the age of the pill through what would become known as the Hull Family Survey. Among other discoveries, the Hull Family Survey reported that male methods were used twice as much as female methods, and that the findings of previous studies on levels of illegitimacy rates were incorrect.[24]

So far as the condom business was concerned, London Rubber continued to respond to changing conditions. Rising costs and wages reduced profitability, and management consultants Urwick, Orr & Partners were brought in to reorganise the group in 1966.[25]

The Unsettled 1970s

In March 1970, a *Sunday Times* report on sex and marriage estimated that 51 per cent of couples used 'protectives' as their main form of contraception, 30 per cent used the pill, 10 per cent the diaphragm, and the remaining 9 per cent other methods. At this stage of the game, then, condoms were still ahead of the pill. The pattern of retail distribution carried on pretty much as in the 1960s, except that the restrictive period in retail chemists' promotion of contraceptives, which had begun with the PSGB's 1953 statement, ended in 1970 when clause 10 was rescinded.[26] This opened up sales promotion to condoms, and would gradually open press advertising. Retail shops began to introduce self-selection displays for customers, improving the prospects for brand competition, and, thereby, new entrants to the condom market.[27] London Rubber continued to expand its range, which included the first condom made from coloured latex, the Durex Black Shadow, and Fourex animal skin condoms imported from Julius Schmid, New York. The quality control standard (BS3704) was updated in respect of the new-style anatomically shaped condoms now available. While the standard minimum sizing (175 mm length and 49 mm width) remained unchanged, provision was now made for the glans as well as the penis shaft in terms of fit. Shaped condoms, BS3704 1972 said, should not exceed 70 mm at the widest point.[28] The FPA, which had began to thaw somewhat on the issue of male contraception under the leadership of Caspar Brook, took advantage of the new retail climate by launching its own-brand condoms that same year, through Family Planning Sales Ltd, a retail company set up by Gordon Snow for this purpose.[29] Unpackaged condoms were purchased from London Rubber and the Akwell Corporation in Ohio.[30] These were branded as the 'Forget me not' (a condom) and 'Two's Company' (a condom and vaginal pessary packaged together). The latter used a design scheme created by the popular illustrator Quentin Blake, who is better known for his work on children's books.[31] As before, only a very small percentage of condoms were actually sold at FPA clinics,[32] but the association's move into the condom business supports Ben Mechen's assertion that in the 1970s, condoms were finally becoming 'normalised'.[33]

Up until 1973, London Rubber was the only full-line contraceptive house producing every major birth control device on the British market. At this time, Ortho (the contraceptive subsidiary of Johnson & Johnson) began selling Conceptrol Shields condoms in Britain as well as its usual creams, diaphragms, and the Ortho Novin oral contraceptive.[34] Ortho's condoms, which were produced by Akwell, also held the right to display the British Standard kite mark,[35] which had been revised in 1972, although London Rubber remained the only British manufacturer.[36] Mechen has argued that the range of condoms available in the 1970s, and the opening up of consumer advertising, marked the beginning of 'contraceptive consumerism'.[37] However, the Conceptrol Shields venture (being a brand very much geared towards self-selecting consumers) was short lived in Britain: Ortho withdrew the product in 1976, saying that market conditions were not, at that time, receptive to its consumer marketing approach.[38] This is probably because Conceptrol Shields had been rushed out in Canada, where London Rubber's subsidiary Julius Schmid owned 98 per cent of a market in which all condoms were imported. Condom advertising had begun to open up in Canada at the same time as Britain, and it was this, combined with the new-style contoured and coloured condoms pioneered by London Rubber, which led to new entrants in the marketplace. Conceptrol Shields were a direct response to Searle, which brought out Stimula, Conture, and Prime condoms.[39] But Ogilvy's image-heavy Shields campaign, which depended on full-colour packaging featuring close-ups of attractive couples gazing into each other's eyes,[40] was too much, too fast for the British public, who had forgotten the dazzling window displays of the 1920s and did not like to be rushed into changing the way they had been buying condoms for the last thirty years.

The price of branded condoms had long been an issue among socially motivated providers of contraception, which London Rubber countered in 1970 in its evidence to the Select Committee on Science and Technology. An annual supply of even its most expensive condoms, it said, would cost £4 11s, compared to £6 per year for a diaphragm or IUD, or £7 for the oral contraceptive pill.[41] These figures are open to debate, however, when one considers the variables involved. For example, condoms might cost significantly more in the case of a person who only buys packets of three as opposed to the less expensive packets of twelve, or who had penetrative sex more frequently than was suggested by the model (which used the *Sunday Times* figure of ninety times per annum, as opposed to EDA's estimate of 100).[42] Equally, a woman using an oral contraceptive, diaphragm, or IUD might experience complications (such as an ill-fitting device or bad reaction to a particular formulation of hormones), necessitating more trips to her GP or family planning clinic, which would add to costs.

The issue of price would be forced in the 1970s by two interconnected events, namely the provision of free contraception by the NHS and a state investigation into London Rubber's monopolistic practices (see below). In terms of non-commercial contraceptive provision, Dugald Baird's wish for free contraception came to pass when national, state-sponsored family planning services were rolled out as part of the 1974 NHS reorganisation, and the health service began the gradual takeover of FPA clinics.[43] This occurred as part of a wider increase in public sector investment, including the NHS and social security, over 1972–74.[44] The oral contraceptive pill was now free via the NHS, and from 1975 contraceptive services could be accessed through GPs. This service, however, was for women only and did not include condoms, the result of which was that 99 per cent of clinic users were women.[45] From the mid-1970s, pills began to overtake condoms as the most widely used appliance contraceptive method in Britain,[46] and it is likely that free oral contraceptive provision to women – along with a new generation of contraceptive users coming of age – contributed to this shift. Advertising condoms to consumers became all the more necessary, but was still problematic, especially on television: in 1976, the BBC famously pulled live coverage of Formula One because of two sponsored John Surtees vehicles displaying Durex decals.[47] Clearly acceptance still had some way to go.

The 1970s also marked an internal shift at what was now known as the 'London Rubber Company International' group of companies, or 'LRCI'. Angus Reid, the last of the old guard, retired in 1971, with the chair taken over by Lord Mayor of London Edward Howard, also the head of the Eucryl tooth powder company. By this time, London Rubber's portfolio had expanded enormously: in addition to condoms, tooth powder, and wine, the company was involved in soap, brushes, bathing caps, disposable knickers, photographic processing, and Cobalt 60 radiation plants.[48] Diversification away from condoms had begun in the 1960s, when London Rubber anticipated changes in consumer requirements, and this foresight was borne out in the mid-1970s by a dramatic slump in sales. This might arguably be attributed (at least in part) to the introduction of free oral contraceptives by the NHS: at the time, London Rubber blamed the pill and competition from Ortho for flagging demand.[49] However, other extrinsic factors would also have affected profitability. In Malaysia, the

FIGURE 9.1   Forget me not condoms, Family Planning Sales Ltd, in foils and cardboard box, 1970s.

natural rubber industry was enjoying a renaissance, which influenced the cost of the raw material. Between 1972 and 1973, global rubber prices doubled,[50] coinciding with the 'oil shock' that saw the price of a barrel of oil from OPEC producers jump 70 per cent, meaning that the basic manufacturing costs for condoms increased substantially almost overnight. This was in combination with the fact that, over the winter of 1973–74, Britain was faced with an economic crisis as the cumulative effects of the oil shock plus devaluation of the pound, sectarian violence in Northern Ireland, and stock market collapse brought the country to the breaking point.[51] Rolling labour disputes, which had crippled such industries as coal mining, also had repercussions for London Rubber. In May 1975, 150 workers from the Amalgamated Glove and Electronic Testing sections walked out in a five-week dispute, supported by the Transport and General Workers Union, over the deduction of union subs from wage packets.[52] Just weeks later, 200 staff lost their jobs when the Hall Lane glove plant closed, following industrial action from hospital workers which affected sales of surgeon's gloves.[53] It was in the light of the economic crises of the 1970s that the value of earlier diversivication became apparent. When condoms performed badly, LRCI's wide portfolio of products and services created a safety net that kept the London Rubber group of companies afloat. The Sanitas toiletries division, for example, won a contract for supplying recycling toilets for passenger trains over 1975–76, and consumer photographic processing enjoyed an excellent summer in 1975, contributing £2 million to group profits.[54]

Nonetheless, the Monopolies and Mergers Commission (MMC) investigation into anti-competitive practices at London Rubber, which published its damning report in 1975, cast a shadow over recovery. Convened in 1972 following a reference from the Department of Health and Social Security, the MMC was supported by non-profit contraceptive stakeholders including the FPA. The report recommended that London Rubber drastically reduce the price of condoms, leading Leo Abse, MP (who had campaigned for the investigation) to claim, in his flamboyant fashion, that he had 'brought down the cost of loving'.[55] The MMC found that London Rubber's pricing policy operated against public interest because it resulted in excessive profits. The differential price structure of its condoms, the MMC said, was a deterrent to potential competitors, and was exploitative. London Rubber's lawyers fiercely challenged these findings with a High Court action, but the matter was resolved when London Rubber agreed to a less drastically reduced rate of return.[56] After all of this, condom prices were somewhat restored at the cusp of the new decade when their actual profitability fell short of forecasts.[57] This took London Rubber 'off the hook' for the time being, but two further investigations would follow in the 1980s and 1990s.

The Diverse 1980s

The 1980s is often recalled in the popular imagination as a period of money-driven market liberalization, and for LRCI Group, which was by now very much a City company run by financiers, the decade was marked by a divergent spread of corporate interests, high finance, and a greater sense of internationalism. The company's non-contraceptive subsidiary portfolio was taken into surprising new directions as LRCI group continued its diversification programme under a new management team, which included Donald E. Seymour in the chair, and Alan E. Woltz (formerly of Julius Schmid and LRC North America) as chief executive and managing director. LRCI's need to diversify in the 1980s was all the more pressing following a slump in demand for condoms during the previous decade. Contraceptives, balloons, gloves, and toiletries were now made under the 'LRC Products' subsidiary, which replaced 'LRI'.[58] As more business acquisitions were made, the contribution of condoms to LRCI group became proportionately smaller. New business areas included Feminique sanitary towels, and the Royal Worcester Spode fine china division, both of which were aimed at American markets. At home, products included Duraplug electrical accessories, Buttercup syrup, Galloways and Liquifruta cough medicines, Wrights coal tar soap, Beechwood paint brushes, and hot water bottles and bathing caps by Mandelle and Britmarine.[59] In particular, the high-margin photo processing side of LRCI group's business was greatly expanded, this being one of the only British consumer sectors experiencing real growth at the beginning of the 1980s as inexpensive automatic cameras became commonplace.[60] Photo processing involved the production of paper prints from rolls of camera film taken by amateur photographers, 'holiday snaps' and the like, for the consumer market. Films were dropped into high street retailers including Boots and Woolworth's, or sent via mail order to a chain of labs operated by LRCI's photo processing business, ColourCare International Ltd. ColourCare was established by combining the smaller photographic acquisitions built up since the 1970s,[61] and would be expanded further with Spanish acquisitions later in the 1980s,[62] but the division was so significant that by 1983 LRCI became known as 'the contraceptives and photo processing group'.[63] In a 1985 revamp, LRCI changed its name to 'London International Group' ('LIG') reflecting its size, scope, and ambitions in international consumer markets, and its reduced dependency on the traditional contraceptive trade.[64]

The condom market was dominated by the AIDS crisis from 1982 onward. The marketing of condoms for disease protection was an entirely new direction in Britain, and for LIG especially, which had historically sold condoms as contraceptives rather than prophylactics. This was partially because of medical opinion on the subject: London Rubber had pointed out the utility of condoms in VD prophylaxis to the Select Committee on Science and Technology in 1970, but this was by no means the general consensus, and the company, who still eschewed connections to STIs in public, elected not to market them for this purpose.[65] Even into the late 1970s, genito-urinary specialists were pointing out that barrier methods had not been proven to offer complete protection against disease.[66] By the early 1980s, however, there was a widespread, general recognition of the condom's unique ability to protect people against STIs.[67] Indeed, condoms would offer the only known protection against AIDS (or, rather, HIV) at the time,[68] and were officially recognised as having prophylactic (as well as contraceptive) qualities for the first time.[69] LIG had, with great foresight, already introduced new brands that would come to resonate with public feeling, such as Durex Nu-Form Extra Safe, which was launched in 1980.[70] Demand for condoms in Britain, which had declined sharply in 1973, stopped falling.[71] The NHS, which had finally begun supplying condoms in small numbers as part of its free contraceptive programme in the late 1970s, also began buying in more unbranded condoms for distribution via Local Health Authorities in clinics. These were purchased through Family Planning Sales Ltd, which switched from consumer retail sales to clinic and hospital supply, and Lamberts, which were both supplied by LRC.[72] Around 20 per cent of all condom sales in the mid-1980s went to the NHS.[73]

By this time, the AIDS crisis had come to be seen as a public health issue, with the Department of Health calling it 'perhaps the greatest new public health challenge this century',[74] mounting the first AIDS public health campaign in 1986.[75] However, despite the health emergency, government authorities decided against the blanket distribution of free condoms as a preventable measure, reasoning that condoms were already free from clinics and were widely available for consumer purchase.[76] Durex was advertised for the first time on British television in August 1987, expressly because of AIDS: broadcast regulation had been relaxed on account of the crisis.[77] The ability to advertise on television changed the consumer marketplace beyond recognition. Whereas the gradual opening up of consumer advertising in the 1970s had led to a false start for competition (as in the case of Conceptrol Shields), television, combined with the recognised public need for condoms for health and prophylactic purposes, gave competitors a genuine opportunity to vie for market share. Widespread advertising across mass media gave startup competition the opportunity to attract completely new users, which was easier than trying to convert existing ones (condoms being notoriously brand-inelastic).[78] In 1987, Virgin Records founder and sexual health advocate Richard Branson introduced Mates, which were produced by the Australian company Ansell (a subsidiary of Dunlop), for sale through the Virgin company.[79] Unlike premium Durex brands, Mates were sold inexpensively (at around half the price of Durex), and the proceeds were donated to AIDS research.[80] They were advertised on television in November 1987,[81] and the BBC (who ran the non-commercial channels BBC1 and BBC2) agreed to screen them as public service announcements, a huge coup for Virgin.[82] Branson advertised Mates aggressively, and expanded the retail reach of condoms, selling them through his network of Virgin record shops, and in Anita Roddick's cosmetic chain, the Body Shop.[83] According to Alison Payne, who was associate director of planning at Bates Dorland at the time, the advertising agency in charge of LIG's television campaign over 1986–87, the company was 'very afraid of Mates'.[84] However, the market remained difficult and Mates suffered 'a devastating publicity setback' when its products failed Consumers' Association inflation tests in 1989.[85] This was especially problematic for Mates given Durex's long-standing reputation for reliability in the minds of brand-loyal consumers, and given the pressing need for protection from HIV. Mates would operate at a loss until the early 1990s.[86]

The public perception of AIDS as a serious threat to health increased steadily between 1986 and 1989,[87] and condom use grew accordingly.[88] The AIDS crisis also changed sexual practice among gay men,[89] many of whom were not accustomed to using condoms,[90] and were expressly targeted by health campaigns. In 1987, American condom consumption spiked because (so statisticians explained) gay male consumers were entering the marketplace in sizable numbers for the first time, although it was difficult to prove conclusively.[91] This followed a global growth in the condom market which levelled off in 1988.[92] In Britain, governmental organisations and charitable bodies promoted 'safe sex' through the use of condoms, and encouraged their distribution to women and men,[93] but although this presented LIG with opportunities, the transition to a new customer base was culturally problematic for the company.[94] Its dependence on addressing its consumer base through normative stereotypes was well established, and it was reluctant to publicly acknowledge the use of its product outside of the normative heterosexual family.[95] Back in the 1970s, London Rubber had privately stated that it wished to avoid making any public connection with disease.[96] In the 1980s, and while liaising with the company over TV advertising, Alison Payne felt that they exhibited a 'really sleazy attitude to sex and contraception', were reluctant to acknowledge gay condom use, and 'didn't want' the prophylaxis market.[97] 'My experience with LRC [LIG] in the late 80s was that they only felt really comfortable with their product when it was presented as beneficial for stable married couples (preferably already with children)', she told me in 2016. 'It wasn't just AIDS they felt uncomfortable with, it was homosexual sex – disease and buggery just wasn't how they wanted to see the Durex brand – you have to remember that it was a "gay" disease then'.[98] This is Payne's personal opinion based on her own dealings with the company, and although it is impossible to pinpoint how widespread these views were within LIG as a whole, Payne's observation chimes with Paul Jobling's study on twentieth-century Durex advertising, which appraised the company as immovable and 'myopic' in its resistance to acknowledging or accommodating non-normative sexual identities.[99]

On top of this, there was also some question as to whether the company's condoms (which were tested on the basis of vaginal intercourse) would remain safe during anal sex, which was then construed as the type of sex practised by homosexual men.[100] By 1987, however, AIDS had reached a crisis point and concomitant public health campaigning was well underway: condom manufacturers could no longer escape the moral responsibility to acknowledge the condom's role in disease prophylaxis, even if they were reluctant to connect their products to sex outside of heteronormative family life. At last, LIG publicly and proactively associated itself with the subject of AIDS, and, in particular, with AIDS research. MillionAid, LIG's fundraising campaign, aimed to raise £1 million for research charities on the basis that it would donate 10 pence for every kite mark cut out of Durex boxes and returned to the company. Because MillionAid coincided with Branson's non-profit Mates offering, cynics understandably criticised LIG for profiteering from a serious epidemic where others were helping out of altruism. When accused of cashing in on the crisis in order to sell Durex, a spokesperson said, 'We cannot deter people from having sexual relations ... but the least we can do is to ask people to use our product for their own safety'.[101] As had been the case since the company's earliest days, the aim was not to drive or shape sexual culture per se, but to capitalize upon changes and trends in sexual behaviour brought about by extrinsic events, or at least to reluctantly go along with them.

When the AIDS crisis began, London Rubber held between 90 and 95 per cent of the British condom market and had just been given permission to increase its prices following reductions imposed by the 1975 MMC report.[102] Following a second MMC report in 1982, the company was once again found to be a monopoly, and its condoms were placed under enforced governmental price control, effective from September 1983.[103] This coincided with the new demand for barrier prophylaxis, meaning that prices were reduced just as demand surged. Operations had also been rationalised just prior to the AIDS crisis: household and industrial glove production were moved to Malaysia, and the photographic processing side of the business was rapidly expanded.[104] However, once public demand for condoms increased (by 20–25 per cent in Britain, because of AIDS public health campaigns),[105] LIG was able to increase the variety of retail sites, which was central to opening visibility. Condoms became even more commonplace, and were now sold through petrol stations and supermarkets, the latter contributing the most significant area of growth (and accounting for ten per cent of the total market by the decade's end).[106] By 1985, LIG brands included – in addition to Gossamer, Fetherlite, and Nu-Form – Elite, Arouser (which was ribbed), and Gold, which was gold coloured and larger than standard condoms, and was perceived as a 'gay condom' outside of the company.[107] Black Shadow was withdrawn in 1988, and Fiesta, a mixed three-pack of coloured condoms introduced in 1985, was withdrawn in 1990,[108] demand for novelty being limited. The need for different sizes became apparent with the increasing diversity of the marketplace, and the updated British Standard BS3704 1989 divided condoms into new categories according to size and finish. Types A (smooth) and B (textured) were a minimum of 52 mm in width and 160 mm in length. Types C (smooth) and D (textured) were 48 mm wide, at a minimum, and at least 150 mm long. This meant that the minimum length had lost an overall 25 mm on the original 1964 Standard, but manufacturers were free to make condoms longer.[109] The minimum width was a different matter, as condoms that are too large slip off during

FIGURE 9.2   Poster from Durex advertising safer sex, AIDS awareness, and the use of condoms. Durex Information Service, 1990s.

use. Condoms under the new standard lost 1 mm at the lower end of the scale, but now enjoyed a more flexible 2 mm deviation either way.[110] By 1988, British people were using more than 140 million condoms per year, at a cost in excess of £33 million.[111]

Improved demand was initially good for LIG; sales increased by 20 per cent per year during the AIDS crisis. But requirements reached such heights by 1987 that the market became over-supplied, meaning that retailers with stockpiled condoms did not need to replenish stocks to the same degree in 1988, leading to a sudden drop in sales to whole-sale suppliers. Furthermore, analysts speculated that too few teenagers were responding to public health messages and were not using condoms in the desired numbers, meaning that the potential market had fallen short: just three or four sexually active British teenagers out of every ten was using them.[112] Lastly, a consignment of latex used for LIG's American condom production (which had become an important contributor to group profits) was found to be defective, but only after the units had already been produced and had gone through electronic testing, at which stage they were rejected.[113] LIG was saved from the potentially devastating effect of the sudden condom downturn by its other businesses, especially photo processing, which saw an operating profit of £12.7 million on sales of £95 million by the summer of 1989 (an increase of 22 per cent on the previous year), and accounted for almost a third of group sales.[114] Clearly, consumers were taking a lot of photographs. Condoms, on the other hand, accounted for less than a quarter of group sales, as did gloves.[115] Success in photo processing also offset the expense of disposing the loss-making Royal Worcester Spode fine china division, which had haemorrhaged £1.2 million over 1987–89 due to a fall in American tourism to Britain after the crisis in Libya.[116] By the close of the decade, the inventories of condom retailers were returning to normal levels, stabilising the market.[117] LIG's condom brands were strong, and remained international leaders. However, with its diverse portfolio of products and services, LIG had come to depend on other businesses – especially photography – to sustain the group on the whole. Whereas in the 1970s the non-contraceptive companies within the group had saved London Rubber from disaster when condom sales plummeted, by the 1990s LIG had become dependent on the more diverse areas of the business. It was this dependency on other areas that would take LIG to the brink of receivership, leading to the downfall of condom manufacture at Chingford and the end of condom manufacturing in Britain.

1990–94: The Demise of ColourCare

By 1990, LIG had an annual turnover of approximately £350 million, was present in 120 countries, employed 8,000 people, and operated in two core areas: health and personal products (including condoms and surgical gloves), which contributed about two-thirds of global annual sales, and photographic processing, which was mostly concentrated in home markets and accounted for approximately one-third of sales.[118] Condom manufacturing was consolidated into four factories in Britain (Chingford), the US (Anderson, South Carolina), Italy (Bologna), and Spain (Barcelona).[119] Durex Extra Safe was launched, becoming the best-selling Durex condom in Britain. For the first time since the 1970s, condoms were the most popular method of birth control, with 22 per cent of adults between sixteen and fifty-four using them, followed by the pill at 21 per cent of users, although, because of 'safe sex' messages, many couples went 'double Dutch' and used both.[120] After decades of trying to nurture female acceptance, women were finally buying more condoms in response to AIDS. Sales to women rose from 23 per cent in 1983 to 58 per cent in 1991, according to figures gathered by LRC Products,[121] which prompted the company to resume the manufacture of diaphragms and spermicides.[122] Elsewhere, Chartex launched the Femidom female condom with an initial promotional budget of £1 million, indicating how lucrative the potential women's market was. Nonetheless, LRC Products' research suggested that British women had grown accustomed to the uncomplicated, traditional condom, and preferred it to other non-systemic methods. 'Women found the concept of a female condom appealing but when they saw the possible product they were less likely to use it', said Jean Smith, the LRC Product's group manager for family planning. 'Their preference was for a male condom which appealed to women, giving them the freedom to purchase and carry condoms'.[123] It was on this basis that Mates and Durex each launched heavily branded traditional male condoms specifically marketed at women, namely Ladymates (1992) and Durex Assure (1991), a coral-coloured condom in discreet packaging that quickly took 3 per cent of the total British market. The marketplace for barrier protection had opened up so much because of the AIDS crisis that the entire Durex range was repackaged and relaunched in 1992 and included, among the established brands, Safe Play, available in natural, minty, or ribbed, and Allergy, which was hypoallergenic. By this time, condoms were actively marketed to single persons, including young people, who, like women, represented an important potential market. Safe Play and Gold recognised that young people had sex early, met partners casually, changed them regularly. Safe Play Minty, a fun green-tinted product, was initially sold through clinics and vending machines before being launched in pharmacies in November 1991. It was then promoted in nightclubs, in an effort to move young people towards normalised patterns of regular condom purchasing.[124] Later brand hook-ups in nightclubs would also include Swan Vesta matches.[125]

Condoms aside, overall turnover and profit had increased year-on-year throughout the 1980s, and LIG entered the last decade of the century intending to expand its global reach, and to further develop successful areas.[126] Between April 1987 and January 1991, LIG ran a significant capital investment programme amounting to approximately £110 million, focused on the surgeon's glove brand Biogel and the ColourCare photo processing business.[127] Biogel was patented at a cost of £10 million and was produced at a new and dedicated £14 million facility in Malaysia, while £30 million was spent on upgrading technology for photo processing, and a further £17 million was spent on leasing plant and equipment.[128] £20 million was also used for acquisitions for photo processing, and for the health and personal products divisions.[129] It was ColourCare, however, that suffered the most from the economic recession that hit Britain and Europe in the early 1990s, rapidly turning it from a profit-making asset to a loss-making liability. By the close of 1993, and in combination with cash-flow problems aggravated by a company debt of £157 million, senior management called for a strategic review.[130] Operations were completely pared back and rationalised as LIG returned its focus to core businesses of dipped latex products and barrier protection, disposing of non-core brands and all photo processing interests. These measures saved LIG, but resulted in the closure of British manufacturing, and the end of condom production at Chingford in the summer of 1994.

Although LIG had made some rationalisations within ColourCare (closing wholesale photo processing in Bilbao and Barcelona in 1990, for example),[131] the aim at the beginning of the 1990s had been to improve market share, in Britain especially, despite evidence of a downturn in consumer spending on photographs. Consumer 'D&P' ('developing and processing') was very much a seasonal business and represented a discretionary spend for the average consumer, who would take photographs on special occasions such as summer weddings or holidays, the beginning of the school year, or over Christmas.[132] Demand for D&P dropped in line with the general economic recession, wherein consumers reduced spending on nonessential items. LIG nonetheless invested £1.6 million buying laboratories in Bedford, Tunbridge Wells, Worthing, and Cardiff,[133] before purchasing a photographic company in Scotland and building a new lab in Walsall, West Midlands, aiming to gobble up share while the market was depressed. The goal was to get ahead in the 'tremendous price war' that had seen laboratories slash prices to win the business of high street retailers, which included independent photography shops and pharmacies in addition to chains like Boots and Woolworth's. D&P labs were at the mercy of retailers who were cutting prices on the full gamut of their offerings, not just in consumer photography, which left a huge overcapacity in the market and threw some D&P businesses into difficulty.[134] Buying up small outfits when they were cheap allowed Colour-Care to grow its share at home, where the majority of its business took place, and to keep retail D&P (which was being hit by mail-order brands, such as Grunwick's Bonusprint) competitive.

Even as consumer spending dropped, LIG upgraded ColourCare's labs to state-of-the-art technology and increased marketing efforts, banking on having a majority stake in the market by the time it recovered.[135] A continuous flow production system, the 'Maxilab', was installed in the Park Royal laboratory, North London, in Newmarket (Suffolk), and Livingston (Scotland). As with Lucian Landau's Automated Protective plant in the 1950s, the Maxilab was designed on the principle of continuous flow production. It was the most high-speed system available,[136] but this meant that the Maxilab would need continuous high-volume input in order to work efficiently. ColourCare also operated 'minilabs' on-site at high street stores, giving retailers the option of charging a premium for one-hour or one-day services, or a lower rate for sending films off to the main labs.[137] As well as consumers, minilabs served the professional estate agent industry, which produced photographs of properties for sale as part of their essential service, and with whom ColourCare had just secured new D&P contracts over 1989–90.[138] By the autumn of 1991, ColourCare operated more than 230 minilabs in Britain and Northern Ireland, but closures had already begun in the shadow of the threat of war in the Gulf, which affected consumer confidence. An early 90s housing market slump naturally reduced demand for estate agent's services, slashing their own D&P requirements.[139]

As minilabs closed, processing was diverted to the new state-of-the-art Maxilabs (such as one that opened in Mitcham in May 1992), but demand was evidently too low to recoup the substantial capital investment that had been made in equipping them. ColourCare had been grown into the leading low-cost photo processer in the UK with 34 per cent of the market, and by 1992 the business accounted for almost 40 per cent of LIG turnover.[140] In Europe, ColourCare launched the Hot Box disposable camera, expanded into Portugal, and tested retail ventures in France, Holland, and Norway.[141] But the number of films being processed in Britain – ColourCare's main market – had dropped from 92 million in

1989 to 82 million in 1992, aggravating overcapacity and increasing price pressures.[142] LIG closed laboratories and made redundancies in an effort to improve break-even points, while management pitched for business, winning an important supply contract for the 350 Supasnaps retail outlets.[143] Compared with a profit of £6.3 million in 1992, ColourCare ran at an operating loss of £1.1 million in 1993. Turnover fell by £1 million to £72.9 million, at 37 per cent of LIG's total turnover, a fall mitigated somewhat by the Supasnaps contract. But this was not enough to resolve ColourCare's immediate problems, or to reconcile its sudden, negative impact on the group.[144]

D&P was not the only interest to bring the company to its knees, however. LIG also strained under the weight of other debts and obligations at this point in the early 1990s, not least of which was a 4.5 per cent convertible bond about to reach maturity. The bond had been sold in 1987 to finance the purchase of the HATU-ICO condom business in Italy for £50 million.[145] £61.6 million had to be made available to repay the bonds with interest by March 1992, and LIG elected to soften the blow by re-capitalising in what would be the first of several extraordinary rights issues.[146] 'The convertible chickens from corporate Britain's financing boom of the late Eighties', commented the *Times* on 14 January 1991, 'are coming home to roost'. A tense political climate, with war in the Gulf imminent, only made matters worse. LIG made the first announcement of a one-for-four rights issue (or 'rights dump' as the *Times* called it) just as peace talks in Geneva reached a standstill, ruffling the feathers of existing investors and lowering confidence.[147] Although LIG had sufficient banking facilities to meet the bonds redemption, Alan Woltz told shareholders, the issue of 33,283,869 ordinary new shares would allow for the completion of the existing capital investment programme, but would also enable LIG to 'take advantage of attractive acquisition opportunities' made apparent by the economic downturn, and the Gulf War.[148] In other words, the rights issue would allow for the repayment of the bond, plus interest, freeing up existing borrowing arrangements to fund cut-price acquisitions for ColourCare.

By the summer of 1992, however, the slump in photo processing reduced trading profits by 53 per cent. LIG share prices had plummeted, and pre-tax profits fell from £39.3 million to £16.9 million. LIG necessarily began a rapid rationalisation programme. Production of surgeon's gloves was moved to Malaysia at a cost of £13.4 million, and 650 jobs in Chingford and Llanelli, South Wales, were lost. Manufacturing in Anderson,

South Carolina, was also shut down at a cost of £3.7 million, with an additional £4.8 million cost for reorganising these divisions.[149] In the midst of this, the LIG board was also publicly censured by the London Stock Exchange for deliberately leaking a profits warning to analysts, instead of reporting it through official channels. The public flogging rocked confidence even more.[150] As if this wasn't enough, the MMC conducted yet another investigation into the supply of condoms over 1993 (and which was presented to Parliament in May 1994). It was found that one of the company's long-standing trade practices, namely entering into exclusive agreements with customers whereby they agreed only to stock the company's condoms, operated against the public interest.[151] In the final quarter of 1993, LIG's chief executive, Anthony Butterworth, abruptly stepped down, followed by Alan Woltz (who was by now LIG chairman) in December.[152] LIG was clearly in deep trouble. By May 1994, senior management had been entirely replaced under the leadership of Michael Moore as chairman and Nick Hodges as new chief executive, who instigated an emergency strategic review to clean up the mess. The review found that LIG's core strength lay in the thin film barrier technology business: in other words, condoms and gloves.[153] 'If ever there was evidence of the cliché that cobblers should stick to their last', wrote Vincent Lindsay in the *Guardian*, 'LIG is it'.[154]

Getting back to basics was expensive, and called for drastic measures. A rapid sell-off of non-core businesses, such as cough medicines, mostly added to debt in the short term, despite a more conservative accounting system being adopted.[155] Photo processing interests, which were losing money and were not repaying capital investment, were quickly disposed of. But this in itself was also costly, resulting in a loss of £174.9 million, after exceptional charges of £168.3 million.[156] ColourCare, which reputedly held a book value of £30 million, was sold to Nexus Photo, a company founded by ColourCare's former management, for just £1,[157] and Kodak purchased the Boots minilabs for £3.8 million.[158] Meanwhile, LIG's operating profit had crashed from £416 million (in 1993) to £7.5 million, while the share price plunged and left a deficit in shareholder's funds of £10.5 million.[159] By June 1994, and after British closures (including Chingford) had been announced, two extraordinary meetings had been held to approve the sale of photo processing; an increase in share capital; a new one-for-one rights issue; and the reduction of the share premium account of the company.[160] This was the beginning of Nick Hodge's plan for recovery.[161]

July 1994: The Fall of Chingford

In City circles, it had been evident 'to the world and his dog' that the 'disastrous diversification into photo processing' had tipped the scales and put LIG into the red.[162] The loss-making Royal Worcester Spode had also played its part, as had the 1980s corporate financing boom, during which LIG took on borrowing and accrued debt. The threat of AIDS, which changed the condom's fortunes after the pill had taken over as the most widely used contraceptive method, 'should have been a bonanza', *Guardian* journalist Vincent Lindsay wrote. But it 'turned out to be a nightmare [for LIG], all because Woltz was too free with the cheque book'.[163] In terms of its reputation and uptake, the condom had made an astonishing recovery since the 1970s. The image of condoms in the public consciousness had been virtually normalised as 'just another healthcare product', which was greatly assisted by the partial relaxation of advertising restrictions.[164] Its role in protection (for prophylaxis as well as pregnancy protection) was beyond dispute, and there was an extensive world trade in condoms (LIG being the biggest manufacturer), particularly in the form of aid to Global South countries.[165] Disposable gloves also experienced unprecedented growth from the 1980s onward, because of the protection they offered to medics dealing with communicable disease, including AIDS.[166] But the overall contribution of condoms and gloves to group fortunes had been systematically diminished by the deliberate and aggressive growth of uncomplementary business areas in the 1980s and 1990s, including ColourCare.

Of course, City commentators were in a position to trace LIG's troubles back to bad investments. But for staff on the shop floor at Chingford, the shutdown of their factory on Friday 29 July 1994 was distressing and difficult to comprehend.[167] After all, this was the part of the business that was doing well: at the time, LIG's branded condoms held 22 per cent of a world market that was, after the AIDS-related surge in demand, growing at a steady rate of 2–3 per cent per year.[168] The NHS was also a regular purchaser of (discounted) condoms, accounting for over 20 per cent of all sales at home.[169] Having moved most glove production abroad by 1992, LIG Chingford was almost exclusively concerned with condom production, as it had been since the war.[170] Following the AIDS crisis, and the increased public discussion of condoms (which included, for example, now-commonplace television advertising and direct marketing to teenagers and gay men), workers were 'stunned' when the closure was announced because, from their perspective, Durex was a tremendous success.[171] According to local press reports, the general reaction was 'Why us?' underpinned by resentment at what many perceived as evident corporate greed in a period of economic recession, especially the Transport and General Workers Union's 287-strong membership. These workers had reportedly accepted a below-average pay rise of 2 per cent in return for job security,[172] following earlier culls of the workforce (above). 'It has nothing to do with the workers because we have produced what the company wants', shop floor convenor Lil Carter told the *Chingford Guardian*. 'Some departments have been operating on Saturdays and Sundays. Basically they are going for cheap labour abroad. There has been no investment in the factory here for years'.[173]

Carter may not have been privy to what went on in the LIG board-room, but she was astute in her observation that the Chingford factory and its heavily unionised labour force had become a liability. Landau's 1950s AP machines, which were still in use some forty years later, had only received modest capital investment under Alan Woltz, in order to avoid fully replacing them. In 1988, three additional APs had been added to production in anticipation of increased demand because of the AIDS crisis, but this happened just as the market was flooded by global overcapacity in 1987–88.[174] By 1994, the Chingford operation was tired and old, 'beyond redemption', and 'something of a relic'.[175] Electronic condom testing at Chingford still required hand-mounting onto probes, a process that hadn't changed since it was introduced in 1953 and was seen to embody the overall tiredness of the plant and its processes.[176] As well as being costly in itself (at least £8.9 million by LIG estimates),[177] upgrading the Chingford plant would have likely meant temporarily diverting a share of its production to other factories in the global LIG family. Upgrading would also incur 140 redundancies at a cost of £2 million.[178] Even with a saving of approximately £1.8 million per year that such a programme might achieve, the return would be too low to make a full renovation viable. LIG had explained this to MMC investigators. Over ten years, LIG said, an upgrade as outlined above would achieve an internal rate of return of 9 per cent at then-current price levels, but would only receive internal approval if it were forecast to bring in 30 per cent. For this to be achieved, the retail price of condoms would need to be increased by 17 per cent, which was impossible, if only because of repeated sanctions from the MMC.[179] Plans were also afoot to widen the North Circular Road, the twenty-five-mile motorway circling central London and which ran directly past the Chingford factory. The road had been turned into a three-lane dual carriageway in 1973, bringing London Rubber's plant closer to contaminants generated by vehicle traffic.[180] A further widening of this road, which LIG objected to at the public inquiry, would have had a detrimental affect on product quality by greatly increasing the potential for debris to contaminate liquid latex.[181] Moving the factory further back on the same site would have been impossible because of the Banbury Reservoir to the rear (an Edwardian structure in use by the Thames Water company), and heavy development in the adjacent areas.

If LIG were to keep jobs in Chingford, a new site would be needed and the entire factory would have to be relocated, as well as upgraded. Given LIG group's desperate situation, and the cold reality that alternative production would have to take over from Chingford one way or the other, Nick Hodges bit the bullet and shut Chingford down along with other British operations. In addition to 600 redundancies in Chingford, the 240 remaining workers at the Llanelli glove-packing factory were fired, and sixty workers were left jobless in Dundee as the cough mixture brands were sold off. This left LIG with a small administrative staff at Head Office in Chingford, some R&D personnel in Cambridge,[182] and closure costs of £19 million.[183] Job cuts in Britain were followed by 1,000 abroad, reducing the global workforce to 5,000, a quarter of its former glory.[184] Hodges, who had joined the company as sales director of LRC Products in 1982 and himself managed Chingford between 1987 and 1991, told the *Chingford Guardian*, 'This has been the most painful decision of my career. I ran LRC for four years and closing it is very much a wrench'.[185] The shutdown came quickly: plant was dismantled and shipped abroad, and production moved to Spain, Italy, and Thailand, which was closer to the source of natural latex, and where a new state-of-the-art factory was already under construction as part of a joint venture.[186] Although the official closing day was 29 July, most of the workforce left the week before, having little to do. 'We ran out of work', Lil Carter said. 'The machines were gone and we were just scraping around for something to do. So we just picked up our pay cheques and went home'.[187]

After Chingford: Durex Lives On

The first phase of Hodge's recovery programme effectively decimated LIG's net assets through sell-offs, closures, and the payment of debts, refinancing the company through the sale of shares. The next stage was to reconstitute LIG as a 'leaner and fitter' company with a global command of its core products, attacking costs and improving productivity.[188] LIG was redesigned as the worldwide leader in personal protection products using thin film barrier technology.[189] The survival of the Durex brand was integral to this plan, as LIG strove to make it the first global condom brand. This process had already begun some years earlier by attaching the Durex name to the American brands Ramses and Sheik. Going forward, LIG's mission was to make clear the Durex parentage of its other international brands by adding the 'Durex Seal of Quality' to packaging. Central to the globalisation of Durex was the creation of a global supply chain structure through investment and acquisition, allowing LIG to supply condoms to any market, from any factory.[190] In 1995, the new condom factory in Bangpakong, Thailand, was completed.[191] To this was added two refurbished and upgraded factories in India, the Mister condom business in Malaysia, Androtex in Spain, the Aladan glove and condom manufactory in America, and Dua Lima in Indonesia over 1995–97.[192] LIG was positioned to develop operations in the fast-growing economies of Taiwan, Vietnam, and Indonesia, where it saw a growing market for its products. The introduction of square packaging in 1995 (which replaced lozenge-shaped metal foils) moved global Durex brands towards uniformity and economies of scale, while Durex Avanti, the first non-latex polyurethane condom produced in conjunction with Okamoto Industries, Japan, marked LIG's ongoing commitment to R&D.[193]

Increased investment in Durex had a tangible effect on LIG's performance in the years following refinancing and the closure of Chingford. Sales of family planning products rose by 15.2 per cent over 1995–96,[194] and 7.2 per cent over 1996–97, by which time Durex was sold in over 130 countries and was the leader in over forty markets. The globalization of condom markets was also indicated by the substitution of the old British Standard 3704 with a new European Standard, EN600 1996 (later to become an international standard, ISO4047, in 2002). A multi-million pound global marketing and sponsorship contract with MTV (for the youth market), sponsorship of the 11th Annual AIDS Conference in Vancouver, and the annual Durex Global Survey all 'successfully emphasised the exciting and modern profile of Durex'.[195] In 1996, the brand also laid claim to an ultra-modern first: being the first condom with a presence on the World Wide Web, at durex.com.[196] By the close of the 1990s, LIG had consolidated its condom manufacture to Virudhungar and Pallavaram, India; Rubi, Spain; Bangpakong, Thailand; and Qingdao, China. Small-scale R&D production was still carried out in Cambridge, England.

Although LIG had managed to stay afloat following the events of 1994, it ran into difficulties again at the cusp of the millennium. The Italian factory in Bologna was closed because of overcapacity, and American sales suffered following the launch of Durex in the US in 1998. Back in the 1960s, London Rubber had secured its place in the American market through the acquisition of Julius Schmid. By the 1990s, LIG felt the time had come to phase out the existing Schmid brands to make room for Durex, but American consumers did not respond well to having their trusted brands replaced. This led to a sudden slump in sales, forcing LIG to pull out of the American consumer market. In Germany, reconfiguration of pack sizes to accommodate the new, uniformly square condom foil resulted in lost merchandising space (because packets were now bigger and fewer could be placed on the shelf) and an overall reduction in sales. Italian sales decreased also, just as the Bologna factory was shut down. Added to this, sales of medical examination gloves suffered in America following an influx of low-cost gloves from Asia; the collapse of Asian currencies further depressed prices. This left all manufacturers of medical examination gloves with significant overcapacity, leading to fierce price competition, and LIG closed its glove and condom factories in Dothan, Alabama.[197]

Although the Durex brand remained strong outside of the US, LIG's overall recovery was severely hampered. On 24 May 1999, the board of LIG announced that it had agreed to the terms of a merger with Seton Scholl Healthcare PLC, manufacturer of Dr Scholl's foot care products.[198] A new healthcare company, SSL International Plc., was formed in June of that year, after which Nick Hodges, Michael Moore, and the rest of the board resigned.[199] LIG was re-registered as a private company in April 2001, and became a holding company under SSL International, which would continue the Durex brand until SSL was itself purchased by Reckitt Benckiser in 2010.[200] The principal activity of LIG, as it currently exists, is to act as an intermediary holding company for Reckitt Benckiser, which now produces condoms under the Durex brand but is otherwise unconnected to the London Rubber Company and its historic activities. LIG no longer makes money. Durex, which, for all intents and purposes, left Britain in 1994 and took condom manufacturing with it after fifty-five years, remains the best-selling condom in Britain, and (its current makers claim) the most popular brand in the world.[201] As for the Family Planning Association, which continued to exist as an information and advocacy group after its clinics were absorbed into the NHS in the 1970s, the difficulty in attracting income did not improve. It was liquidated on 15 May 2019.[202]

Conclusion

The story of the modern, disposable condom in Britain is really the story of the London Rubber Company and its advantage as a 'first mover', which is to say its status as a near-monopoly producer, and its mission to stamp out, exploit, or otherwise control competition, both within the contraceptives industry and beyond.[1] It is also the story of an image programme, run over many decades, which ostensibly sought to gain public acceptance for the condom but was also subject to the often-conflicting emotions of consumers, restrictions from advertising vendors and retailers, and the unspoken benefits of stigmatisation for deflecting market competition. This book has attempted to set condoms within the many-shaded, complex, and fluid environment that London Rubber negotiated during its first fifty years of operation. It has also summarised events over the following decades, up to 2001, describing the intersecting twists and turns that kept the Durex brand alive through times of adversity. As has been shown, the success and availability of the condom has been affected by changing sexual and social mores and by technological innovation, but also by the professionalization of pharmacy and public relations, by advertising, by HIV and AIDS, and even by such disparate forces as the Gulf War, photographic processing, and English pottery. But what does all this tell us about the supply of contraceptives in modern Britain? And what significance does it have for the reproductive and sexual freedoms that so many of us enjoy today?

One important finding of this study is that the birth control industry was, in many ways, as responsive and reactive as it was complex, a pattern that is borne out in the ongoing search for the perfect contraceptive, indicating that strong continuities have run concurrently with (what are widely understood to be) watershed moments in birth control history, such as the disruptively innovative birth control pill. The case of London Rubber shows us that there is ultimately no 'magic bullet' in contraception (or prophylaxis for that matter), no single product type that will fulfil a universal criterion, and no foolproof means of persuading people into patterns of use.

It also suggests that that top-down models of power, which are so often invoked in reproductive politics, have limited application – at least in this particular story. It is true that the London Rubber Company operated at a near-monopoly through virtually all of its existence. This is partly attributable to its size, its aggression, and its ruthless crusade to squash competition wherever it appeared, but monopolistic conditions existed because of an interconnecting set of conditions and coincidences. Perhaps it was providence that plucked Lucian Landau from the family soap business in Warsaw and placed him on a rubber technology course at the North London Polytechnic, just as Pirelli mailed over samples of liquid latex. But it was a combination of business acumen, marketing savvy, new media opportunity, regulatory development, commercial openings, hostility, and the very particular social and cultural conditions of the time that allowed London Rubber to blossom over the coming decades. Some conditions of the monopolistic landscape arose because of forces beyond the company's control (such as the Second World War), and some came about by design (such as the practice of substituting competitors' brands), but a policy of responsive action was one of London Rubber's great strengths. It was also the company's folly.

While it is tempting to see large, successful, monopolistic companies as exercising complete expertise over their markets and customers, the case of London Rubber shows us that even the powerful rely on trial and error, act on misinformation, make bad judgements, and can be risk-happy or risk-averse depending on the climate, often displaying behaviours that might be considered counterintuitive. London Rubber's strategic response to crisis and future planning was pragmatic and changeable in the first fifty years, then prescriptive and less flexible in the decades up to 2001. Its business practices, which were sometimes shady and sometimes benefitted from sleaze and stigmatisation, often appeared to run contrary to common sense. In the 1930s, the company supported the proposed Contraceptives (Regulation) Bill with the aim of restricting distribution to professionalised chemists and debarring automatic vending. In the 1940s, it moved into less profitable rubber gloves and balloons (the former venture becoming successful and holding its own during the AIDS crisis). In the 1950s it supported the FPA, an organisation as committed to female methods of birth control as it was opposed to selling contraceptives for profit. In the 1960s, London Rubber got into bed with the enemy by producing and actively marketing its own oral contraceptive pill, even as it waged a multifaceted underground public relations campaign to undermine the pill in the public sphere. Precautionary diversification of its business areas in the 1960s carried London Rubber through tough times in the 1970s, set the pattern for the 1980s, and almost undid it in the 1990s. Courtship of healthcare providers resulted in resistance and rebellion at the same time as it created a dependency – for London Rubber, this meant an uneasy relationship with the FPA in the 1950s and 1960s, and three investigations by the MMC in the 1970s, 1980s, and 1990s (which were supported by the FPA and the Department of Health) as condoms became considered a health necessity for everyday life, which thus needed to be less expensive. In the case of London Rubber, the long-sought-after official endorsement of condoms (by social activists and medical professionals as an alternative to consumer advertising) turned out to mean more social responsibility, constant pressure on prices, and watchful surveillance by the very authorities it had previously sought to win over. Be careful what you wish for.

The *longue durée* picture further shows us that, far from being a social engineer intending to change British sexual habits, London Rubber preferred to toe the mainstream line in order to gain much-coveted access to publicity. The expansion of the British contraceptive market was a desirable outcome, but completely overhauling social attitudes was not. In her study on margarine, another difficult-to-sell product with negative cultural connotations in the post-war period, Jane Hand has shown how Unilever completely transformed margarine 'from a product perceived inferior to butter to a product with health benefits at complete odds with butter'.[2] London Rubber similarly sought to reverse the popular perception of condoms, casting them as the antithesis of extramarital sex by repeated association with married family life, reinforcing (rather than challenging) the sexual norms of the day. In his 1997 paper on Durex condom advertising, Paul Jobling observed that London Rubber 'tended to harp on normative stereotypes', recognising 'neither the fluid sexual politics of the period nor the multicultural nature of British society'.[3] That much was evident through London Rubber's public communications, and, as this book has also shown, it reflected a long-standing strategy to avoid 'rocking the boat' on sexual matters. However, this was only one approach among many, and the company continued to benefit from the extramarital trade on the quiet until such a time that the casual, unmarried user actually became the target consumer because of extrinsic forces, including, for example, the gradual acceptance of cohabitation and the provision of birth control supplies and advice to unmarried women. In the first fifty years, however, London Rubber was passive about the problem of social stigma, even though (as EDA's research had suggested) pushing the envelope in the 1960s may have led to greater acceptance of condoms and condom advertising in later decades. In the end, it was brand competition in the 1970s (opened up by relaxed rules on retail display and print advertising) and the AIDS public health emergency in the 1980s (which forced recognition of non-normative users and opened the market to new brands) that pushed London Rubber into challenging the status quo. For many years, the company had refused to acknowledge the casual user, or the potential use of condoms for medical prophylaxis against sexually transmitted infections (STIs). At the same time, in the first half of the twentieth century at least, it comfortably reaped the benefits of the all-male barbershop trade. The putatively seedy side of the business was allowed to coexist with respectable distribution through retail pharmacists and the FPA, and London Rubber continued to wear two hats. These activities were intended to work in the company's favour, either by providing conduits into potential new markets, such as the middle-class married woman, or by keeping the condom business impenetrable to competitors. In the 1980s, London Rubber was forced to take a position on self-protection against disease and non-normative sexual practice, because society demanded it. But by this time a culture of finance and speculation, combined with a drop in sales fuelled by free contraceptive pills from the NHS in the previous decade, gradually shrunk the condom's role in keeping the company afloat. In the end, London Rubber came full circle, not only returning to the specialised business of making condoms, but also reconciling itself to the historic primary function of penis barriers that predated its own existence, namely, the prevention of transmission of disease. The Chingford factory was sacrificed in order that the Durex brand might go on.

So what difference does it actually make to know how the modern latex condom came to be? And does it actually matter? I would argue that having the long view casts a critical perspective on the material reality of personal protection, behoving us as a society to remember the complexity involved in supplying that which we simply take for granted. At the time of writing, supermarket shelves the world over are being cleared out of toilet paper in a wave of panic buying amid the COVID-19 coronavirus pandemic, despite manufacturers holding plentiful stocks (in Britain, at least). Because of the supermarket's system of 'just in time' replenishment, shelves cannot be refilled fast enough to meet extreme demand, which shoppers read as scarcity. Hand sanitizer has become impossible to get hold of and hospitals and care homes are reporting the theft of their supplies every day. We ask ourselves: is the collective consumer psyche fundamentally so volatile? What do we really require to meet our needs, to keep ourselves and our loved ones safe? We might equally ask: how do material necessities get to the supermarket (or hospital) shelves in the first place, and what factors might impede this process? Back in 1987, a world rush on condoms actually led to over-supply, seriously affecting the ability of London Rubber and other manufacturers to level out production: longer term, the knock-on effects prompted some very bad business decisions. As we have learned, condoms and toilet paper are historically 'unmentionable' products, but in times of mass panic, crowds reach out for the basic, 'functional' items that make them feel in control of their bodies.[4] What is more, they expect those items to be readily available. Recalling the complicated and sometimes surprising technological and cultural journey of the condom might help us to better appreciate the basic protective function it performs, and how much we value our ability to self-protect, and also self-fulfil, at the moment of our choosing.

Today, in most developed countries, reproductive freedom is upheld and defended. The World Health Organization's primary mandate, which is to provide assistance to its members in achieving the highest attainable standard of health for all, is underpinned by a commitment to universal sexual and reproductive health.[5] In 2012, the United Nations declared access to family planning a human right.[6] International standards dictate minimum levels of quality and safety to which condoms must conform, wherever in the world they are produced and consumed.[7] However, this was not always the case, and while socially motivated contraceptive providers of the twentieth century had high ideals, for-profit industry laid much of the groundwork for the delivery of today's reproductive freedoms. The British Family Planning Association, which was recently liquidated after running into financial difficulty, is a case in point: the money always has to come from somewhere. Right now, value sales of condoms are decreasing in Britain as consumers move away from using them for personal protection against pregnancy or disease.[8] The use of pre-exposure prophylaxis or 'PrEP', which is to say an antiretroviral medicine to prevent acquisition of HIV, has become very popular. And for many sexually active people today, HIV and AIDS is thought of less as a present danger and more as a moment in history, as something from the past. Consequently, the market research firm Mintel tells us, the 'scare factor' attatched to STIs – a known motivator for condom use – has declined.[9] Public Health England recommends combining PrEP and condoms for protecting against HIV and other STIs, such as chlamydia, gonorrhoea, and syphilis.[10] And according to the *Sunday Times* of 15 March 2020, the

NHS has announced that it intends to supply PrEP as part of essential healthcare services. In the meantime, the number of condoms used for prophylactic purposes is dropping, despite continued advances in comfort. In the 1950s diaphragms were sold in increments of 2.5 mm: today, under ISO4047 2015, condoms are produced in different widths to ensure a good fit and therefore safety (which is to say 45–50 mm, 50–6 mm, 56–65 mm, 65–75 mm). Their employment as a contraceptive, though still significant, has nonetheless entered a downturn. Birth control pills have (since the 1960s) competed with condoms for the top spot in contraceptive use, and until very recently condoms had resumed their place as the frontrunner. At the time of writing, however, oral contraceptives have once again become the most widely employed birth control method in Britain. Meanwhile, diagnoses of STIs continue to rise, particularly among the over-sixties. Following on from selling condoms as contraceptives to middle-class marrieds in the 1960s, then cohabiting couples in the 1970s, then pitching them as prophylactics to unmarried youths and gay men in the 1980s and 1990s, today's recommended target market for Durex and other condoms is sexually active seniors.[11] If makers are to continue supplying free condoms for social and health care, and branded products at all price points on the retail market while continuing to turn a profit, then they must continue to be open minded in their marketing. Without the profit incentive, the free supply of condoms would be severely hampered and so would R&D, which is necessary to improve the user experience and, it is hoped, the uptake of condom use. Presently, journalist Mark Hay tells us, 'the condom industry is a minefield of innovation bottlenecks and stumbling blocks'.[12] The present search for a disruptor in condom technology was instigated six years ago with a series of small grants made by the Bill and Melinda Gates Foundation, but has yet to generate something truly groundbreaking. Small-scale innovators are more plentiful than they were in London Rubber's day, but only the biggest companies are in the position to undertake extensive prototyping, development, and testing, and to underwrite risky new products with other investments or alternative forms of income.[13] They also have the expertise in mass production. Some things, then, have not changed: non-profits push for increased acceptance and uptake, while the commercial sector supplies the means. As *Protective Practices* suggests, this relationship has long been symbiotic.

Perhaps this point is especially pertinent in the case of the oral contraceptive pill and women's contraception more widely. This study has demonstrated that, far from being separate entities, male and female contraceptives were very much interconnected in the years leading up to the introduction of the pill, in terms of production and supply. Diaphragms and condoms were not made in the same moulds, but their parentage was the same, and in London Rubber's case, domination of the diaphragm market helped to keep it under control. The company deployed Feminor in the same way. In lieu of any other significant player in the British condom industry, London Rubber would continue to reference oral contraceptives as its main competitor in the 1970s, 1980s, and 1990s.[14] But even the pill had a role in protecting the monopoly by making entry into the traditional contraceptive market all the more formidable.[15] Although the pill was materially unlike the condom, it was also the product of a different industry – pharmaceutical medicine – which was directly linked to its administration scheme and therefore its mode of distribution through prescribing doctors. This imbued the pill with a set of values that stood apart from what the condom represented, lending it to broad and involved discussion in mass media. London Rubber agitated by circulating 'disinterested' information that, though not strictly disinformation, nonetheless used the now-recognisable techniques of 'fake news'.[16] Mass media enthusiasm for the pill as an object of enquiry accelerated the acceptability of contraception, ahead of London Rubber's own efforts, which the company belatedly tried to exploit. 'Disruption', in this sense, came not simply from the physical reality of pill-taking as opposed to condom use, but in the springboarding of the new product into the public imagination.

Pulling back from the British picture, this book has also shown that the home contraceptive industry had more in common with its American counterparts than previously thought. In *Devices and Desires*, Andrea Tone suggests that success in the appliance contraceptive market was an American phenomenon, and that Julius Schmid's 'rags-to-riches ascent' was a uniquely American success story.[17] The original Schmid, née 'Schmidt', was a poor German Jew who worked in a sausage factory in New York before creating a condom empire managed by generations of the same family.[18] Meanwhile, in London, the Russian-Jewish Jacksons, née Jacobys, scratched out a living before hitting the big time with contraceptive wholesaling and ultimately providing jobs for the extended Jackson family. Tone says that when oral contraceptives came along, birth control was 'medicalized',[19] but perhaps it is also the case, in Britain at least, that contraceptive supply and distribution was professionalised, too. In this sense, the 'pharmaceutical turn' in contraception, as we might call it, threatened to take personal protection out of the hands of long-established condom families, who learned business on the job and had been responsible for developing their own markets and technologies. If anything, what we learn from the similarities between the Schmids, the Jacksons, and also Lucian Landau is that early contraceptive businesses were driven not by ideology, but by opportunity – especially in the case of entrepreneurial immigrants building new lives in new lands. Parallels between America and Britain can also be found elsewhere, for example in London Rubber's difficult codependency with the Family Planning Association. Rosemarie Holz's work on the relationship between contraceptive companies and American Planned Parenthood clinics has demonstrated the 'malleable relationship between business and charity, the malleable definition of birth control, and the guerrilla-style flexibility of the form and function of the local birth control clinic'.[20] Holz's work shows that the experience of London Rubber was not unlike that of commercial outfits across the pond, which sought to support the charitable provision of birth control in order that the whole subject might be made more acceptable, thus benefitting the for-profit sector as a whole. As is the case today, off-brand, cut-price, or free contraception is subsidised by the profits of premium consumer lines: without them, and without attractive incentives offered through the supply chain, the WHO and United Nations' ideal of reproductive freedom and sexual health for all would be out of reach.

So far as Britain is concerned, the uniqueness of the London Rubber case lies in its status as the dominant manufacturer and distributor, which saw it holding close to 100 per cent of the market for most of its existence. Whereas the American condom market was split (Julius Schmid and Youngs Rubber being the dominant companies in the first half of the twentieth century), London Rubber experienced specific, extraordinary conditions during the Second World War, which allowed it to become the biggest dipped latex outfit in the country almost overnight. The British case is also unique from the standpoint of everyday contraceptive visibility. The British medical historian Claire L. Jones demonstrates that contraceptives were more noticeable on the British high street than had previously been thought.[21] *Protective Practices* goes some way to unpacking the stratification of the retail market. It has found that changes in retail display regulation permeated the entire trade, forcing London Rubber to take drastic measures to convey the availability of its products to both new and established consumers. More work needs to be done on this idea of visibility, however, if only to investigate how closely contraceptive consumers of the past, looking into bright displays of birth control products and marriage manuals in shop windows, resemble today's average customer, pondering over condoms and sex aids in the aisles of Superdrug or Boots. Is it the case that the attitudes of contraceptive consumers have really progressed so much? Or have they simply returned to what they were a century ago when the contraceptive retail trade was thriving, before it was interrupted by a small but vocal wave of public morality? Perhaps consumers have, like London Rubber, also come full circle. 'It is not the availability of technology that determines patterns of contraceptive use', Andrea Tone observes, 'but the specific contexts in which women and men encounter it'.[22] This was certainly the case in terms of how London Rubber tried to direct the users of diaphragms and oral contraceptives towards alternative methods of contraception by appropriating information channels and borrowing reputational clout from such organisations as the FPA and BSI.

Technology, however, did absolutely underpin London Rubber's success as a company and, perhaps most importantly, the condom's success as a high-margin consumable. As *Protective Practices* has shown, nothing beat the condom for ease of manufacture or profitability once the correct technology was developed and implemented. Like Killian's automatic condom machines in America, Landau's sophisticated Automated Protective lines were protected by patents, and by the size of capital investment needed to get them up and running. Together with the Durex brand name, forever synonymised with 'condom' in the British mindset following the Second World War, Landau's APs constituted the strongest barrier to competition wielded by London Rubber, making it impossible for extant manufacturers to recover after the war, or for smaller companies to get a foothold. Diaphragms were never going to match the return on investment, but London Rubber was able to produce them in many varieties without affecting its main operation. Because of this, the company was able to hold FPA clinics to ransom: in other words, the supply of inexpensive, high-quality diaphragms was directly linked to the efficiency of London Rubber's condom dipping, and to its willing network of distributors, shady or otherwise. The company anticipated change, and tried to reduce its dependency on its core product, firstly in the 1960s when the pill gathered pace, then in the 1980s when other consumer markets looked promising. Ultimately, though, London Rubber ended as they had begun: by sticking to what they did best, and making high quality and technologically advanced condoms for the mass market.

Appendices

TABLE A.1   London Rubber Chingford home production and sales
of condoms by volume (actual and estimated figures) 1935–66.

Source: Family Planning Association Papers, Wellcome Library, London;
Christopher Tietze, *The Condom as a Contraceptive* (New York: National Committee
on Maternal Health, Inc., 1960); B.E. Finch and Hugh Green, *Contraception through
the Ages* (London: Peter Owen, 1963); John Peel, 'The Manufacture and Retailing of
Contraceptives in England,' *Population Studies* 17 (1963); Consumers' Association,
'Contraceptives,' *Which?* Supplement, 15 November 1963; Economist Intelligence
Unit, 'Contraceptive Products,' *Retail Business Survey* 92 (1965); London Rubber
Company papers, Waltham Forest Local Studies Centre, London; Monopolies and
Mergers Commission, *Contraceptive Sheaths* (London: HMSO, 1975).

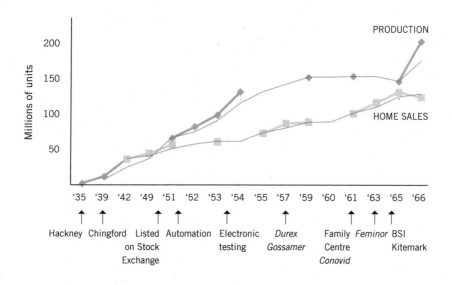

TABLE A.2   London Rubber Group financial health 1955–65.

Source: LRC annual reports and accounts.

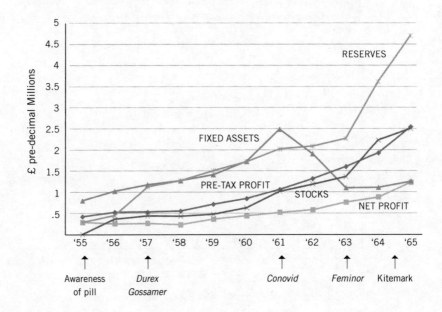

TABLE A.3 Falling distributive margins on three-packs of London Rubber condoms, in shillings and pence, before and after Resale Price Maintenance (1964). Figures in parentheses refer to figures given in MMC report.

Source: Family Planning Association Papers, Wellcome Library, London; Christopher Tietze, *The Condom as a Contraceptive* (New York: National Committee on Maternal Health, Inc., 1960); B.E. Finch and Hugh Green, *Contraception through the Ages* (London: Peter Owen, 1963); John Peel, 'The Manufacture and Retailing of Contraceptives in England,' *Population Studies* 17 (1963); Consumers' Association, 'Contraceptives,' *Which?* Supplement, 15 November 1963; Economist Intelligence Unit, 'Contraceptive Products,' *Retail Business Survey* 92 (1965); London Rubber Company papers, Waltham Forest Local Studies Centre, London; Monopolies and Mergers Commission, *Contraceptive Sheaths* (London: HMSO, 1975).

	Price to retailer/ gross	Pack price to retailer	Suggested retail price	Realised profit £	Realised profit %	LR gross sales revenue*	Distributive Margin (estimated)
pre-1939 No.76 Durex	33/0d	8d.	2/6d	1/10d	72%	No data	≥1/3d
post-RPM No.76 Durex	55/	1/2d	3/	≥ 1/	62%	≥1/	≥2/6
pre-RPM Durex Gossamer	85.	1/9d	3/9	≥ 11d	≥ 53% (57%)	≤1/6d	≥2/
post-RPM Durex Gossamer	85.	1/9d	3/	≥9d	c.44% (53%)	≤1/6d	≥10d

* from which production, quality control, selling costs, and overheads are deducted

Guide to Subsidiaries 1950–65

1950 Elarco Ltd
Latex Industries Ltd
Essex Rubber Industries Ltd
The London Rubber Company (A.G.) Ltd

1952 Lewis Knight and Company Ltd (toy balloons, London)

1955 Lea Bridge Rubber Works (toy and advertising
balloons, London)

1956 Young and Fogg Rubber Company Ltd (toy and
advertising balloons)

1958 Rimbacher Gummiwaren-Fabrik, G.m.b.H.*
(rubber manufacturers, Rimbach bei Odenwald,
Mönchengladbach, Germany)

1959 Broad Street Securities Ltd (investments: for purchase
of B.E. Bird Ltd)
Argent Securities Ltd (investments)
The Scotch Hoose (Cambridge) Ltd (restaurant and
cocktail bar)
Supreme Surgical Hosiery (London) Ltd

1960 London Rubber Company (Nederland) N.V. (Leerdam)
E.W. Edwardson and Company (Ware) Ltd (adhesives
and glues)
Churchill and Williams Ltd (wines and spirits,
Northampton)
B.E. Bird Ltd (wines and spirits, Northampton)
Valentine Charles Ltd (wines and spirits,
Northampton)

* Converted to London Rubber Company G.m.b.H.,1959

1961   J. Allen Rubber Company Ltd (Lydney); London Rubber
Industries (London)
Family Centre Ltd (London)

1962   London Rubber Company A.B. (Stockholm)

1963   London Rubber Company (India) Private Ltd (Pallavaram,
Madras)
Julius Schmid Incorporated (New York)
Julius Schmid of Canada Ltd (Toronto)

1964   London Rubber Company Linz Ges.m.b.H. (Austria)
Autonumis Ltd (machine vending, Tetbury)
Menz Vending Ltd

1965   Marigold Italiana S.p.A. (washing-up gloves, Cuveglio, Milan)
Lewis Gilder and Company Ltd (trade wholesalers of protective
clothing, London)
Veedip Ltd (surgical, household, and industrial gloves, Slough)
Tetbury Automats Ltd (machine vending)

Guide to Primary Sources

At the time of writing, there is no publicly available archive of corporate records relating to the London Rubber Company known to the author. As such, this work has necessarily drawn from dispersed sources, the most important of which are detailed below, with a list of archival collections and interviews at the end of this appendix.

Family Planning Association/Wellcome Collection

This archive has been used to map a temporal framework for *Protective Practices*. The FPA kept good records of its dealings with manufacturers (the 'manufacturers files'), including correspondence, notes of meetings, visits and telephone calls, and, occasionally, samples of literature, print publicity (proofs, drafts, and clippings), and catalogues, as relevant to the conversation at the time. The London Rubber manufacturers files are catalogued under FPA/A7/71-85 (excepting 77, which is currently closed) and cover the period 1934–62. Recently catalogued FPA papers pertaining to the FPA and the Council for the Investigation of Fertility Control, namely C/F/7/1/14-5, pick up where the manufacturers files leave off, covering London Rubber's early interest in the pill and the testing of Feminor over 1959–68. Being central to contraceptive supply in Britain, London Rubber naturally pops up elsewhere in the FPA archive. For cxample, A13/20 is dedicated to FPA correspondence concerning the London Foundation for Marriage Education over 1962–65, and reference to dealings with the company can be found throughout the Executive Committee Minutes. It has not been possible to conduct a complete file-by-file search for London Rubber material as the FPA archive is extensive and is still being catalogued, but readers may consult the notes section of this work for specific instances of files where London Rubber makes isolated appearances as pertinent to the remit of this study.

Wellcome Collection also holds the Robert J. Hetherington papers, an extensive collection relating to the oral contraceptive pill in Britain. This collection includes extensive marketing collateral for oral contraceptives in the UK, as collected by Hetherington (a geriatric specialist from Birmingham) during the 1960s and 1970s. This resource is especially rich in visual material, and presents an excellent overview of the oral contraceptive marketplace in Britain. It also includes extensive clippings from news and print media. In respect of London Rubber, files A4/1-2 contain print marketing and circulars used to sell Feminor (1963–68).

Market Research
Market research reports produced on behalf of London Rubber by Ernest Dichter Associates in 1961, via Crane Advertising, are held within the Ernest Dichter Papers, Hagley Museum and Library, Wilmington, Delaware. The available documents are: *1380a: Proposal for a Psychological Survey on Protective Contraceptives* (the original pitch made to win London Rubber's business); *1380c: A Motivational Research Study on Rubber Contraceptives* (the pilot research study); and *1739e: Some Remarks on the Questions Raised on the Contraceptive Research* (a follow-up to the pilot research, suggesting further work). It would appear from these documents that London Rubber did not pursue motivational research beyond the pilot study, *1380c*. The 1961 market research report produced by The Pulse, London, and which is entirely separate from the EDA work, can be found in the FPA papers at the Wellcome Collection, in FPA/A7/81. In addition, the Economist Intelligence Unit produced special reports on the contraceptive industry via its journal, *Retail Business Survey* (later *Retail Business*), namely, 'Contraceptive Products' (October 1965), 'Contraceptives' (August 1969), and 'The UK Contraceptive Market' (August 1975). Although not wholly concerned with London Rubber per se, these reports are an invaluable resource for understanding the commercial contraceptive trade in mid-twentieth-century Britain, which was, for all intents and purposes, dominated by London Rubber.

Official Documents and Reports
As a public company, London Rubber published annual reports from 1950 onward. These are available at Guildhall Library, London; London Stock Exchange Annual Reports and Accounts: Commercial and Industrial Reports; the Bodleian Library, University of Oxford; and through Companies House. No single repository holds a full run, and reports for the years 1953–55 and 1962 could not be located. Officially filed paperwork including annual reports from 1973 and articles of association can be obtained

through Companies House, under the company number 488344. Unfortunately, degraded reprographics means that reports from the 1970s onwards contain many illegible pages. In these cases, some figures can be corroborated though the financial press. Trademark and patent information can be obtained through the Intellectual Property Office. Between 1975 and 1994, London Rubber was subject to three investigations by the Monopolies and Mergers Commission: *Contraceptive Sheaths. A Report on the Supply of Contraceptive Sheaths in the United Kingdom* (1975); *Contraceptive Sheaths. A Report on the Supply of Contraceptive Sheaths in the United Kingdom* (1982); and *Contraceptive Sheaths. A Report on the UK Supply of Supply of Contraceptive Sheaths* (1994). The reports were published by Her Majesty's Stationary Office.

Personal Testimony
This book has used personal testimony in the shape of verbatim quotes from two former London Rubber staff members, John Harvey and Angela Wagstaff, recorded in conversation with the author over 2016 and 2017. At the time of writing, the Waltham Forest Oral History Workshop is preparing transcripts of interviews with former staff London Rubber staff members, which will be available for research use upon request. I was also greatly helped by personal conversations with Dr Alison Payne. Lucian Landau's autobiography, *Normal, I Suppose: A Rather Strange Story* was published by the Macaw Press, London, in 2001, in an apparently small print run. The British Library's copy was consulted for this book. Landau also detailed some of the technical aspects of his work at London Rubber in a special booklet, *Natural Rubber Latex and Its Applications No. 3: The Manufacture of Dipped Rubber Articles from Latex*, produced for the British Rubber Development Board in 1954.

Company Materials
Copies of London Rubber's internal magazine, *London Image*, for 1964–74, were kindly loaned to the author by Angela Wagstaff. Digital scans of these magazines have been deposited with the Waltham Forest Local Studies Centre, Vestry House Museum, London Borough of Waltham Forest. Vestry House also holds the London Rubber photo albums, a unique and invaluable collection documenting the genesis of the company. A selection of photographs from these albums is reproduced here by the kind permission of Vestry House Museum.

London Rubber produced several educational films in the 1960s. In particular, *According to Plan* (1964) includes a montage showing condom production at Chingford. *According to Plan* has been digitised by Wellcome Collection and can be viewed online at https://wellcomelibrary.org/item/ b2847868x#. Information on London Rubber's brief sponsorship of the Nutrition Department of Queen Elizabeth College, London, can be found in the Queen Elizabeth College Archive, King's College London Archives, including the Liddell Hart Centre for Military Archives, in file QAS GPF3/1.

Select Archival Collections

Admiralty Papers, National Archives, Kew
Author's collection (objects and ephemera)
BBC Written Archives, Caversham
Contraceptive Object Collection, Division of Medical Sciences,
    Smithsonian National Museum of American History, Washington, DC
C.P. Blacker Papers, Wellcome Collection
Ernest Dichter Papers, Hagley Museum and Library, Wilmington,
    Delaware
Ernest Dichter Papers, University of Vienna Library
Eugenics Society Papers, Wellcome Collection
Family Planning Association Papers, Wellcome Collection
Google Patents (online)
Historic Hansard HC and HL Debates (online)
Home Office Files, National Archives, Kew
House of Commons Parliamentary Papers (online)
Institute of Public Relations Papers, History of Advertising Trust,
    Raveningham, Norfolk
JISC Media Hub (online) (decommissioned 1 September 2016)
London Stock Exchange Annual Reports and Accounts: Commercial and
    Industrial Reports, Guildhall Library, London
LRC Photo Albums, Papers and Ephemera, Waltham Forest Local Studies
    Centre
London Image 1964–74. Private collection of Angela Wagstaff
Media Archive for Central England
Medical Research Council Papers, National Archives, Kew
Monopolies and Mergers Commission Papers, National Archives, Kew
National Institutes of Health Library, Bethesda, Maryland
Nuffield Foundation Papers, National Archives, Kew

Percy Skuy Papers, Dittrick Medical Museum, Cleveland
Public Morality Council Archive, London Metropolitan Archive
Queen Elizabeth College Archive, King's College London Archives,
    including the Liddell Hart Centre for Military Archives
Robert J. Hetherington Papers, Wellcome Collection
Roche Historical Museum and Archive, Basel
Syntex Papers, Division of Medical Sciences, Smithsonian Institution
Viscount Dawson of Penn Papers, Wellcome Collection

Conversations and Interviews

John Harvey. In conversation with the author, Chingford, London,
    8 December 2016; 3 November 2017; 13 November 2017 (in the
    presence of Angela Wagstaff).
Lucian Landau. In conversation with Mary Rose Barrington, n.d. (likely
    1990s). DVD transfer, courtesy of the Society for Psychical Research
    and Mary Rose Barrington.
Alison Payne. In conversation with author, 19 May 2014; email
    correspondence July 2016.
Ray Russell-Fell. Interview conducted by Alice Mackay, 20 July 2015,
    Archives of the Waltham Forest Oral History Workshop.
Percy Skuy. Skype conversation with author, 27 August 2014.
Angela Wagstaff. In conversation with author, Chingford, London,
    3 November 2017, 13 November 2017 (in the presence of John Harvey);
    9 June 2017.

EPIGRAPH

Samuel A. Baker, 'Advertising Male Contraceptives', in *The Condom: Increasing Utilization in the United States*, edited by Myron H. Redford (San Francisco, CA: San Francisco Press, 1974), 115.

FOREWORD

1 Jeannette Parisot, *Johnny Come Lately: A Short History of the Condom*, translated and enlarged by Bill McCann, new material and revisions by Geraldine Rudge (London: Journeyman Press, 1987), ix and *passim*.
2 Anna Clark, *Desire: A History of European Sexuality* (New York and Oxford: Routledge, 2008), 6–7.
3 Rachel M. Pierce and Griselda M. Rowntree, 'Birth Control in Britain Part I', *Population Studies* 15, no. 1 (July 1961): 3–31, 'Part II', no. 2 (November 1961), 121–60; Francois Lafitte, 'The Users of Birth Control Clinics', *Population Studies* 16, no. 1 (July 1962): 12–30; John Peel, 'The Manufacture and Retailing of Contraceptives in England', *Population Studies* 17, no. 2 (November 1963): 113–25; C.M. Langford, 'Birth Control Practice in Great Britain: A Review of the Evidence from Cross-Sectional Surveys', *Population Studies* 45 (1991): 49–68.
4 Based on the letters held at the Wellcome Collection: D. Cohen, 'Private Lives in Public Spaces: Marie Stopes, the Mothers' Clinics and the Practice of Contraception', *History Workshop* 35, no. 1 (1993): 95–115; C. Davey, 'Birth Control in Britain during the Inter-War Years: Evidence from the Stopes Correspondence', *Journal of Family History* 13, no. 3 (1988): 329–45; E. Faulkner, '"Powerless to Prevent Him": Attitudes of Married Working-Class Women in the 1920s and the Rise of Sexual Power', *Local Population Studies* 49 (1992): 51–61; L.A. Hall, *Hidden Anxieties: Male Sexuality 1900–1950* (Cambridge: Polity Press, 1991); '"A Deep Debt of Gratitude for Your Heroic Frankness": Marie Stopes, Marriage Advice, and Readers' Reactions', in *La Mediazione Matrimoniale: Il terzo (in)comodo in Europa fra Otto e Novecento*, edited by Bruno Wanrooij (Rome: Edizioni di Storia e Letteratura, 2004), 323–36; R. Hall, *'Dear Dr Stopes': Sex in the 1920s* (London: Deutsch, 1978); E. Holtzmann, 'The Pursuit of Married Love: Women's Attitudes towards Sexuality and Marriage in Great Britain, 1918–1939', *Journal of Social History* 16, no. 2 (1982): 39–52; G. Jones, 'Marie Stopes in Ireland: The Mothers' Clinic in Belfast', *Social History of Medicine* 5, no. 2 (1992): 255–77; P. Neushul, 'Marie C. Stopes and

the Popularization of Birth Control Technology', *Technology and Culture* 39, no. 2 (1998): 245–72.

5 Kate Fisher, *Birth Control, Sex, and Marriage in Britain 1918–1960* (Oxford: Oxford University Press, 2006); Simon Szreter, *Fertility, Class and Gender in Britain 1860–1940* (Cambridge: Cambridge University Press, 1996); Simon Szreter and Kate Fisher, *Sex before the Sexual Revolution: Intimate Life in England 1918–1963* (Cambridge: Cambridge University Press, 2010).

6 Claire L. Jones, 'Under the Covers? Commerce, Contraceptives and Consumers in England and Wales, 1880–1960', *Social History of Medicine* 29, no. 4 (2015): 734–56.

7 Foundational works on this topic include: Norman Himes, *Medical History of Contraception* (Baltimore: The Williams and Wilkins Company, 1936); J.A. and Olive Banks, *Feminism and Family Planning in Victorian Britain* (Liverpool: Liverpool University Press, 1964); Peter Fryer, *The Birth Controllers* (London: Secker and Warburg, 1965); Angus McLaren, *Birth Control in Nineteenth Century England* (London: Croom Helm, 1978); Richard A. Soloway, *Birth Control and the Population Question in England, 1877–1930* (Chapel Hill, NC: University of North Carolina Press, 1982).

8 William Hudson, *Greevz Fisher of Youghal & Leeds: From Quaker to Individualist and Freethinker* (Austin, TX: William Husdon, 2013); Frank Poller, *Holmes of Hannay* (East Hannay, Oxfordshire: Hannay History Group, 1993); Home Office files, 'Indecent Literature: Pseudo-medical Pamphlets', HO144/238 A52538-9, National Archives, Kew.

9 Fryer, *The Birth Controllers*, 123–31.

10 Muriel Box, ed., *The Trial of Marie Stopes* (London: Femina, 1967), 364.

11 Doris H. Linder, *Crusader for Sex Education: Elise Ottesen-Jensen (1886–1973) in Scandinavia and on the International Scene* (Lanhan, NY and London: University Press of America, 1996), 112–13.

12 'Voluntary Parenthood Society (John Strachey), 1928', Eugenics Society papers, SA.EUG.D.202-203, Wellcome Collection.

13 'W.J. Rendell, 1948–1964', Family Planning Association Papers, FPA/A7/106-107, Wellcome Collection; see also Natasha Szuhan, 'Sex in the Laboratory: The Family Planning Association and Contraceptive Science in Britain, 1929–1959', *The British Journal for the History of Science* 51, no. 3 (2018): 487–510.

INTRODUCTION

1 Alexander Wilson and Christopher West, 'The Marketing of "Unmentionables"', *Harvard Business Review* 59, no. 1 (1981): 91–102.

2 Alfred D. Chandler, *Shaping the Industrial Century: The Remarkable Story of the Evolution of the Modern Chemical and Pharmaceutical Industries* (Cambridge, MA and London: Harvard University Press, 2005), 7–8.

3 Clayton M. Christensen, *The Innovator's Dilemma: When New Technologies Cause Great Firms to Fail* (Brighton, MA: Harvard Business Review Press, 2013).

4 For a discussion of Durex condoms and 'safe sex', see Ben Mechen, '"Closer Together": Durex Condoms and Contraceptive Consumerism in 1970s Britain', in *Perceptions of Pregnancy from the Seventeenth to the Twentieth Century*, edited by Jennifer Evans and Ciara Meehan, 213–36.

5 David Barlow, 'The Condom and Gonorrhoea', *Lancet* 310, no. 8042 (1977): 811.

6 Paul Jobling, 'Playing Safe: The Politics of Pleasure and Gender in the Promotion of Condoms in Britain, 1970–1982', *Journal of Design History* 10, no. 1 (1997): 68.

7 Andrea Tone, *Devices and Desires: A History of Contraceptives in America* (New York: Hill and Wang, 2002), 106–7.

8 Text from the VD act is reproduced from Alexander Wilson, *Advertising and the Community* (Manchester: Manchester University Press, 1968), 217 (appendix A).

9 The correlation between contraception, contraceptive information, and fertility rates is much debated, and is notoriously difficult to assess because of the many variables affecting it (such as abortion practice, infant mortality, patterns of labour change, war, disease, etc.). Conclusive evidence supporting links between contraceptive availability and fertility decline is limited. Hera Cook gives an explanation of fertility rates and a useful summary of the surrounding debate in *The Long Sexual Revolution: English Women, Sex and Contraception 1800–1975* (Oxford: Oxford University Press, 2004), 14–19.

10 Janet Roebuck, *The Making of Modern English Society from 1850* (London: Routledge and Kegan Paul, 1973), 132; John Peel, 'The Hull Family Survey', *Journal of Biosocial Science* 2, no. 1 (1970): 59.

11 Tone, *Devices and Desires*, 239.

12 Pierce and Rowntree, 'Birth Control in Britain Part I', and 'Part II'; Fisher, *Birth Control, Sex and Marriage*.

13 Roebuck, *Modern English Society*, 132; A.M. Carr-Saunders et al., *A Survey of Social Conditions in England and Wales as Illustrated by Statistics* (Oxford: Oxford University Press, 1958), 28–9; Pierce and Rowntree, 'Birth Control in Britain Part I'; Cook, *Sexual Revolution*, 14–19.

14 David Kynaston, *Family Britain, 1951–1957* (London: Bloomsbury, 2010).

15 'Annual Number of Births and Deaths, England and Wales, 1915–2014', *Trends in Births and Deaths over the Last Century*, Office for National Statistics, accessed 13 November 2019, https://www.ons.gov.uk/peoplepopulationand community/birthsdeathsandmarriages/livebirths/articles/trendsinbirthsand deathsoverthelastcentury/2015-07-15; 'Marriage Rates in the UK', Datablog, *The Guardian*, accessed 12 November 2019, https://www.theguardian.com/ news/datablog/2010/feb/11/marriage-rates-uk-data.

16 Pierce and Rowntree, 'Birth Control in Britain Part I', and 'Part II'.

17 Michael Murphy, 'The Contraceptive Pill and Women's Employment as Factors in Fertility Change in Britain 1963–1980: A Challenge to the Conventional View', *Population Studies* 47, no. 2 (1993): 223.

18 Bill Bayliss, 'The London Rubber Co.', received 28 August 2014, Lost Wal-
    thamstow Trades, Walthamstow Memories, accessed 12 November 2019,
    http://www.walthamstowmemories.net/html/losttrades.html; Leonard Davis
    'The London Rubber Co.', Chingford Notes Extras (London: Chingford Histor-
    ical Society, 1998).

19 Peel, 'Manufacture and Retailing'.

20 Jones, 'Under the Covers?'; Mechen, '"Closer Together"'; Jobling, 'Playing
    Safe'.

21 Jobling, 'Playing Safe'.

22 Mechen, '"Closer Together"'. See also Mechen's forthcoming book, *Responsible
    Pleasures: Liberalism and the Sexual Revolution* (Berkeley: University of Califor-
    nia Press).

23 Jones, 'Under the Covers?' 737.

24 Ibid., 738.

25 For example, Cook, *Sexual Revolution*; Fisher, *Birth Control, Sex and Marriage*.

26 In addition to Jones's ongoing work, several histories of contraception have
    sections that incorporate the production and/or sale of condoms. For example,
    B.E. Finch and Hugh Green present a chapter on the historical condom taken
    largely from Himes, but also provide an account of discoveries made by E.J.
    Dingwall (on British skin condoms) and also E. Lennard Bernstein (on the ety-
    mology of 'condom') in the 1950s and 1960s. Finch and Green do give a brief
    account of twentieth-century condom production, which comes from the Lon-
    don Rubber Company; Angus McLaren appraises the condom in terms of the
    medical establishment's response to the gamut of commercially retailed con-
    ception control in *Nineteenth Century*.

27 Aine Collier, *The Humble Little Condom* (Amherst, NY: Prometheus, 2007);
    Parisot, *Johnny Come Lately*.

28 Claire L. Jones, *The Business of Birth Control: Contraception and Commerce in
    Britain before the Sexual Revolution* (Manchester: Manchester University Press,
    2020).

29 Rose Holz, *The Birth Control Clinic in a Marketplace World* (Rochester, NY and
    Woodbridge, Suffolk: University of Rochester Press and Boydell and Brewer,
    2012).

30 Himes, *Medical History*, chapter 8, 'History of the Condom or Sheath', 186–206;
    For a more up-to-date history of contraception, see Donna J. Drucker, *Contra-
    ception: A Concise History* (Cambridge, MA: Massachusetts Institute of Technol-
    ogy Press, 2020).

31 Tone, *Devices and Desires*, 183–202. Tone also made the case for the significance
    of business in 'Making Room for Rubbers: Gender, Technology, and Birth
    Control Before the Pill', *History and Technology* 18, no. 1 (2002): 51–76. Joshua
    Gamson has mapped the conflicting public face of condoms in 'Rubber Wars:
    Struggles over the Condom in the United States', *Journal of the History of Sexual-
    ity* 1, no. 2 (1990): 262–82.

32 Wilson and West, '"Unmentionables"', 93.

33 Ibid.

34 Holz, *The Birth Control Clinic in a Marketplace World*, 146.

35 For example, see Rickie Solinger, *Pregnancy and Power: A Short History of Reproductive Politics in America* (New York: New York University Press, 2005).

36 Jeffrey Weeks, *Sexuality* (New York: Routledge 2010 [1986]), 38.

37 Jobling, 'Playing Safe', 61–2.

38 Ibid.

39 Tone, 'From Naughty Goods to Nicole Miller: Medicine and the Marketing of American Contraceptives', *Culture, Medicine and Psychiatry* 30, no. 2 (2006): 252–4, 257.

CHAPTER 1

1 Percy Skuy, *Tales of Contraception* (Cleveland, OH: Dittrick Medical Museum, 1995), presents illustrated examples of historic and unusual penis coverings from around the world in conjunction with examples from the comprehensive contraceptive object holdings from the historical contraceptive collections at the Dittrick Medical Museum in Cleveland, Ohio.

2 Himes, *Medical History*, 86; Finch and Green, *Contraception through the Ages* (London: Peter Owen, 1963), 46–7; McLaren, *Nineteenth Century*, 21; Jeffrey Weeks, *Sex, Politics, and Society* (London and New York: Longman, 1989), 46.

3 Himes, *Medical History*, 188.

4 Milton Lewis, 'A Brief History of Condoms', in *Condoms*, edited by Adrian Mindel (London: BMJ Books, 2000), 2.

5 Ibid., 3.

6 Beryl Suitters, *The History of Contraceptives*. Prepared for the Medical Committee by Beryl Suitters, Librarian, International Planned Parenthood Federation (London: International Planned Parenthood Federation, 1967), 18.

7 Finch and Green, *Through the Ages*, 50; Himes, *Medical History*, 190.

8 Himes, *Medical History*, 87.

9 Ibid., 199.

10 Finch and Green, *Through the Ages*, 50, 197–200.

11 Eric Dingwall, 'Early Contraceptive Sheaths', *British Medical Journal* 3, no. 4800 (1953): 40–1. For a live-action demonstration of skin condoms being made, see iO9, 'We Made Old-Fashioned Condoms from Scratch, and They Were Gross', YouTube, accessed 13 November 2019, https://www.youtube.com/watch?v=_R39Ehpbrdg.

12 Finch and Green, *Through the Ages*, 51; Peter Fryer, *The Birth Controllers* (London: Corgi, 1967), 30–1.

13 James S. Murphy, *The Condom Industry in the United States* (Jefferson and London: McFarland, 1990), 10.

14 Lewis, 'A Brief History of Condoms', 7; Peel, 'Manufacture and Retailing', 117.

15 McLaren, *A History of Contraception: From Antiquity to the Present Day* (London: Blackwell, 1992), 184; Tone, 'Black Market Birth Control: Contraceptive Entrepreneurship and Criminality in the Gilded Age', *The Journal of American History* 87, no. 2 (2000): 439–40.

16 Greg Grandin, *Fordlandia: The Rise and Fall of Henry Ford's Forgotten Jungle City* (London: Icon, 2010), 26.

17 Peel, 'Manufacture and Retailing', 117.

18 Cecil Voge, *The Chemistry and Physics of Contraceptives* (London: Jonathan Cape, 1933), 206; Vern L. Bullough, 'A Brief Note on Rubber Technology and Contraception: The Diaphragm and Condom', *Technology and Culture* 22, no. 1 (1981): 108; Peel, 'Manufacture and Retailing', 117: Tone, *Devices and Desires*, 61–2.

19 Tone, *Devices and Desires*, 61–2.

20 Monopolies and Mergers Commission, *Contraceptive Sheaths* (London: HMSO, 1975) [henceforth MMC 1975], 11; Peel, 'Manufacture and Retailing', 117.

21 Lesley Hall, 'The Condom Page', accessed 12 November 2019, http://www.lesleyahall.net/jgreevzf.htg/jgreevzf.gif.

22 Jones, 'Under the Covers?' 738.

23 McLaren, *Nineteenth Century*, 225.

24 Jones, 'Under the Covers?' 738; Peel, 'Manufacturing and Retailing', 119.

25 Himes, *Medical History*, 187.

26 Ibid., 202.

27 Peel, 'Manufacturing and Retailing', 117; Tone, *Devices and Desires*, 186.

28 Aly Götz and Michael Sontheimer, *Fromms: How Julius Fromm's Condom Empire Fell to the Nazis* (New York: Other Press, 2009), 28.

29 Himes, *Medical History*, xvii, 100, 201; Fryer, *Birth Controllers*, 68.

30 John Hadfield, 'The Manufacture of Dipped Goods', *India Rubber World* 1 (July 1921): 710.

31 Ibid., 720; Himes, *Medical History*, 202; Murphy, *Condom Industry*, 7; Peel, 'Manufacture and Retailing', 117.

32 Peel, 'Manufacture and Retailing', 117.

33 Thea Horton, *The French Letter King* (Bloomington, IN: Author House, 2014), 29.

34 'Document on the London Rubber Company', 24 January 1968, c24.5, Waltham Forest Local Studies Centre, London; MMC 1975, 16.

35 Peel, 'Manufacture and Retailing', 117; Götz and Sontheimer, *Fromms*, 8, 28; Peel, 'Manufacture and Retailing', 117; James Woycke, *Birth Control in Germany 1871–1933* (London: Routledge, 1988), 39.

36 Tone, *Devices and Desires*, 188.

37 Ibid., 50–1.

38 Ibid., 108, 185, 188.

39 Ibid., 102–3.

40 Voge, *Chemistry and Physics*, 207–8; Peel, 'Manufacture and Retailing', 122.

41 Dingwall, 'Early Contraceptive Sheaths', 40.

42 Christopher Tietze, *The Condom as a Contraceptive* (New York: National Committee on Maternal Health, Inc., 1960), 6n4.

43 Jessica Borge, '"Wanting it Both Ways": The London Rubber Company, the Condom and the Pill 1915–1970'. PhD thesis, Birkbeck, University of London, 2017, 67.

44 Lucian Landau, *Natural Rubber Latex and Its Applications No. 3: The Manufacture of Dipped Rubber Articles from Latex* (London: The British Rubber Development Board, 1954), 6.

45 Tone, *Devices and Desires*, 193.

46 Ibid.

47 Landau, *Natural Rubber Latex*, 6.

48 Voge, *Chemistry and Physics*, 207; Himes, *Medical History*, 202.

49 Voge, *Chemistry and Physics*, 207; Himes, *Medical History*, 202–3; Murphy, *Condom Industry*, 10; Tone, *Devices and Desires*, 196.

50 Edward S. Killian, 'Apparatus for Manufacturing Thin Rubber Articles', US Patent 1923733A (1931), Google Patents, accessed 12 November 2019, https://patents.google.com/patent/US1923733A/en.

51 Randolph Cautley, 'Report to the National Committee on Maternal Health', ca. 1935, cited in Himes, *Medical History*, 202–3. Cautley also reported the lesser 'Shunk Process' of vertical dipping (Shunk being a minor American producer), which was not fully automated and yielded 100,000 units daily.

52 Tone, *Devices and Desires*, 194.

53 Ibid., 193–5.

54 Ibid. and Murphy, *Condom Industry*, 10. Prior to this, Youngs had outsourced production to Killian.

55 Peel, 'Manufacture and Retailing', 122; Collier, *The Humble Little Condom*, 201.

56 Lucian Landau, *Normal, I Suppose: A Rather Strange Story* (London: Macaw Press, 2001), 40.

57 'Document on London Rubber'.

58 Peel, 'Manufacture and Retailing', 122; G. Barry Carruthers, 'Memorandum of Visit to the London Rubber Co.', 1954, FPA/A7/73.

59 John Peel and Malcolm Potts, *Textbook of Contraceptive Practice* (Cambridge: Cambridge University Press, 1969), 55.

60 'Document on London Rubber'.

61 Peel and Potts, *Textbook*, 211.

62 H. Bardot, *Ut Prosim*, catalogue (London: H. Berdot, 1904).

63 Hugh Linstead to Lord Dawson, 7 April 1933, Viscount Dawson of Penn Papers, BED/B.2, Wellcome Collection.

64 J.C.M. McWalter, correspondence, 'About Abortifacients and Antigestatory Appliances', *Chemist and Druggist* (10 July 1897): 64.

65 John Londei, *Shutting up Shop: The Decline of the Traditional Small Shop* (Stockport: Dewi Lewis, 2007), 36–7.

66 Peel, 'Manufacture and Retailing', 124.

67 Ada Willis, *How to Limit Your Family* (London: The Stockwell Hygienic Co. Ltd, N.D.), ca. 1940, 53.

68 Himes, *Medical History*, 326.

69 Peel, 'Manufacturing and Retailing', 119; Jones, 'Under the Covers?' 15; Szreter and Fisher, *Sex Before*, 239–40.

70 Chief constable, Leeds C.I.D., to Dawson, February, 1933, BED/B.2.

71 Ibid.

72 Jones, 'Under the Covers?' 746–7.

73 Hansard. Bermondsey Borough Council (Street Trading) Bill (By Order). House of Commons Debates, 13 May 1926, vol. 195, col. 1071.

74 R.L. Matthews to Dawson, 27 February 1933, BED/B.2.

75 Dawson to Mr Wilson, 15 December 1932, BED/B.2.

76 Prentif shared a number of directors with George's. Memo, November 1937, FPA/A7/100.

77 Paul Ferris, 'Contraception, an Observer Enquiry', *The Observer*, 12 June 1966.

78 John Harvey, in conversation with the author (in the presence of Angela Wagstaff), Chingford, London, 8 December 2016.

79 Ibid.

80 Note on National Retail Union of Tobacconists, ca. 1933, BED/B.2.

81 Economist Intelligence Unit [henceforth EIU], 'Hairdressers as Retailers', *Retail Business Survey* 113 (1967): 44; EIU, 'The UK Contraceptive Market', *RBS* 210 (1975): 28.

82 EIU, 'Contraceptive Products', *Retail Business Survey* 92 (1965): 17; Peel, 'Manufacturing and Retailing', 116.

83 Peel, 'Manufacturing and Retailing', 116.

84 Women barbers provoked caution when they appeared. 'Female Barber', ATV, 27 February 1968, Media Archive for Central England, accessed 12 November 2019, http://www.macearchive.org/films/atv-today-27021968-female-barber.

85 EIU, 'Hairdressers', 44–5, 47.

86 Auld Committee, *The Shops Act Late Night and Sunday Opening: Report of the Committee of Inquiry into Proposals to Amend the Shops Acts Cmnd 9376* (London: HMSO, 1984), 2. The Hairdressers' and Barbers' Shops (Sunday Closing) Act 1930 was the result of a private member's bill supported by the hairdressing trade, possibly as an anti-competitive measure. An exception was made for Scotland in the 1950 Shops Act, whereby Jewish barbers or hairdressers were permitted to open on a Sunday providing they did not open on Saturdays and informed the Local Authority.

87 Peel, 'Manufacturing and Retailing', 124.

88 Londei, *Shutting up Shop*, 36–7.

89 Himes, *Medical* History, 201.

90 Green, *Curious History*, 94.

91 McLaren, *Nineteenth Century*, 222; Claire L. Jones, *The Medical Trade Catalogue in Britain 1870–1914* (London: Pickering and Chatto, 2013), 57; McLaren, *Nineteenth Century*, 221; Jones, 'Under the Covers?'

92 D.V. Glass, 'Introduction', in Fryer, *British Birth Control Ephemera 1879–1947* (London: Barracuda, 1969), 2; Howard M. Tyrer to Dawson, 17 January 1934, BED/B.2.

93 Hancock's literature bundle, BED/B.2.

94 Glass, 'Introduction', 2.

95 Robert Jütte, *Contraception: A History* (London: Polity, 2008), 117–34, cited in Jones, 'Under the Covers?' 741–2.

96 David Edgerton, *Shock of the Old* (London: Profile, 2008), 24.

97 Lewis, 'A Brief History of Condoms', 1.

98 Lucy Bland, *Banishing the Beast: Feminism, Sex and Morality* (London: Tauris Parke, 2002), 244.

99 Lesley A. Hall, 'Venereal Diseases and Society in Britain, from the Contagious Diseases Acts to the National Health Service', in *Sex, Sin and Suffering*, edited by Roger Davidson and Lesley A. Hall (London: Routledge, 2001), 123–4.

100 Weeks, *Sex, Politics*, 188.

101 Llewellyn-Jones, *Sex and V.D.* (London: Faber and Faber, 1974), 43–6, 57–62.

102 Ibid., 16; Hall, *Hidden Anxieties*, 36.

103 Mark Harrison, 'The British Army and the Problem of Venereal Disease in France and Egypt during the First World War', *Medical History* 39, no. 2 (1995): 140.

104 Hall, *Hidden Anxieties*, 37.

105 This phrase was also used in America. Tone, *Devices and Desires*, 91.

106 Hall, 'Venereal Diseases', 120–36. Richard Davenport-Hines presents a useful discussion of attitudes towards VD in *Sex, Death, and Punishment* (London: Collins, 1990), chapter 5, 'Venus Decomposing'.

107 Antje Kampf, '"Controlling Male Sexuality": Combatting Venereal Disease in the New Zealand Military during Two World Wars', *Journal of the History of Sexuality* 17, no. 2 (2008): 257; David Michael Simpson, 'The Moral Battlefield: Venereal Disease and the British Army during the First World War'. PhD thesis, University of Iowa, 1999, 11, 183; Davenport-Hines, *Sex, Death*, 196–8.

108 Davenport-Hines, *Sex, Death*, 234–5; Bland, *Banishing*, 197.

109 Hall, 'Venereal Diseases', 126.

110 Simpson, 'Moral Battlefield', 183.

111 Ibid., 403.

112 Tone, *Devices and Desires*, 91.

113 Hall, '"War Always Brings It On": War, STDs, the Military, and the Civilian Population in Britain, 1850–1950', *Clio Medica/The Wellcome Series in the History of Medicine* 55, no. 1 (1999): 214.

114 Simpson, 'Moral Battlefield', 120, 122.

115 Ibid.

116 Ibid., 123.

117 Ibid., 124; Halliday Sutherland, 'A Plan for the Control of Venereal Disease in HM Forces', *Public Health* 56 (February 1943): 58.

118 *Final Report of the Commissioner, Royal Commission on Venereal Disease* (London: HMSO 1916), 40; Simpson, 'Moral Battlefield', 124.

119 Harrison, 'British Army', 148.

120 Tone, *Devices and Desires*, 91.

121 *Final Report of the Commissioner*, 173, appendix 24.

122 Lord Trevethin's Committee, 'Inquiry on Venereal Disease', *British Medical Journal* 1, no. 3258 (1923): 976–9.

123 Medical director-general, minutes of a meeting ref. MDG.32/10/60/A, 15 November 1960, ADM1/27662, Admiralty Papers, National Archives, Kew.

124 Cook, *Sexual Revolution*, 137, 276–7.

125 Cautley et al., 'Rubber Sheaths as Venereal Disease Prophylactics', *American Journal of the Medical Sciences* 195, no. 2 (1938): 155–63.

126 Voge, *Chemistry and Physics*, 208.

127 Ibid.; London Rubber and FPA, correspondence, 1937–1941, FPA/A7/71.

128 Cautley et al., 'Rubber Sheaths', 158.

129 Wilson, *Advertising and the Community*, 217.

130 The Public Morality Council [henceforth PMC], *A Report as to Efforts to Secure the Prohibition of the Display and Advertisements of 'Birth Prevention Accessories'*, 1932, A/PMC/67, Public Morality Council Archive, London Metropolitan Archives.

131 C.H. Rolph, ed., and British Social Biology Council, *Women of the Streets: A Sociological Study of the Common Prostitute* (London: Secker and Warburg, 1955), 93.

132 Ibid., 97.

133 Julia Laite, *Common Prostitutes and Ordinary Citizens* (Basingstoke and New York: Palgrave Macmillan, 2012), 146n74.

134 Rolph et al., *Women of the Streets*, 97.

135 Ibid.

136 Ibid.

137 Ibid. The British brand Dettol is a medical and household disinfectant equivalent to Lysol in America, which was also used as a contraceptive douche. For more information on the use of Lysol as a vaginal douche in America, see Tone, *Devices and Desires*, 170–3.

138 For more on Aletta Jacobs, see Drucker, *Contraception*, 4–5, 18–19.

139 Barbara Brookes, *Abortion in England 1900–1967* (Beckenham: Crook Helm, 1988), 3, 14; Marcus Collins, *Modern Love* (London: Atlantic, 2003), 107; Cook, *Sexual Revolution*, 274–5, 277; Audrey Leathard, *The Fight for Family Planning* (London: Palgrave MacMillan, 1980), 5, 10.

140 Marie Carmichael Stopes, *Contraception (Birth Control). Its Theory, History and Practice. A Manual for The Medical and Legal Professions* (London: John Bale, Sons and Danielson, Ltd, 1923), 16, 76, 235.

CHAPTER 2

1 'Document on London Rubber'; MMC 1975, 11, 16.

2 Dr Vera Norris and Mrs Conrad, Confidential Report of Visit to London Rubber Company, 1952, FPA/A7/73.

3 York in conversation, *Business Daily*, BBC World Service, 27 August 2018.

4 Harvey, in conversation with the author (in the presence of Angela Wagstaff), Chingford, London, 3 November 2017.

5 Ibid.

6 Bayliss, 'The London Rubber Co'; 'Lionel Alfred Jackson, ca. 1894–1934', Jewish Lives Project, accessed 12 November 2019, https://www.jewishlivesproject.com/profiles/lionel-alfred-jackson.

7 'Central Criminal Court, Nov. 4', *The Times* (London), Friday 5 November 1886, 10.

8 Bayliss, 'London Rubber', 1.

9 Ibid.; Davis, 'London Rubber', 2; Finch and Green, *Through the Ages*, 54; MMC 1975, 16; 'Document on London Rubber'; '1929–1965: From Aldersgate St. to Hall Lane', *London Image* (spring/summer 1966): 22. Copies of *London Image* supplied by Angela Wagstaff.

10 MMC 1975, 16; 'Document on London Rubber'; 'Careers for All at London Rubber', *Walthamstow Guardian*, 6 August 1971, 1.

11 Bayliss, 'London Rubber', 1; Peel, 'Manufacture and Retailing', 122; 'Aldersgate St. to Hall Lane', 22.

12 'To Err … Is Human', *London Image* (winter 1969/1970): 21; 'A R Reid Retires', *London Image* (autumn 1971): 5.

13 T.A.B. Corley, 'British Entrepreneurs and Brand Names', *Oxford Dictionary of National Biography* online, edited by Lawrence Goldman, accessed 12 November 2019, http://www.oxforddnb.com/view/10.1093/ref:odnb/9780198
614128.001.0001/odnb-9780198614128-e-92738?rskey=IcGhLd&result=1.;
Ilana Löwy, 'Defusing the Population Bomb in the 1950s: Foam Tablets in India', *Studies in History and Philosophy of Science* 43, no. 3 (2012): 589–93, 586.

14 'Elkan M. Jackson. Late Chairman of London Rubber', *London Image* (spring 1971): 22–3; 'Aldersgate St. to Hall Lane', 22.

15 'History of Durex', Durex Information Service, accessed 12 November 2019, https://www.durex.com.sg/history-of-durex/.

16 Landau, *Normal*, 39–40.

17 Ibid., 12–17; Denise Iredell, 'Obituary: Lucian Landau 1912–2001', *Journal of the Society for Psychical Research* 65, no. 4 (October 2001): 285–7, 285. My thanks to Christopher Josiffe for bringing this source to my attention.

18 National College of Rubber Technology Archive (1948–1986), accessed 12 November 2019, https://archiveshub.jisc.ac.uk/search/archives/5dfa25da-9317-3f70-be1d-cc2d6359ed57.

19 Landau, *Normal*, 35.

20 Ibid., 38.

21 Tone, *Devices and Desires*, 194.

22 'Change of Name', *The London Gazette*, 6 September 1932, 5693. Landau was naturalized in 1937.

23 Landau, *Normal*, 38.

24 Ibid., 39.

25 UK Trademark 502932, 'Durex' (filed 22 May 1929), *Trade Marks Journal* 2677 (17 July 1929).

26 Landau, *Normal*, 40.

27 Ibid., 40–1.

28 Ibid.; 'Document on London Rubber'; MMC 1975, 16; London Rubber Photo Albums.

29 Landau, *Normal*, 41.

30 Ibid.

31 Landau, in conversation with Mary Rose Barrington, n.d. (likely 1990s). DVD transfer, courtesy of the Society for Psychical Research and Mary Rose Barrington.

32 Landau, *Normal*, 41; Notes on London Rubber Co., following meeting of Lord Dawson and A.R. Reid, March 1933, BED/B.2.

33 Chandler, *Industrial Century*, 7–8.

34 Ibid.

35 Austin Coates, *The Commerce in Rubber: The First 250 Years* (Oxford: Oxford University Press, 1987), 267–90; Purdie, 'The British Agency House in Malaysia and Nigeria: Evolving Strategy in the Commodity Trade,' PhD thesis, University of Glasgow, 2018, 95–6.

36 The Rubber Grower's Association, Inc., *Rubber Latex*, 4th ed. (London: Rubber Grower's Association, Inc., 1936), 87.

37 Ibid., 86.

38 Landau, *Normal*, 41; London Rubber Photo Albums, Waltham Forest Local Studies Centre, London; 'Document on London Rubber'; MMC 1975, 16.

39 'The General Supply Stores (Frank Turner), Chemists' Sundriesman', mail order catalogue, ca. 1944. Author's Collection.

40 Landau, *Normal*, 42.

41 Ibid., 45, 47.

42 Ibid., 41; *Rubber Latex*, 86.

43 Landau, *Normal*, 42.

44 Ibid., 45.

45 Iredell, 'Obituary', 286.

46 Lord Dawson and A.R. Reid, March 1933, BED/B.2.

47 Stopes, *Contraception*, 156, 164, 180.

48 Landau, *Normal*, 46.

49 London Rubber Company Ltd, *Director's Report and Statement of Accounts* (1965), 4; Harvey, in conversation, 3 November 2017; Landau, *Normal*, 46; MMC 1975, 16.

50 MMC 1975, 16.

51 Landau, *Normal*, 46–7.

52 Ibid.

53 Harvey, in conversation, 3 November 2017.

54 'Elkan M. Jackson', 22–3.

55 'Double Strength Female Capsules' contained apiol steel and pennyroyal, which were known abortifacients. London Rubber Company, *London Rubber Home and Export Price List* 1936, FPA/A7/72.

56 'Document on London Rubber'; Peel, 'Manufacture and Retailing', 122; Landau, *Normal*, 51; *London Rubber Home and Export Price List*, 3; Lord Dawson and A.R. Reid, correspondence, March 1933, BED/B.2.

57 Dawson and Reid, correspondence; Szreter and Fisher, *Sex Before*, 240n35.

58 Minutes, meeting with medical director general, Royal Navy, 15 November 1960, ADM1/27662; C.F. Cullingham to Miss Holland, 26 July 1934, FPA/A7/71.

59 Ibid. London Rubber declared itself an Admiralty contractor on letterheads from the late 1930s.

60 'Document on London Rubber'.

61 Landau, *Normal*, 49.

62 *Lamberts Prorace Ltd*, catalogue, 1941.

63 'Document on London Rubber'; MMC 1975, 11, 16. The remainder of the market at this time was divided between Lamberts, Harrison Kent Ltd (Prentif brand), Selka Rubber, and other small producers.

64 Landau, *Normal*, 50.

65 Laite, *Common Prostitutes*, 152; Cate Haste, *Rules of Desire: Sex in Britain World War I to the Present* (London: Vintage, 1992, 2002), 120–8.

66 Joshua Levine, *The Secret History of the Blitz* (London: Simon and Schuster UK, 2015), 211–36.

67 Ibid., 213.

68 PMC Executive Committee, minutes, 1940–1941. A/PMC/4.

69 'Document on London Rubber'; Landau, *Normal*, 50.

70 Landau, *Normal*, 54.

71 Ibid.

72 Landau, *Normal*, 50; 'Careers for All'; Interview with Ray Russell-Fell, conducted by Alice Mackay, 20 July 2015. Courtesy of the archives of the Waltham Forest Oral History Workshop.

73 Landau, *Normal*, 50.

74 Haste, *Rules of Desire*, 113.

75 MMC 1975, 11.

76 'Document on London Rubber'.

77 Peel, 'Manufacture and Retailing', 122.

78 The first National Service (armed forces) Act conscripted all males aged 18–41 on 3 September 1939 (the day Britain declared war on Germany). 'Conscription: The Second World War', Living Heritage, Parliament, accessed 12 November 2019, https://www.parliament.uk/about/living-heritage/transformingsociety/private-lives/yourcountry/overview/conscriptionww2/.

79 Executive Committee, minutes, 30 September 1943, A/PMC/5.
80 Minutes, 28 September 1944, A/PMC/5.
81 Purdie, 'The British Agency House', 105.
82 T.S. Harrison to Miss Holland, 25 May 1944, FPA/A7/100; Landau, *Normal*, 50.
83 Landau, *Normal*, 50.
84 Barbara Evans, *Freedom to Choose* (London: Bodley Head, 1984), 206–7; Margaret Pyke to Harrison, 27 May 1944, FPA/A7/100.
85 Margaret Pyke to Harrison.
86 Harrison to Pyke, 31 May 1944, FPA/A7/100; Harrison to Holland.
87 MMC 1975, 11; Prentif and FPA, correspondence, May 1944, FPA/A7/100.
88 Harrison to Pyke; Harrison to Holland.
89 Harrison to Holland.
90 Harrison to Pyke; Harrison to Ministry of Supply, 23 May 1944, FPA/A7/100.
91 Götz and Sontheimer, *Fromms*, 8, 31.
92 Woycke, *Birth Control*, 51–2, 68.
93 Götz and Sontheimer, *Fromms*, 30.
94 Woycke, *Birth Control*, 113; Lewis, 'A Brief History of Condoms', 8.
95 Götz and Sontheimer, *Fromms*, 4.
96 Woycke, *Birth Control*, 39, 59.
97 Ibid., 50, 113.
98 'Messrs. Herbert Fromm', trade advertisement *Pharmaceutical Journal*, 1 October 1937, 12; Memo of telephone call with Mr Harrison, 1 October and 8 October 1937, FPA/A7/100.
99 Götz and Sontheimer, *Fromms*, 16, 20, 30, 53, 76–7, 91.
100 UK Patents 442835, 'A Box or Packing Device for Preservatives', 1935; 442069, 'An Improved Method of Producing Teething Rings for Children', 1935; 445997, 'Improvements in or Relating to Inflatable Life-Belts', 1935; 448214, 'A Process for the Formation of Rough Surfaces on Rubber Goods', 1935; US Patents 2084636, 'Life or Swimming Belt', 1935; 2096296, 'Process for the Production of Slippery Rubber Goods', 1935. Espacenet.
101 Götz and Sontheimer, *Fromms*, 94.
102 'Deaths June 1945', Free BMD, accessed 13 November 2019, http://www.freebmd.org.uk/cgi/information.pl?cite=82SzDAhJuoZ%2F7pmIso84iw&scan=1.
103 Following the end of the war, British officials granted Bachmann and Co., near Zeven, an operating licence to manufacture under the Fromms Act brand for the three Western zones as the former Fromms factory fell to the Soviets, who had taken East Berlin. Eventually, it was absorbed by the German Democratic Republic and nationalised. The factory continued condom production into the 1950s, but ceased to be a viable supplier or competitor for London Rubber because of its position inside the Soviet zone. Götz and Sontheimer, *Fromms*, 161, 64–9.
104 Sir Eric MacFadyen, 'Rehabilitation of Rubber Estates in Malaya', *Rubber Developments* 1, no. 1 (1947): 3–5.

105 Ibid., 5.

106 Dominic Sandbrook, *Never Had It So Good: A History of Britain from Suez to the Beatles* (London: Abacus, 2005), 47–8.

107 Ibid.

108 MMC 1975, 11; Reid to Tietze, 2 February, 1959, FPA/A7/78; Tietze, *Condom as a Contraceptive*, 20.

109 Marks, *Sexual Chemistry*, 188.

110 'London Rubber Co. Ltd vs Durex Products', 4 March 1963, Indian Kankoon, accessed 12 November 2019, http://indiankanoon.org/doc/1333219/.

111 Wilson and West, '"Unmentionables"', 100.

112 MMC 1975, 11.

113 Harvey, in conversation, 8 December 2016.

114 MMC 1975, 17.

115 P.M.C. Watkins to Mrs Smith, 5 June 1957, FPA/A7/69.2.

116 Harvey, in conversation with the author (in the presence of Angela Wagstaff), Chingford, London, 13 November 2017.

117 Ibid.; Willis, *How to Limit Your Family*; British Standards Institution correspondence, 1953–60, FPA/A7/23.2.

118 Harvey, in conversation, 13 November 2017; A 1960 *Lloyds* catalogue can be found FPA/A7/70.

119 For example, UK Trademark 659505, 'Ariel' (filed 27 May 1947), *Trade Marks Journal* (18 August 1948); 662899, 'Pyvex' (filed 1 October 1947), *Trade Marks Journal* (22 September 1948).

120 London Rubber Company, *Annual Reports 1959–1972*.

121 Harvey, in conversation, 8 December 2016.

122 London Rubber Company Ltd, *Directors' Report and Statement of Accounts* (1956), 5. Lea Bridge had specialised in barrage balloons during the Second World War, and now made toy balloons.

123 Harvey, in conversation, 8 December 2016.

124 Ibid.

125 Manufacturer's Files, FPA/A7/72-73. Elarco disappeared from FPA clinics in the early 1950s.

126 Harvey, in conversation, 8 December 2016.

127 UK Trademark 680609, 'Duracreme' (filed 28 June 1949), *Trade Marks Journal* (21 December 1949).

128 Mechen, '"Closer Together"', 220.

129 'Document on London Rubber'.

130 UK Trademark 289288, 'Lam-Butt' (filed 4 January 1907), *Trade Marks Journal* (20 March 1907).

131 'British Latex Products, Ltd.', *The London Gazette*, 38422 (5 October 1948): 5303; London Rubber Letterhead, 25 March 1949, A7/74.

132 E.M. Jackson, 'Chairman's Review', London Rubber Company Ltd, *Report of the Directors and Statement of Accounts* (1951), 3; 'London International Group Ltd, Company number 00488344', Companies House, accessed 12 November 2019,

https://beta.companieshouse.gov.uk/company/00488344; Davis, 'London Rubber', 5.

133   Charles Sweeny, 'Obituary', *The Herald,* 19 March 1993, accessed 12 November 2019, https://www.heraldscotland.com/news/12615419.charles-sweeny/.

134   Landau, *Normal,* 55.

135   Ibid.

136   BBC Radio 4, 'The Malayan Emergency', *Witness History,* podcast, 3 May 2019; see also Anthony Short, *The Communist Insurrection in Malaya, 1948–1960* (London, 1975); Purdie, 'The British Agency House', 117–20.

137   London Rubber Company Ltd, *Director's Report and Statement of Accounts* (1950), 3.

138   John Tully, *The Devil's Milk: A Social History of Rubber* (New York: Monthly Review Press, 2011), 348; London Rubber Company Ltd, *Directors Report and Statement of Accounts* (1952), 3.

139   London Rubber, *Directors Report* (1952), 3.

140   London Rubber Photo Albums.

141   Trademark 702657, 'LONDON RUBBER CO. LTD. LONDON The Name You Can Trust' (filed 14 November 1951), *Trade Marks Journal* (6 February 1952).

142   Landau, *Normal,* 57.

143   Condoms are consistently referenced as the company's core product in Annual Reports from 1959–1972.

144   Harvey, in conversation, 8 December 2016; This complaint was raised by the *Investor's Chronicle* of 23 July 1965, in response to London Rubber's 1965 annual report. Press Clippings, FPA/A17/100.

145   In London Rubber's 1968 annual report, principal activities were broken down as follows: protectives (condoms), surgeon's, house, and industrial gloves (66 per cent total sales, £2,138,000 contribution to group profit before taxation), pharmaceuticals and other products (11 per cent, £453,000), wines and spirits (22 per cent, £113,000), and vending machines (1 per cent, £45,000). London Rubber Company Ltd, *Report and Accounts* (1968), 6.

146   Davis, 'London Rubber', 2, 7; MMC 1975, 22; Elkan Jackson to Ordinary Shareholders, 7 January 1958, Box 3278, London Stock Exchange Annual Reports and Accounts, Guildhall Library, London.

147   Landau, *Normal,* 55.

148   UK Patent 668382, 'Improvements in or Relating to the Manufacture of Toy Balloons and Like Articles made by Dipping', 1950; MMC 1975, 58.

149   Ibid., 16.

150   Ibid., 22.

151   Ibid.

152   Murphy, *Condom Industry,* 19.

153   G. Barry Carruthers, Memorandum, 15 September 1954, FPA/A7/73.

154   Davis, 'London Rubber', 7; MMC 1975 reported that electronic testing was introduced in 1950 (MMC 1975, 22). However, 1953 is the likely correct date as corroborated by two FPA reports of visits to Chingford (above).

155 'Document on London Rubber'; Davis, 'London Rubber', 4.

156 Norris and Conrad, 'Confidential Report'.

157 MMC 1975, 58.

158 Reid to Tietze, 2 February, 1959, FPA/A7/78; Tietze, *Condom as a Contraceptive*, 20.

159 Landau, *Normal*, 54.

160 Ibid.

161 Ibid., 59–60.

162 Ibid., 60.

163 Ibid.

164 Ibid., 47; Landau, in conversation with Mary Rose Barrington.

165 Landau, *Normal*, blurb; Iredell, 'Obituary', 286.

166 'To Err … Is Human'; 'Long Service Awards', *London Image* (spring 1962): 6; 'Aldersgate St. to Hall Lane'; 'Document on London Rubber'; 'Elkan M. Jackson. Late Chairman of London Rubber'; Peel, 'Manufacture and Retailing', 122.

167 Peel, 'Manufacture and Retailing', 122.

168 Kenneth O. Morgan, *Britain since 1945: The People's Peace* (Oxford: Oxford University Press, 2001), 199; Edgerton, *The Rise and Fall of the British Nation: A Twentieth Century History* (London: Penguin Books, 2019), 313.

169 Edgerton, *Rise and Fall*, 321.

170 Lonon Rubber Company *Report and Accounts* (1956), 3.

171 'A R Reid Retires', 5.

172 Harvey, in conversation, 8 December 2016.

173 Harvey, in conversation, 3 November 2017.

174 'A R Reid Retires', 5.

175 Harvey, in conversation, 3 November 2017.

176 Harvey, in conversation, 8 December 2016.

177 Ibid.; Harvey, in conversation, 3 November 2017.

178 Harvey, in conversation, 8 December 2016.

179 Ibid.; 'Aldersgate St. to Hall Lane', 22.

180 Harvey, in conversation, 8 December 2016.

181 Ibid.

182 'Prop' being short for 'prophylactic'. Wagstaff, in conversation with the author, Chingford, London, 9 June 2017.

183 Harvey, in conversation, 8 December 2016.

184 London Rubber Photo Albums; Harvey, in conversation, 13 November 2017.

185 *London Image* (autumn 1968): 29.

186 Wagstaff, in conversation, 9 June 2017.

187 London Rubber Photo Albums.

188 *London Rubber Company International People. Chingford* (3 April 1973): 1.

189 *London Image* (spring 1968): 11.

190 *London Image* (winter 1967): 29.

191 Harvey, in conversation, 8 December 2016.

192 Ibid.

193 Ibid.

194 'Company Personalities Marry', *London Image* (autumn 1971): 32.

195 'To Err … Is Human'

196 *London Image*, 1962–1974.

197 Ibid.

198 Harvey, in conversation, 3 November 2017.

199 London Rubber Company Ltd, *Director's Report and Statement of Accounts* (1959), 4.

200 Wagstaff and Harvey, in conversation, 3 November 2017.

201 Harvey, in conversation, 3 November 2017.

202 Wagstaff, in conversation, 9 June 2017.

203 Ibid.

204 Conversation with anonymous delegate, Business Archives Council annual conference, Royal Albert Hall, London, 13 November 2014.

CHAPTER 3

1 'God's Church for God's World', Lambeth Conference 2020, accessed 13 November 2019, https://www.lambethconference.org/.

2 'Index of Resolutions from 1908', Anglican Communion, accessed 13 November 2019, https://www.anglicancommunion.org/resources/document-library/lambeth-conference/1908/lambeth-conference-archives-1908-index?author=Lambeth+Conference&year=1908.

3 Ibid.; 'Index of Resolutions from 1920', Anglican Communion Office, accessed 13 November 2019, https://www.anglicancommunion.org/resources/document-library/lambeth-conference/1920/lambeth-conference-archives-1920-index?author=Lambeth+Conference&year=1920.

4 'Index of Resolutions from 1930', Anglican Communion Office, accessed 13 November 2019, https://www.anglicancommunion.org/resources/document-library/lambeth-conference/1930/lambeth-conference-archives-1930-index?author=Lambeth+Conference&year=1930.

5 Hansard. Simmonds, Contraceptives (Regulation), Bill. HC Deb, 16 December 1938, vol. 342, col. 2425.

6 J.C.M. McWalter, Correspondence, 'About Abortifacients and Antigestatory Appliances', *Chemist and Druggist* (10 July 1897): 64; Jones, 'Under the Covers?' 738–9. The bill was first read in the House of Lords in 1933.

7 Adrian Bingham, *Family Newspapers?* (Oxford and New York: Oxford University Press, 2009), 57; Public Morality Council, *A Report*.

8 Ibid.; Lesley Hall, 'Sex, Religion and Royalty: Also Dairy Farming', Wellcome Blog, accessed 13 November 2019, http://blog.wellcomelibrary.org/2012/12/sex-religion-and-royalty-also-dairy-farming/.

9 'Parliament', *The Times* (London), 28 February 1934: 7.

10 'Contraceptives Bill', *The Times* (London), 29 February 1934: 7.

11 Ibid.

12 John Peel, 'Contraception and the Medical Profession', *Population Studies* 18, no. 2 (1964): 139; Finch and Green, *Through the Ages*, 20. Dawson's speech was published as *Love-Marriage-Birth Control* (London: E. Nisbet and Co. Ltd, 1922).

13 Bingham, *Family Newspapers*, 57; Green, *Curious History*, 20.

14 Raymond Pierpoint, ed., *Report on the Proceedings of the Fifth International Neo-Malthusian and Birth Conference, Kingsway Hall, London. July 11th to 14th, 1922* (London: William Heinmann Medical Books Ltd, 1922), 290.

15 Hansard. Contraceptives (Regulation) Bill, col. 2420.

16 Ibid., 2422.

17 'Parliament', *The Times* (London), 17 December 1938: 7.

18 'Another attempt to introduce Comstockery here incited by the Roman Catholics', *The Birth Control News* 16, no. 10 (May 1938): 117–22.

19 General Secretary to Miss Steel, 21 March 1947, A/PMC/67.

20 PMC Executive Committee, Minutes, 25 July 1940, A/PMC/4.

21 Thanks to Graham Keen, General Manager, Autonumis Ltd, Stroud, who alerted me to the use of vending machines as sites for brand advertising.

22 EIU, 'Contraceptive Products', 17; Jones, 'Under the Covers?' 752–4.

23 Jones, 'Under the Covers?' 752–4; Dawson, correspondence with campaigners, December 1932, BED/B.2.

24 Jones, 'Under the Covers?' 754.

25 Ibid.; Hansard. Contraceptives (Regulation) Bill, col 2422.

26 Jones, 'Under the Covers?' 752–4; R.L. Matthews to Carlton Oldfield, 2 December 1932 and Reid to Dawson, 9 March 1933, BED/B.2.

27 Matthews to the Right Reverend Lord Bishop of Ripon, 28 January 1933, BED/B.2.

28 Detective Inspector Frank Webster to Leeds Chief Constable, 6 April 1933, BED/B.2.

29 EIU, 'Contraceptive Products', 17.

30 Ibid.; Jones, 'Under the Covers?' 753.

31 EIU, 'Contraceptive Products', 17.

32 Norman St. John-Stevas, 'Birth Control: Morals, Law, and Public Policy', in *Religion and Public Order, 2*, edited by Donald A. Gianella (Chicago: University of Chicago Press, 1964), 42n27.

33 Ibid.

34 Jones, 'Under the Covers?' 753; EIU, 'Contraceptive Products', 17–18.

35 'Parliament', *The Times*.

36 S.W.F. Holloway, 'How the Royal Pharmaceutical Society Got to Where It Is Today', *Pharmaceutical Journal* 268, no. 7201 (2002): 811. Cited in Annie McAuley Brownfield-Pope, 'From Chemist Shop to Community Pharmacy: An Industry Wide Study of Retailing Chemists and Druggists, ca. 1880–1960'. PhD thesis, University of East Anglia, 2003, 205, 209–10.

37 Xrayser, 'Ethics in Business', *Chemist and Druggist* (22 April 1939): 443.

38 'Council Meeting. Statement upon Matters of Professional Conduct. Appendix I', *Chemist and Druggist* (15 April 1939): 430.

39 'Pharmacy and Medicines Bill', *Chemist and Druggist Supplement* (5 July 1941): 7.

40 Reid to FPA, 29 August 1952, FPA/A7/73.

41 'Professional Conduct. Second Revised Draft Statement', *Chemist and Druggist* (28 March 1953): 313. Clause 10 passed without amendments and was adopted in May 1953.

42 'Pharmaceutical Society's Annual Meeting', *Chemist and Druggist* (23 May 1953): 513–14, 513.

43 Ibid.

44 Stuart Anderson, 'Community Pharmacy and Sexual Health in 20th Century Britain', *The Pharmaceutical Journal* (online), 6 January 2001, accessed 13 November 2019, http://www.pharmaceutical-journal.com/community-pharmacy-and-sexual-health-in-20th-century-britain/20003974.article.

45 'Document on London Rubber'; Landau, *Normal*, 40–1; MMC 1975, 16; London Rubber Photo Albums.

46 Reid and Dawson, correspondence, March–May 1933, BED/B.2.

47 London Rubber Company Ltd, *Report and Accounts* (1965); 'LRC Products', Grace's Guide, accessed 13 November 2019, https://www.gracesguide.co.uk/LRC_Products.

48 London Rubber Company Ltd, *Report and Accounts* (1968), 6.

49 Reid and Dawson, correspondence, March–May 1933; EIU, 'Contraceptive Products', 17.

50 Harvey, in conversation, 8 December 2016.

51 Ibid.

52 EIU, 'Chemists', RBS (March 1962): 6.

53 Ibid.

54 MMC 1975, 74.

55 Peel, 'Manufacturing and Retailing', 123.

56 Harvey, in conversation, 8 December 2016; MMC 1975, 16. This changed when Durex Gossamer was launched in 1957.

57 MMC 1975, 80; Note from Mr Harrison, Prentif, 14 June 1938, FPA/A7/72; Harvey, in conversation, 8 December 2016; When Ortho launched condoms in Canada in the 1970s, this strategy was used against its competitor, Julius Schmid (by then owned by London Rubber). Percy Skuy (former CEO of Ortho Canada), Skype conversation with the author, 27 August 2014.

58 Ibid, 73; EIU, 'Contraceptives', RBS 138 (1969): 20; EIU, 'UK Contraceptive Market', 23.

59 MMC 1975, 73.

60 EIU, 'UK Contraceptive Market', 24.

61 Tone, *Devices and Desires*, 190.

62 EIU, 'Chemists', 9.

63 Harvey, in conversation, 8 December 2016.

64 EIU, 'Chemists', 10.

65 Harvey, in conversation, 8 December 2016.

66 EIU, 'Chemists', 14.

67 Wilson and West, '"Unmentionables"', 100.

68 Sample shelf strips, FPA/A7/129.

69 EIU, 'Contraceptive Products', 17; Peel, 'Manufacturing and Retailing', 123.

70 Szreter and Fisher, *Sex Before*, 240, 259–60.

71 Harvey, in conversation, 8 December 2016.

72 MMC 1975, 74.

73 Harvey, in conversation, 8 December 2016.

74 Jones, 'Under the Covers?'

75 Anderson, 'Community Pharmacy'; Jobling, 'Playing Safe', 58; Mechen, '"Closer Together"', 221; Peel, 'Manufacturing and Retailing', 124; Edgerton, *Shock of the Old*, 24.

76 Stanley Chapman, 'The Sexual Revolution', *Southwell Folio* 19 (February 2013): 32–3, 32; MMC 1975, 12.

77 EIU, 'Chemists', 17; Jon Stobart, *Spend, Spend, Spend: A History of Shopping* (Stroud: Tempus, 2008), 198.

78 EIU, 'Self Service', RBS (August 1961): 6; EIU, 'Chemists' Shops Retail Trade Review', RBS 102 (August 1966): 6.

79 EIU, 'Chemists' Shops', 6.

80 Chapman, 'Sexual Revolution', 32.

81 EIU, 'Chemists' Shops', 14.

82 Londei, *Shutting up Shop*, 36–7.

83 Ibid.

84 EIU, 'Chemists', 14.

85 Prentif files, FPA/A7/104.

86 Chapman, 'Sexual Revolution', 32.

87 Kenneth G. Wright, *The Shopkeeper's Security Manual* (London: Tom Stacey, 1971), 9.

88 T.C.N. Gibbens and Joyce Prince, *Shoplifting* (London: Institute for the Study and Treatment of Delinquency, 1962).

89 Ibid.

90 Simon Phillips, Andrew Alexander, and Gareth Shaw, 'Consumer Misbehavior: The Rise of Self-Service Grocery Retailing and Shoplifting in the United Kingdom c. 1950–1970', *Journal of Macromarketing* 25, no. 1 (2005): 66–75; Dawn Nell, Simon Phillips, Andrew Alexander, and Gareth Shaw, 'Helping Yourself: Self-Service Grocery Retailing and Shoplifting in Britain, c. 1950–75', *Cultural and Social History* 8, no. 3 (2011): 371–91.

91 *Murphy Condom Industry*, 38, 40, 44; Deborah M. Roffman, Carl E. Speckman, and Nathan I. Gruz, 'Maryland Pharmacists Ready for Family Planning Initiative', *Family Planning Perspectives* 5, no. 4 (1973): 245.

92 Robert D. Winsor, Sheb L. True, and Chris Manolis, 'Current Condom Merchandising Strategies and Their Implications for Male and Female Shoppers', *Allied Academies International Conference, Academy of Marketing Studies, Proceedings* 8, no. 45 (2003): 45–50.

CHAPTER 4

1 Peel, 'Abortion and Family Planning in England', *Medical Gynaecology and Fertility Abstracts* 4, no. 11 (1965): 3; 'Manufacturing and Retailing', 123.

2 Peel, 'Manufacture and Retailing', 114.

3 Jones, 'Under the Covers? Commerce, Condoms and Consumers in Britain, 1860–1960'. Presentation at History and Technology Seminar, King's College, London, 8 October 2014.

4 London Rubber Company, 'Population Growth in the United Kingdom', 306.

5 Leathard, *Fight for Family Planning*, 100.

6 Cook, *Sexual Revolution*, 316.

7 Lellor Secor Florence, *Progress Report on Birth Control* (London: William Heinman, 1956), 131.

8 Peel, 'Hull Family Survey', 59.

9 Jobling, 'Playing Safe', 61.

10 Peter Miskell, 'Cavity Protection or Cosmetic Perfection? Innovation and Marketing of Toothpaste Brands in the United States and Western Europe, 1955–1985', *Business History Review* 78 (spring 2004): 55, 57.

11 Ibid., 52–3.

12 Ibid., 45–50.

13 Peel, 'Manufacture and Retailing', 114.

14 Cook, *Sexual Revolution*, 276–7.

15 Graham Wootton, *Pressure Groups in Britain 1720–1970* (London: Allen Lane, 1975), 98.

16 Namely, the Society for the Provision of Birth Control Clinics, founded 1924, the Birth Control International Information Centre (1929), the Worker's Birth Control Group, which joined the NBCA in 1930, and the Birth Control Investigation Committee.

17 Public Relations Sub Committee, minutes, 14 September 1955, FPA/A5/45.

18 Cook, *Sexual Revolution*, 275–7.

19 Gordon Snow (former commercial manager, Family Planning Sales Ltd), in conversation with the author, Oxford, 13 January 2015.

20 FPA clinics promoted oral contraceptives from early 1962, and IUDs from 1965.

21 François Lafitte, *Family Planning* (1959), chapters 3.2, 4, cited in Cook, *Sexual Revolution*, 276n21.

22 Lafitte, 'The Users of Birth Control Clinics', 16; Peel and Potts, *Textbook*, 59.

23 Szuhan, 'Sex in the Laboratory', 500.

24 Harvey, in conversation, 8 December 2016; For more on the role of women in the British family planning movement, see Caroline Rusterholz, *Mine Is Women's Medicine: Sex, Family Planning and British Female Doctors in Transnational Perspective (1920–70)* (Manchester: Manchester University Press, 2020).

25 Secretary to the London Rubber Company, 18 March 1938, FPA/A7/71.

26 Pyke to Reid, 31 May 1939, FPA/A7/71.

27 Barbara Evans, *Freedom to Choose* (London: Bodley Head, 1984), 146.

28 Ilana Löwy, '"Sexual Chemistry" before the Pill: Science, Industry and Chemical Contraceptives, 1920–1960', *The British Journal for the History of Science* 44, no. 2 (2011): 245–74, 255.

29 Mr Harrison, correspondence with FPA, spring–summer, 1938, FPA/A7/72.

30 Harvey, in conversation, 8 December 2016.

31 Correspondence, FPA and London Rubber, 1948–1952, FPA/A7/74.

32 NBCC and Prentif, correspondence, 1934–1936, FPA/A7/99.

33 Harrison to Miss Holland, 15 November 1934; Prentif circular, 23 March 1935, FPA/A7/99.

34 Correspondence, FPA and London Rubber.

35 Lamberts briefly continued to supply cervical caps, FPA/A7/74.

36 Transcript of telephone conversation, Margaret Howard and Mrs Wagstaff (Hackney Branch), 28 February 1951, FPA/A7/74.

37 Muriel Groom to Mrs Arnold (Richmond Mothers' Advisory Clinic), 25 July 1950, FPA/A7/74.

38 Norris and Conrad, 'Confidential Report'.

39 Prentif also made sprung diaphrams of 2.5 mm increments, but offered less favourable deals than London Rubber. Table of manufacturer's discounts, 1954, British Standards Institution correspondence 1953–4, FPA/A7/23.1.

40 Harvey, in conversation, 8 December 2016.

41 Szuhan, 'Sex in the Laboratory', 509.

42 Ernest Dichter Associates [henceforth EDA], 1739e: Some Remarks on the Questions Raised on the Contraceptive Research (London: EDA, 1961), 1, Box 78, Ernest Dichter Papers, Hagley Museum and Library, Wilmington, DE 19807.

43 E.C. Corderoy to H. Hill, 10 February 1967, FPA/C/F/7/1/15.

44 London Rubber to NBCA, 1 March 1939, FPA/A7/71.

45 Table of manufacturer's discounts, 1954.

46 London Rubber, 'Clinic Price List', January 1954, FPA/A7/76.

47 Memorandum to Branch Secretaries, 5 November 1965, FPA/A7/81.

48 EIU, 'Contraceptive Products', *RBS* 138 (1969): 23; Lafitte, *Family Planning and Family Planning Clinics* (FPA Working Party Report), May 1962, chapter 5, 21. Cited in Peel, 'Manufacturing and Retailing', 124.

49 F. Johnson to London Rubber, 13 November 1951, FPA/A7/74. Also FPA/A7/74/79 and 81.

50 Dai Hayward to Clifford-Smith, 23 May 1960, FPA/A7/79.

51 FPA memorandum to Branch Secretaries.

52 'Item 543, London Rubber Company', minutes of National Executive Meeting, 16 April 1964, FPA/A7/81.

53 Suzanne White Junod and Lara Marks, 'Women's Trials: The Approval of the First Oral Contraceptive Pill in the United States and Great Britain', *Journal of the History of Medicine and Allied Sciences* 57, no. 2 (2002): 117–60, 134; Szuhan dates the first Approved List to 1937. Szuhan, 'Sex in the Laboratory', 494.

54 Pyke to Reid, 6 December 1946, FPA/A7/74.

55 Szuhan, 'Sex in the Laboratory', 494.

56 Pyke circular, 25 November 1937, FPA/A7/71.

57 *London Rubber Home and Export Price List*, 8.

58 Brookes, *Abortion in England*, 119.

59 FPA and London Rubber, correspondence, 1930s–1960s, FPA/A7/71–72, 74, and 83.

60 Szuhan, 'Sex in the Laboratory', 507–8; British Standards Institution correspondence.

61 Harvey, in conversation, 8 December 2016.

62 Reid to FPA, 3 July 1951, FPA/A7/74.

63 Unknown correspondent to Pyke, 1 April 1941, FPA/A7/72.

64 Pyke to Reid, 10 September 1952, FPA/A7/73; J. Weber to 'Eric' [an employee of London Rubber], 28 February 1962, and Gladys Bowmel to Elstone, 5 March 1962, FPA/A7/82.

65 MMC 1975, 8.

66 Szuhan, 'Sex in the Laboratory', 495.

67 Bingham, *Family Newspapers?* 83.

68 Leathard, *Fight for Family Planning*, 100.

69 13 and 10 per cent disapproved. 30 and 35 per cent 'didn't know'. Gallup, cited in EDA, *1380c: A Motivational Research Study on Rubber Contraceptives* (London: EDA, 1961), 171, 198–9, Box 78, Ernest Dichter Papers, Hagley.

70 Ibid.

71 Reid to Clifford-Smith, 10 August 1956, FPA/A7/ 75.

72 Notes, 1955, FPA/A7/75.

73 Pyke to N. Berry, London Rubber advertising manager, 10 August 1955, FPA/A7/ 75.

74 *London Rubber Home and Export Price List*, 3.

75 Berry to Beryl Northage, 15 December 1959, FPA/A7/ 79.

76 Examples include a request to the Barrow branch asking whether a non-Approved List item could be advertised, FPA/A7/78. The *British Medical Journal* also contacted the association for approval on proposed London Rubber ads: Letter to Berry, 23 January 1961, FPA/A7/80.

77 Blairman to FPA, 19 April 1955, FPA/A7/73.

78 Note, conversation with Miss Gardner, FPA/A7/75.

79 *Practical Family Planning, Revised* (London: Planned Families Publications, 1959), FPA/A7/84; Newsight, 'It's Simply Known as the Pill', *Daily Mail*, 21 September 1965, press clippings, FPA/A7/100.

80 For examples, see '7 out of 10 of Your Married Customers Believe Family Planning to Be Essential', advertisement, *Chemist and Druggist* (6 May 1961): 24.

81 Hansard. Birth Control Booklets. HC Deb, 19 June 1940, vol. 362, col. 144.

82 Leathard, *Fight for Family Planning*, 86.

83 Ibid., 93; Hansard. Luke Teeling, MP, 'The Week's Good Cause' (appeals). HC Deb, 1 July 1959, vol. 608, col. 452.

84 Bingham, *Family Newspapers?* 83.

85 Leathard, *Fight for Family Planning*, 93.

86 Kynaston, *Family Britain*, 563; Hall, *Sex, Gender and Social Change in Britain since 1880* (London: Palgrave Macmillan, 2000, 2013), 139–40.

87 Evans, *Freedom to Choose*, 163.

88 Borge, 'Family Planning and Broadcast Television in Post-War Britain.' Unpublished manuscript, 2020.

89 G. Aird Whyte, 'The Eugenics Society', *Eugenics Review* 46, no. 1 (April 1954): 19.

90 Bingham, *Family Newspapers?* 83.

91 Leathard, *Fight for Family Planning*, 94; '24 Hours', transcript, BBC, 1 November 1965, BBC Written Archives, Caversham.

92 Author's survey of broadcast coverage using the *Radio Times* database, BBC Genome.

93 Bingham, *Family Newspapers?* 83.

94 Sheila J. Himsworth, 'The Archives of the Family Planning Association. Introduction and Review', May 1976, Wellcome Collection (library catalogue), accessed 13 November 2019, http://archives.wellcome.ac.uk/DServe/dserve. exe?dsqIni=Dserve.ini&dsqApp=Archive&dsqCmd=Show.tcl&dsqDb=Catalog &dsqPos=0&dsqSearch=%28AltRefNo%3D%27SA/FPA%27%29; Leathard, *Fight for Family Planning*, 86–94.

95 Ibid., 93.

96 Jane Lewis, 'Private Counselling versus Public Voice, 1948–68', in *Whom God Hath Joined Together: The Work of Marriage Guidance*, edited by Lewis et al. (London and New York: Tavistock/Routledge, 1992), 101.

97 Bingham, *Family Newspapers?* 82.

98 'Contraception: History of Christian Attitudes', BBC, accessed 13 November 2019, http://www.bbc.co.uk/religion/religions/christianity/christianethics/ contraception_1.shtml; Leathard, *Fight for Family Planning*, 96.

99 Ibid.; Rev. Dr Kenneth Greet, secretary of the Christian Citizenship Department of the Methodist Church, served on the Executive Committee from 1956 to 1964. Rev. S.R. Birchwall, vicar of Chingford, sat from 1955–64 and on the National Council 1964–71. Himsworth, 'Archives'.

100 Teeling, 'Good Cause', col. 453.

101 Leathard, *Fight for Family Planning*, 100; Himsworth, 'Archives'.

102 Elstone to Reid, 9 January 1961; Reid to Elstone, 17 January 1961, FPA/A7/80.

103 See, for example, 'New Literature on Family Planning', advertisement, *British Medical Journal* 2, no. 5245 (1961): 11.

104 N.L. Wintergill to London Rubber, 7 November 1958, FPA/A7/78.

105 Reid to Russell Brain, 13 January 1961, FPA/A7/78.

106 Reid to Clifford-Smith, 9 February 1960, FPA/A7/78.

107 FPA and London Rubber, correspondence, 1957–1960, FPA/A7/76; Elstone to Reid, 9 March 1961, FPA/A7/80.

108 Correspondence, FPA/A7/76/79.

109 Pyke to Mrs Nicholls, 16 November 1959, FPA/A7/79.

110 Mrs Parker to all Area Organisers, 5 July 1960, FPA/A7/76.

111 Berry to Clifford-Smith, 23 December 1959, FPA/A7/79.

112 Memo, 9 December 1959, FPA/A7/79.

113 Hayward to Clifford-Smith, 5 November 1959, FPA/A7/79.

114 Hayward to Parker, 15 February 1960, FPA/A7/79.

115 Parker to Hayward, 20 November 1959, FPA/A7/79.

116 Hayward to Elstone, 18 April 1961, FPA/A7/80.

117 Elstone to Hayward, 24 April 1961, FPA/A7/80.

CHAPTER 5

1 London Rubber (Industries) Ltd, *Memorandum of Association* (1961).

2 'Well Protected', *The Economist*, 27 August 1966.

3 London Rubber Company Ltd, *Report and Accounts* (1959), 4.

4 This phrase was popularised following Reginald Maudling's 1963 budget, which aimed for greater expansion of the economy.

5 Edgerton, *Rise and Fall*, 310.

6 'Document on London Rubber'.

7 *Report and Accounts* (1959), 4.

8 Ibid.

9 London Rubber Company Ltd, *Director's Report and Statement of Accounts* (1960), 4.

10 Ibid., 5; London Rubber Company Ltd, *Director's Report and Statement of Accounts* (1961), 4.

11 Sandbrook, *Never Had It So Good*, 236.

12 *London Image* (winter 1968–69): 29.

13 Harvey, in conversation, 8 December 2016.

14 Anthony Sampson, *Anatomy of Britain* (London: Hodder and Stoughton, 1962, 1963), 496–8.

15 *Memorandum of Association*.

16 London Rubber Company Ltd, *Director's Report and Statement of Accounts* (1963), 4.

17 'Document on London Rubber'.

18 MMC 1975, 18; London Rubber Company Ltd, *Report and Accounts* (1967), 6.

19 Durex Information Service for Sexual Health, *History of the Condom* (Broxbourne: London International Ltd, 1994), 6. Percy Skuy Papers, Dittrick Medical Museum, Cleveland, Ohio.

20 MMC 1975, 19, 22; Davis, 'London Rubber', 7.

21 These figures do not make clear whether prices are derived from bulk buying, e.g., packs of twelve condoms, or the more expensive and more common 'packet of three'. London Rubber Company International Ltd, memorandum

of evidence, 'Population Growth in the United Kingdom', in *Select Committee on Science and Technology, Session 1969–70: Population*. Minutes of Evidence and Appendices (London: HMSO, 1970), appendix 13, 305.

22 Harvey, in conversation, 8 December 2016.

23 Consumers' Association [henceforth CA], 'Contraceptives', *Which?* supplement (15 November 1963): 38.

24 MMC 1975, 69, 73.

25 London Rubber Industries, 'Enormous Public Demand for Durex Gossamer', advertisement, *Chemist and Druggist Supplement* (4 March 1961): 63. Italics in original.

26 Author's experiments with own Durex object collection.

27 Elstone to Berry, 16 January 1961, FPA/A7/80.

28 CA, 'Contraceptives', 7.

29 EIU, 'Contraceptive Products', 12.

30 MMC 1975, 29.

31 London Rubber Company Ltd, *Report and Accounts* (1963), 4; *London Image* (autumn/winter 1964): 22.

32 David Reynolds, *One World Divisible* (London: Penguin, 2001), 142.

33 *London Image* (spring 1962): 15; FPA/A7/81; London Rubber International Ltd, *Report and Accounts* (1970), 9.

34 London Rubber Company Ltd, *Director's Report and Statement of Accounts* (1958), 4.

35 Linder, *Crusader for Sex Education*, 207.

36 Snow, in conversation with author.

37 London Rubber to Members and shareholders, 1963.

38 'Document on London Rubber'.

39 Raymond L. Belsky and Alfred. D. Sollins, 'Commercial Production and Distribution of Contraceptives', *Reports on Population/Family Planning*, no. 4 (June 1970): 5–6.

40 London Rubber Company Ltd, *Director's Report and Statement of Accounts* (1964), 4.

41 'Document on London Rubber'; EIU, 'Contraceptive Products', 13.

42 Reid to the Editor, *Sunday Times*, 19 June 1968, press clippings, FPA/C/F/7/1/15.

43 Sampson, *Anatomy of Britain*, 251–3.

44 Condom returns slips from Navy medical officers, January–February 1961, ADM1/27662. London Rubber's annual output in the 1930s was 2 million. John Peel, 'Manufacture and Retailing', 122.

45 Sampson, *Anatomy of Britain*, 251–4.

46 Minutes, meeting with medical director general, Royal Navy, 15 November 1960, ADM1/27662.

47 Sampson, *Anatomy of Britain*, 251–4.

48 Hansard. Emanuel Shinwell, MP, Contraceptives (Supply). HC Deb 15 November 1949, vol 469 c184w.

49 Medical director general of the Navy Fleet Order MDG.32/10/60/A, December 1960, ADM1/27662.

50 Returns slips, ADM1/27662.

51 CA, 'Contraceptives', 37–45. The report went on sale to *Which?* subscribers as a supplement on 17 January 1964.

52 FPA secretary to Prentif, Ltd, 10 February 1937, FPA/A7/100.

53 Beryl Suitters, *Be Brave and Angry* (London: International Planned Parenthood Federation, 1973), 73, 106–8.

54 FPA and Premier Laboratories, correspondence 1959–1964, FPA/A7/98.

55 IPPF, *Medical Handbook* (London: International Planned Parenthood Federation, 1962), 9.

56 Lawrence Black, 'Which? Craft in Post-War Britain: The Consumers' Association and the Politics of Affluence', *Albion: A Quarterly Journal Concerned with British Studies* 46, no. 1 (2004): 52–81, 71.

57 Bingham, *Family Newspapers*, 82–7.

58 Press clippings, 1963–1964; *Which?* press release, 15 November 1963, FPA/A17/109.

59 Among those circulating teasers were the *Guardian*, *Observer*, *Daily Mail*, *Times*, *New Society*, *Northern Echo*, *Yorkshire Post*, *News of the World*, *Spectator*, *New Statesman*, *Glasgow Herald*, and *Financial Times*.

60 *Which?* press release, 15 November 1963, FPA/A17/109.

61 Ibid.

62 CA, 'Contraceptives', 40–1. The London Rubber retail brands examined were Durapac, Durex Coral Supertrans, Durex Gossamer, Durex Nu-Pac, Durex Protectives, Ona Protectives, Ona Coral Supertrans, Velsan, Betall's Veribest Golden Pack, and Prevax. Clinic brands also manufactured by London Rubber were CBC Lubricated, CBC Teat, and Transyl. Brands from other manufacturers were Lam-Butt no.9a, Morfi, Parico, Phelps Ivory, Perfection Third Quality, Prentif Silver Pack, Silvexa, Star, Waverly Pearl, Arloid Coralex, Arloid Crystalex, Lloyd's Grade B, and Premex Coral Superfine.

63 Ibid., 45.

64 *Pharmaceutical Journal*, 23 November 1963: 532.

65 Minutes, British Standards Institution Technical Committee 9GC/17, Surgical Rubber and Plastic Appliances, November 1958, FPA/A7/23.2.

66 CA, 'Contraceptives', 38.

67 Ibid., 36.

68 Ibid.

69 Lawrence Black, *Redefining British Politics. Culture, Consumerism and Participation, 1954–70* (Basingstoke: Palgrave Macmillan, 2010), 14–45; Matthew Hilton, *Consumerism in Twentieth Century Britain. The Search for a Historical Movement* (Cambridge: Cambridge University Press, 2008), 137–64.

70 *Which?* press release.

71 *Which?* clippings files, FPA/A17/109.

72 Ibid.

73 British Standards Institution, *British Standard for Rubber Condoms BS3704* (London: British Standards Institution, 1964).

74 Durex Information Service, *History of the Condom*.

75 *The Times* (London), 17 July 1959.

76 'Document on London Rubber'; British Standards Institution correspondence.

77 London Rubber retained exclusive use of the kite mark until Ortho introduced own-brand condoms in the 1970s. EIU, 'Contraceptive Products', 3.

78 British Standards Institution correspondence; BSI, 'First Contraceptive Standard Laid Down by BSI', press release, 8 April 1964, FPA/A7/81; BSI, *BS3704*, 4.

79 Ibid.

80 BSI 'First Contraceptive Standard', 7; John J. Dumm et al., 'The Modern Condom: A Quality Product for Effective Contraception', *Population Reports*, Series H/2 (1974): 30.

81 London Rubber and National Birth Control Association, correspondence 1937–1941, FPA/A7/71.

82 Harvey, in conversation, 8 December 2016.

83 BSI, *BS3704*, 6.

84 Miskell, 'Cavity Protection', 46–50.

85 Elstone to Premier Laboratories, 28 August 1964, FPA/A7/98.

86 Invitation to BSI Licence Award Ceremony, Waldorf Hotel, 9 April 1964, FPA/A7/81.

87 BSI, *BS3704*, 4.

88 Wendy B. Murphy, *Science and Serendipity* (White Plains, NY: Benjamin Co. Inc., 1994), 9–10.

89 Marks, *Sexual Chemistry*, 5.

90 Milton Silverman, 'Wonderful Medicine Plant', *Saturday Evening Post* (21 February 1953): 28.

91 Syntex Laboratories, *A Corporation and a Molecule: The Story of Research at Syntex* (Palo Alto, CA: Syntex Laboratories, 1966), 31.

92 Junod and Marks, 'Women's Trials', 128–9.

93 Daniel Carpenter, *Reputation and Power* (Princeton, NJ: Princeton University Press, 2010), 185–8, 535.

94 Junod and Marks, 'Women's Trials', 146; G.D. Searle and Co., *Annual Report* (1961), 10.

95 Searle and Co., *Annual Report* (1961), 10.

96 For more information on this process, see Carpenter, *Reputation and Power*, 536–7; Junod and Marks, 'Women's Trials', 128–33, 144.

97 Searle and Co., *Annual Report* (1961), 10.

98 Syntex Laboratories, *A Corporation and a Molecule*, 31.

99 Norman Applezweig, 'The Big Steroid Treasure Hunt', *Chemical Week* (31 January 1959): 38.

100 MMC 1975, 18.

101 Marks, *Sexual Chemistry*, 243.

102 Renee Michelle Courey, 'Participants in the Development, Marketing and Safety Evaluation of the Oral Contraceptive, 1950–1965: Mythic Dimensions of a Scientific Solution'. PhD thesis, University of California, Berkeley, 1994, 91.

103 Marks, *Sexual Chemistry*, 122.

104 Bingham, *Family Newspapers?* 84.

105 Sue Hawkins, 'The Pharmaceutical Industry, Doctors and the Pill'. Master's thesis, Imperial College, London, 2002, 5.

106 Correspondence, December 1958–February 1959; Pyke to Professor W.C.W. Nixon, 4 February 1959, FPA/A17/44.

107 Harvey, in conversation, 8 December 2016.

108 Ann Cartwright, *Parents and Family Planning Services* (New York: Atherton, 1970), 17.

109 Junod and Marks, 'Women's Trials', 134.

110 London Rubber to Clifford-Smith, 2 May 1957, FPA/A7/75.

111 Reid and Eleanor Mears, correspondence, May–July 1959, FPA/C/F/7/1/14. Free sampling of Gossamer through the FPA, rather than the CIFC, was implemented in 1962. R. Ross-Turner to Margaret Howard, 7 March 1962, FPA/A7/82.

112 Reid and Helena Wright, correspondence, June–July 1958, FPA/C/F/7/1/14.

113 Note of telephone conversation with Mr Turner, 19 June 1959, FPA/C/F/7/1/14.

114 Mears to Reid, 14 September 1959, FPA/C/F/7/1/14. Underline in original.

115 Borge, 'According to Plan: Strategic Film Production at the London Rubber Company in the 1960s', *Cahiers d'Histoire du Cnam* 12, no. 2 (2019): 73–103.

116 Murphy, *Condom Industry*, 10–12.

117 Tone, *Devices and Desires*, 239.

118 Jonathan Eig, *The Birth of the Pill* (New York: Norton, 2014), 275.

119 London Rubber Ltd to members and shareholders, 11 October to 11 December 1963, Box 3261, Guildhall.

120 Ibid.

121 Elizabeth Siegel Watkins, *On the Pill* (Baltimore and London: Johns Hopkins University Press, 1998), 42.

122 Junod and Marks, 'Women's Trials', 128–9.

123 Tone, *Devices and Desires*, 239.

124 Ibid., 196; London Rubber Ltd to members.

125 *Drug Topics Red Book 1945–6*, 145; Supreme Court of India, 3.

126 Supreme Court of India, 11.

127 Ibid.

128 Author's survey of *Drug Topics Red Book* and *American Druggist Blue Book*, 1940–1974, and also of contraceptive collection objects, conducted over February–June 2015 at the Division of Medical Sciences, Smithsonian Institution.

129 *American Druggist Blue Book 1940–1*, inside cover.

130 Author's survey.

131 'Disruptive Technologies: Fertility Control Pills in the Past, Present and Future' (seminar supported by the Centre for Parenting Studies, Centre for the Interdisciplinary Study of Reproduction and Kent Law School, 20 March 2019).

132 Christensen, *Innovator's Dilemma*.

133 Ibid., xviii.

134 MMC 1975, 18.

135 London Rubber Company Ltd, *Report and Accounts* (1959), 5.

CHAPTER 6

For the chapter-opening epigraph: EDA, *1380c*, 160.

1 EIU, 'Contraceptive Products', 19; MMC 1975, 12–13.

2 Leathard, *Fight for Family Planning*, 108.

3 EIU, 'Contraceptive Products', 10 (table 1: aggregate figures from Pierce and Rowntree, 'Birth Control in Britain').

4 Peel, 'Hull Family Survey', 65; Murphy, *Condom Industry*, 135.

5 EIU, 'Contraceptive Products', 11, 19.

6 MMC 1975, 61.

7 EIU, 'Contraceptive Products', 10.

8 Marks, *Sexual Chemistry*, 116–37.

9 The British Pharmaceutical industry's 1958 marketing code prohibited the advertising of prescription medicines directly to the public in order to distance manufacturers from patent medicine. *Code of Sales Promotion Practice for Medical Specialties in the United Kingdom* (London: Association of the British Pharmaceutical Industry, 1958). Supplied by Gillian Reeves, communications officer, ABPI, June 2014.

10 'The Contraceptive Pill', *British Medical Journal* 2, no. 5254 (1961): 754–5.

11 Leathard, *Fight for Family Planning*, 107; press clippings, RJH/A11/2.

12 Pierce and Rowntree, 'Birth Control in Britain Part I' and 'Part II'.

13 'Symposium on Oral Contraception', *Queen's Medical Magazine* 53 (1961): 215–26.

14 National Economic Development Office, *Focus on Pharmaceuticals* (London: HMSO, 1972), 117.

15 EDA, *1380c*, 171.

16 Peel, 'Manufacture and Retailing', 113–25, 124.

17 Ibid.

18 EIU, 'Contraceptive Products', 20.

19 Baker 'Advertising Male Contraceptives', 116.

20 Skuy, Skype conversation, 27 August 2014.

21 Bernard Asbell, *The Pill: A Biography of the Drug that Changed the World* (New York: Random House, 1995), xvi; Cook, *Sexual Revolution*, 48.

22 Wilson and West, '"Unmentionables"', 99.

23 Lafitte, 'Users of Birth Control Clinics', 12–30; Pierce and Rowntree, 'Birth Control in Britain Part I' and 'Part II'.

24 The Pulse London Ltd. [henceforth TPL], *Family Planning Enquiry* [henceforth FPE] (London: The Pulse Ltd, February, 1961), FPA/A7/81.

25 TPL, *1959a. Independent Television London Viewership Survey, no. 1* (spring 1959) and *No. 2* (August–September 1959), produced on behalf of Associated Rediffusion, British Library, London. With thanks to Alison Payne for suggesting this citation.

26 Hayward to Elstone, 24 March 1961, FPA/A7/80.

27 *Modern Family Planning* [henceforth MFP] (London: Family Counsel, 1961), FPA/A7/76.

28 Ibid., 8.

29 Marks, *Sexual Chemistry*, 141.

30 Ibid., 138.

31 Hetherington's papers are held at Wellcome Collection, under reference RJH.

32 Author's correspondence with Julia Larden, Hetherington's daughter, November 2013; Jessica Borge, 'The Oral Contraceptive Trade in Britain: Print Marketing Collateral, 1961–1969', Arts and Humanities Research Council Digital Image Gallery, accessed 13 November 2019, http:/www.ahrc.ac.uk/research/readwatchlisten/imagegallery/2014galleries/theoralcontraceptivetradein britain/.

33 *MFP*, 12–14.

34 Committee on the Safety of Drugs, *Report for 1969 and 1970* (London: HMSO 1971).

35 TPL, *FPE*, 1.

36 Ibid., 2, 14, table 8.

37 Ibid., 2.

38 Eig, *Birth of the Pill*, 171–2; Cook, *Sexual Revolution*, 292; Marks, *Sexual Chemistry*, 75, 105, 131–5, 138, 207–15; Robert J. Hetherington Papers, series 'C'.

39 TPL, *FPE*, 3, 16.

40 EIU, 'UK Contraceptive Market', 28.

41 TPL, *FPE*, 17. Other brands mentioned were Volpar, the minimally successful product of the FPA's collaboration with British Drug Houses (4 per cent), Ona (an London Rubber brand distributed only through barbershops, 2 per cent), Ortho (who produced several contraceptive products but not condoms, 2 per cent), and Gynomin (2 per cent).

42 Ibid., 14, table 11.

43 Ibid., 3.

44 Ibid., 16, table 13.

45 Ibid., 4. 76 per cent reported a favourable response to *MFP*.

46 Ibid. One person mentioned 'the part about the pill', and the other person refused to explain their objection.

47 For an examination of the entangled nature of privately and publicly funded sex education in America, see Alexandra M. Lord, *Condom Nation: The U.S.*

Government's Sex Education Campaign from World War I to the Internet (Baltimore: Johns Hopkins University Press, 2009).

48 TPL, *FPE*, 26–8, appendix B, 'Verbatims'.

49 Hayward to Elstone, 24 March 1961, FPA/A7/80.

50 TPL, *FPE*, 4.

51 EIU, 'Motivational Research', *RBS* 131 (1969), 29.

52 'New Literature on Family Planning'.

53 Ibid.

54 London Rubber memo on *MFP*, 15 December 1961, FPA/A7/84.

55 EIU, 'Motivational Research', 30.

56 Winston Fletcher, *Powers of Persuasion* (Oxford and New York: Oxford University Press, 200), 58; Stefan Schwarzkopf, '"Culture" and the Limits of Innovation in Marketing: Ernest Dichter, Motivation Studies and Psychoanalytic Consumer Research in Great Britain, 1950s–1970s', *Management and Organizational History* 2, no. 3 (2007): 219–36, 222.

57 Institute of Motivational Research [henceforth IMR], *999c: A Motivational Research Study of the Sales and Advertising Problems of Perception and Delfen* (Croton-on-Hudson, NY: IMR, 1958), Box 45, Ernest Dichter Papers, Hagley.

58 Ibid., 15.

59 Ibid., 16.

60 IMR, *1485c: The Place of the Condom in the Present Cultural Climate* (Croton-on-Hudson, NY: IMR, July 1962), University of Vienna Library.

61 Ibid., 14.

62 Ibid., 96–7.

63 IMR, *985.11e: Memorandum of Physician's Attitudes towards the Treatment of Female Disorders* (Croton-on-Hudson, NY: IMR, July 1960), Box 44, Ernest Dichter Papers, Hagley.

64 EDA, *1380a: Proposal for a Psychological Survey on Protective Contraceptives* (London: EDA, 1961), Box 78, Ernest Dichter Papers, Hagley.

65 EDA, *1380c*.

66 EDA, *1739e*.

67 EDA, *1380a*, 5–6.

68 Ibid., 1.

69 Ibid., 2.

70 EDA, *1380c*, 7.

71 Pierce and Rowntree, 'Birth Control in Britain Part I', 127, table 1; Moya Woodside, 'The Contraceptive Practices of an English Working-Class Group', *Human Fertility* 12, no. 1 (1947): 12, table 1.

72 EDA, *1739e*, 9.

73 EDA, *1380c*, 169.

74 EDA, *1739e*, 8.

75 Ibid., 11.

76 McLaren, *A History of Contraception*, 235–6; Cook, *Sexual Revolution*, 48.

77 Elizabeth Draper, *Birth Control in the Modern World: The Role of the Individual in Population Control* (London: Penguin, 1965), 124–5.

78 EDA, *1380c*, 54.

79 Ibid.

80 Laite, *Common Prostitutes*, 174.

81 Ibid., 5.

82 Bingham, *Family Newspapers?* 164–9.

83 Hall, *Sex, Gender and Social Change*, 142–4.

84 EDA, *1380c*, 52, 54, 55, 61, 63, 66, 70–1.

85 Ibid., 9.

86 Ibid., 75

87 Ibid., 18.

88 Ibid., 14, 90.

89 Ibid., 74. Underscore in original.

90 EDA, *1739e*, 8; EDA, *1380c*, 166.

91 Ibid.

92 Anderson, 'Community Pharmacy'; Jobling, 'Playing Safe', 58; Mechen, '"Closer Together"', 215–17; Peel, 'Manufacturing and Retailing', 124.

93 Both Suzie Hayman and Paul Jobling have conflated consumer approval of family planning education with the approval of commercial advertising. Hayman, *Advertising and Contraceptives* (London: Birth Control Trust and Brook Advisory Centres, 1977), 12; Jobling, 'Playing Safe', 58.

94 TPL, *FPE*, 1.

95 Under pressure from social stakeholders to 'produce evidence' of consumer resistance, the Independent Broadcasting Authority commissioned independent audience research in 1980. The majority of the 1,003-strong cohort strongly disagreed with contraceptive advertising. Health Education Council executive to FPA executive (identities protected), 28 November 1977, FPA/C/B/3/11/1.

96 John U. Farley and Harold J. Leavitt, 'Population Control and the Private Sector', *Journal of Social Issues* 23, no. 4 (1967): 136.

97 Leo Abse, MP, Hansard. National Health Service (Family Planning), Bill. HC Deb, 17 February 1967, vol. 741, col. 965.

98 Ibid.

99 Wilson and West, '"Unmentionables"', 99.

100 Ibid., 92.

101 Ibid.

102 Ibid., 100.

103 Edgerton, *Shock of the Old*, 24.

104 Asbell, *The Pill*, xvi.

105 Harvey, in conversation, 8 December 2016.

106 EDA, *1739e*, 8.

107 Ibid., 9.

108 Ibid.

109 Ibid.

110 Ibid.

111 TPL, *FPE*, 3, 4, 15, 16, 18; EDA, *1380c*, 33, 167.

112 EDA, *1380c*, 33.

113 For a detailed discussion of the historic medicalization of contraception through the pill, see Andrea Tone, 'Medicalizing Reproduction: The Pill and Home Pregnancy Tests', *Journal of Sex Research* 49, no. 4 (July 2012): 319–27. For an examination of the doctor's role in circulating oral contraceptive knowledge, see Agata Ignaciuk, 'Doctors, Women, and the Circulation of Knowledge of Oral Contraceptives in Spain in the 1960s–1970s', in *Gendered Drugs and Medicine*, edited by Teresa Ortiz-Gómez and María Jesús Santesmases (Farnham and Burlington: Ashgate, 2014), 147–66.

114 EDA, *1739e*, 9.

115 EDA, *1380c*, 10.

116 Ibid., 11–12.

117 Ibid.

118 John Pearson and Graham Turner, *The Persuasion Industry* (London: Eyre and Spottiswoode, 1965), 177; EDA, *1739e*, 6, 8.

119 'Number of Marriages, Marriage Rates and Period of Occurrence, 11 June 2014', table 3, *Historic Marriage Numbers and Rates, 1862–2011*, Office for National Statistics, accessed 13 November 2019, https://www.ons.gov.uk/people populationandcommunity/birthsdeathsandmarriages/marriagecohabitation andcivilpartnerships/datasets/numberofmarriagesmarriageratesandperiod ofoccurrence; EDA, *1380c*, 71.

CHAPTER 7

For the chapter-opening epigraph: Insight, 'The Rise and Fall of an Undercover Pressure-group', *Sunday Times*, 20 June 1965, Press Clippings. FPA/A7/100.

1 Editorial, 'Hands off the Loop', *Medical Gynaecology and Fertility Abstracts* 4, no. 4 (1965): 1; 'Obituary', *Medical Gynaecology and Fertility Abstracts* 4, no. 3 (1965): 1.

2 EIU, 'Contraceptive Products', 20–1.

3 'The Rise and Fall'; Leslie Geddes-Brown, 'The Campaign to Knock the Pill', *Northern Echo*, 23 June 1965, press clippings, FPA/A7/100.

4 'It's Simply Known as the Pill'.

5 Mechen, '"Closer Together"', 220.

6 'The Rise and Fall'.

7 Jeremy A. Greene and David Herzberg, 'Hidden in Plain Sight: Marketing Prescription Drugs to Consumers in the Twentieth Century', *American Journal of Public Health* 100, no. 5 (2010): 800.

8 EDA, *1739e*, 8.

9 Ibid.; EDA, *1380c*, 166.

10 EDA, *1380c*, 169–71; TPL, *FPE*, 16, table 13.

11 EDA, *1380c*, 10, 138.

12 Peel, 'Contraception and the Medical Profession', 133.

13 Tamasin Cave and Andrew Rowell, *A Quiet Word* (London: Bodley Head, 2014), 200–1.

14 Ibid.

15 Noel Wilkinson, 'Let's End This Image of Women with Beards', *Evening Star*, 13 September 1965, press clippings, FPA/A7/100. A useful account of women's attitudes to oral contraceptive safety (encompassing the 1960s debate), can be found in Marks, *Sexual Chemistry*, 207–14.

16 For an overview of the thalidomide tragedy in Britain, see Gordon E. Appelbe, 'From Arsenic to Thalidomide: A Brief History of Medicine Safety', in *Making Medicines: A Brief History of Pharmacy and Pharmaceuticals*, edited by Stuart Anderson (London and Chicago; Pharmaceutical Press, 2001), 243–9.

17 'The Rise and Fall'.

18 Institute of Public Relations, *Do You Need Planned Public Relations?* (London: IPR, 1961), 3. IPR Papers, History of Advertising Trust, Raveningham, Norfolk. Italics in original.

19 S.E. Finer, *Anonymous Empire: A Study of the Lobby in Great Britain* (London: Pall Mall Press, 1966), 137.

20 Sampson, *Anatomy*, 594.

21 Jacquie L'Etang, *Public Relations in Britain: A History of Professional Practice in the 20th Century* (Mahwah, New Jersey: Lawrence Erlbaum Associates, 2004), 136.

22 L'Etang, *Public Relations in Britain*, 170.

23 CA, 'Contraceptives', 90; Finer, *Anonymous Empire*, 137–8; MMC 1975, 26; Leathard, *Fight for Family Planning*, 106–7.

24 GSU *Bulletin*, 2 December 1964, 1.

25 Editorial, *Daily Mail*, 22 July 1964, 6, cited in Bingham, *Family Newspapers*, 85; Appelbe, 'From Arsenic to Thalidomide', 257–8.

26 For evidence of this PR campaign see, for example, Christopher George, 'Drugs: The Political Threat', *Yorkshire Post*, 13 May 1964, press clippings, FPA/A17/99. See also: Association of the British Pharmaceutical Industry, *Facts about Pharmaceutical Expenditure under the N.H.S.* (London: ABPI, 1964); *How Equivalent Is an Equivalent* (London: ABPI, 1963); *The Human and Economic Contribution of Drugs* (London: ABPI, 1963).

27 GSU *Bulletin*, 4; Committee for the Safety of Drugs, *Annual Report for the Year Ending December 1966* (London, 1967), 6, cited in Marks, *Sexual Chemistry*, 142.

28 'The Rise and Fall'.

29 Sampson, *Anatomy of Britain*, 598.

30 Correspondence, *The Ampleforth Journal* 69, part 3 (October 1964): 264–6.

31 GSU *Bulletin*, 6.

32 'The Rise and Fall'.

33 Ibid.

34 Ibid.

35 'London Rubber Industries Helps New Techniques in Surgery', *London Image* (summer 1973): 15–16; Interview with Ray Russell-Fell.

36 'Help for the Handicapped', *London Image* (autumn/winter 1964): 12–13.

37 Interview with Ray Russell-Fell.

38 Press clippings, FPA/A17/100.

39 Ibid.

40 Barbara Seaman, *The Doctor's Case against the Pill* (New York: P.H. Wyden, 1969), is considered to be a foundational text of the Women's Health Movement of the 1970s; GSU *Bulletin*, 2.

41 'The Rise and Fall'; MMC 1975, 26.

42 Borge, 'According to Plan'.

43 MMC 1975, 26; 'Family Centre', circular to doctors, November 1961, FPA/A7/81.

44 Patricia McLaughlin, 'Report on the Seventh International Conference on Planned Parenthood: February, 10th–16th, 1963, Singapore', *Journal of the Institute of Health Education* 1, no. 3 (1963): 1.

45 International Planned Parenthood Federation, British Committee Second Draft of Appeal Leaflet Embodying Suggestions of Mrs Pyke and Mr Aird, 24 July 1955. C.P. Blacker Papers, CPB/C.4/3, Wellcome Collection.

46 C.P. Blacker, Draft report on the IPPF 7th International Conference in Singapore, February, 1963, CPB/C.4/9.

47 Files detailing this collaboration are currently closed to researchers until 1 January 2021, FPA/A10/22.

48 Later called *Medical Gynaecology and Fertility Abstracts*. Hard copies of *Fertility Abstracts* were consulted at the National Library of Medicine, National Institutes of Health, Bethesda, Maryland, and the British Library, London.

49 EDA, *1380c*, 169.

50 Casey to C.P. Blacker, correspondence, 1961, CPB/C.4/7.

51 Ibid.

52 Ibid.; A.S. Parkes to Blacker, 20 February 1961, CPB/C.4/7.

53 'Fertility Abstracts', subscription form, March 1962, FPA/A7/82.

54 'Honouring Dr George Barry Carruthers MD', the Royal Society of Medicine Wall of Honour, accessed 13 November 2019, http://www.rsm-wallofhonour. com/dr-george-barry-carruthers-md.aspx.

55 Subscription form; *Fertility Abstracts* emulated a similar journal, *Tydings*, which had been published by Julius Schmid in America between 1950 and 1954. Julius Schmid (USA and Canada) joined the London Rubber Group in 1963. *Tydings* consulted at the National Library of Medicine.

56 FPA and London Rubber, correspondence, May–August 1962, FPA/A7/82.

57 'Honouring Dr George Barry Carruthers MD'.

58 Northage to Margaret Howard, 1 August 1962. FPA/A7/82; Carruthers to Elstone, 22 May 1962; 'Fertility Abstracts', subscription form.

59 *Fertility Abstracts* 3, no. 1 (1964).

60 'Obituary', 1; Carruthers, 'The Sequential Oral Contraceptive: A Clinical Study', *Fertility Abstracts* 4, no. 2 (1965): 3–6.

61 FPA and London Rubber, correspondence, 1954–1957, FPA/A7/73–75.

62 Elstone to Morrell, 12 February 1962, FPA/A7/82.

63 'Note of Conversation with Miss Gardner, Advertising Agency', 18 July 1955, FPA/A7/75.
64 Elstone to Reid, 29 April 1960; Norman Berry to Clifford-Smith, 27 November 1959; Berry to Clifford-Smith, 4 January 1960, FPA/A7/79.
65 MFP.
66 'Conversation with Miss Gardner'.
67 Ibid.
68 FPA/A7/129.
69 'When a Patient Asks about Family Planning ...' advertisement, Lancet (17 February 1962): 30.
70 EDA, 1380c, 171.
71 The Plain Facts about Family Planning (London: H.F. Booklets, 1961), 4.
72 Marriages Are Made (London: London Rubber Industries, 1965), 15–16.
73 Ibid., 15–23.
74 EDA, 1380c, 14.
75 Marriages Are Made, 23.
76 Ibid.
77 London Foundation for Marriage Education, Some Religious Views on Contraception (London: Counsel Publications, 1965), 14–15.
78 Paul R. Ehrlich, The Population Bomb (New York: Ballantine Books, 1968); Leslie Woodcock Tentler, Catholics and Contraception: An American History (Ithaca and London: Cornell University Press, 2004), 137.
79 Alana Harris, '"The Writings of Querulous Women": Contraception, Conscience and Clerical Authority in 1960s Britain', Recusant History 32, no. 4 (October 2015): 557–85.
80 Patrick Russell and James Piers Taylor, Shadows of Progress (London: British Film Institute, 2010), 60–100; EDA, 1739e, 8.
81 Reid to Clifford-Smith, 4 September 1958, FPA/A7/78.
82 Elstone to Reid, 2 April 1958, FPA/A7/78; Sylvia Ponsonby, 'London Federation Public Relations', Family Planning 11, no. 3 (1962), 65.
83 Reid and Elstone, correspondence, August–September 1962, FPA/A17/38.
84 'London Rubber Film Unit Points the Way to Family Planning', London Image (winter 1968/1969): 4–9. FPA area organiser's report, 23 March 1966, FPA/A7/81. The London Rubber films were: According to Plan (1964); Learning to Live (1964); Sex Instruction: Man and Woman (1964); Family Planning – A Medical Approach (1964); London Image (1965).
85 Press clippings, FPA/A7/100.
86 EDA, 1380c, 16.
87 Michael Schofield, The Sexual Behaviour of Young People (Harmondsworth: Penguin, 1968), 87–8, 139, 256 (appendix 3). Based on some 2000 interviews held in England, 84 per cent of boys and 82 per cent of girls claimed some knowledge of contraception.
88 Ibid., 180; EDA, 1380c, 16.
89 Sandbrook, Never Had It So Good, 435.

90 *According to Plan*, embedded video, Wellcome Collection, accessed 13 November 2019, https://wellcomelibrary.org/item/b2847868x#?c=0&m=0&s=0&cv=0.

91 Fisher, *Birth Control, Sex, and Marriage*, 59–60; EDA, *1380c*, 191; EDA, *1739e*, 8.

92 EDA, *1739e*, 8; EDA, *1380c*, 44.

93 EDA, *1380c*, 75.

94 Ibid., 7; EDA, *1739e*, 8.

95 EDA, *1380c*, 7.

96 Ibid., 9.

97 Ibid., 9–10.

98 'Obituary', *Medical Gynaecology and Fertility Abstracts* 4, no. 3 (1965): 1.

99 *According to Plan*, 07:17; Jessica Borge, 'Making and Marketing Condoms', Wellcome Blog, accessed 13 November 2019, http://blog.wellcomelibrary.org/2016/10/making-and-marketing-condoms/.

100 EDA, *1380c*, 10.

101 *Oral Contraceptives: An Eminent Doctor's View. From a BBC Broadcast in 'Woman's Hour'*, transcript reprint, 19 September 1960, no attribution, FPA/A7/84.

102 Ross-Turner to Howard, 7 March 1962, FPA/A7/82.

103 Barrow-In-Furness papers, spring 1962, FPA/A7/J17.

104 Ibid.

105 Mrs Froda Parker to Dr M.C. Waind, 21 May 1962, FPA/A7/J17.

106 Northage to Elstone, 18 January 1962, FPA/A7/84; FPA Barrow-in-Furness papers.

107 Elstone to Reid, 26 October 1962, FPA/A7/82.

108 Ibid.

109 Cartwright, *Parents and Family Planning Services*, 3.

110 Ibid., 133.

111 Marks, *Sexual Chemistry*, 37.

112 Examples of Peel's early work on contraception include 'Birth Control and the British Working-Class Movement: A Bibliographical Review', *Bulletin of the Society for the Study of Labour History* 7 (autumn 1963): 16–22; 'Manufacture and Retailing'; 'Contraception and the Medical Profession'.

113 Simpson to Reid, 10 April 1962, FPA/A7/82.

114 Ibid.

115 'Sociological Research Foundation: The S.R.F. and That Speech', *London Image* (autumn 1968): 37–41; 'Swedish Visit: Promoting Ententes Cordiales' (autumn 1970): 13.

116 Peel, 'The Protective in Family Planning: An Evaluation', *Medical Gynaecology and Fertility Abstracts* 4, no. 1 (1965): 5–7; 'Intrauterine Contraceptive Devices: An Assessment', *Medical Gynaecology and Fertility Abstracts* 4, no. 3 (1965): 3–7; 'Abortion and Family Planning', 2–7.

117 Peel, 'Abortion and Family Planning', 6.

118 Peel, 'The Protective', 7; Peel and Potts, *Textbook*, 59.

119 'Durex Gossamer in the Post-Partum Period', advertisement, *British Medical Journal* 1, no. 5286 (1962): 8.

120 Peel, 'The Protective', 7.

121 Alderman, 'Pressure Groups: A Mixed Blessing', *Contemporary Record* 2, no. 1 (1988): 4.

122 Marc Mulholland, 'McLaughlin (Florence), Patricia Alice (1916–1997)', *Oxford Dictionary of National Biography* online, edited by Lawrence Goldman, accessed 13 November 2019, http://www.oxforddnb.com/view/article/64703.

123 Sampson, *Anatomy*, 598.

124 Mulholland, 'McLaughlin'.

125 Ibid.

126 'How Safe Are Oral Contraceptives?' Handwritten note, 22 October 1964, FPA/A7/81.

127 Morris Davis, 'Some Neglected Aspects of British Pressure Groups', *MidWest Journal of Political Science* 7, no. 1 (February 1963): 43; See also Finer, *Anonymous Empire*.

128 Vance Oakley Packard, *Hidden Persuaders* (New York: D. McKay Co., 1957); Pearson and Turner, *Persuasion Industry*. See also Sampson, *Anatomy*, 594–9.

129 Ibid., 179.

130 Institute of Public Relations, *Articles of Association* (1963), appendix A, Code of Professional Conduct 31, IPR Papers; 'Suspension', *Public Relations* 18, no. 2 (1966): 5, cited in L'Etang, *Public Relations in Britain*, 179n86.

131 In June 1968, the *Sunday Times* followed up with an article claiming that prices for condoms supplied to clinics 'could be halved'. Reid and Caspar Brook, correspondence, June 1968, FPA/C/F/7/1/15.

132 This is the second of Steven R. Van Hook's three rules for approaching a PR crisis. The first is to avoid a crisis in the first place, and the third is to 'seek possible ways to turn your crisis into an opportunity'. Van Hook, 'Crisis Management Moments: Making the Most of a Bad Situation', accessed 19 November 2019, http://aboutpublicrelations.net/aa021701a.htm.

133 Ibid.

134 'The Rise and Fall'.

135 John Peel and Robert E. Dowse, 'The Politics of Birth Control', *Political Studies* 13, no. 2 (1965): 179–97.

136 Ibid., 179.

137 Ibid., 196.

CHAPTER 8

1 EIU, 'Contraceptive Products', 16.

2 EDA, *1739e*, 8–9, emphasis in the original.

3 Ibid.

4 Thanks to Adrian Bingham and Alana Harris for this observation.

5 Harvey, in conversation, 8 December 2016.

6 Ibid.

7 'Well Protected', *The Economist*, 27 August 1966, 850.

8 Langford, 'Birth Control Practice', 60; Jones, 'Under the Covers?' 745.

9 Ibid., 754.

10 ITV Late Evening News, 'Contraceptive Pill: To Be Put on Market', broadcast 3 March 1960, 10:47 and 11 p.m.; Leathard, *Fight for Family Planning*, 106.

11 Hawkins, 'The Pharmaceutical Industry', 30–2.

12 Ibid.; James McMillan and Bernard Harris, *The American Takeover of Britain* (London: Leslie Frewin, 1968), 44–55. Marks, *Sexual Chemistry*, 88; Norolen file, RJH/A8/1; One third of the British drugs market was British, one third American, and the remainder made up of European companies. Brian Inglis, *Doctors, Drugs and Disease* (London: Deutsch, 1965), 12.

13 Megestrol acetate or 'MGA' was used in combination with the oestrogen ethinyl estradiol in *Volidan*. Vladimir Petrow and Sir Frank Hartley, 'The Rise and Fall of British Drug Houses, Ltd.', *Steroids* 61, no. 8 (1996): 476–82, 77–8; Löwy, '"Sexual Chemistry"', 253–7.

14 'The Sequential Approach: Feminor Sequential', circular to doctors, January 1966, RJH/A4/2. Mead Johnson's share was 34 per cent.

15 The nutrition department was world famous at the time. Neville Marsh, *History of Queen Elizabeth College: One Hundred Years of University Education in Kensington* (London: King's College London, 1986), 271. For a history of pharmaceutical firms in the field of neuroscience outsourcing research work to universities, see Mark Dennis Robinson, *The Market in Mind: How Financialization Is Shaping Neuroscience, Translational Medicine, and Innovation in Biotechnology* (Cambridge, MA: Massachusetts Institute of Technology Press, 2019).

16 'Subjects of Main Research Projects in Progress', Statement of Development Policy-Quinquennium 1957–1962, 1955, QAP/GF6/10, Queen Elizabeth College Archive, King's College London Archives including the Liddell Hart Centre for Military Archives. Yudkin's work on contraception was the result of a collaboration with infertility specialist B.P. Wiesner. Wiesner and Yudkin, 'Inhibition of Estrus by Cultivated Gromwell', *Nature* 170, no. 4320 (16 August 1952): 274; Sam Gordon Berkow et al., 'Oral Contraception', *Obstetrics and Gynecology* 20, no. 3 (1962): 324; Marks, *Sexual Chemistry*, 49–50; Yudkin, 'Outline of Research Project to the Nuffield Foundation' (ca. 1953), FD1/4841, Nuffield Foundation Papers, National Archives, Kew.

17 Florence, *Progress Report on Birth Control*, 232.

18 Yudkin to Mrs Houghton, 12 June 1958, FPA/A14/202. Capitalisation in original; Yudkin continued to search for a contraceptive agent together with Margaret A. Sanders. Sanders, Wiesner, and Yudkin, 'Control of Fertility by 6-Azauridine', *Nature* 189, no. 4769 (1961): 1015–16.

19 'Subjects of Main Research Projects in Progress, Statement of Development Policy-Quinquennium 1957–1962', 1955, QAP/GF6/10; Marks, *Sexual Chemistry*, 49–50.

20 Florence, *Progress Report*, 233.

21 W.H. Heath and Diana M. Grylls, correspondence, May 1960; Grylls to Kenneth Brown Baker Baker [solicitors], 16 May 1960, QAS/GPF3; Angus Reid to QEC,

14 March 1961, QAS/GPF3; Queen Elizabeth College Council Minutes, 10 May 1960, QA/C/M13.

22 Lillian Whitworth to Grylls, 15 February, 1961, QAS/GPF3/1.

23 Grylls, notes on visit from Dr Carruthers, 3 May 1963, QAS/GPF3/1.

24 G.B. Barlow and A.J. MacLeod, 'Use of γ-Lactones in the Synthesis of Amino-Acids', *Journal of the Chemical Society (Resumed)* (January 1963): 141–3.

25 QAS/GPF3/3/4/6.

26 Grylls's notes; Perham to Grylls, 31 March 1964, QAS/GPF3/1; Financial Committee Reports 1961–1965, QA/F/M9, QEC.

27 EDA, *1380c*, 191.

28 Circular to doctors.

29 'Family Centre', *London Image* (spring 1962): 16.

30 Carruthers and Gerald Swyer, 'Oral Contraceptive Trials', correspondence, *British Medical Journal* 1, no. 5289 (1962): 1418; FPA and London Rubber, correspondence 1960–1962, FPA/A7/76/19/80/81/82; FPA/A13/40.

31 *Lamberts Prorace Catalogue A. Latest Price List of Approved Contraceptive Appliances* (London: Lamberts of Dalston, 1935); CA, 'Contraceptives', 90.

32 *A Planned Family* (Portsmouth: Lloyd's Surgical Department Ltd, 1960), 7, FPA/A7/70.

33 'Family Centre'; 'Visit the Family Centre: London's New Clinic for Engaged and Married Couples', leaflet, March 1962, FPA/A7/82.

34 CA, 'Contraceptives', 94–6; 'Family Centre'.

35 Family Centre, advertisement, *Fertility Abstracts* 2 (1963): back cover; *Fertility Abstracts* 1 (1962): inside cover.

36 Jesse Olszynko-Gryn, 'Pregnancy Testing in Britain, C. 1900–67: Laboratories, Animals and Demand from Doctors, Patients and Consumers'. PhD thesis, Cambridge University, 2014, chapters 4 and 5, 122–203; 'When Pregnancy Tests Were Toads: The Xenopus Test in the Early NHS', *Wellcome History* 51 (2013): 1–3.

37 'Visit the Family Centre'; Family Centre advertisement.

38 *Queen* magazine, 10 March 1965, press clippings, FPA/A17/100; Family Centre advertisement; Marks, *Sexual Chemistry*, 159.

39 Carruthers, 'Sequential', 3–6; 'Trial of a New Form of Oral Contraceptive', *British Journal of Clinical Practice* 19, no. 8 (1965): 455–60.

40 'Family Centre', 17.

41 Ibid., 16; Maurice Katz, 'Gerald Isaac MacDonald Swyer', Lives of the Fellows, Royal College of Physicians, accessed 13 November 2019, http://munksroll. rcplondon.ac.uk/Biography/Details/4321.

42 'Family Centre', 16–17.

43 Later known as *Medical Gynaecology and Fertility Abstracts*; Carruthers 'Sequential', 4–5.

44 J. Abraham and Courtney Davis, 'Testing Times: The Emergence of the Practolol Disaster and Its Challenge to British Drug Regulation in the Modern Period', *Social History of Medicine* 19, no. 1 (2006): 127–47, 133.

45 Junod and Marks, 'Women's Trials', 136–7.
46 Clifford-Smith to Swyer, 15 October 1957, FPA/A14/200; for a history of FPA contraceptive testing, see Szuhan, 'Sex in the Laboratory'.
47 Junod and Marks, 'Women's Trials', 136.
48 Abraham and Davis, 'Testing Times', 129.
49 Family Planning Association, *Approved List* (London: FPA, 1965), FPA/A17/100; EIU, 'Contraceptive Products', 16.
50 Eleanor Mears and Carruthers, correspondence, September to October 1964, FPA/C/F/7/1/14.
51 'New Medicines', *MIMS* (November 1964): XV; 'Announcements', *Practitioner* (October 1964): A129; *Lancet*, 21 September 1964: 3; *GP* (October 1964): 12.
52 'Woman years' was an established statistical device for counting menstrual cycles. Marks, *Sexual Chemistry*, 111–12; Carruthers 'Sequential', 3–6.
53 Ibid.
54 Ibid.; Carruthers, 'Trial', 455–60.
55 Mears to Carruthers, 19 October 1964, FPA/C/F/7/1/14.
56 Ibid.
57 CIFC Minutes of the Clinical Trials Committee [henceforth CTC], 5 May 1965; Carruthers to Mears, 15 June 1965; Dr Hilary Hill to Carruthers, 21 July 1965, FPA/C/F/7/1/14.
58 Mears to Carruthers, correspondence, May–March 1965, FPA/C/F/7/1/14; CIFC CTC, 10 August 1964, FPA/A5/160/1.
59 Hill and Carruthers, correspondence, July–September 1965, FPA/C/F/7/1/14.
60 Trials were set to continue with Dr Silva Chinnatanby in Ceylon.
61 EIU, 'Contraceptives', 15; CIFC CTC minutes, 10 August 1964.
62 Marks, *Sexual Chemistry*, 77–8.
63 EIU, 'Contraceptives', 18; NEDO, *Focus on Pharmaceuticals*, 118.
64 British Drug Houses made this point. CIFC CTC minutes, 20 June 1963, FPA/A5/160/1.
65 Ibid.
66 CIFC CTC, 5 May 1965, FPA/A5/160/1.
67 Ibid. This led to a glut of sequentials. British Drug Houses' Secrovin was marketed in Canada in 1965, while Serial 28 (also BDH) launched in Britain in 1966 and was presented alongside Volidan and Nuvacon, using the BDH progestogen, MGA. Serial 28 was offered as a low-oestrogen combined pill from 1967. Eli Lilly's C-Quens (aka Sequens), and Ortho's Ortho-Novin SQ would join the British race in 1966, as would Organon's Ovanon in 1968; Petrow and Hartley, 'The Rise and Fall', 478; Syntex Papers, British Drug Houses Box 1 BC/GT25, Division of Medical Sciences, Smithsonian Institution; R.J. Hetherington, handwritten notes, RJH/A1/6.
68 CIFC CTC minutes, 10 August 1965; EIU, 'Contraceptives', 23.
69 EIU, 'UK Contraceptive Market', 16–31, 23.
70 EIU, 'Contraceptive Products', 19.

71 Financial Committee Reports 1961–1965, QA/F/M9; Grylls to London Research Foundation, 17 April 1964, QAS/GPF/3/1.

72 Lord Sainsbury (chairman), *Report of the Committee of Enquiry into the Relationship of the Pharmaceutical Industry with the National Health Service 1965–1967* (London, HMSO: 1967), 55; EIU, 'Contraceptive Products', 18. For an overview of the drug pricing debate, see Judy Slinn, 'Patents and the UK Pharmaceutical Industry between 1945 and the 1970s', *History and Technology* 24, no. 2 (2008): 191–205.

73 Harvey, in conversation, 8 December 2016.

74 Ibid.

75 Reid, 'Oral Contraceptives', *London Image* (autumn/winter, 1964): 2.

76 EIU, 'Contraceptive Products', 25; author's survey of *Statistical Review of Advertising* (June 1964–March 1965).

77 Reid, 'Oral Contraceptives', 2.

78 Ibid.

79 Marks, *Sexual Chemistry*, 116–37.

80 Peel, 'Contraception and the Medical Profession', 133.

81 Harvey, in conversation, 8 December 2016.

82 EDA, *1739e*, 8.

83 Bingham, *Family Newspapers?* 84; Marks, *Sexual Chemistry*, 138–82.

84 Marks, *Sexual Chemistry*, 138–82.

85 Press clippings, FPA/A17/100.

86 Ibid., *Birmingham Mail*, 7 July 1965.

87 Harvey, in conversation, 8 December 2016; accounts of the day-to-day routine of American medical representatives can be found in Jeremy A. Greene, 'Attention to "Details": Etiquette and the Pharmaceutical Salesman in Postwar America', *Social Studies of Science* 34, no. 2 (2004): 271–92.

88 Harvey, in conversation, 8 December 2016.

89 Ibid.

90 *London Image* (autumn/winter 1964): 6.

91 *London Image* (autumn 1966): 11; Feminor advertising, RJH/A4/1.

92 Hall, 'Venereal Diseases', 123–4; McLaren, *A History of Contraception*, 235–6.

93 London Rubber Industries Ltd, Medical Division detail pack, ca. 1966, RJH/A4/1; Cook, *Sexual Revolution*, 278–9.

94 Cook, *Sexual Revolution*, 281.

95 London Rubber Company Ltd, *Feminor Sequential: The First British 'Second Generation' Oral Contraceptive* (London: London Rubber, 1965), 5, RJH/A4/1.

96 Ibid., 11.

97 Ibid., 12. Italics in original. A useful account of women's attitudes to oral contraceptive safety (encompassing the 1960s debate) can be found in Marks, *Sexual Chemistry*, 207–14; oral contraceptive press clippings.

98 Cardiac patients and lactating women were also singled out for attention. London Rubber, *Feminor Sequential*, 15–17.

99 EDA, *1739e*, 8–9. Product literature for all oral contraceptives available in the UK in the 1960s can be found in Series A: Oral Contraceptives, their Producers and Products, RJH Papers.

100 London Rubber, *Feminor Sequential*, 14–15. Italics in original.

101 *London Image* (autumn 1966): 20; *According to Plan*; Feminor marketing collateral, RJH/A4/1/2.

102 'Obituary', *Medical Gynaecology and Fertility Abstracts* 4 (1965): 1–3.

103 Marks, *Sexual Chemistry*, 207–14.

CHAPTER 9

1   MMC 1975, 15.

2   Ferris, 'Contraception'.

3   MMC 1975, 19.

4   LRI to Mrs Howard, 31 March 1967, FPA/C/F/7/1/15.

5   MMC 1975, 46; Mrs Howard to Mr Baker, 14 April 1967, FPA/C/F/7/1/15.

6   Leo Abse, MP, Hansard. Contraceptive Industry. HC Deb, 24 May 1968, vol. 765, col. 1192–8; press clippings 1963–4, FPA/17/81.

7   G. Fricker to Mr. Edsall, 8 June 1967, FPA/C/F/7/1/15.

8   EIU, 'Contraceptive Products', 20; EIU, 'Contraceptives', 23.

9   MMC 1975, 12.

10 'Breakthrough in Contraceptive Advertising', *London Image* (summer 1969): 34.

11 MMC 1975, 27.

12 Twenty-one-day schemes meant that users stopped and started their administration routine on the same day of the week, as opposed to different days for the established twenty-day regimens, which caused confusion.

13 Cook, *Sexual Revolution*, 281.

14 Syntex Papers.

15 For more information on the effect of the encyclical, see David Geiringer, *The Pope and the Pill: Sex, Catholicism and Women in Postwar England* (Manchester: Manchester University Press, 2019).

16 Advertisement, *British Medical Journal* 3, no. 5610 (1968): 131; Hetherington, notes, RJH/A1/6.

17 Marks, *Sexual Chemistry*, 237–65.

18 NEDO, *Focus on Pharmaceuticals*, 122.

19 F. Shubeck and R.L. Belsky, *Intrauterine Contraceptive Devices* (Cambridge, MA: Massachusetts Institute of Technology, 1971), 53.

20 'Committee for Doctors', National Council, memo, 10 February 1967, FPA/C/F/7/1/15.

21 EIU, 'Contraceptive Products', 19; *Chemist and Druggist* (3 January 1970): 2, 5; MMC 1975, 26; Marks, *Sexual Chemistry*, 77–8. Only two of the first generation sequentials (Serial 28 and Ovanon), remained by 1975. The Feminor brand

name has since re-emerged as an emergency 'morning after' contraceptive in Nepal, produced by Lomus Pharmaceuticals PvT. Ltd. 'Feminor', International Consortium for Emergency Contraception, accessed 13 November 2019, https://www.cecinfo.org/country-by-country-information/status-availability-database/pills/feminor/.

22 A.P. Sam, 'Controlled Release Contraceptive Devices: A Status Report', *Journal of Controlled Release* 22, no. 1 (1992): 42.

23 Richard Davies, invitation to launch, June 1968, FPA/C/F/7/1/15; 'Sociological Research Foundation'; MMC 1975, 26.

24 'The Hull Family Survey', *London Image* (winter 1972): 12–13; John Peel, 'Hull Family Survey', 45–70; 'The Hull Family Survey II: Family Planning in the First 5 Years of Marriage', *Journal of Biosocial Science* 4, no. 3 (1972): 333–46; John Peel and Griselda Carr, *Contraception and Family Design: A Study of Birth Planning in Contemporary Society* (Edinburgh and London: Churchill Livingstone, 1975).

25 London Rubber Company Ltd, *Report and Accounts* (1966), 5.

26 MMC 1975, 13.

27 The Monopolies and Mergers Commission, *Contraceptive Sheaths: A Report on the Supply in the United Kingdom of Contraceptive Sheaths* (London: HMSO, November 1982), 8 [henceforth MMC 1982].

28 British Standards Institution, *Specification for Rubber Condoms* (London: British Standards Institution, 1972), 2.

29 Family Planning Sales Ltd, 'Memorandum and Articles of Association', 26 July 1972; Snow, 'Condom Marketing in the United Kingdom', in *The Condom: Increasing Utilization in the United States*, 1–4.

30 Gordon Snow, in conversation with the author.

31 FPA/CB/11/15.

32 Office of Health Economics, *Family Planning in Britain* (London: Office of Health Economics, 1972), 11.

33 Mechen, '"Closer Together"'.

34 EIU, 'UK Contraceptive Market', 24.

35 EIU, 'Contraceptive Products', 3.

36 MMC 1982, 2.

37 Mechen, '"Closer Together"'.

38 MMC 1982, 9.

39 'The "Unmentionable" Contraceptive Wins Respectability', *Financial Post* (Toronto), 3 September 1977.

40 'Informing without Offending', *Stimulus* (Toronto), February 1973; Ortho clippings files, Dittrick Medical Museum, Cleveland, Ohio.

41 London Rubber Company International Ltd, memorandum of evidence, 305.

42 EDA, *1739e*, 1. Both estimates put the rate of intercourse at around just under two instances per week.

43 Leathard, *Fight for Family Planning*, 200, 227–9.

44 Edgerton, *Rise and Fall*, 459.

45 MMC 1982, 7.

46 Murphy, 'The Contraceptive Pill', 223.

47 Wilson and West, '"Unmentionables"', 100.

48 London International Ltd, *Report and Accounts* (1971).

49 MMC 1982, 5.

50 Purdie, 'The British Agency House', 230–1.

51 Sandbrook, *Seasons in the Sun. The Battle for Britain, 1974–1979* (London: Penguin, 2013), 8–9.

52 'LR Strike Moves', *Chingford Guardian and Independent*, 19 May 1975.

53 '200 Sacked in Trade Slump', *Chingford Guardian and Independent*, 16 May 1975.

54 LRC International Ltd, *Report and Accounts* (1976), 5.

55 'Profit Rule Shrinks Durex Margins', *The Guardian*, 17 October 1975; *The Monopolies Commission's Report on the Supply of Contraceptive Sheaths in the United Kingdom*, Draft Submission to Minister of State, November 1974, Monopolies and Mergers Commission Papers, FV73/51, National Archives, Kew.

56 Monopolies and Mergers Commission, *Contraceptive Sheaths: A Report on the Supply in the UK of Contraceptive Sheaths* (London: HMSO, 1994), 3 [henceforth MMC 1994].

57 F.W. Glaves-Smith, deputy director general, Office of Fair Trading, 15 August 1979, Memorandum, 'LRC International Contraceptive Sheaths: Proposed Price Increases', FV73/53.

58 LRC International Ltd, *Report and Accounts* (1978), 5.

59 LRC International Ltd, *Report and Accounts* (1982).

60 'LIG Revived by Second Half Rally', *The Times*, 16 June 1989; LRC International Ltd, *Annual Report and Accounts* (1983), 7.

61 Competition Commission, *Eastman Kodak Company and ColourCare Ltd, A Report on the Proposed Merger* (London: HMSO, December 2001), 7; Beryl Downing, 'Printing Problems Need Greater Exposure', *The Times*, 20 July–5 August 1983.

62 'LIG Expands in Spain', *The Times*, 2 March 1989.

63 'LRC Profits Up by a Third', *The Times*, 28 June 1983.

64 Advertisement, 'A New Name … A Powerful Track Record', *The Times*, 18 November 1985.

65 London Rubber Company International Ltd, memorandum of evidence, 306; London Rubber representative (identity protected), correspondence with Suzie Hayman Advertising and Contraceptives Project, FPA/C/B/11/1–3.

66 Barlow, 'The Condom and Gonorrhoea', 811.

67 MMC 1994, 1.

68 Ibid., 11.

69 Ibid.

70 LRC International Ltd, *Annual Report and Accounts* (1981), 7.

71 MMC 1975, 99.

72 MMC 1982, 10, 27.

73 MMC 1994, 15.

74 Ibid., 5.

75 Kaye Wellings, *Assessing AIDS Prevention in the General Population. EC Concerted Action. Assessment of AIDS/HIV Preventive Strategies. Final Report of the General Population Working Group* (University Institute of Social and Preventive Medicine, Lausanne, Switzerland, June 1992), 14.

76 Virginia Berridge, *AIDS in the UK: The Making of Policy, 1981–1994* (Oxford: Oxford University Press, 1996), 121.

77 Jobling, 'Playing Safe', 58; MMC 1994, 6–7.

78 Murphy, *Condom Industry*, 135.

79 MMC 1994, 9, 22.

80 'Threat of Aids Helps LIG to £15m Profit', *The Times*, 13 November 1987; *The Grocer*, 4 July 1987: 11.

81 Jobling, 'Playing Safe', 58.

82 Collier, *Humble Little Condom*, 309.

83 Ibid., 307, 310.

84 Alison Payne, in conversation with author, London, 19 May 2014.

85 MMC 1994, 72.

86 Ibid.

87 Wellings, *Assessing AIDS*, 39.

88 Ibid., 47.

89 Murphy, *Condom Industry*, 96.

90 See, for example, Michael Schofield, 'Social Aspects of Homosexuality', *British Journal of Venereal Disease* 40, no. 2 (June 1964): 132; Lode Wigersma and Ron Oud, 'Safety and Acceptability of Condoms for Use by Homosexual Men as a Prophylactic against Transmission of HIV during Anogenital Sexual Intercourse', *British Medical Journal* 295, no. 6590 (1987): 94; John McGarry, 'Gay Birmingham Remembered', The Gay Birmingham History Project, accessed 13 November 2019, http://gaybirminghamremembered.co.uk/interview/48/.

91 Murphy, *Condom Industry*, 129.

92 Ibid.

93 MMC 1994, 5.

94 Jobling, 'Playing Safe', 61–2.

95 Ibid.

96 Advertising and Contraceptives Project, FPA/C/B/11/1–3.

97 Payne, in conversation.

98 Payne, email correspondence with author, July 2016.

99 Jobling, 'Playing Safe', 62.

100 Berridge, *AIDS in the UK*, 121.

101 'LRC in Fund-Raiser to Bid to Beat AIDS', *Waltham Forest Guardian*, 21 August 1987: 14.

102 MMC 1994, 3.

103 Ibid., 1, 3; *Report and Accounts* (1983), 7.

104 MMC 1994, 52.

105 'Threat of Aids'.

106 MMC 1994, 5; *The Grocer*, 11 March 1989: 46; *The Grocer*, 3 November 1993: 42.

107 MMC 1994, 133.

108 MMC 1994, 133.

109 BSI, *BS3704*, 6.

110 British Standards Institution, *British Standard Specification for Natural Rubber Latex Condoms* (London: British Standards Institution, 1989), 2–3.

111 Collier, *Humble Little Condom*, 311.

112 Martin Waller, 'LIG Concern as Aids Message Fails', *The Times*, 17 September 1988.

113 Ibid.

114 'LIG Ahead of Expectations', *The Times*, 16 November 1988; London International Group PLC, *Annual Report and Accounts* (1989), 7.

115 Ibid.

116 Rosemary Unsworth, 'LIG to Sell Royal Worcester Spode', *The Times*, 3 June 1988.

117 *Report and Accounts* (1989), 9.

118 London International Group PLC, *Annual Report and Accounts* (1990), 3; London International Group PLC *Annual Report and Accounts* (1991), 5; MMC 1994, 51.

119 *Report and Accounts* (1990), 11, 16.

120 'Safety First', *Chemist and Druggist* (5 December 1992): 1021–4.

121 Ibid.

122 *Report and Accounts* (1990), 16.

123 'Safety First'.

124 Ibid.; MMC 1994, 133.

125 *The Grocer*, 23 January 1993: 34.

126 *Report and Accounts* (1991), 7.

127 Alan E. Woltz to Ordinary Shareholders, 10 January 1991.

128 Ibid.

129 Ibid.

130 Neil Bennett, 'LIG Faces Cash Call as Revamp Cuts 1,000 Jobs', *The Times*, 20 April 1994.

131 Woltz to Ordinary Shareholders.

132 Competition Commission, *Eastman Kodak*, 35.

133 'LIG Buys Film Labs for £1.6m', *The Times*, 4 January 1990.

134 *Report and Accounts* (1990), 25; Vincent Lindsay, 'Rubber Baron on Trial at LIG', *The Guardian*, 24 April 1994; Downing, 'Printing Problems'.

135 *Report and Accounts* (1991), 7, 10, 19–20; London International Group PLC, *Annual Report and Accounts* (1992), 8.

136 *Report and Accounts* (1990), 25.

137 Competition Commission, *Eastman Kodak*, 33, 40.

138 *Report and Accounts* (1990), 25.

139 Ibid.; *Report and Accounts* (1991), 19–20.

140 Lindsay, 'Rubber Baron'; London International Group PLC, *Annual Report and Accounts* (1992), 5; London International Group PLC, *Annual Report and*

Accounts (1993), 6, 29; 'LIG to Shed a Fifth of Its Workforce', *The Times*, 10 December 1993.

141 London International Group PLC, *Annual Report and Accounts* (1993), 30.

142 Ibid., 11.

143 Ibid., 6, 28–9.

144 'LIG to Shed a Fifth'.

145 'LIG Pays £4.7m for Italian Health Firm', *The Times*, 19 September 1987.

146 Woltz to Ordinary Shareholders; 'LIG and Saatchi Face Up to the Premium Put Problem', *The Times*, 14 January 1991.

147 'LIG', *The Times*, 11 January 1991.

148 Woltz to Ordinary Shareholders.

149 Jon Ashworth, 'LIG Force Shares Down', *The Times*, 19 June 1992.

150 Carl Mortishear, 'LIG Censured over Briefings to Analysts', *The Times*, 15 May 1993.

151 MMC 1994, 2.

152 Ben Laurance, 'Durex Maker to Seek £70m', *The Guardian*, 20 April 1994.

153 London International Group PLC, *Annual Report* (1997), 2.

154 Lindsay, 'Rubber Baron'.

155 London International Group PLC, *Annual Report* (1995), 3; London International Group PLC, *Annual Report* (1994), 1–3.

156 *Annual Report* (1994), 1–3.

157 Laurance, 'Durex Maker to Seek £70m'; Competition Commission, *Eastman Kodak*, 7.

158 *Annual Report* (1995), 17.

159 *Report and Accounts* (1994), 1–3.

160 Ibid.

161 Paul Durman, 'LIG Braced for Trouble over Italian Closure', *The Times*, 29 May 1998.

162 Carl Mortishead, 'ColourCare Loss Holds LIG Down to £27.8m', *The Times*, 26 June 1993; 'LIG Faces Cash Revamp'; Clare Stewart, 'LIG Profits Improve 72% after Change in Strategy', *The Times*, 31 May 1996.

163 Lindsay, 'Rubber Baron'.

164 MMC 1994, 17.

165 Ibid., 19.

166 *Report and Accounts* (1987), 10.

167 Doreen Friend, 'No Bouncing Back for Sad Rubber Staff', *Chingford Guardian*, 4 August 1994.

168 Laurance, 'Durex Maker to Seek £70m'; 'LIG Faces Cash Revamp'.

169 MMC 1994, 24.

170 Ibid., 52.

171 'No Bouncing Back'; '600 Jobs Go as LRC "Makes a Packet"', *Waltham Forest Yellow Advertiser*, 29 April 1994: 1.

172 'LRC to Close', *Chingford Guardian*, 21 April 1994: 1.

173 Ibid.

174 MMC 1994, 52, 61.

175 Lindsay, 'Rubber Baron'.

176 Ibid.

177 MMC 1994, 62.

178 Ibid.

179 Ibid.

180 *LRC International News*, 'Chingford' (summer 1972): 1.

181 'LRC to Close'.

182 MMC 1994, 52.

183 Laurance, 'Durex Maker to Seek £70m'; 'LRC to Close'.

184 'LRC to Close'.

185 *Annual Report* (1994), 6; 'No Bouncing Back'.

186 'LRC to Close'; '600 Jobs Go'; MMC 1994, 52; LRC International Ltd, *Report and Accounts* (1999), 21.

187 'No Bouncing Back'.

188 *Annual Report* (1995), 3, 6.

189 London International Group PLC, *Annual Report* (1996), 1

190 *Annual Report* (1995), 4–5, 11–12.

191 Ibid.

192 *Annual Report* (1996), 2; *Annual Report* (1997), 2.

193 *Annual Report* (1995), 12, 14; *The Grocer*, 11 June 1994: 18.

194 *Annual Report* (1996), 4.

195 *Annual Report* (1997), 5–6, 14.

196 *Annual Report* (1996), 14.

197 *Report and Accounts* (1999), 4–5, 18–19, 22.

198 Ibid., 4.

199 Office of Fair Trading, *Condoms. Review of the Undertakings Given by LRC Products Ltd.* (March 2006), 13; London International Group PLC, *Accounts for the Year Ended 31 March 2000*, 1.

200 Companies House, 'Certificate of Incorporation on Re-registration of a Public Company as a Private Company', 30 April 2001.

201 'Changing Sexual Wellbeing', Durex, Reckitt Benckiser Group, Plc., accessed 13 November 2019, https://www.rb.com/brands/durex/.

202 'McCorquodale (Midlands) Ltd to Supply Publications and Resources after FPA Liquidation', FPA press release 14 June 2019, accessed 13 November 2019, https://www.fpa.org.uk/news/mccorquodale-midlands-ltd-supply-publications-and-resources-after-fpa-liquidation.

CONCLUSION

1 Chandler, *Industrial Century*, 7–8.

2 Jane Hand, 'Marketing Health Education: Advertising Margarine and Visualising Health in Britain from 1964–c. 2000', *Contemporary British History* 31, no. 4 (April 2017): 17–18 (online version).

3 Jobling, 'Playing Safe', 60–1.

4 Interview with Charlene Chan, consumer psychology researcher, Nanyang School of Business, Singapore. BBC World Service, Business Daily, 'The psychology of panic buying', 10 March 2020 (podcast edition).

5 'Ensuring Human Rights in the Provision of Contraceptive Information and Services', World Health Organization Guidance and Recommendations 2014, accessed 13 November 2019, https://www.who.int/reproductivehealth/publications/family_planning/human-rights-contraception/en/.

6 'State of World Population 2012', United Nations Population Fund, accessed 23 May 2020, https://www.unfpa.org/publications/state-world-population-2012.

7 At the time of writing, the current international standard for condoms is ISO 4074:2015. '11.200 – Birth Control. Mechanical Contraceptives', Standards catalogue, International Standards Organisation, accessed 16 November 2019, https://www.iso.org/ics/11.200/x/.

8 Mintel Group Ltd, Brochure for 'Sexual Health UK' report (August 2019), accessed 16 March 2020, https://store.mintel.com/uk-sexual-health-market-rep.

9 Ibid.

10 Charlotte O'Halloran, Suzy Sun, Sophie Nash, Alison Brown, Sara Croxford, Nicky Connor, Ann K. Sullivan, Valerie Delpech, and O. Noel Gill, *HIV in the United Kingdom: Towards Zero HIV Transmissions by 2030 (2019 Report – Data to End 2018)* (London: Public Health England, 2019), 79

11 Ibid; Mintel Group Ltd, brochure for 'Sexual Health UK'.

12 Mark Hay, 'Why Big Condom Makers Aren't Interested in Big Condom Innovations', *Forbes* online, accessed 16 March 2020, https://www.forbes.com/sites/markhay/2018/10/29/why-big-condom-makers-arent-interested-in-big-condom-innovations/.

13 Ibid.

14 MMC 1975; MMC 1982; MMC 1994.

15 MMC 1975, 50.

16 For more information on the use of disinformation techniques in contemporary America, see '2019 IPR Disinformation in Society Report', Institute for Public Relations [Florida], accessed 12 November 2019, https://instituteforpr.org/ipr-disinformation-study/.

17 Tone, *Devices and Desires*, 187–8.

18 Ibid.

19 Ibid.; 'The Medicalization of Contraceptives', 203–84.

20 Holz, *The Birth Control Clinic in a Marketplace World*, 146.

21 Jones, 'Under the Covers?'; *Business of Birth Control*.

22 Tone, *Devices and Desires*, 289.

equity of, 114, 171; brand premium, 50–1, 82–3, 88, 91, 127, 201; development of, 31–2, 34–5; diaphragm, 98; export trade, 120; Extra Safe, 206; Fetherlite, 191; Formula One, 196; Gossamer, 84–5, 114–17, 122–4, 126, 133, 148; Nu–Form, 192, 200; postpartum use, 186; Ramses, 214–15; Sheik, 214–15; rubber gloves, 138; as synonym for condom, 49, 138, 144, 145, 224; trademark, 35, 132; transfer of brand, 215; wartime supply, 47–9. *See also* competitors: Durex Products Inc.

Elarco, 22, 40–1, 51–2
Ernest Dichter Associates, 96, 146–50, 152–3, 154, 156, 166, 174
eugenics, 40, 104

Family Centre. *See* clinics; fertility; front organisations
family planning: as concept, 30, 71, 74, 78, 91, 117, 122, 139; as controversial topic, 104, 153, 177; as human right, 220; acceptance of condoms in, 171; exploitation of, 124–5, 145, 151, 153, 162, 189; NHS adoption, 177; public opinion, 145, 150Family Planning Association, 30, 89–108; Approved List, 99–100, 102, 122–3; contraceptive preference, 30, 93, 139, 195; contraceptive testing, 122–7; expansion, 89, 105; liquidation, 215; LRC's courtship of, 89–96, 102–3, 106–8, 161–2; as National Birth Control Association, 30, 92, 94, 99, 126; oral contraceptive pill, 131, 134–7, 167; paper bombing, 166–8; Pharmaceutical Society of Great Britain, 77, 84; poached staff, 168; power struggle, 99–101, 191; Silver Jubilee, 104, 106; as woman-centred, 30, 90, 92. *See also* clinics; Contraceptives (Regulation) Bill; Council for the Investigation of Fertility Control; Family Centre; Feminor; front organisations; medical authorities; public relations; women

Family Planning Association clinics: branches, 77, 99, 102, 191; Darlington, 107; Hackney, 95; handover to NHS, 196; North Kensington, 104, 106; Wigan, 96
Family Planning Sales, 194, 197, 200
female condoms, 17, 206
Feminor, 192–3; as anti-pill device, 185–7; as commercial flop, 184–5; development, 173–8; medical trials, 180–3; product literature, 188–9. *See also* Council for the Investigation of Fertility Control; Family Centre; *Fertility Abstracts*; medical authorities; market share; oral contraceptive pill
fertility, 5, 104, 130, 149; Family Centre remit, 178, 180; Yudkin and, 177
Fertility Abstracts, 160–2, 169–9, 180–2; obituary to the pill, 189
film, 106–7, 131, 165, 170, 172, 174
Fromms Berlin, 18, 46–8, 79; Julius Fromm, 46, 48
front organisations: Counsel Publications, 162–3, 169; Genetic Studies Unit, 158–60, 169, 171, 173; London Foundation for Marriage Education, 165–6, 169; Sociological Research Foundation, 193; the Family Centre, 160–2, 169, 170, 178–80, 183, 185, 193. *See also* *Fertility Abstracts*; Planned Families Publications

Germany, 17–18, 34, 41–2, 119, 215, 222; imports from, 18, 41, 48, 58, 78. *See also* retailing; prophylaxis
gloves: household, 51, 53, 110–11, 138; surgical, 138, 198, 205, 209–11, 215
Great War, 18, 26–31
Grey, Timothy, 155, 159, 171
gynaecology, 23, 137; examinations, 17, 21, 96, 166; therapies, 128–9, 138, 143, 187

Harvey, John, 11, 33, 40, 49, 60–5, 80–5, 114–15, 185–7
Hayward, Dai, 106–7, 145
homosexuality, 4, 91, 148, 192, 201–3, 211. *See also* markets

hormones: progesterone, 128–9, 176, 182; oestrogen, 182, 184, 186, 193; steroids, 129, 161, 176, 188

imports, 34–5, 41, 49, 78–9
India, 49, 117, 132, 160
Institute of Public Relations, 157, 171
International Planned Parenthood Federation, 106, 122–3, 130, 160
intrauterine devices, 21, 160, 169, 193; cost to consumer, 195; Saf-t-coil, 193

Jackson, Elkan, 33–4, 40–2, 52, 58, 64, 67
Jackson, Lionel, 31–3, 34–5, 40; death of, 58, 68
Jewish manufacturers, 18, 46, 48, 164, 222
Julius Schmid, 119–20, 131–2, 193, 194, 195, 199, 222–3

Landau, Lucian, 20, 32–6, 39–42, 52–3, 58–60
latex: artificial limbs, 159; competition, 37; contamination, 28, 205, 207, 213; development of dipped condoms, 19–20, 34–41, 44–6, 50–7; dipping process, 54–5; domination of, 111–13; injection moulding, 95; storage, 111–12, 141; supply, 43–5, 48, 50, 53, 111; surgical service, 159; transportation, 37; wartime supply of, 44–6, 48. *See also* manufacturing
London 21: Chancery Lane, 21; Clerkenwell, 33–4, 40; Euston, 21; Hackney, 35–41, 95; High Holborn, 21; Holloway 30, 178; North Kensington, 104, 106; South Tottenham, 50; Stockwell, 21; Victoria, 21; West End, 16, 21, 23, 72. *See also* Chingford
London International Group, 200
London Rubber Industries, 109–14
LRC International, 196–200
LRC Products, 199
lubrication, 61–2, 64, 101

MacLeod, Iain, 104–6
mail order, 23–5, 31, 50, 83, 89. *See also* catalogues; Planned Families Publications

Malaysia: Malayan emergency, 53, 111; as source for latex, 37, 41, 43, 48, 53; transference of production to, 203, 207, 209, 214.
Malthusian League, 30, 74, 172
manufacturing: Automated Protective (AP) lines, 20, 51–8, 85, 125, 224; automation, 19–20, 31–2, 52–5, 58–9; barriers to, 51, 224; early automation, 19–20; end of British, 207, 121–2; Killian's chain, 16–20, 35, 40; output, 20, 41, 43, 58; rotoseal, 114, 119; semi-mechanised, 29, 41; with solvents, 19, 20, 32. *See also* latex; rubber
Marc Quinn Associates, 157, 159, 171
Marker, Russell, 128
market research studies: by Ernest Dichter Associates, 146–50, 152–3; motivational research, 146; quantitative, 141, 149; by The Pulse, London, 141–6
market share, 32, 42, 50, 90, 203, 223; of ColourCare, 207–8, 211; of Feminor, 184; of oral contraceptives, 155, 181; of retailers, 24. *See also* Julius Schmid
marketing, 51, 88, 110–11, 150, 195, 200, 206; on MTV, 214; social marketing, 184–5; British Standard, 125–7. *See also* advertising
markets: American, 120, 132, 214–15, 222–3; black market (wartime), 42, 58; British, 81–2, 116, 120, 136, 181, 195, 203, 206; Catholic, 193; clinic, 95; disruption of, 133–5, 221–2; European, 111, 118–19; expansion of, 90–1, 107, 115, 133, 176, 191; gay, 201–2, 219; hormone, 128–9; Indian, 132; liberalization of, 81, 90, 136, 147, 186, 193, 199, 205; prophylaxis, 202, 206; seniors, 221; uncertainty of, 134–5; value of, 116, 136; women's, 26, 93, 133, 147, 175, 185, 193, 206; world, 37, 120, 193, 201, 211, 214; youth, 165, 214, 221. *See also* medical authorities; oral contraceptive pill; market share; packaging
married persons: LRC couples, 64; clinic users, 104–5, 178; *Marriages Are Made*, 163–4, 168; popularity of, 153; pre-marital couples, 153, 165; proviso

packaging, 16, 71, 139, 146–7, 166, 192, 195, 206; envelopes, 19, 103, 114, 115, 116–17; repackaging, 35, 50, 194; pocket packs, 114–16; square foils, 215

Peel, John, 168–9, 172, 193

penises, 27–8, 139, 194

Pharmaceutical Manufacturers: British Drug Houses, 94, 176, 193; Schering, 131, 138, 182; Searle, 129–31, 137–8, 165, 168, 195; Syntex, 128–9

Pharmaceutical Society of Great Britain, 76–9, 81–4; Statement upon Methods of Professional Conduct, 76–7, 83–4, 86, 90, 103, 194

pharmacies. See chemists

photographic processing, 198–200, 203, 205, 207. See also ColourCare

Planned Families Publications, 162–3, booklets, 102–3, 106, 141–6, 153–4, 162, 163–5. See also Fertility Abstracts; print booklets; mass media

population, 92, 117, 129, 130, 132, 134, 150–1, 164

Population Investigation Committee, 137, 139, 147–8

postwar expansion, 49–58, 67, 79, 111, 196, 199, 203, 207

pregnancy: accidental, 87, 182; sexual anxiety over, 163–4; termination of, 21, 25, 41, 77, 100, 168–9, 192; testing, 92, 100, 178, 180; pricing, 82, 115, 151, 185–6, 198, 199, 201, 203–4. See also animal products; fertility; thalidomide; women

print booklets, 25, 89, 103, 146, 150, 162–4, 174, 188. See also Feminor; Fertility Abstracts; mass media; Planned Families Publications

profitability, 50, 53, 116–17, 185, 196; of AIDS crisis, 202–3; of condoms, 51, 82–3, 93, 111, 113–6, 199, 211, 224; ColourCare, impact on, 207, 209; of diaphragms, 95; disapproval of, 21, 30, 74, 93, 145, 150–1, 162–6, 191; of Durex brands, 33, 88, 114–16; and employee share scheme, 65; of European subsidiaries, 119–20; of Feminor, 184–5;

for FPA, 93–4, 96, 191; for funding research and development, 53, 220, 221, 223; of haircutting, 25; leaked warning, 210; low profit areas, 51; LRC Group profits, 112–14, 198, 205, 210, 228; of machine vending, 80; of North American Operations, 120, 132, 205; resale price, 94, 115; Which? criticism of, 122, 124–5. See also market share; Monopolies and Mergers Commission

prophylaxis: barrier, 15, 18, 27–9, 200–4, 206, 207; and condom efficacy, 4, 28–9, 31, 200, 202; vs contraception, 4–5, 11, 27, 30, 31, 45, 91, 186; in Germany, 46, 48; moral, 26–7; normalization in the Navy, 28; PrEP, 220–1; prophylactic packs 27–8; reduced concern for, 220–1; topical 27–8. See also AIDS

prostitutes, 16, 29–30, 91, 148; cultural association with, 12, 15, 26, 148–9, 151; foreign girls, 29; foreign ports, 121; pimps, 29; and public relations, 157; and condoms, 29; during wartime, 42; Wolfenden Committee, 148

protectives. See condoms

public health. See AIDS

public image: image programme, 90, 157, 166, 211; old-fashioned, 138, 153–4, 164, 166; as problematic, 26, 122, 135, 138, 149, 154

Public Morality Council, 29, 44, 71, 74, 75

Public Relations: Family Planning Association, 102–4, 106–7; LRC, 152, 155–73

Pyke, Margaret, 99, 100–1, 104–5

quality control, 28, 122, 124, 126–7; defective products, 28, 201; electronic testing, 53, 123, 125, 141, 166, 212; failure rates, 123, 126, 182, 184; Family Planning Association, 99–100, 122–3, 125, 127; inflation testing, 37–8, 55, 94, 97, 125, 140, 201; perception of quality, 11, 64, 192, 214. See also Council for the Investigation of Fertility Control; regulation; standards

Queen Elizabeth College, 177–8. *See also* Feminor

Quinn, Marc, 159, 171. *See also* Marc Quinn Associates

rationalisation of industry scheme, 4–5, 43, 46, 48, 75

regulation: advertising, 4–5, 11, 39, 150, 201, 211; benefits of, 78–81; drugs 180–1; Family Planning Association Approved List, 84, 99, 122; LRC, support of, 69, 78, 88; perception of, 150; vending machines, 75–6, 80. *See also* Contraceptives (Regulation) Bill; Council for the Investigation of Fertility Control; standards; Pharmaceutical Society of Great Britain

Reid, Angus Roderick, 33–4, 40–2, 58–61, 78–9, 196

Resale Prices Act (1964), 115. *See also* profitability

research and development, 95, 129, 159, 184, 186, 192, 214, 221; of Automated Protective lines, 53–4; of Durex, 34–8; of Feminor, 177–8

respectability, 21, 30, 83–5, 101, 107, 129, 157. *See also* cultural acceptability

retail display, 21, 69, 74–5, 83, 99, 107, 126, 217. *See also* condoms; Pharmaceutical Society of Great Britain

retailing, 20–6; barbershops, 24–5, 33, 48, 79, 83–5, 90, 103, 115; Boots the Chemist, 86–7, 191–2, 199, 208, 210, 224; chemists' shops, 23–5, 72, 81–8, 103, 194; clinics, 51, 93, 96, 99, 100–1, 116, 126, 200; 'cundum' warehouses, 15–16, 21, 25; distribution, 16, 20, 24, 31, 120, 167, 194; hairdresser-tobacconists, 23–4, 31, 33, 34, 40, 78–9; herbalists, 23–4, 79, 82, 84, 115; in Germany, 48; LRC's first shop, 34; petrol stations, 23, 75, 203; pharmacy (liberal period), 53–4; pharmacy (professionalization), 76–9, 86–8; pharmacy (restrictive period), 54, 194; pubs, 23, 75; record shops, 201; self service, 83, 86, 87, 194–5; separation

of chemists' shops, 77; on streets, 23, 29; supermarkets, 203; surgical/rubber/hygiene stores, 17, 21, 25, 50, 72–3, 87, 90; 'under the counter' debate, 86–8; in West End, 73. *See also* Pharmaceutical Society of Great Britain; vending machines

RFSU (Riksforbundet for Sexuell Upplysning), 118–19

rubber: Brazilian boom, 16; cement process, 17–19, 31–2, 35, 40, 132; North London Polytechnic, 34–5; pessaries, 21; pricing, 53, 198; sheet rubber, 17, 45, 46, 95; slumps, 37, 53; spikes, 37, 198; sponges, 21, 35; technological revolutions, 31; vulcanization, 16–17, 54, 55. *See also* latex

sales representatives, 23, 33, 81–3, 101, 167–8; medical, 187

sales volume, 23, 80, 96, 114–17, 120, 204–6, 214, 227. *See also* clinics; consumption volume; market share

sampling, 99, 103, 139, 148, 165, 167

Second World War, 43–9, 53, 63

sex: advice, 77; and arousal, 30; casual, 26, 27–9, 72, 121, 146, 148, 166, 192; counselling 104, 105; cultures, 90, 203, 206, 216; education, 165; extra-marital sex, 26–7, 29, 42, 70–1, 152–3, 206, 218; fear, 74; frequency of, 42, 96, 111, 115, 194–5, 206; and impotence, 21, 25, 77; play, 163–4; and messiness, 148, 188; normative, 11, 90, 202, 218–9; oral contraceptive as shorthand for, 139; safe, 4, 8, 200, 202, 204, 206; selfish, 26, 149, 154; shameful, 152–3; spontaneous, 19, 149. *See also* consumer emotions; condom; homosexuality; teenagers; prostitutes; marriage; men; women

shares, 58, 65, 90, 124–5, 173; convertible bond, 209; extraordinary rights issues, 209; public flotation 52–3

shoplifing, 87–8

shops. *See* retailing

sizing. *See* standardization

social class, 60, 63, 90–3, 107, 135, 143–4, 153. *See also* market research studies

social stigmatization, 11, 28–9, 84, 152, 217–18

sperm, 163; semen absorption, 30

spermicides, 93, 142, 146, 206; confused with lubricant, 87; Duracreme, 51, 96, 131; Durafoam, 133; Duragel, 83, 99; Frommag, 48; Volpar, 94

spiritualism, 59

standardization: British Standards, 122–7, 149, 194–5, 214, 221–7; condom sizing, 126–7, 194, 203; date-stamping, 100, 126; diaphragm sizing, 95–6; European standard, 214; kite mark, 125–6, 127, 191, 195, 202

Stopes, Marie, 30, 40, 90, 92

subsidiaries, 111, 113–14, 117, 119–20, 133, 199, 230–1; international, 119–20. *See also* Autonumis; Elarco; Julius Schmid; London Rubber Industries

teenagers, 71, 75; knowledge of contraception, 205. *See also* markets; men; sex; women

termination of pregnancy. *See* pregnancy

thalidomide, 156, 158, 159, 178; artificial limbs, 159

The Pulse, London, 141–8, 150–4, 156

trademarks, 35, 40, 51–2, 132, 138

unmentionableness, 9, 139, 144, 149–52, 151, 168, 220

vaginas: barriers, 20–3, 51, 95, 144, 194; douching, 21, 29; intercourse, 202; intravaginal ring, 193; semen absorption, 30; trichomoniasis 169, 187. *See also* diaphragms

vending machines, 74–6, 231; Autonumis, 80–1; for chocolates, 75, 80; as competitive threat, 80–1, 130; and model bylaw, 76, 80. *See also* anti-competitive practices; Contraceptives (Regulation) Bill; profitability

venereal disease: and condoms, 15–16, 24–5, 26, 29, 30, 138, 148, 219; gonorrhea, 26–7, 220; during Great War, 26–9; LRC reluctance to acknowledge, 5, 91, 153, 200–2; and prostitution, 4, 11, 16, 26, 29, 42; during Second World War, 42, 44–5; syphilis, 15, 26, 220; Venereal Disease Act (1917), 4–5, 29; conflation with yeast infections, 187. *See also* AIDS

Wagstaff, Angela, 65–7

Which? magazine. *See* Consumers' Association

wholesaling, 12, 24, 31–2, 34, 40–1, 51, 205

wine, 88, 134.

withdrawal. *See coitus interruptus*

women: awareness of condoms, 144; awareness of oral contraception, 143, 190; cheapened by condoms, 148; condom consumers, 21, 23, 29, 31, 147, 156, 206; contraceptive consumers, 71, 82, 87, 147, 176, 196, 206; contraceptive controllers, 30, 93, 156, 164; contraceptive knowledge, 64, 66, 87, 144, 164; contraceptive use, 147–8, 166, 204–6; employees, 63–4; factory girls, 35–6, 43–4; feminism, 26, 30, 92; film explainers, 165; housewives, 61, 71, 145, 160; influence of medical authorities on, 144, 156; as business proprietors, 16, 22–3, 25, 40, 50; wage differential, 64; working mothers, 64; working with men, 61. *See also* prostitutes

Yudkin, John, 177